Kiss Me at the Stroke of Midnight

Rin Mikimoto

5

Contents

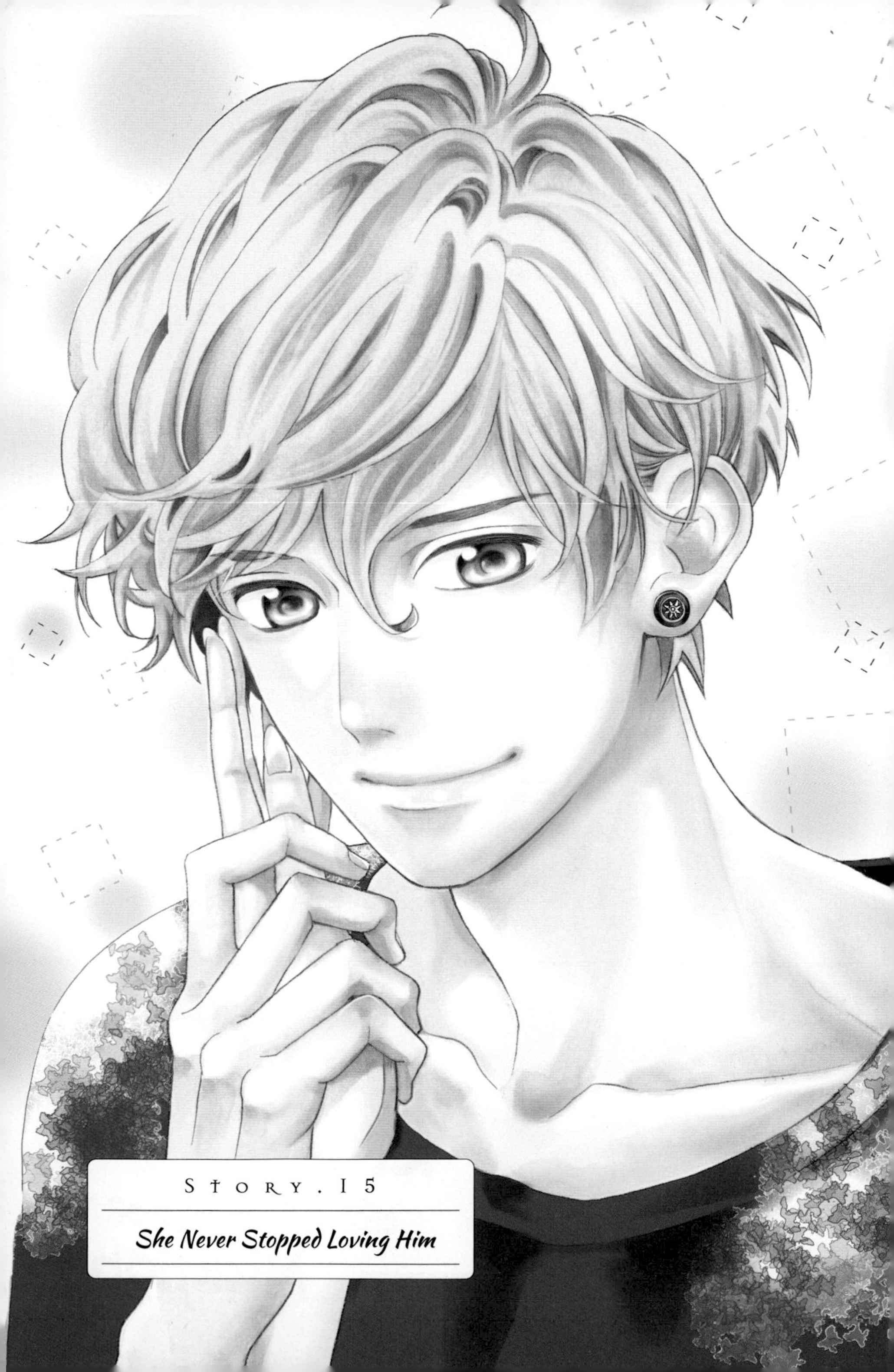

STORY . 15

She Never Stopped Loving Him

Kiss Me at the Stroke of Midnight

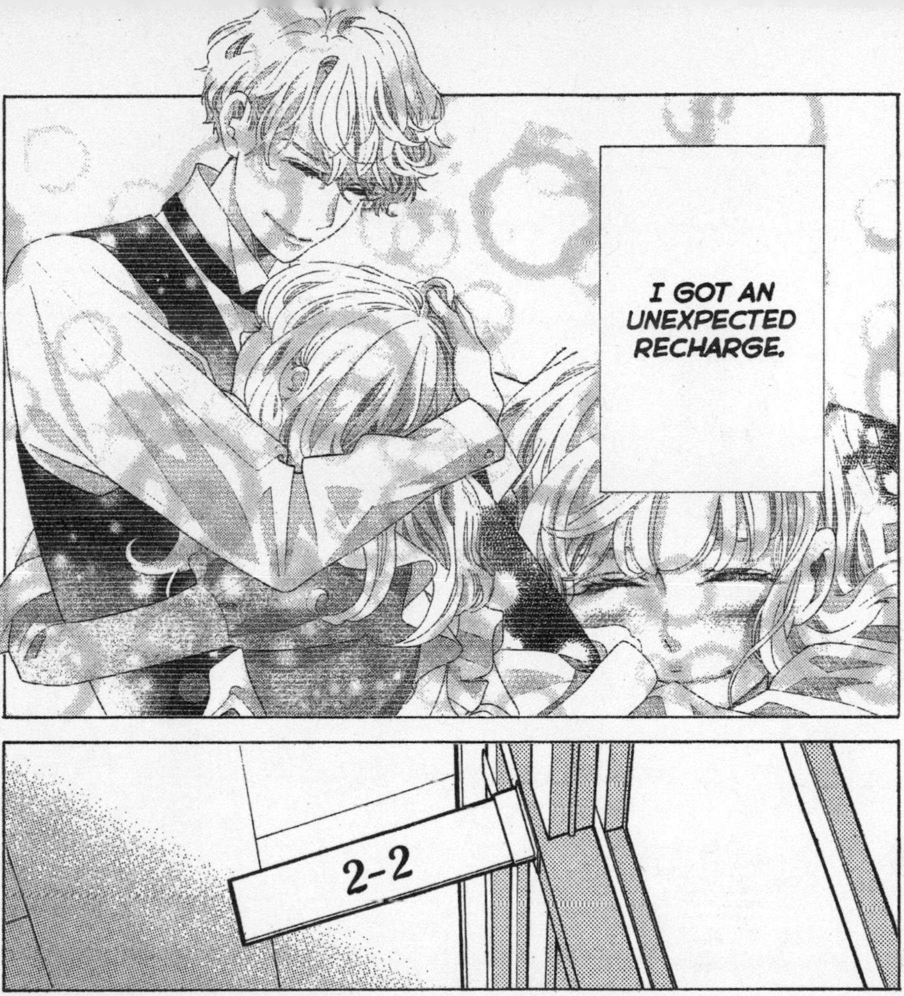
I GOT AN UNEXPECTED RECHARGE.
2-2

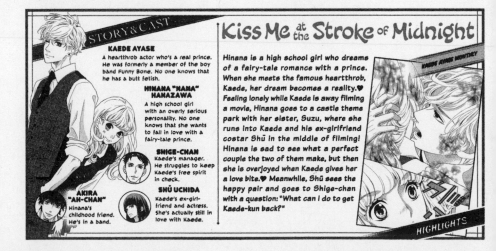

STORY & CAST

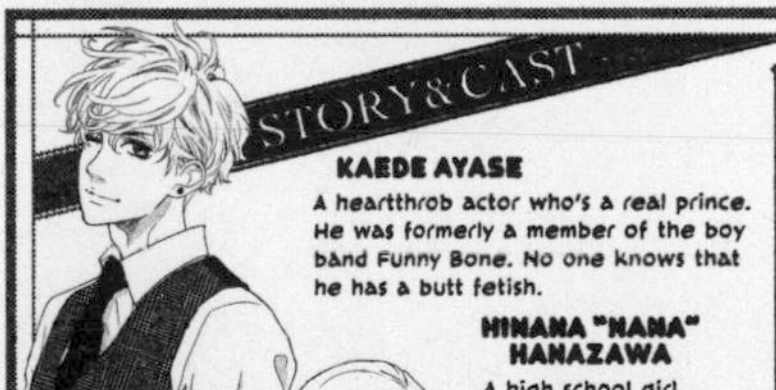

KAEDE AYASE
A heartthrob actor who's a real prince. He was formerly a member of the boy band Funny Bone. No one knows that he has a butt fetish.

HINANA "NANA" HANAZAWA
A high school girl with an overly serious personality. No one knows that she wants to fall in love with a fairy-tale prince.

SHIGE-CHAN
Kaede's manager. He struggles to keep Kaede's free spirit in check.

SHŪ UCHIDA
Kaede's ex-girlfriend and actress. She's actually still in love with Kaede.

AKIRA "AH-CHAN"
Hinana's childhood friend. He's in a band.

Kiss Me at the Stroke of Midnight

Hinana is a high school girl who dreams of a fairy-tale romance with a prince. When she meets the famous heartthrob, Kaede, her dream becomes a reality.♥ Feeling lonely while Kaede is away filming a movie, Hinana goes to a castle theme park with her sister, Suzu, where she runs into Kaede and his ex-girlfriend costar Shū in the middle of filming! Hinana is sad to see what a perfect couple the two of them make, but then she is overjoyed when Kaede gives her a love bite.♥ Meanwhile, Shū sees the happy pair and goes to Shige-chan with a question: "What can I do to get Kaede-kun back?"

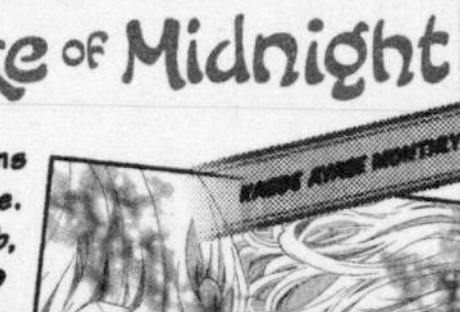

HIGHLIGHTS

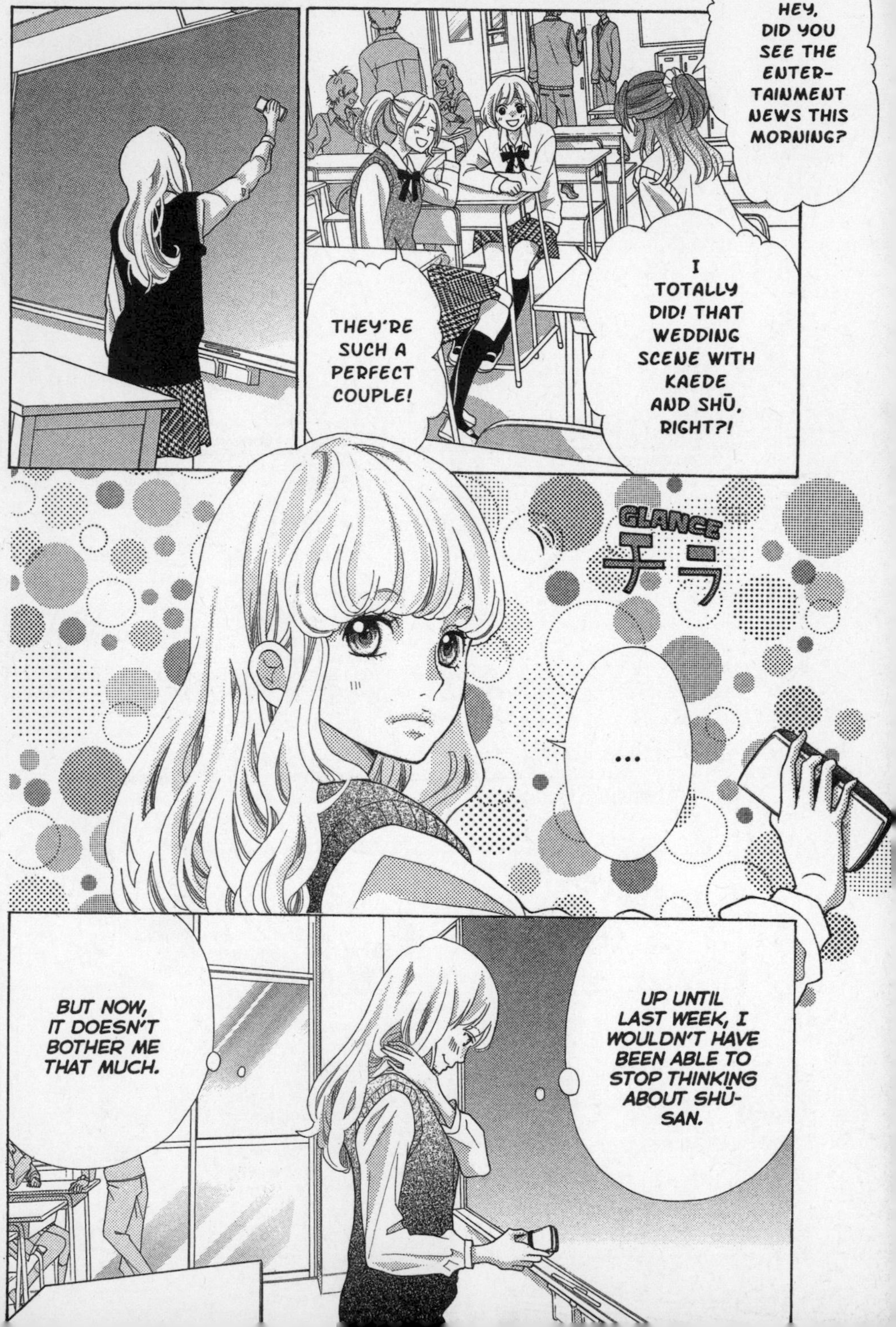
HEY, DID YOU SEE THE ENTER-TAINMENT NEWS THIS MORNING?
I TOTALLY DID! THAT WEDDING SCENE WITH KAEDE AND SHŪ, RIGHT?!
THEY'RE SUCH A PERFECT COUPLE!
GLANCE
チラ
...
UP UNTIL LAST WEEK, I WOULDN'T HAVE BEEN ABLE TO STOP THINKING ABOUT SHŪ-SAN.
BUT NOW, IT DOESN'T BOTHER ME THAT MUCH.

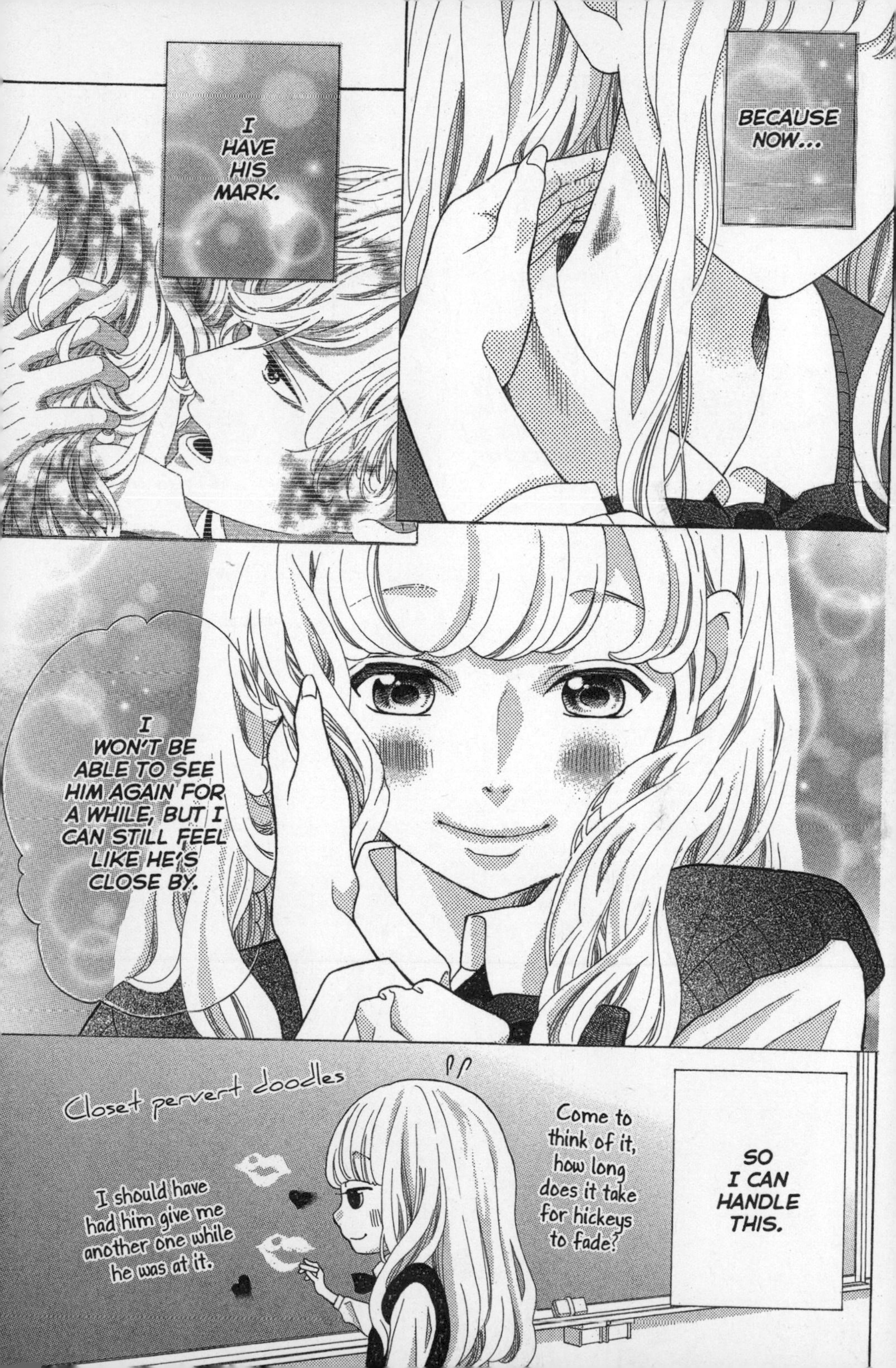
BECAUSE NOW...
I HAVE HIS MARK.
I WON'T BE ABLE TO SEE HIM AGAIN FOR A WHILE, BUT I CAN STILL FEEL LIKE HE'S CLOSE BY.
SO I CAN HANDLE THIS.
Come to think of it, how long does it take for hickeys to fade?
Closet pervert doodles
I should have had him give me another one while he was at it.

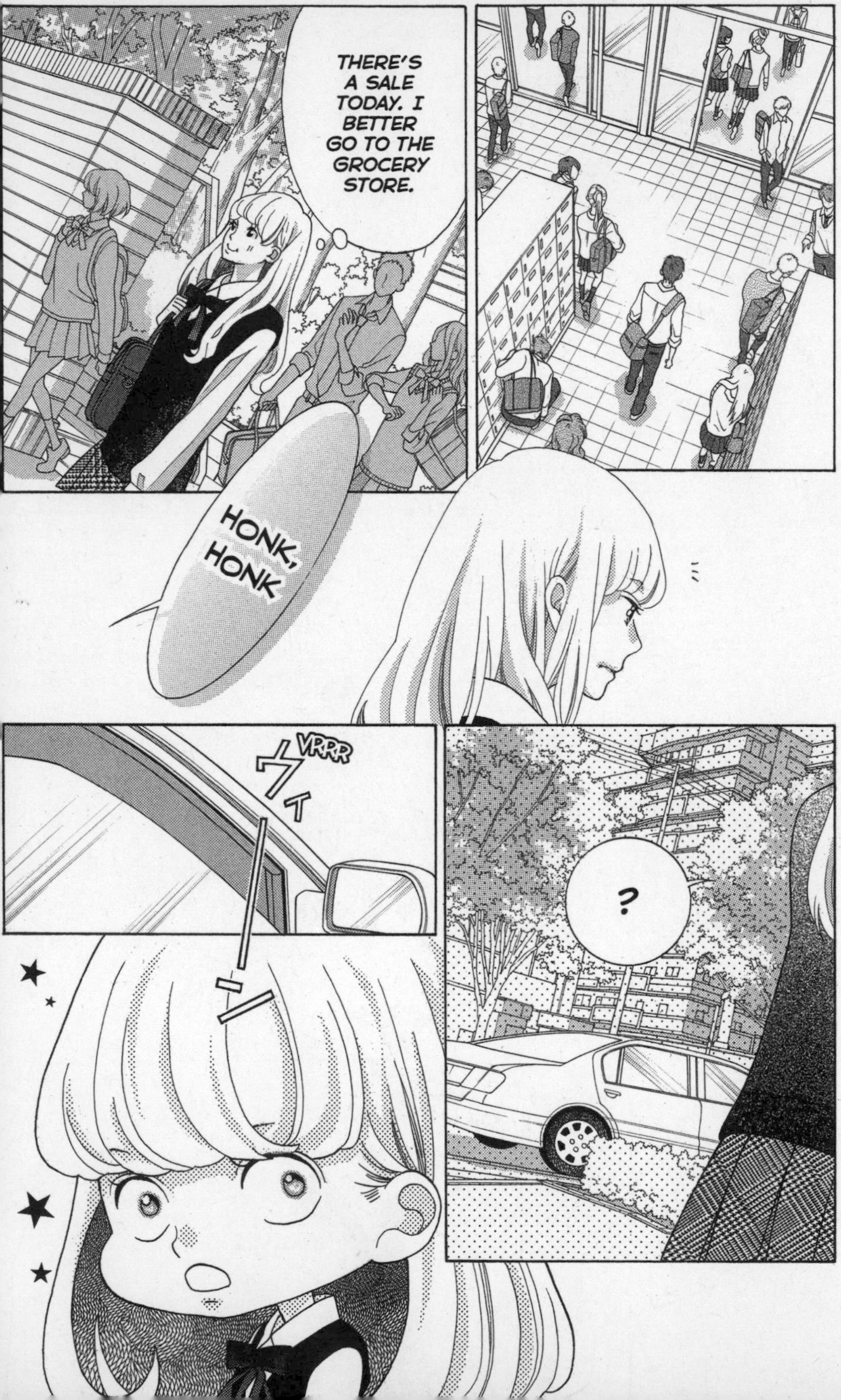
THERE'S A SALE TODAY. I BETTER GO TO THE GROCERY STORE.
HONK, HONK
?
VRRR

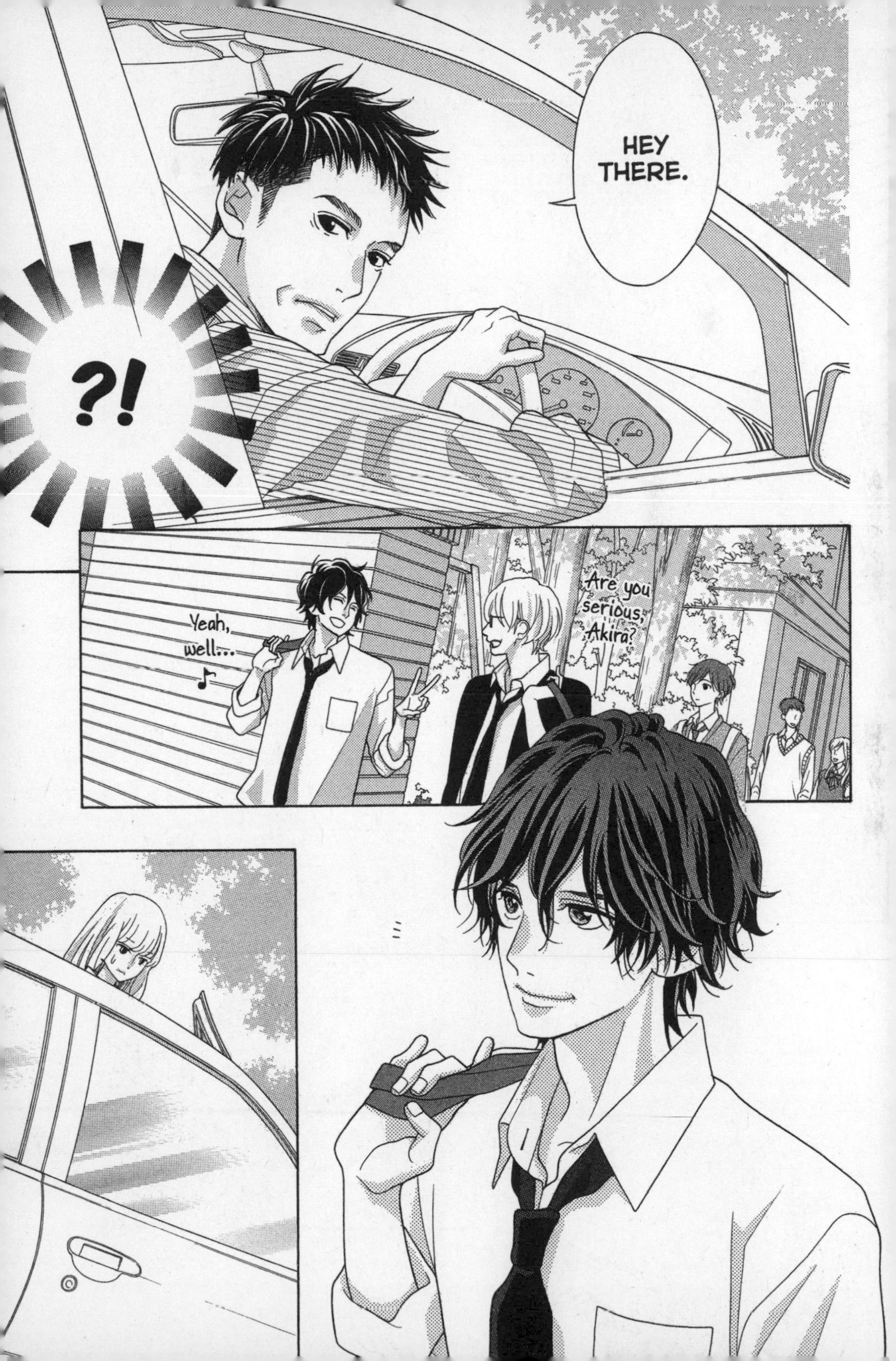
HEY THERE.
?!
Are you serious, Akira?
Yeah, well... ♪

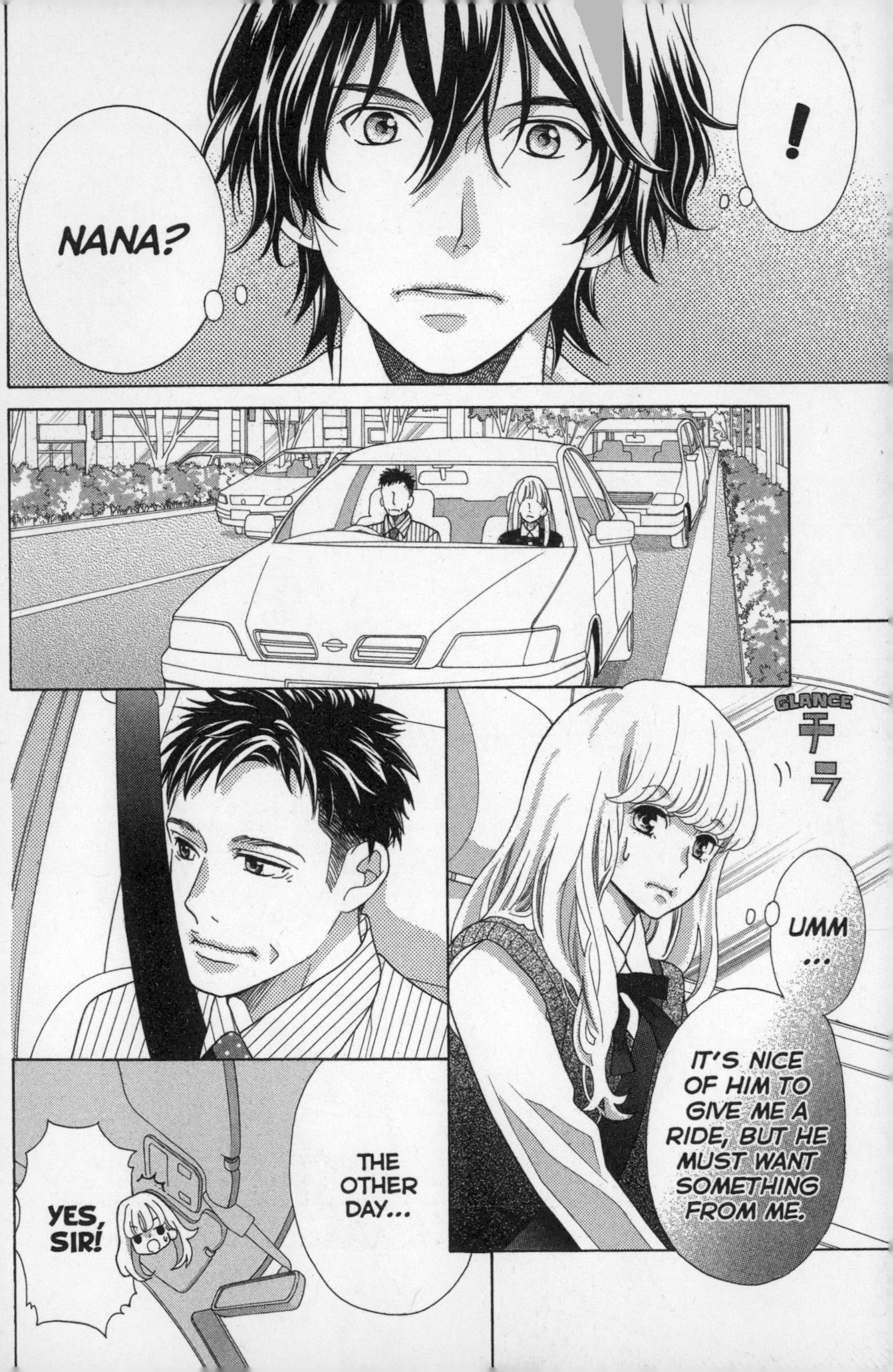
!
NANA?
GLANCE
チラ
UMM...
IT'S NICE OF HIM TO GIVE ME A RIDE, BUT HE MUST WANT SOMETHING FROM ME.
THE OTHER DAY...
YES, SIR!

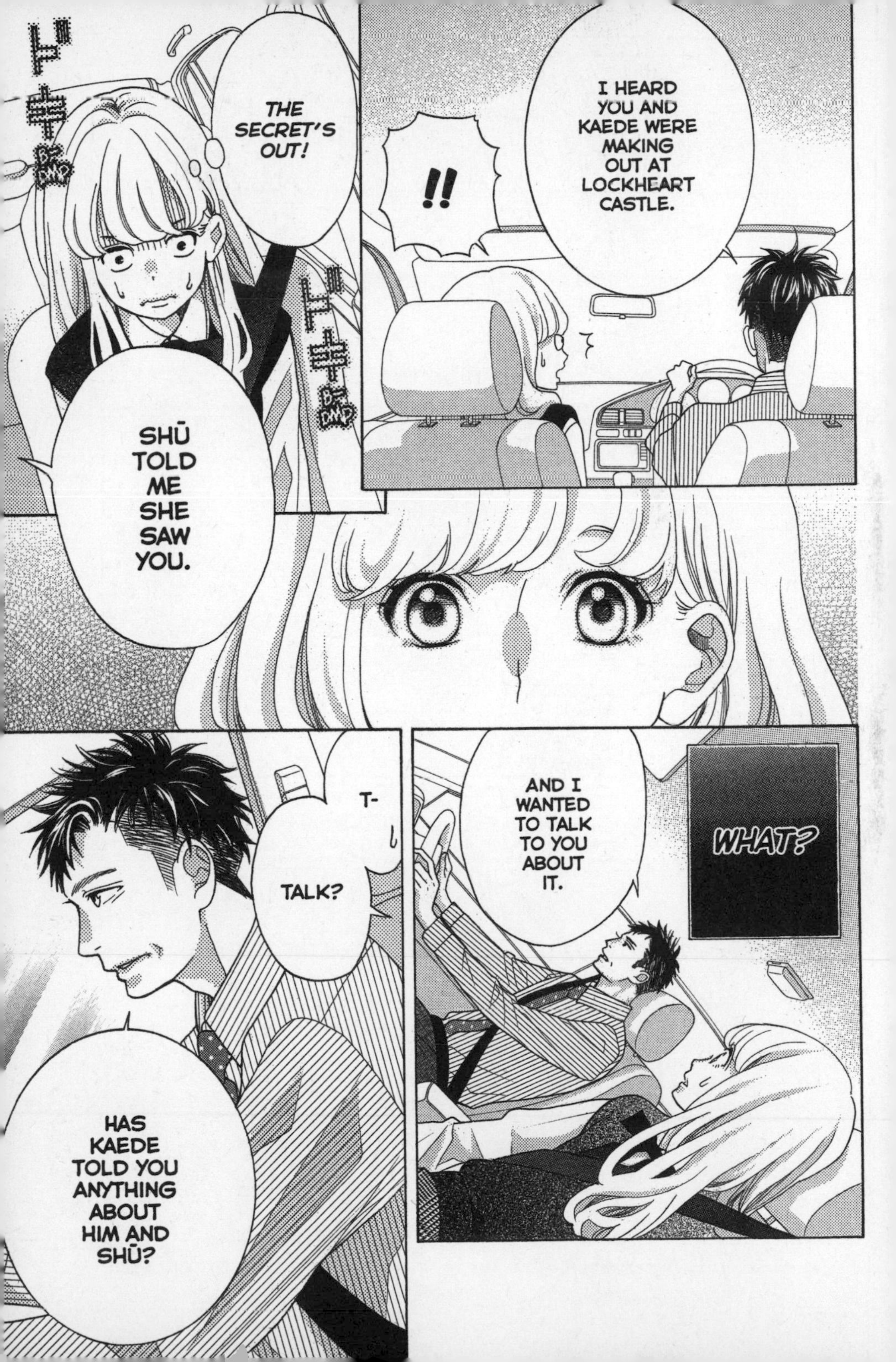
I HEARD YOU AND KAEDE WERE MAKING OUT AT LOCKHEART CASTLE.
!!
THE SECRET'S OUT!
BA-DMP
BA-DMP
SHŪ TOLD ME SHE SAW YOU.
AND I WANTED TO TALK TO YOU ABOUT IT.
WHAT?
T-
TALK?
HAS KAEDE TOLD YOU ANYTHING ABOUT HIM AND SHŪ?

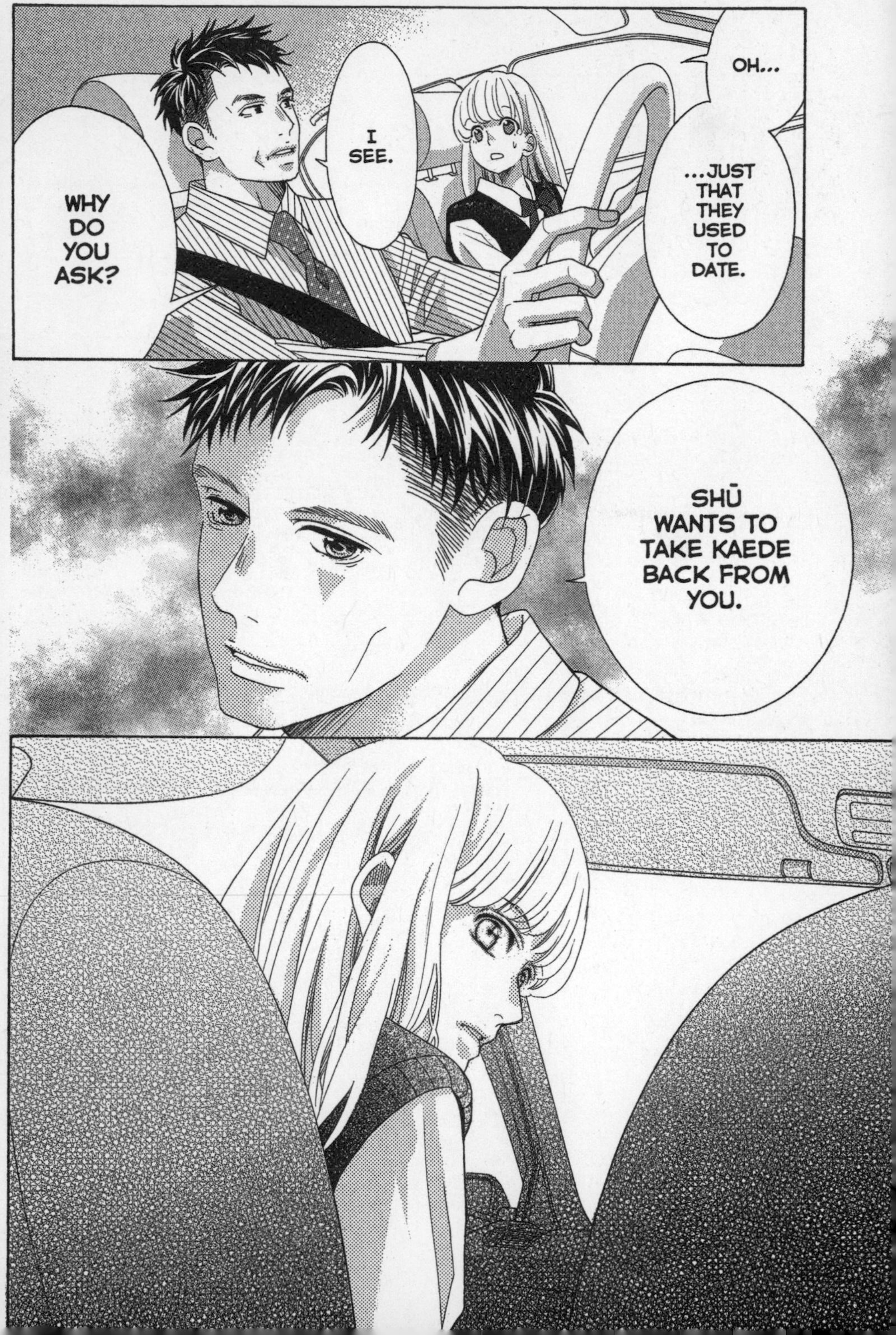
OH...
...JUST THAT THEY USED TO DATE.
I SEE.
WHY DO YOU ASK?
SHŪ WANTS TO TAKE KAEDE BACK FROM YOU.

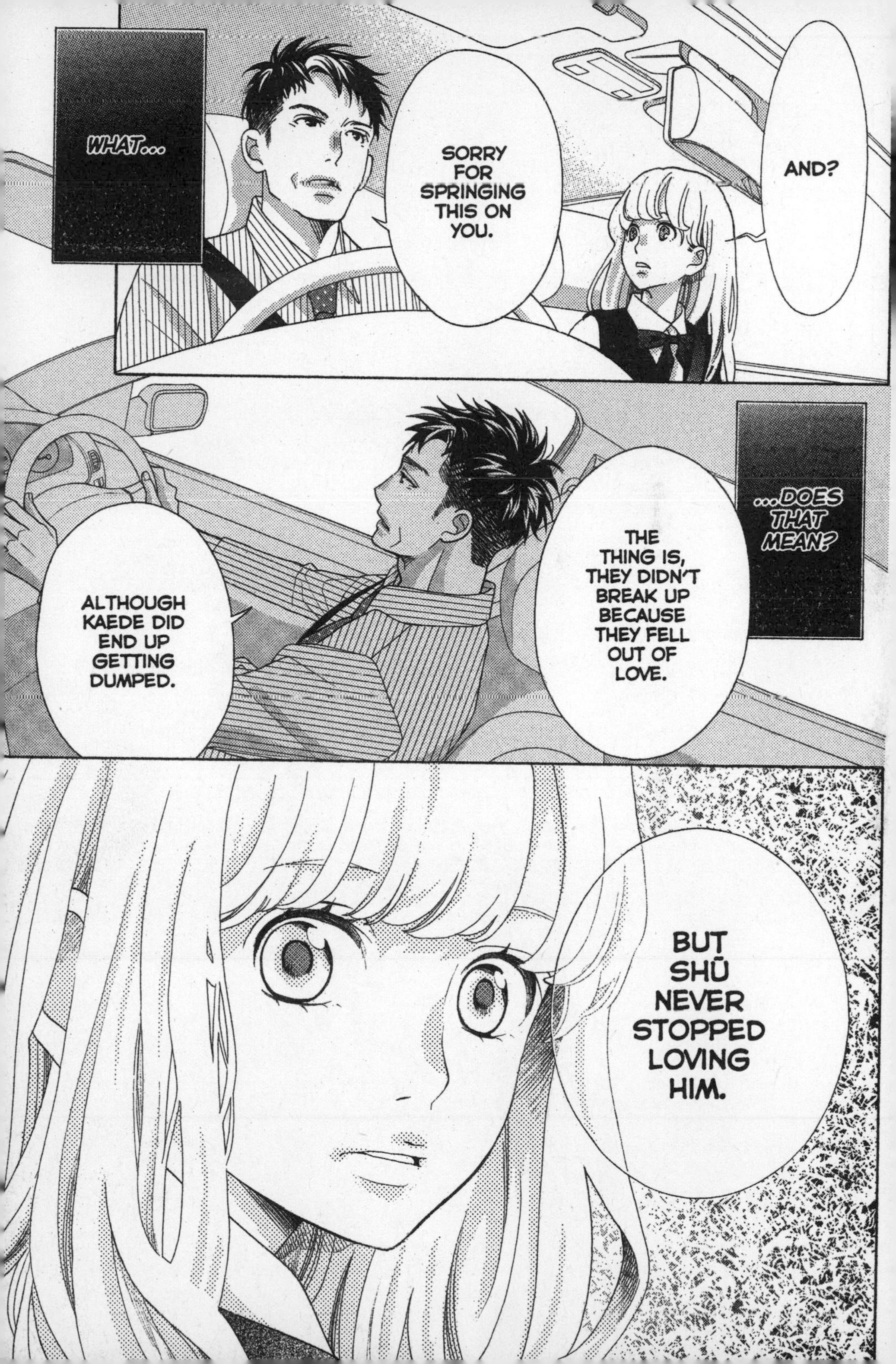
AND?
SORRY FOR SPRINGING THIS ON YOU.
WHAT...
...DOES THAT MEAN?
THE THING IS, THEY DIDN'T BREAK UP BECAUSE THEY FELL OUT OF LOVE.
ALTHOUGH KAEDE DID END UP GETTING DUMPED.
BUT SHŪ NEVER STOPPED LOVING HIM.

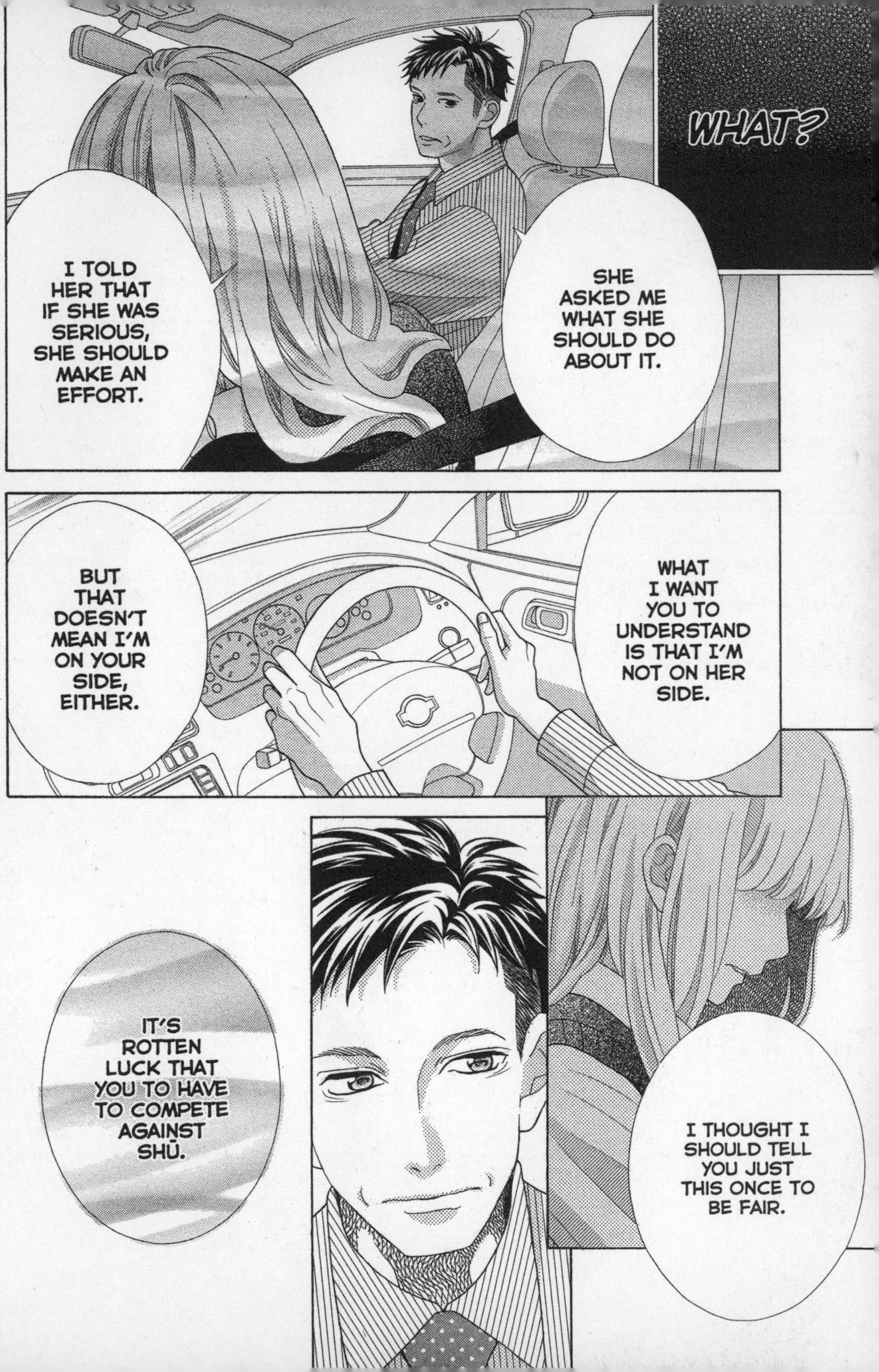
WHAT?
SHE ASKED ME WHAT SHE SHOULD DO ABOUT IT.
I TOLD HER THAT IF SHE WAS SERIOUS, SHE SHOULD MAKE AN EFFORT.
WHAT I WANT YOU TO UNDERSTAND IS THAT I'M NOT ON HER SIDE.
BUT THAT DOESN'T MEAN I'M ON YOUR SIDE, EITHER.
I THOUGHT I SHOULD TELL YOU JUST THIS ONCE TO BE FAIR.
IT'S ROTTEN LUCK THAT YOU TO HAVE TO COMPETE AGAINST SHŪ.

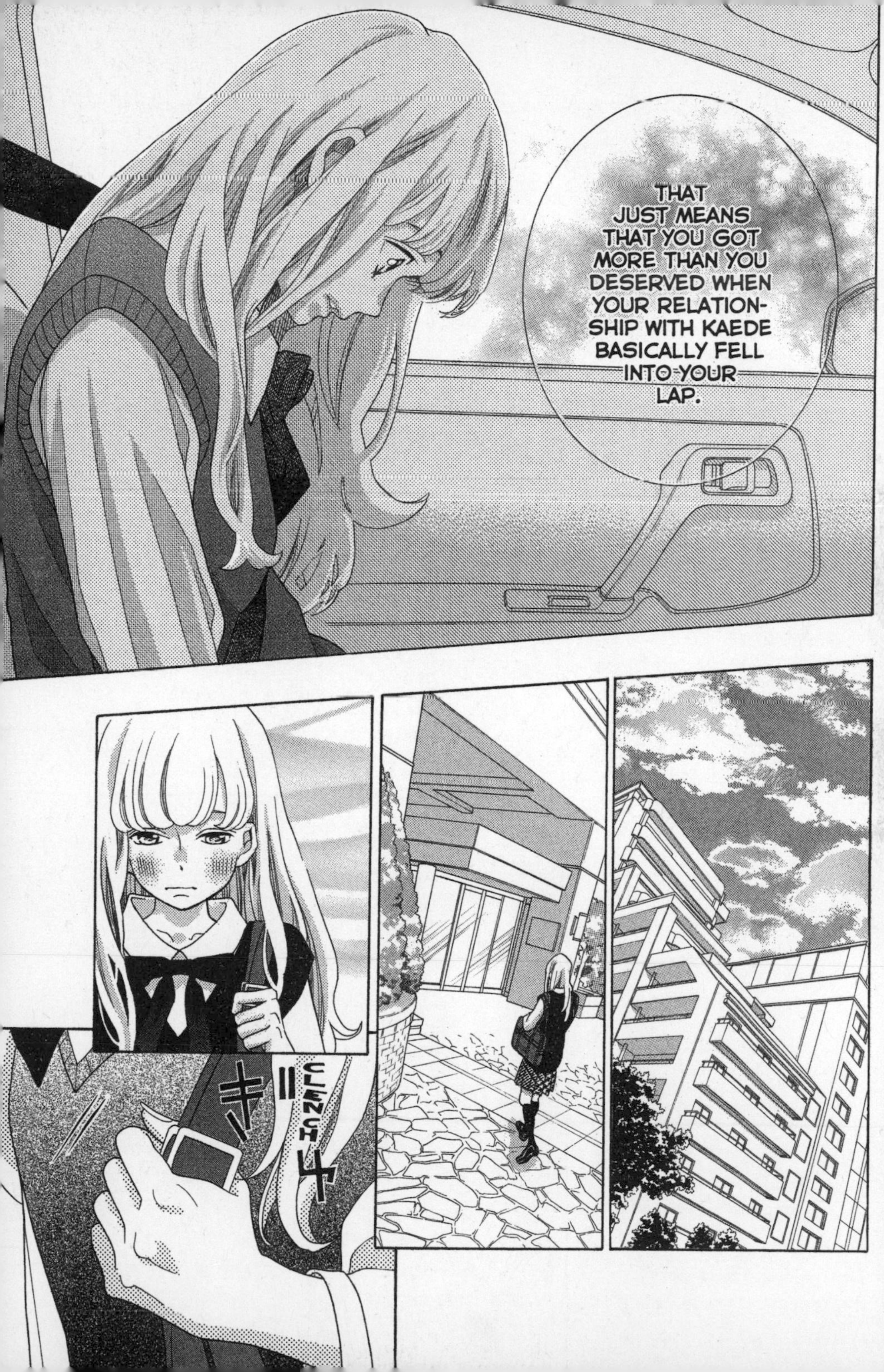
THAT JUST MEANS THAT YOU GOT MORE THAN YOU DESERVED WHEN YOUR RELATION-SHIP WITH KAEDE BASICALLY FELL INTO YOUR LAP.
CLENCH

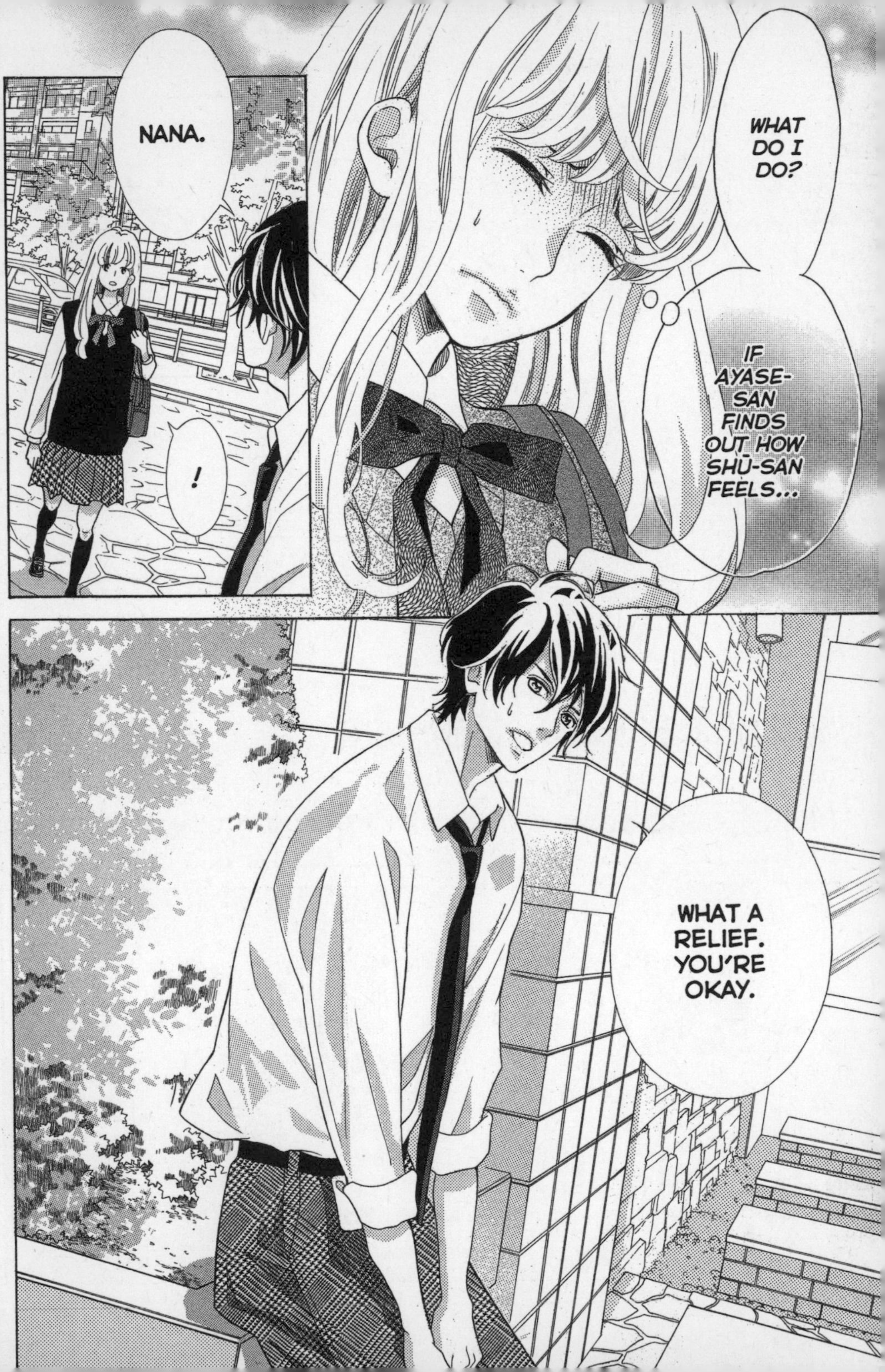
WHAT DO I DO?
IF AYASE-SAN FINDS OUT HOW SHŪ-SAN FEELS...
NANA.
!
WHAT A RELIEF. YOU'RE OKAY.

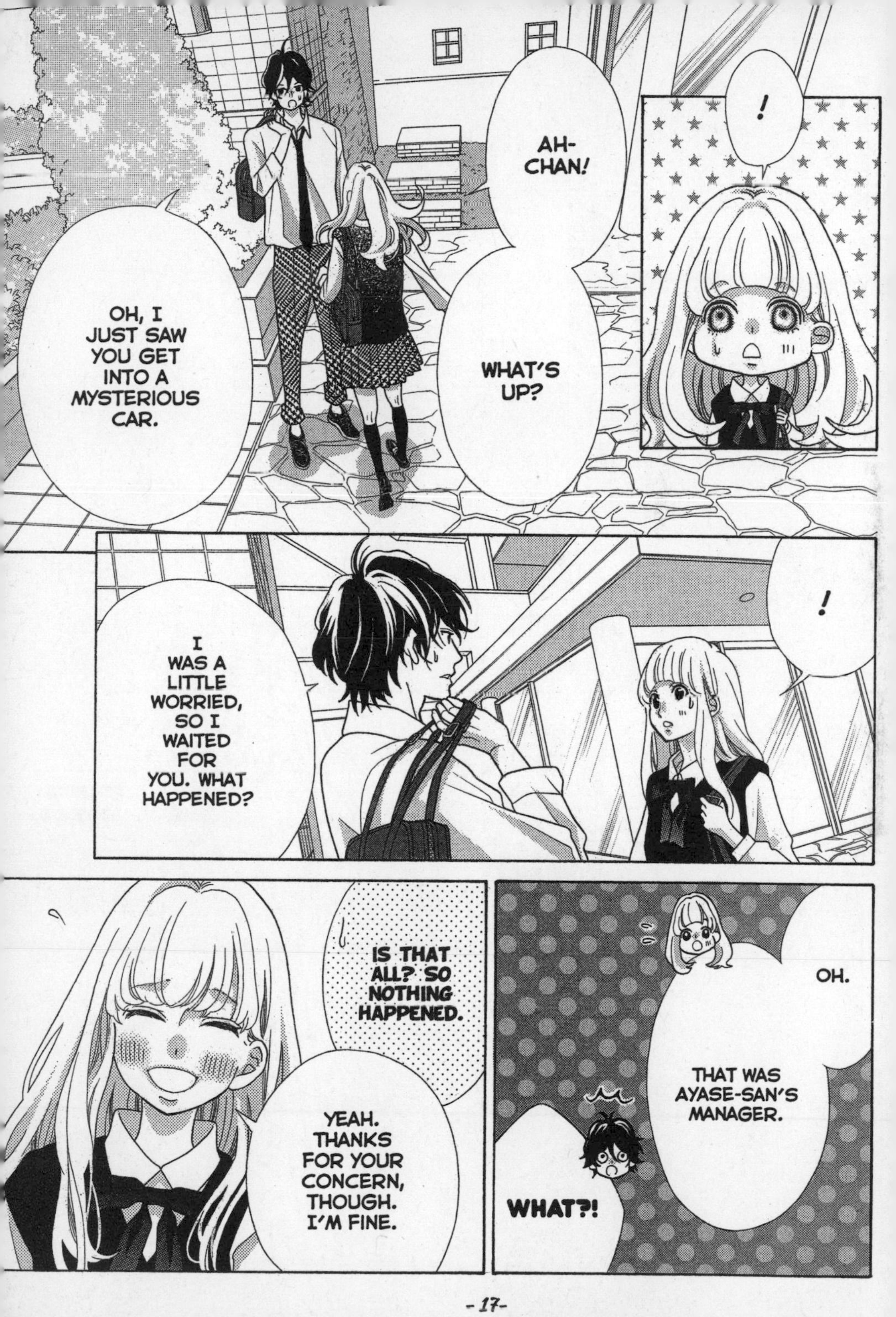
!
AH-CHAN!
WHAT'S UP?
OH, I JUST SAW YOU GET INTO A MYSTERIOUS CAR.
!
I WAS A LITTLE WORRIED, SO I WAITED FOR YOU. WHAT HAPPENED?
OH.
THAT WAS AYASE-SAN'S MANAGER.
WHAT?!
IS THAT ALL? SO NOTHING HAPPENED.
YEAH. THANKS FOR YOUR CONCERN, THOUGH. I'M FINE.

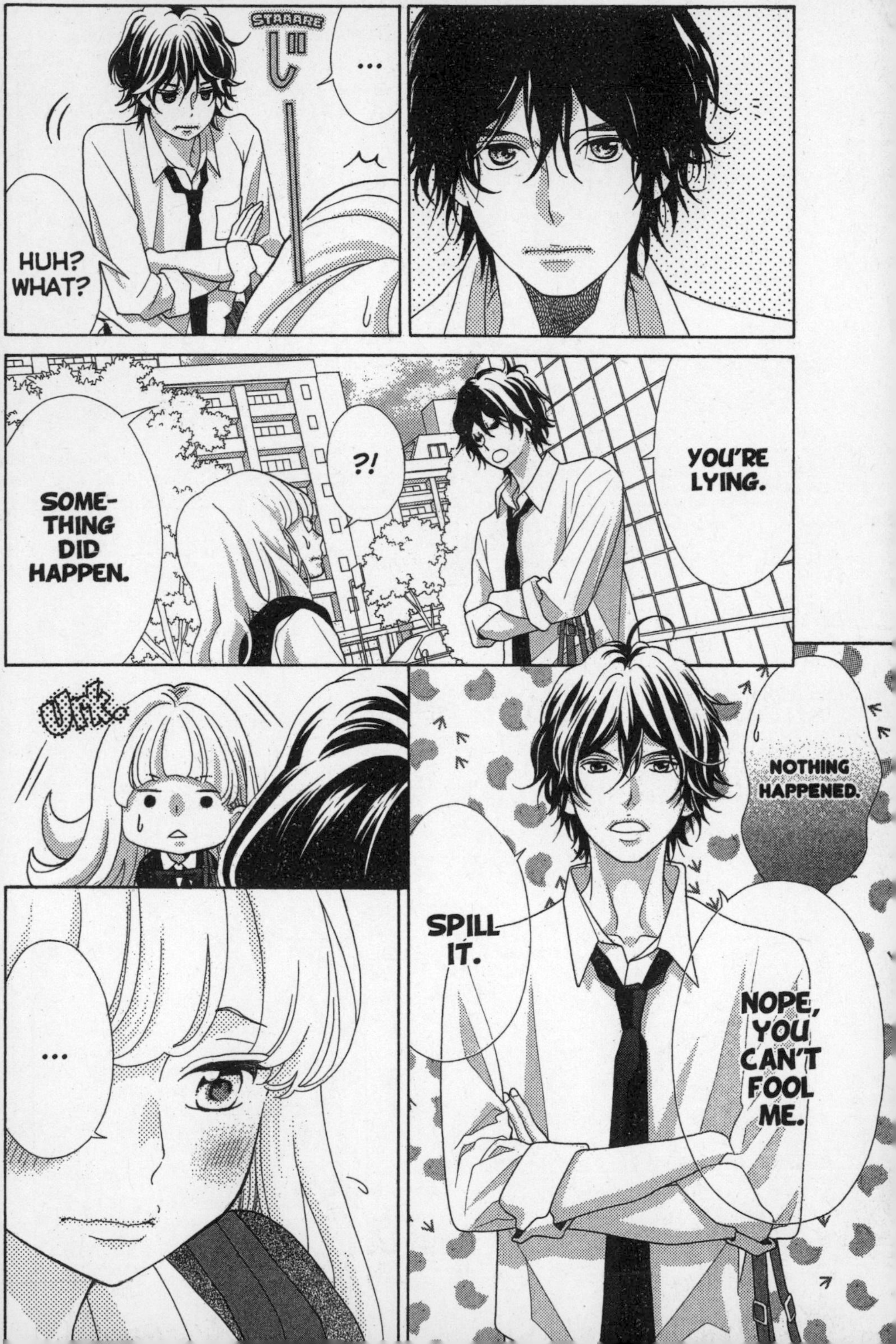
...
STAAARE
HUH? WHAT?
YOU'RE LYING.
?!
SOME-THING DID HAPPEN.
NOTHING HAPPENED.
NOPE, YOU CAN'T FOOL ME.
SPILL IT.
UNK.
...

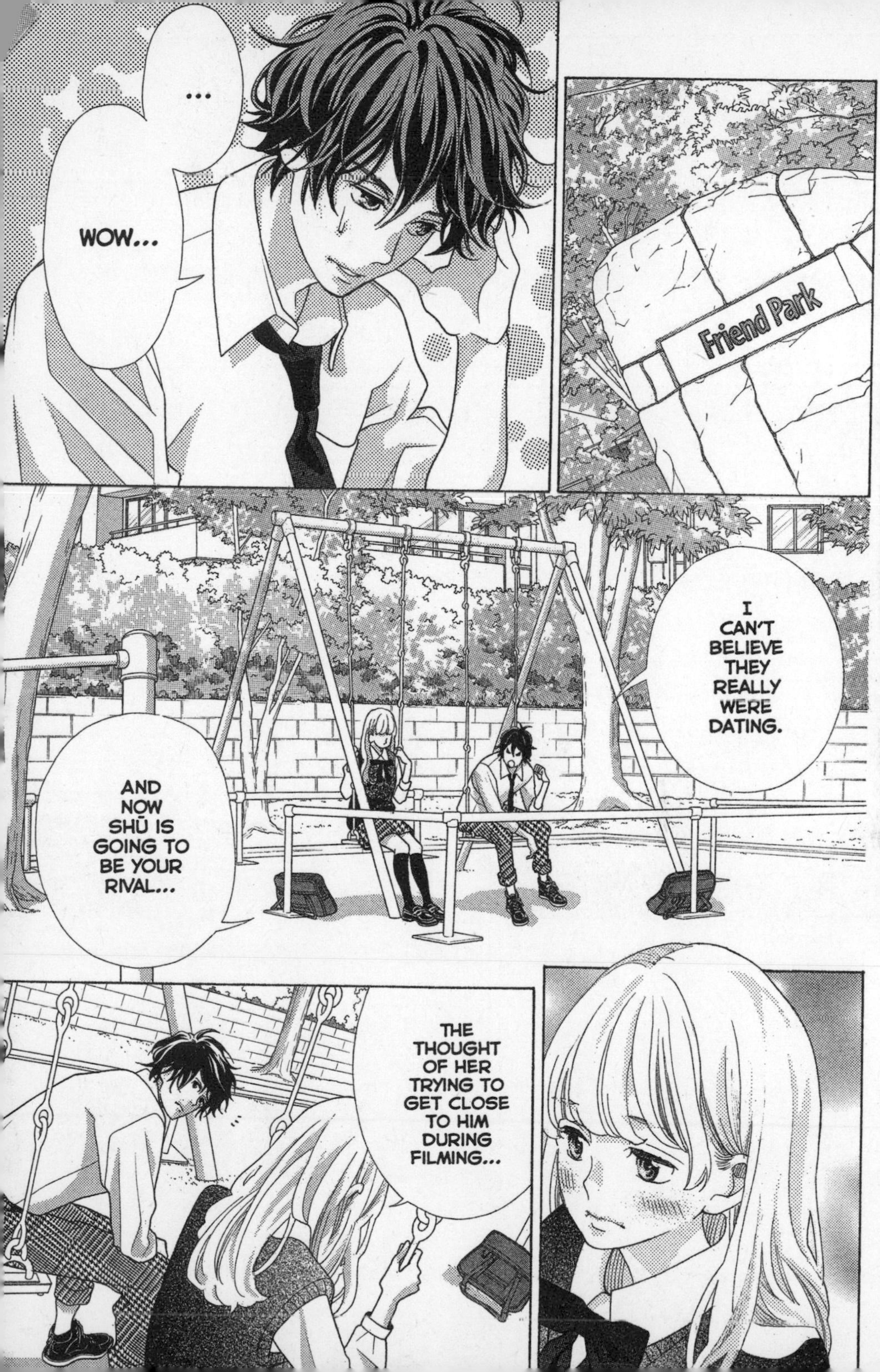
Friend Park
...
WOW...
I CAN'T BELIEVE THEY REALLY WERE DATING.
AND NOW SHŪ IS GOING TO BE YOUR RIVAL...
THE THOUGHT OF HER TRYING TO GET CLOSE TO HIM DURING FILMING...

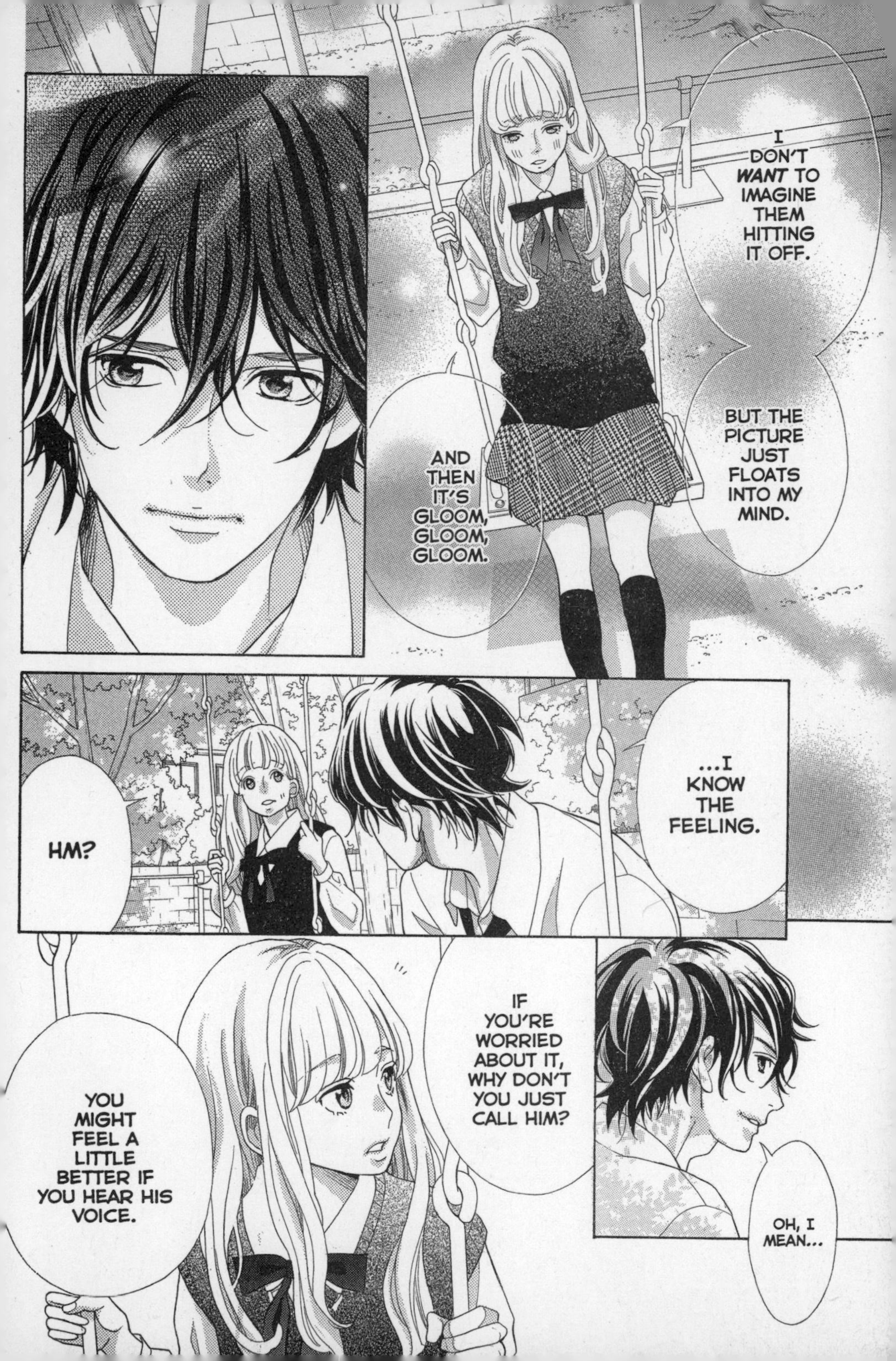
I DON'T *WANT* TO IMAGINE THEM HITTING IT OFF.
BUT THE PICTURE JUST FLOATS INTO MY MIND.
AND THEN IT'S GLOOM, GLOOM, GLOOM.
...I KNOW THE FEELING.
HM?
OH, I MEAN...
IF YOU'RE WORRIED ABOUT IT, WHY DON'T YOU JUST CALL HIM?
YOU MIGHT FEEL A LITTLE BETTER IF YOU HEAR HIS VOICE.

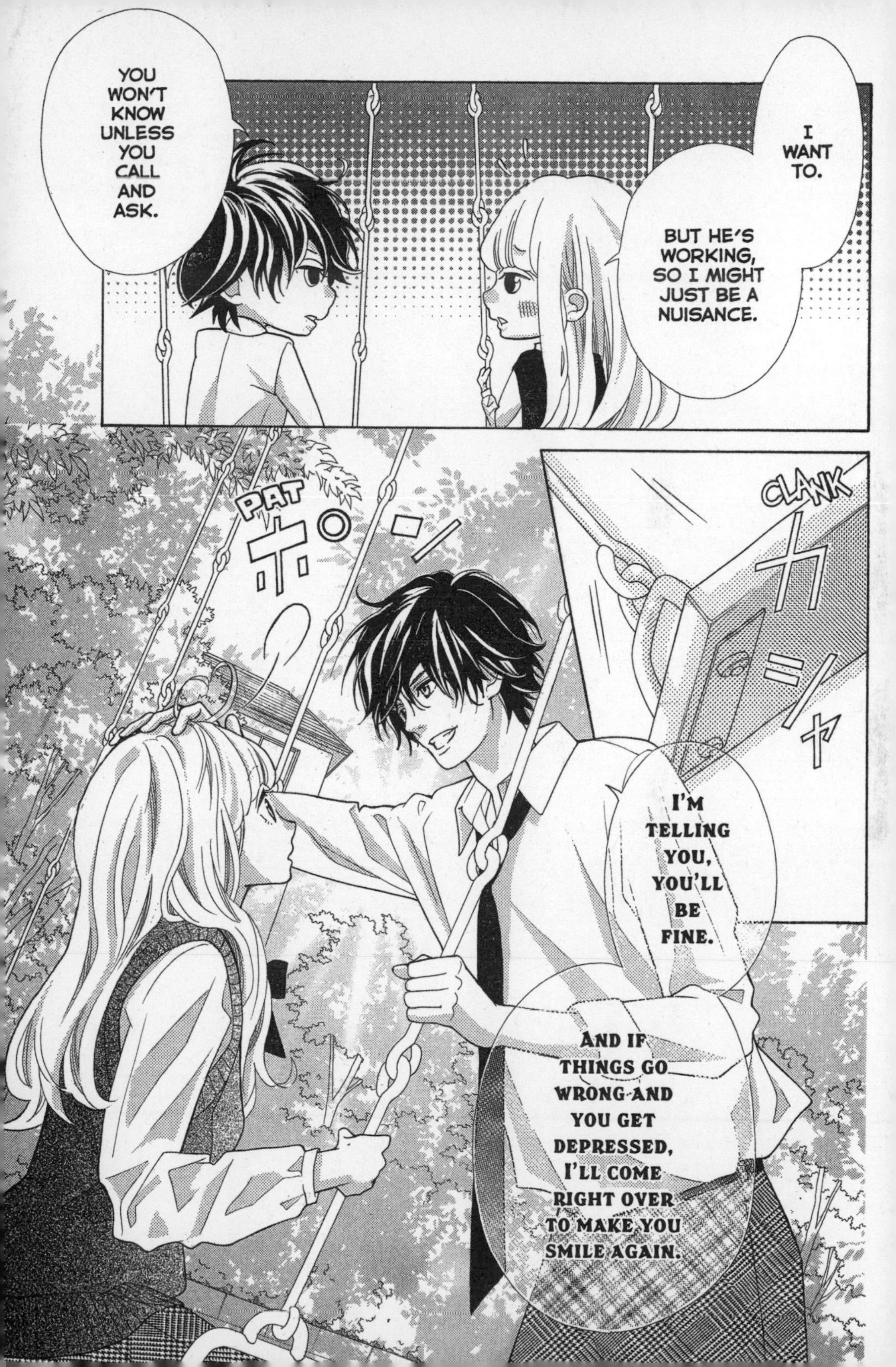
I WANT TO.
BUT HE'S WORKING, SO I MIGHT JUST BE A NUISANCE.
YOU WON'T KNOW UNLESS YOU CALL AND ASK.
CLANK
PAT
I'M TELLING YOU, YOU'LL BE FINE.
AND IF THINGS GO WRONG AND YOU GET DEPRESSED, I'LL COME RIGHT OVER TO MAKE YOU SMILE AGAIN.

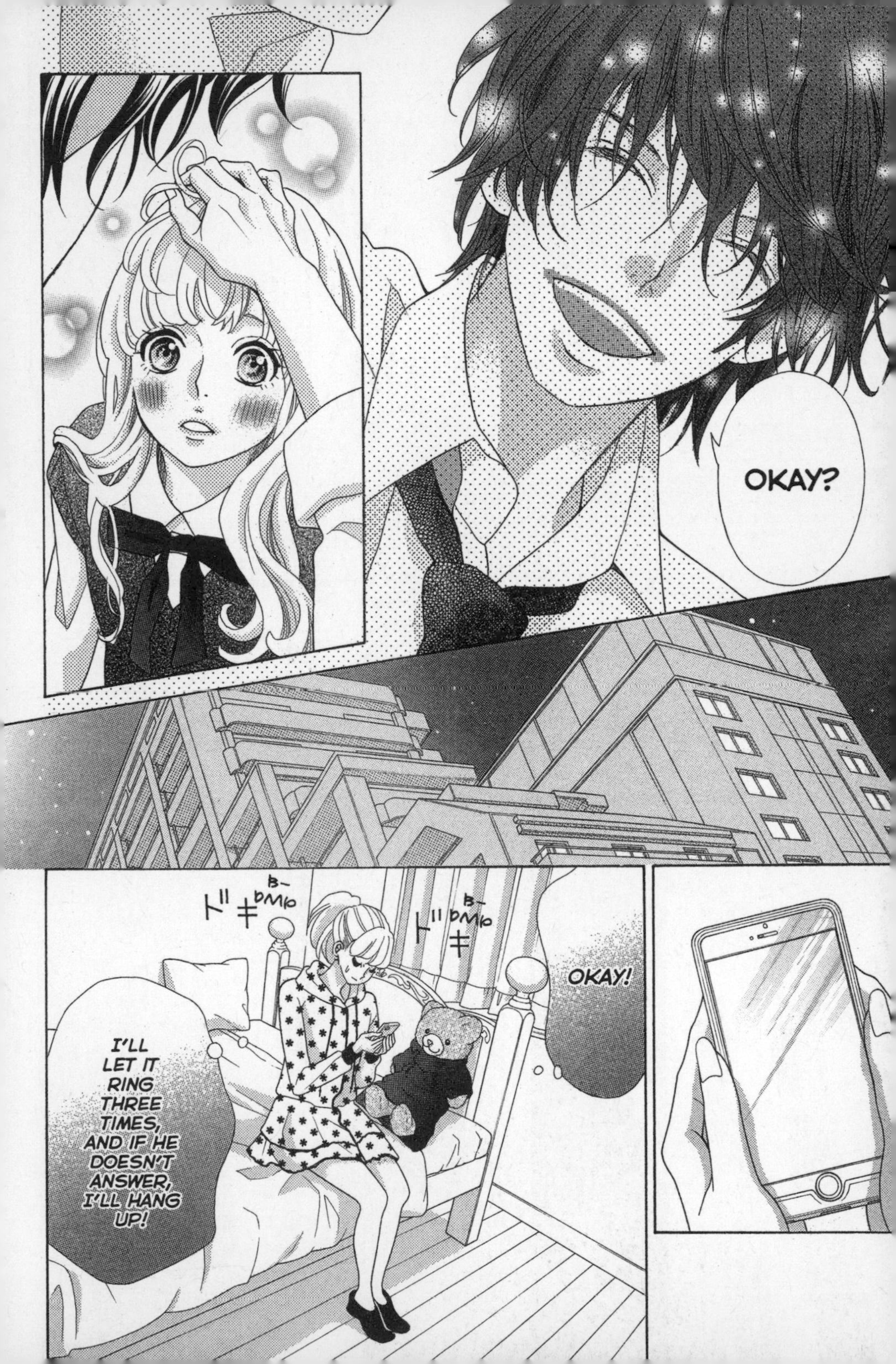
OKAY?
ドキ
B-DMP
ドキ
B-DMP
OKAY!
I'LL LET IT RING THREE TIMES, AND IF HE DOESN'T ANSWER, I'LL HANG UP!

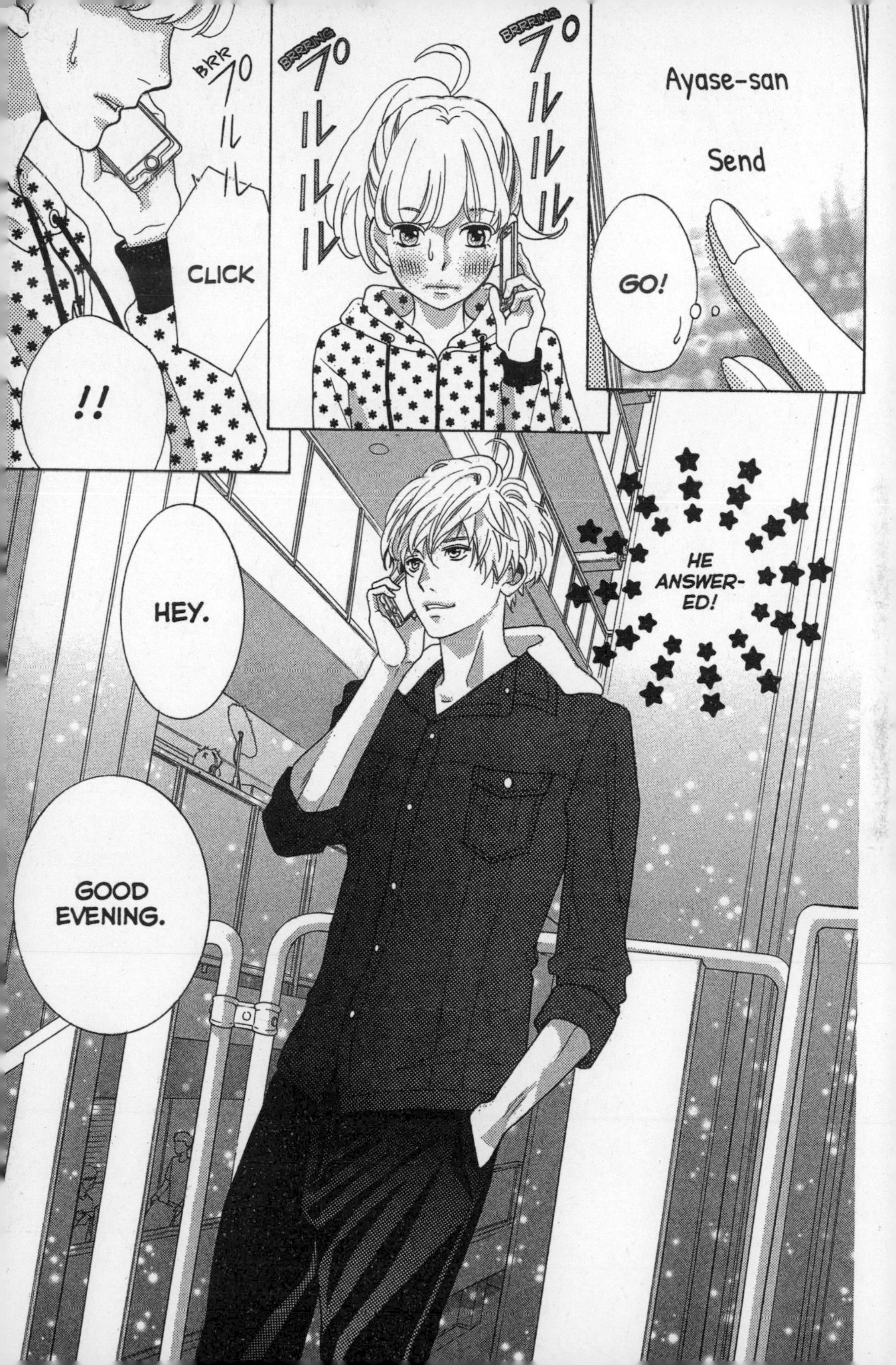

Ayase-san
Send
GO!
BRRRING
プルルル
BRRRING
プルルル
BRR
プルル
CLICK
!!
HE ANSWERED!
HEY.
GOOD EVENING.

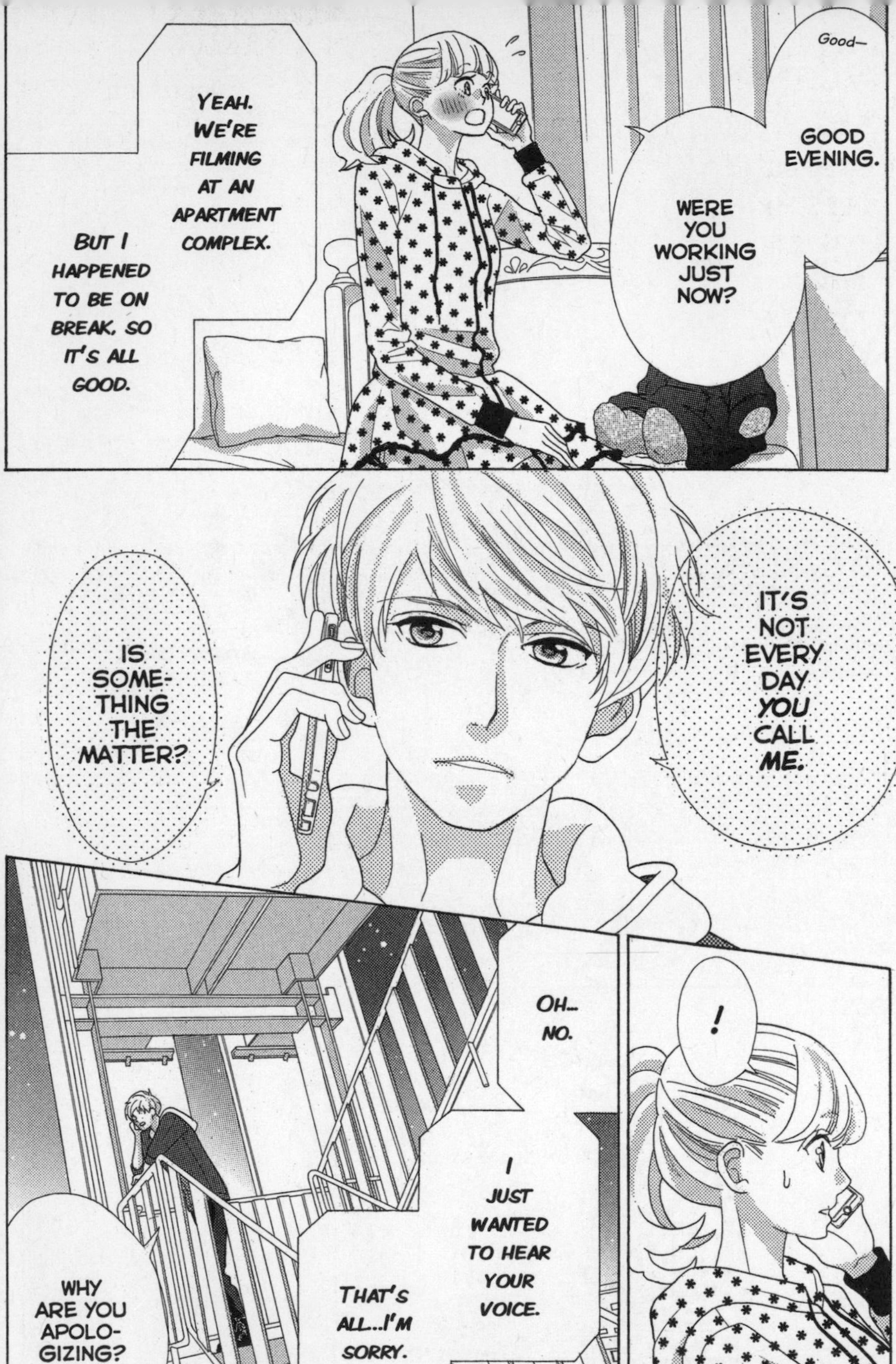
Good—
GOOD EVENING.
WERE YOU WORKING JUST NOW?
YEAH. WE'RE FILMING AT AN APARTMENT COMPLEX.
BUT I HAPPENED TO BE ON BREAK, SO IT'S ALL GOOD.
IT'S NOT EVERY DAY YOU CALL ME.
IS SOMETHING THE MATTER?
!
OH... NO.
I JUST WANTED TO HEAR YOUR VOICE.
THAT'S ALL...I'M SORRY.
WHY ARE YOU APOLOGIZING?

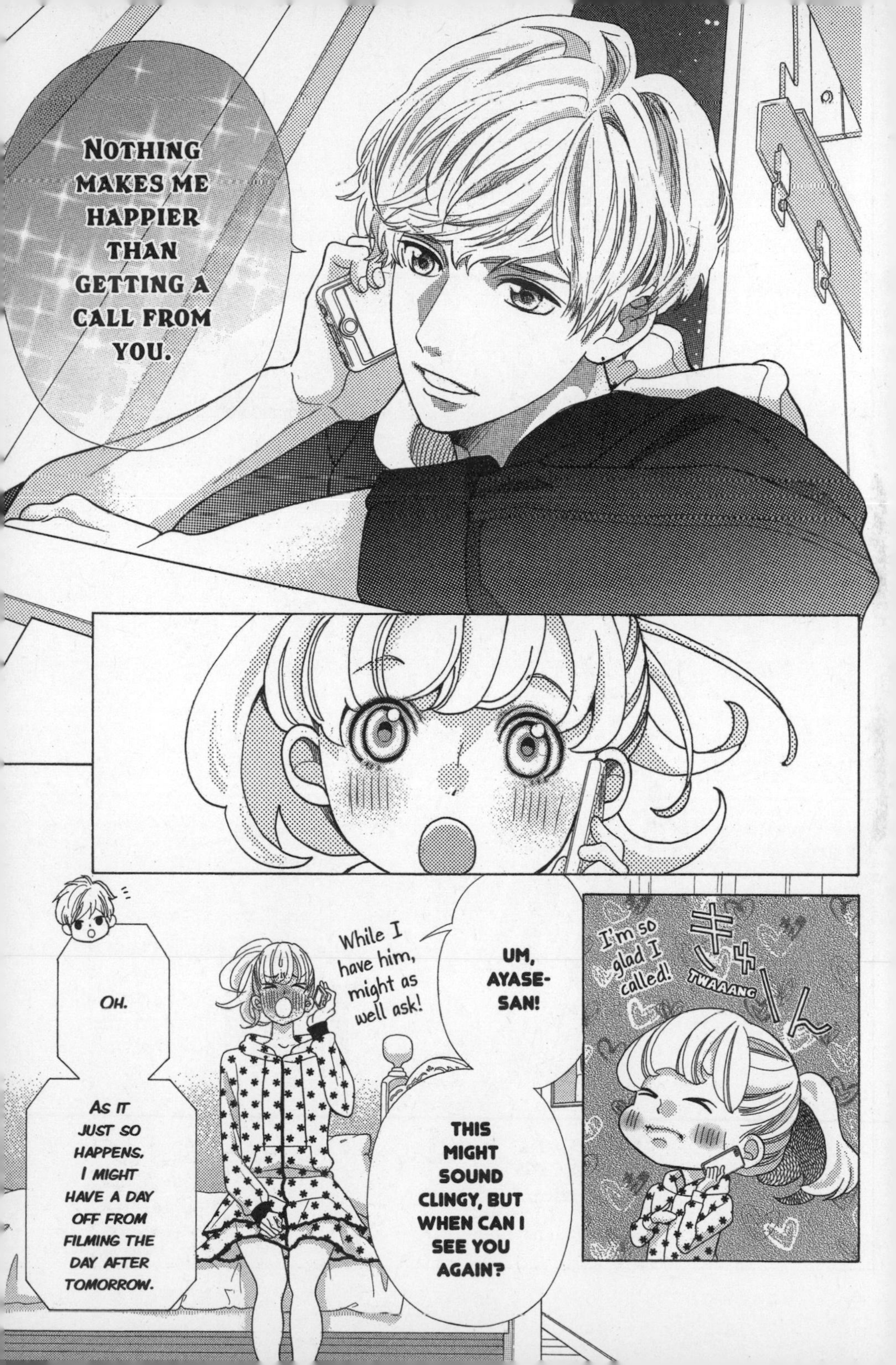
Nothing makes me happier than getting a call from you.
I'm so glad I called!
TWAAANG
Um, Ayase-san!
While I have him, might as well ask!
This might sound clingy, but when can I see you again?
Oh.
As it just so happens. I might have a day off from filming the day after tomorrow.

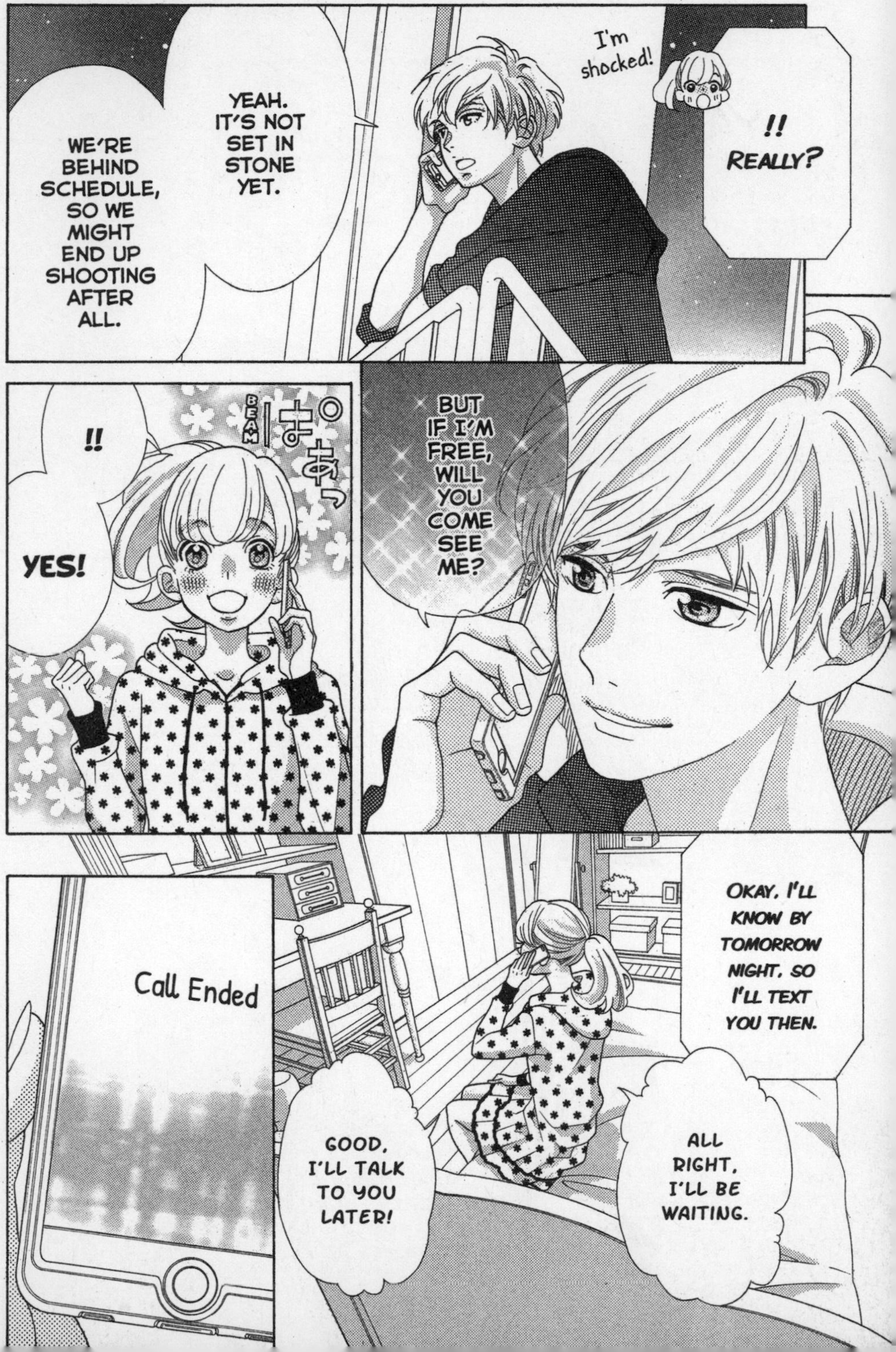
!! REALLY?
I'm shocked!
YEAH. IT'S NOT SET IN STONE YET.
WE'RE BEHIND SCHEDULE, SO WE MIGHT END UP SHOOTING AFTER ALL.
BUT IF I'M FREE, WILL YOU COME SEE ME?
BEAM
!!
YES!
OKAY, I'LL KNOW BY TOMORROW NIGHT, SO I'LL TEXT YOU THEN.
ALL RIGHT, I'LL BE WAITING.
GOOD, I'LL TALK TO YOU LATER!
Call Ended

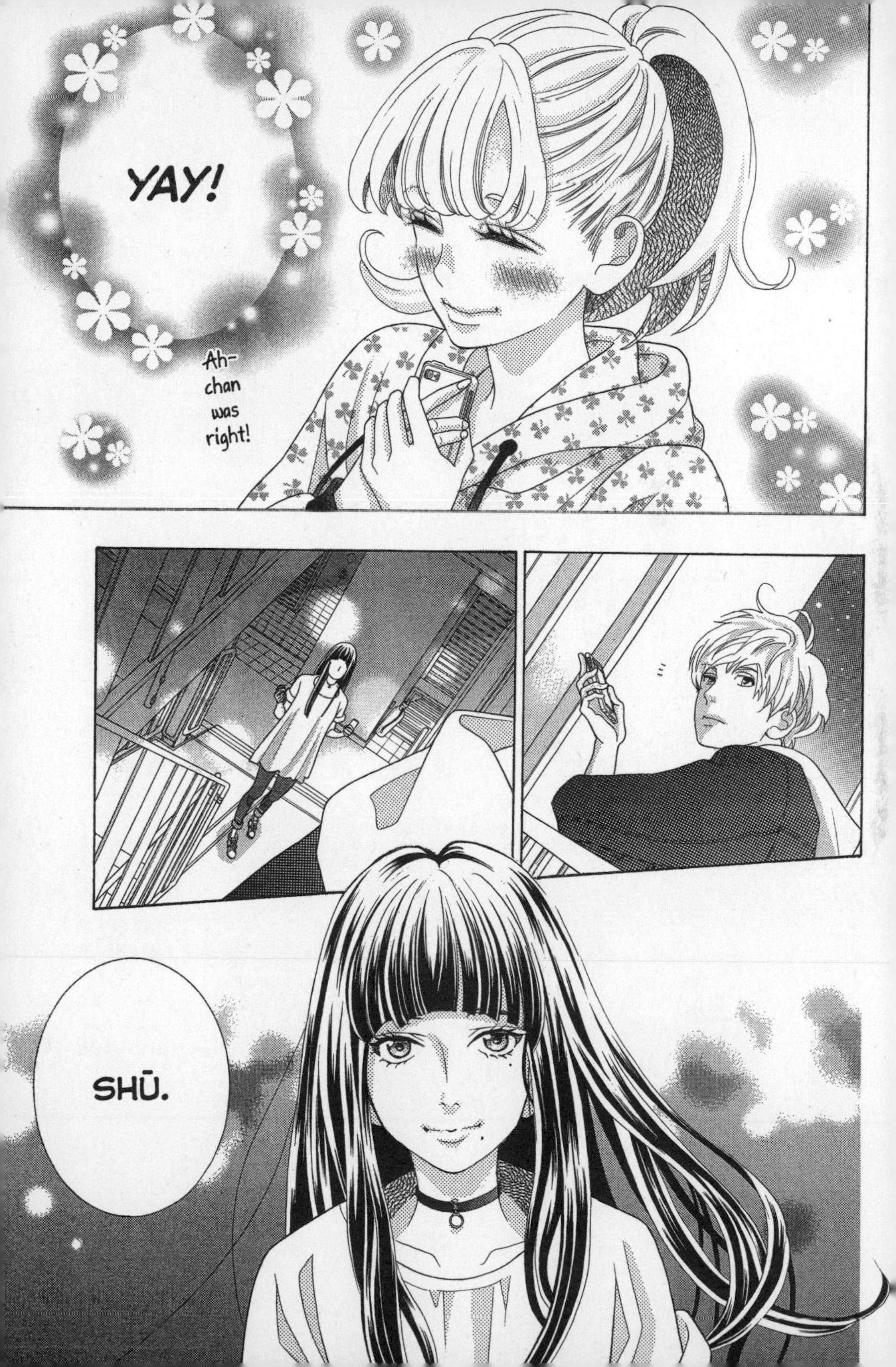
YAY!
Ah-chan was right!
SHŪ.

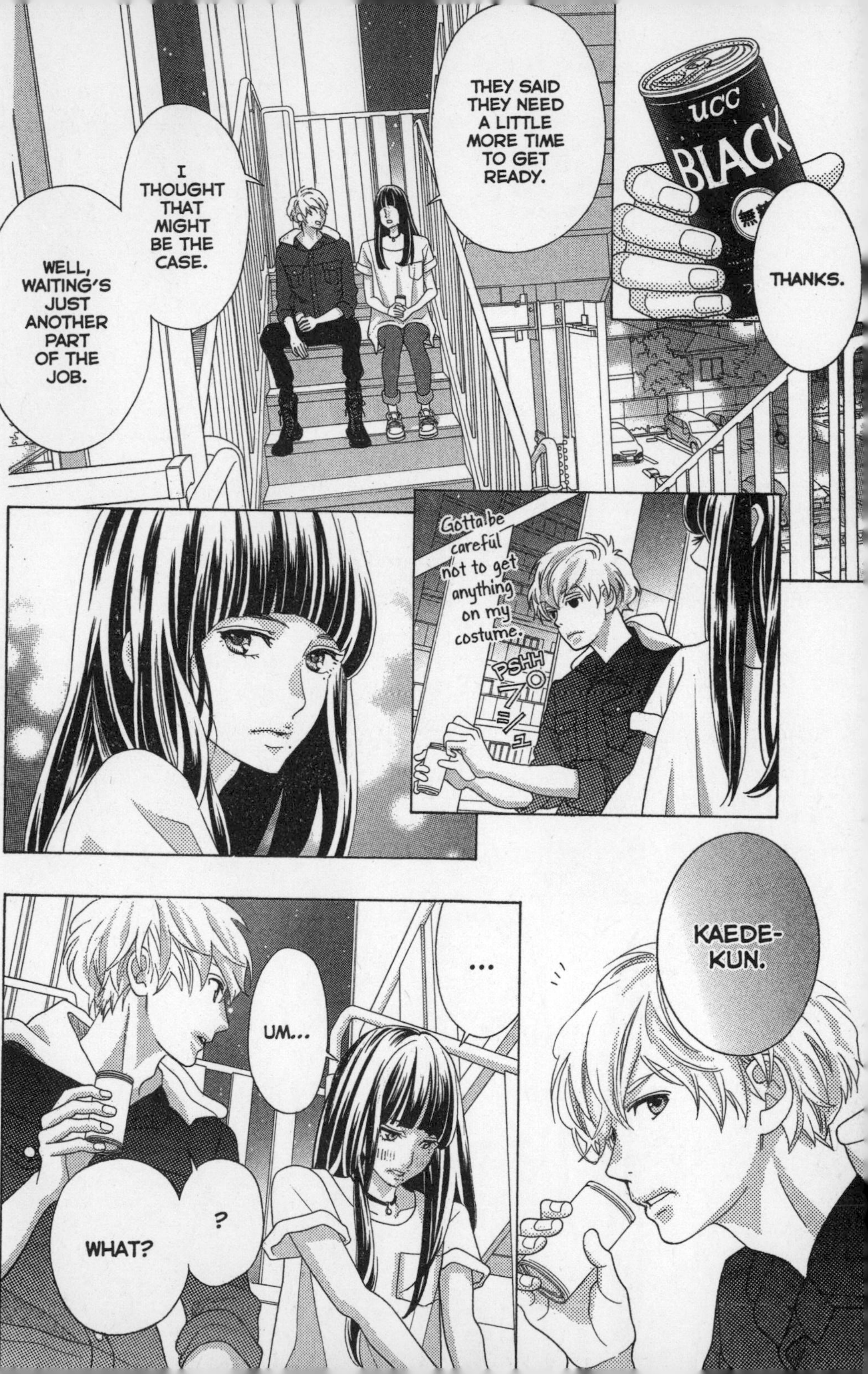
THANKS.
THEY SAID THEY NEED A LITTLE MORE TIME TO GET READY.
I THOUGHT THAT MIGHT BE THE CASE.
WELL, WAITING'S JUST ANOTHER PART OF THE JOB.
Gotta be careful not to get anything on my costume.
PSHH
KAEDE-KUN.
...
UM...
?
WHAT?

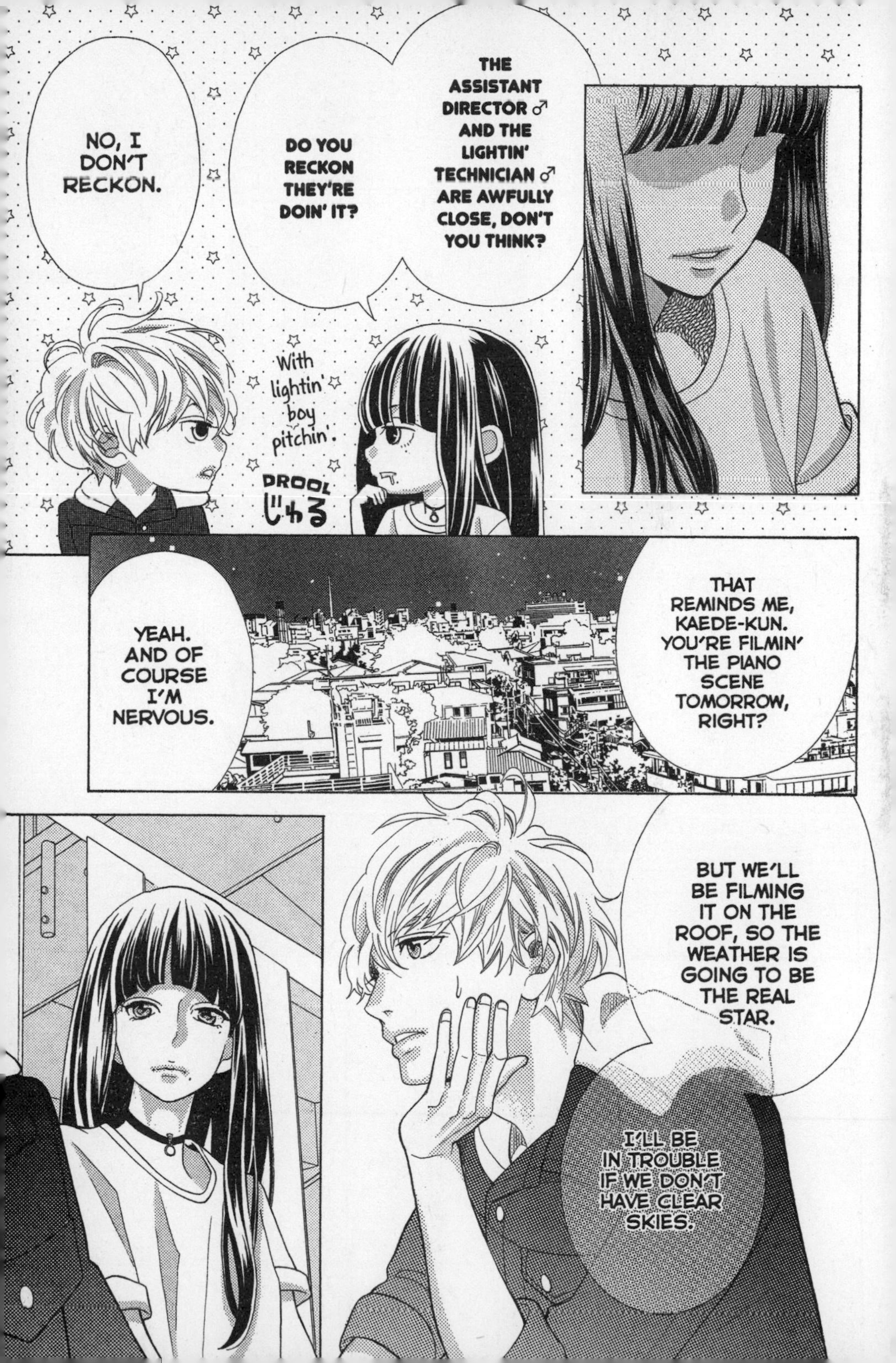
THE ASSISTANT DIRECTOR ♂ AND THE LIGHTIN' TECHNICIAN ♂ ARE AWFULLY CLOSE, DON'T YOU THINK?
DO YOU RECKON THEY'RE DOIN' IT?
NO, I DON'T RECKON.
With lightin' boy pitchin'.
DROOL
じゅる
THAT REMINDS ME, KAEDE-KUN. YOU'RE FILMIN' THE PIANO SCENE TOMORROW, RIGHT?
YEAH. AND OF COURSE I'M NERVOUS.
BUT WE'LL BE FILMING IT ON THE ROOF, SO THE WEATHER IS GOING TO BE THE REAL STAR.
I'LL BE IN TROUBLE IF WE DON'T HAVE CLEAR SKIES.

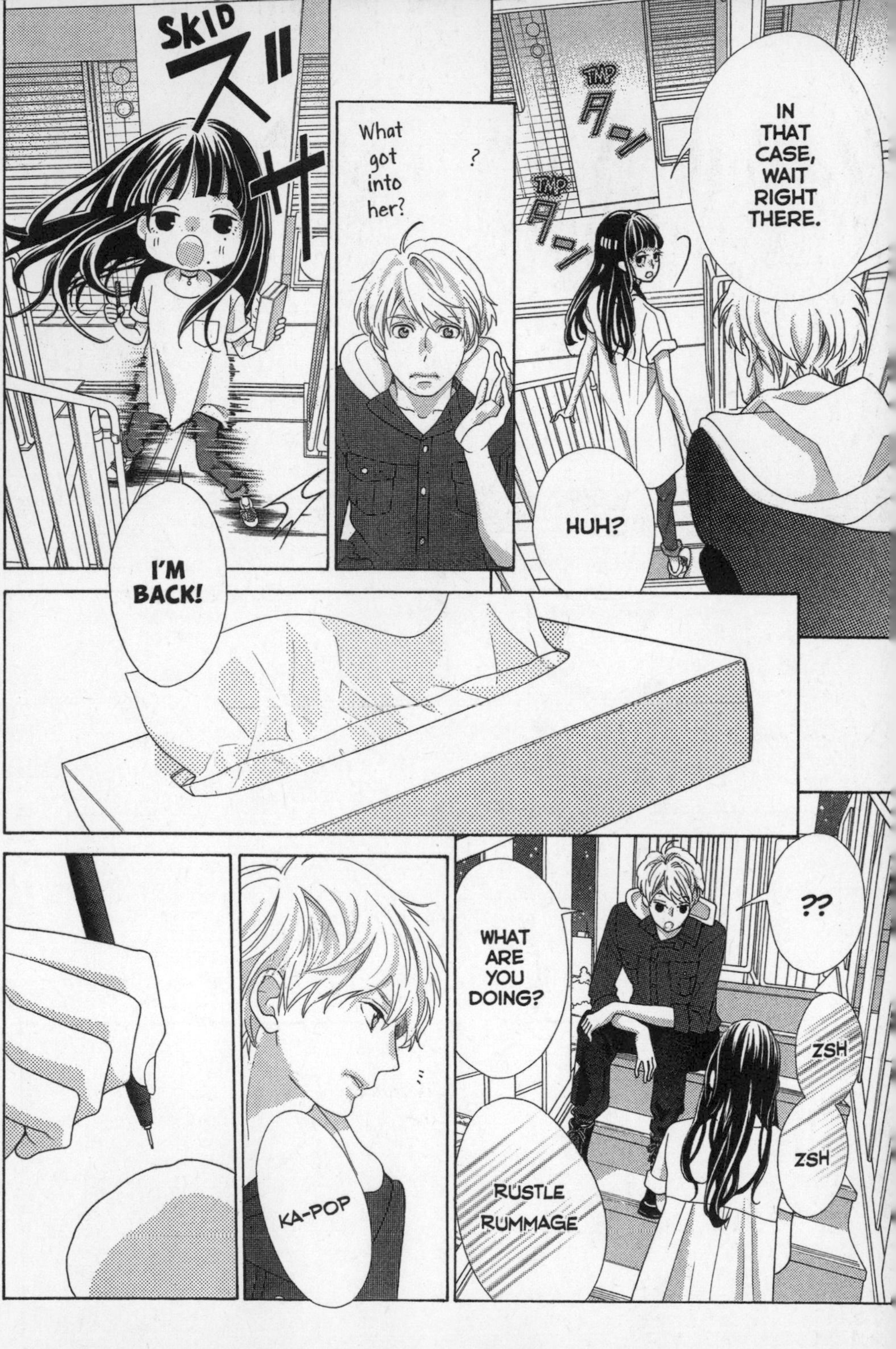
IN THAT CASE, WAIT RIGHT THERE.
TMP
TMP
HUH?
What got into her?
?
SKID
I'M BACK!
??
WHAT ARE YOU DOING?
ZSH
ZSH
RUSTLE RUMMAGE
KA-POP

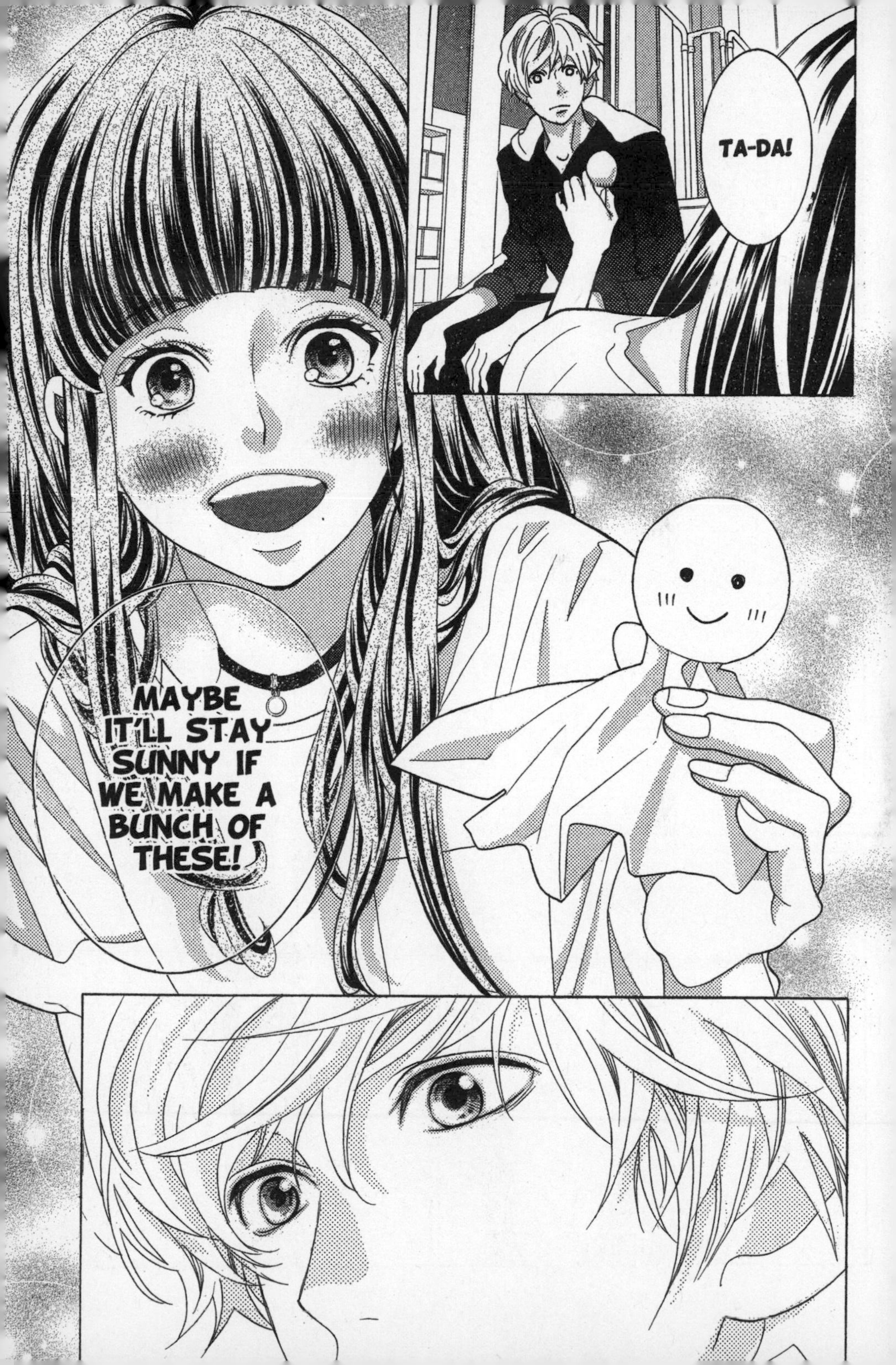
TA-DA!
MAYBE IT'LL STAY SUNNY IF WE MAKE A BUNCH OF THESE!

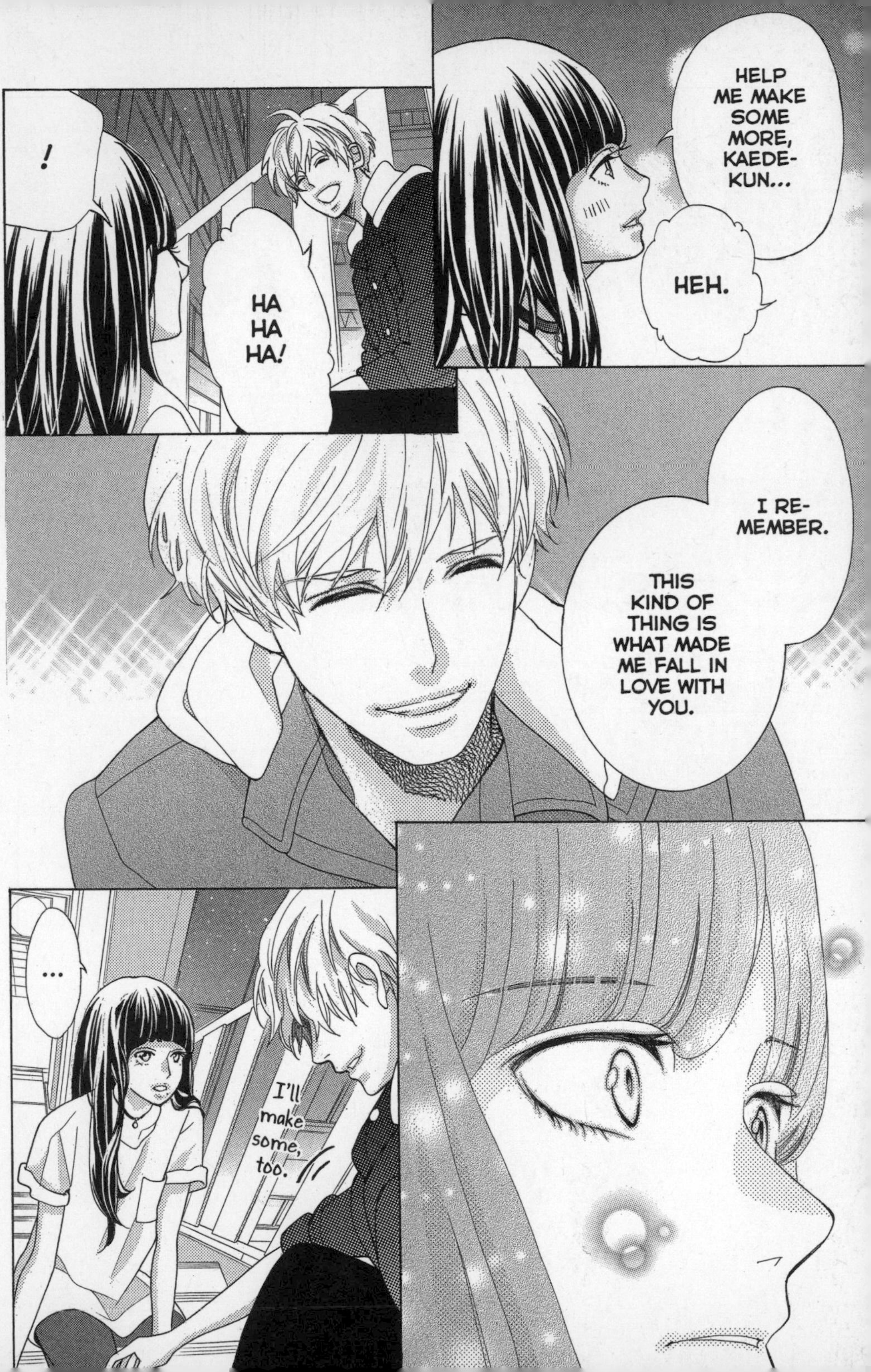
HELP ME MAKE SOME MORE, KAEDE-KUN...
HEH.
HA HA HA!
!
I RE-MEMBER.
THIS KIND OF THING IS WHAT MADE ME FALL IN LOVE WITH YOU.
I'll make some, too.
...

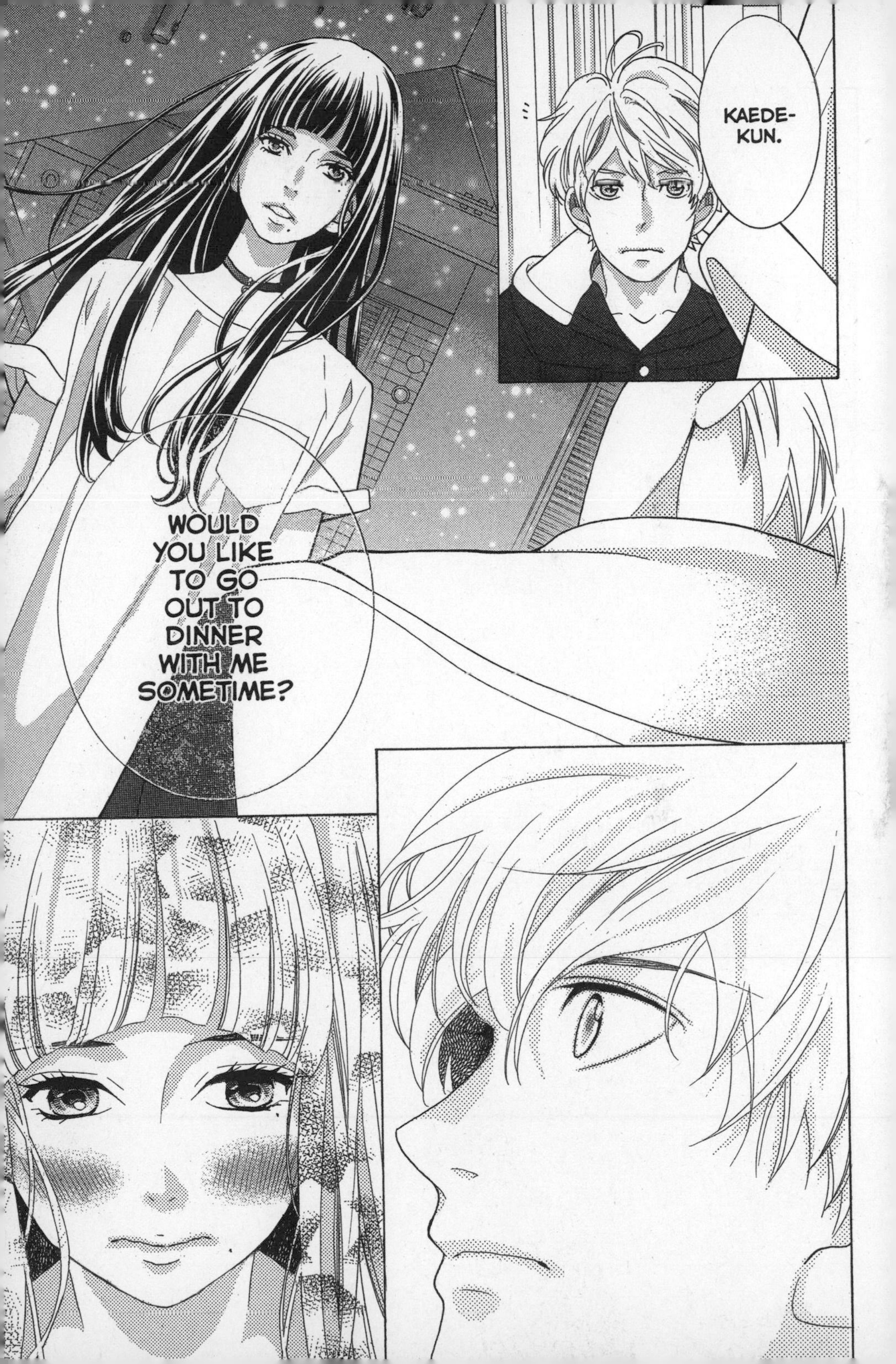
KAEDE-KUN.
WOULD YOU LIKE TO GO OUT TO DINNER WITH ME SOMETIME?

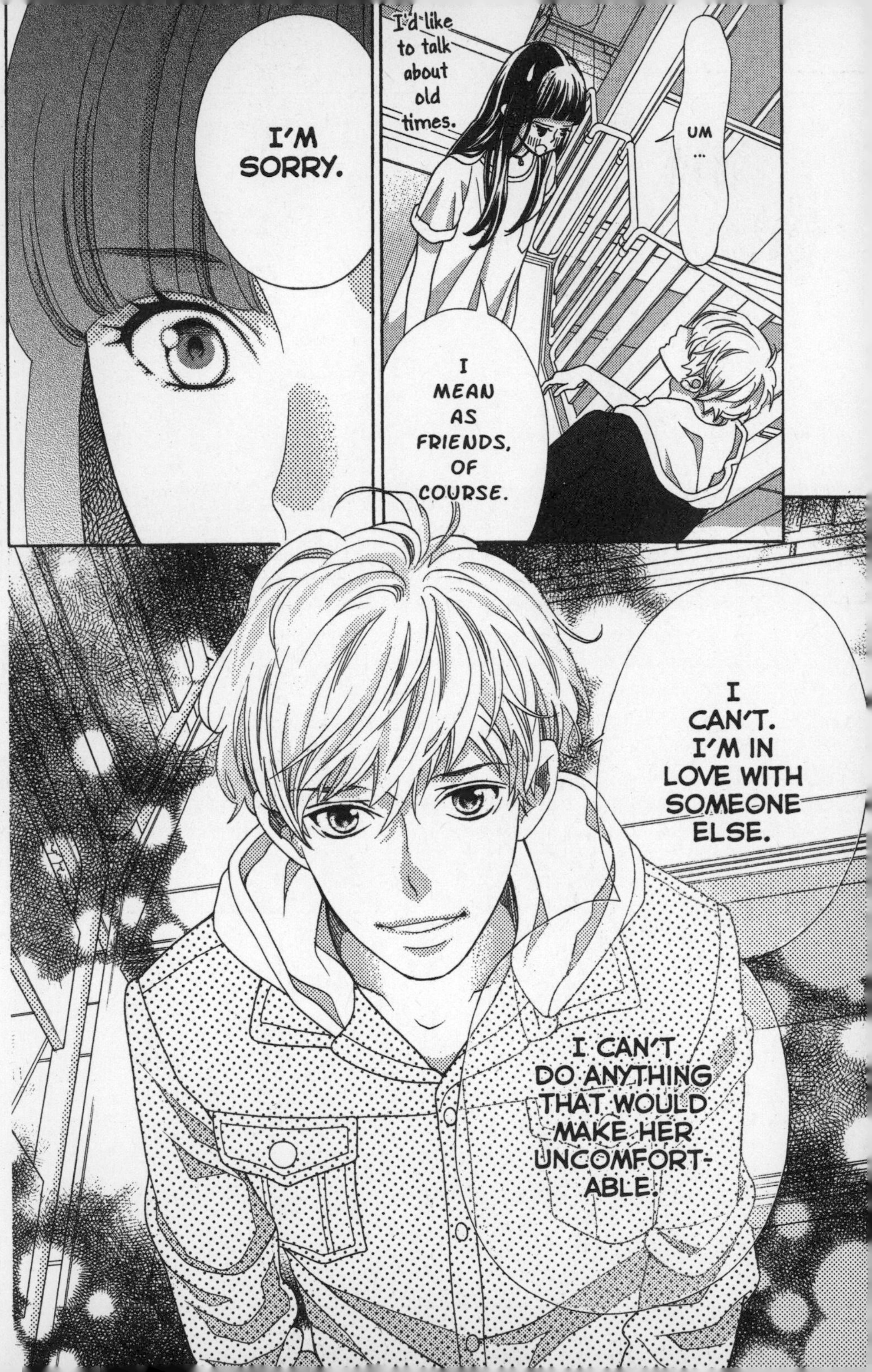
UM ...
I'd like to talk about old times.
I MEAN AS FRIENDS, OF COURSE.
I'M SORRY.
I CAN'T. I'M IN LOVE WITH SOMEONE ELSE.
I CAN'T DO ANYTHING THAT WOULD MAKE HER UNCOMFORT-ABLE.

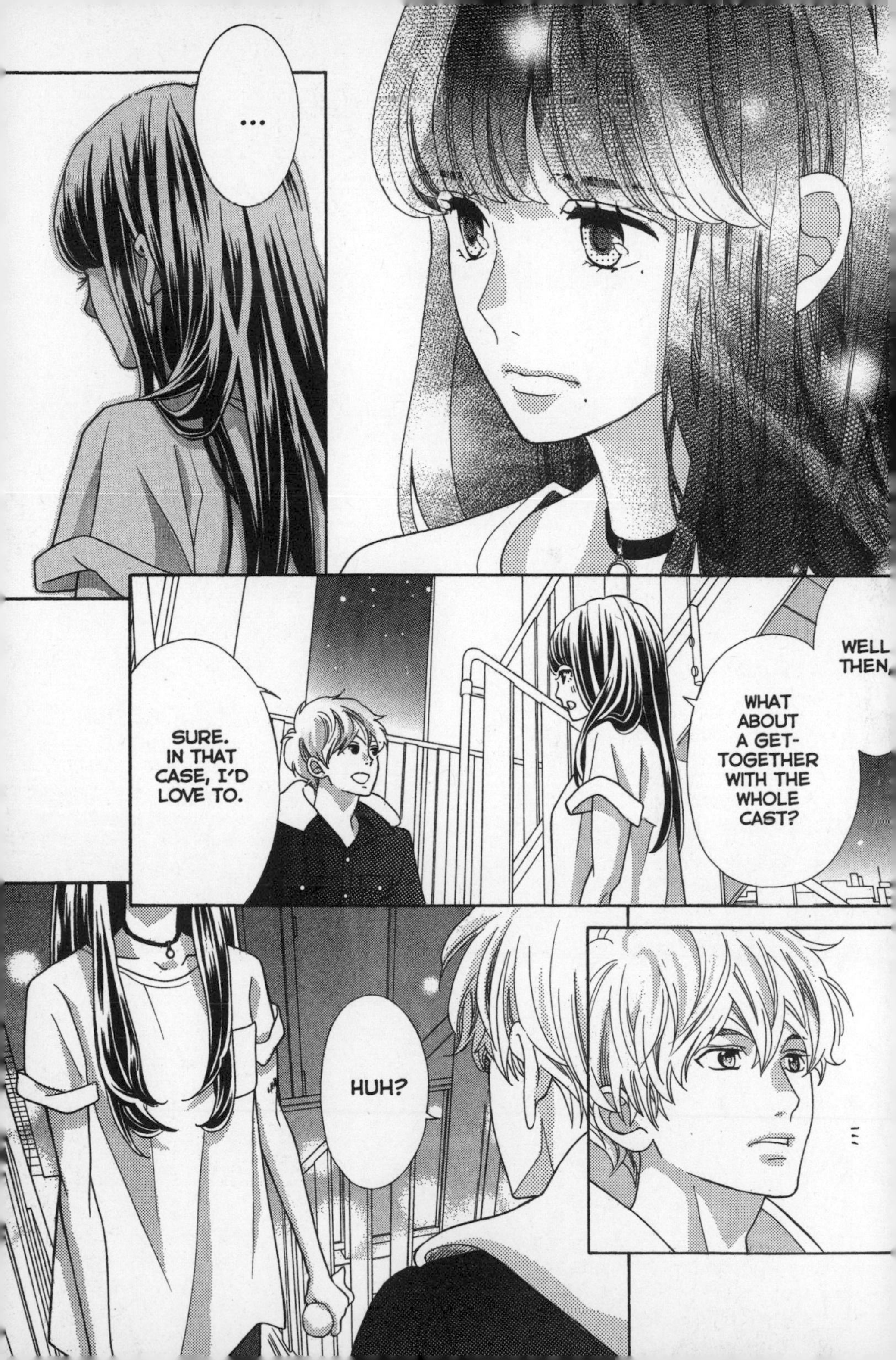
...
WELL THEN,
WHAT ABOUT A GET-TOGETHER WITH THE WHOLE CAST?
SURE. IN THAT CASE, I'D LOVE TO.
HUH?

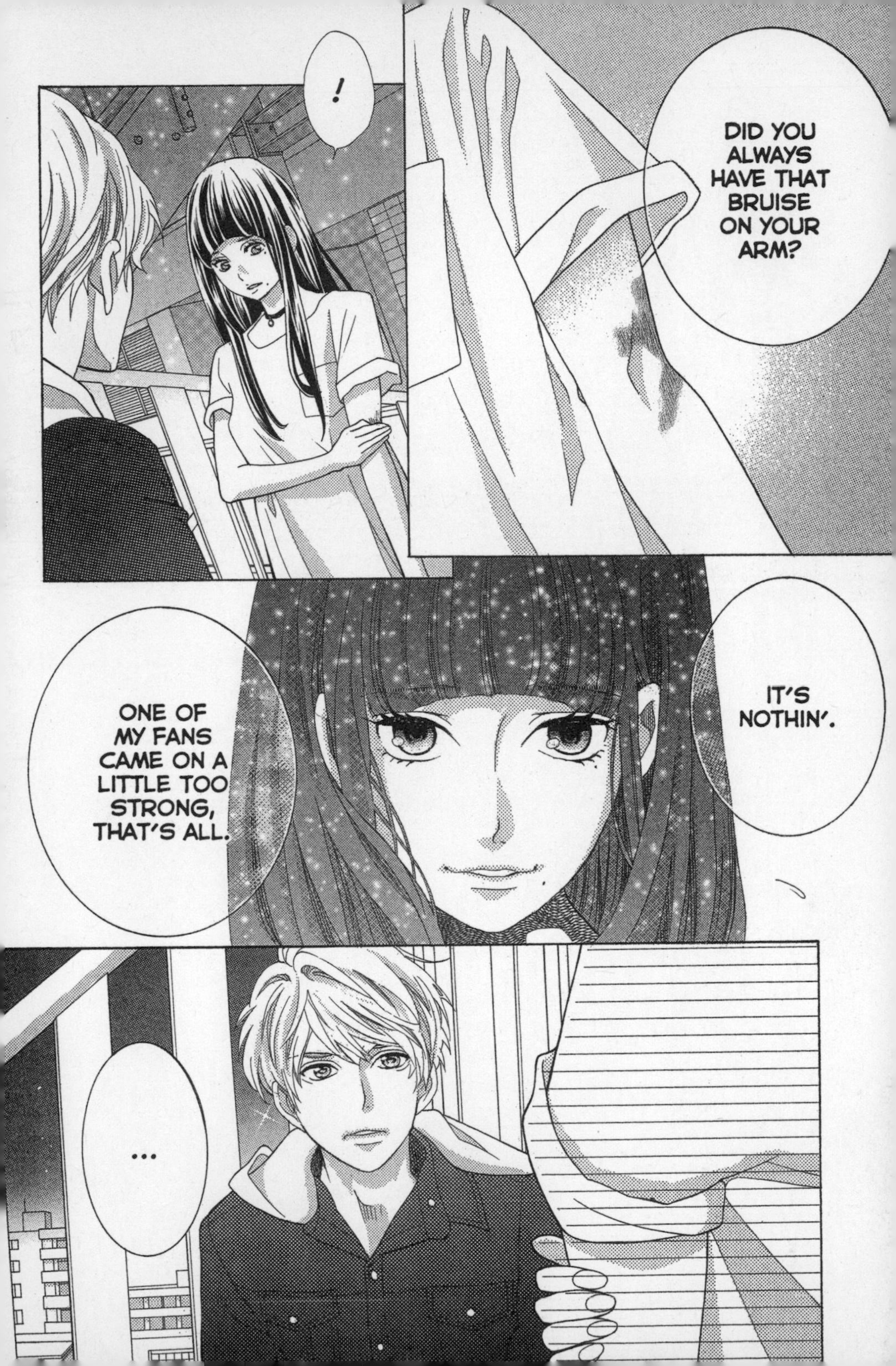
DID YOU ALWAYS HAVE THAT BRUISE ON YOUR ARM?
!
IT'S NOTHIN'.
ONE OF MY FANS CAME ON A LITTLE TOO STRONG, THAT'S ALL.
...

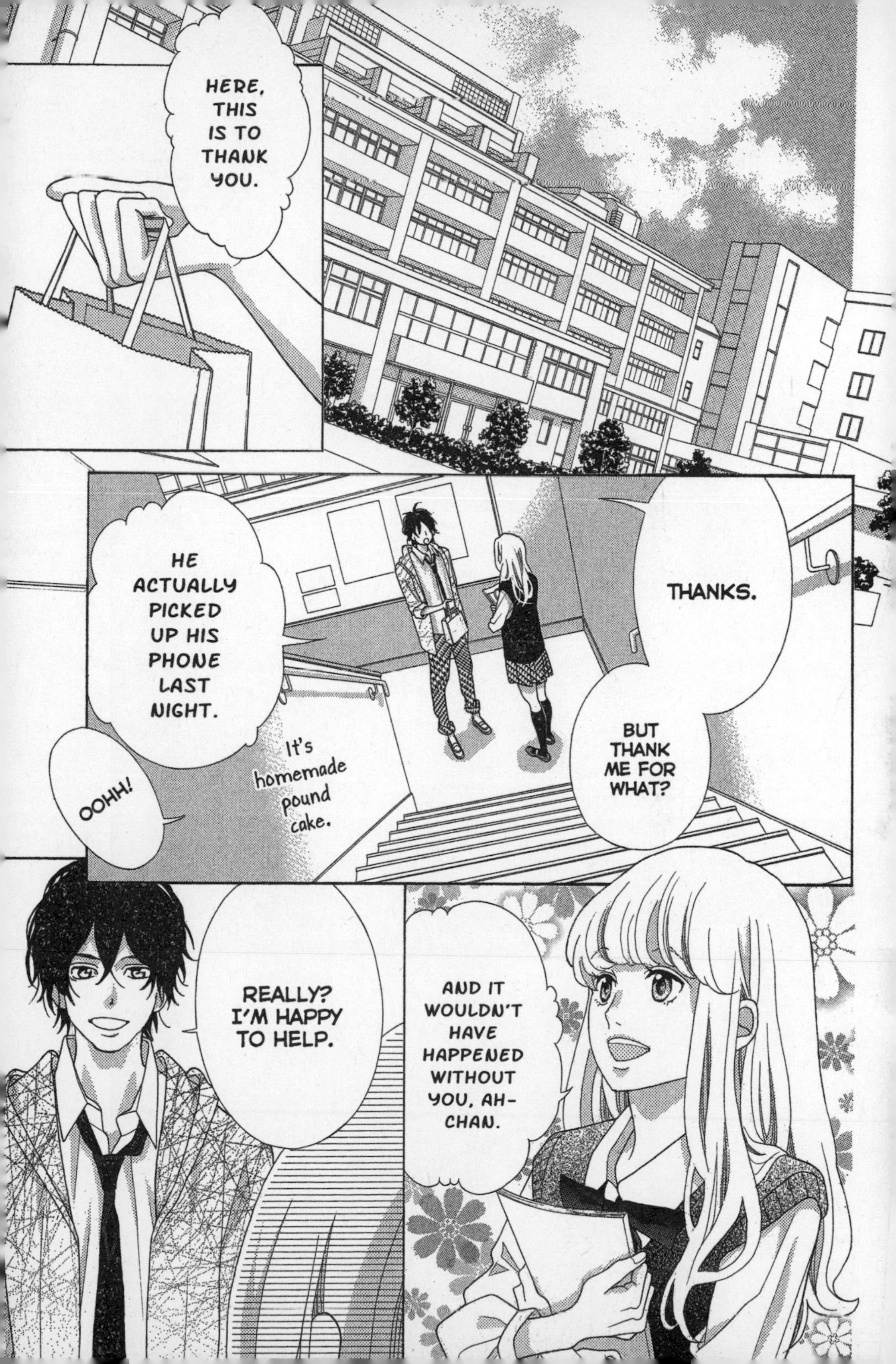
HERE, THIS IS TO THANK YOU.
THANKS.
BUT THANK ME FOR WHAT?
HE ACTUALLY PICKED UP HIS PHONE LAST NIGHT.
It's homemade pound cake.
OOHH!
AND IT WOULDN'T HAVE HAPPENED WITHOUT YOU, AH-CHAN.
REALLY? I'M HAPPY TO HELP.

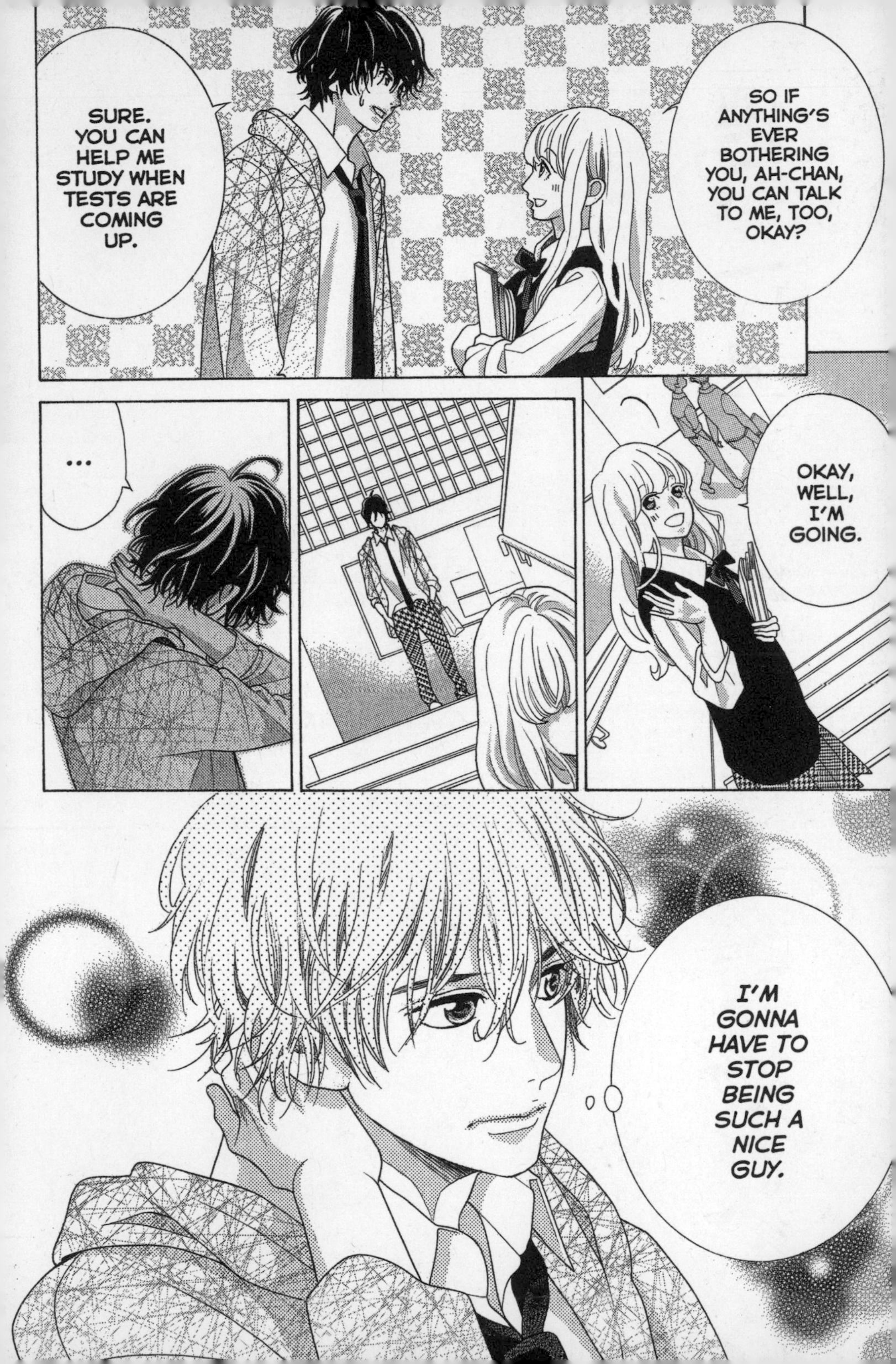
SO IF ANYTHING'S EVER BOTHERING YOU, AH-CHAN, YOU CAN TALK TO ME, TOO, OKAY?
SURE. YOU CAN HELP ME STUDY WHEN TESTS ARE COMING UP.
OKAY, WELL, I'M GOING.
...
I'M GONNA HAVE TO STOP BEING SUCH A NICE GUY.

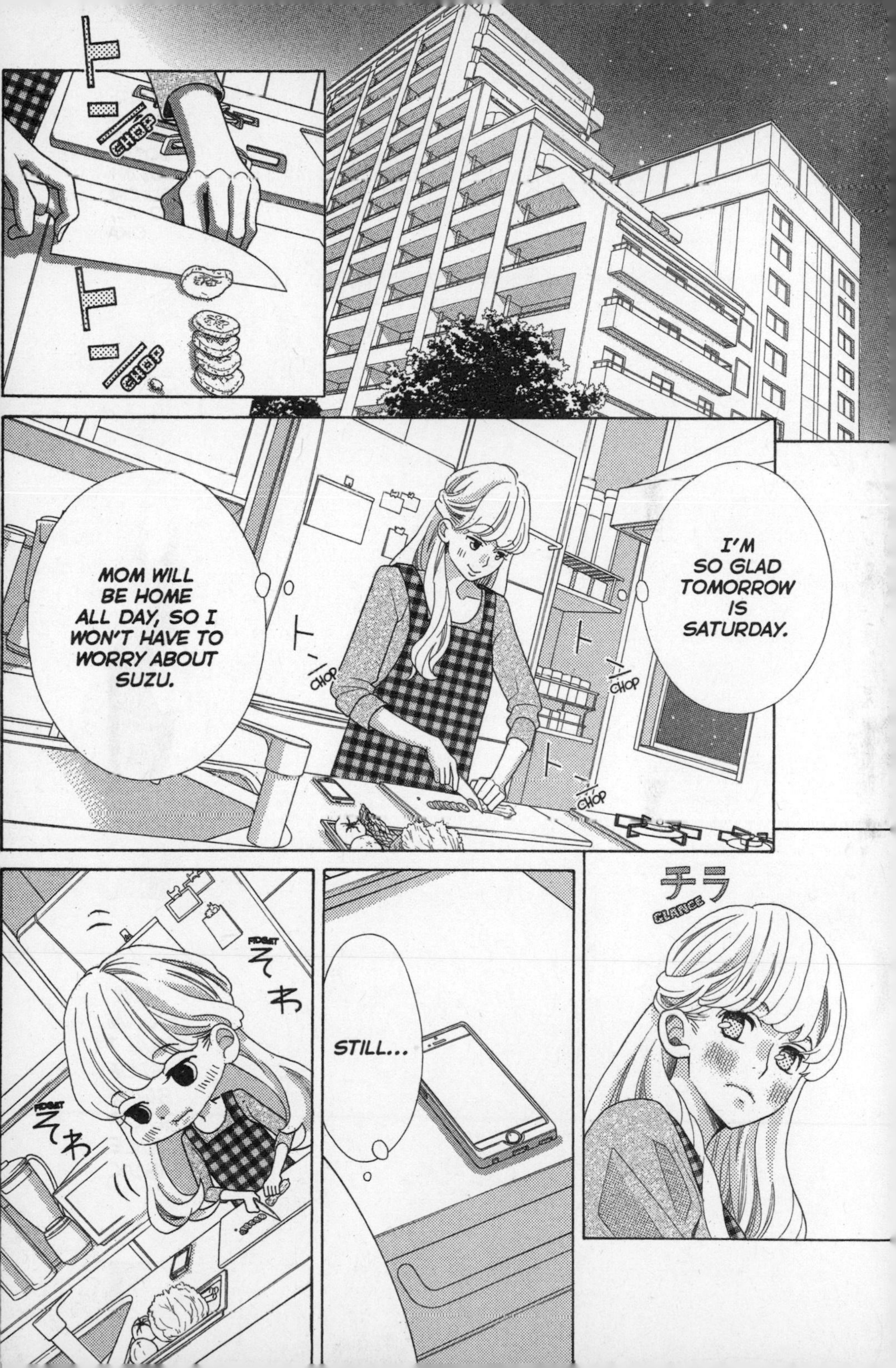
CHOP
CHOP
I'M SO GLAD TOMORROW IS SATURDAY.
MOM WILL BE HOME ALL DAY, SO I WON'T HAVE TO WORRY ABOUT SUZU.
CHOP
CHOP
CHOP
チラ
GLANCE
STILL...
FIDGET
そわ
FIDGET
そわ

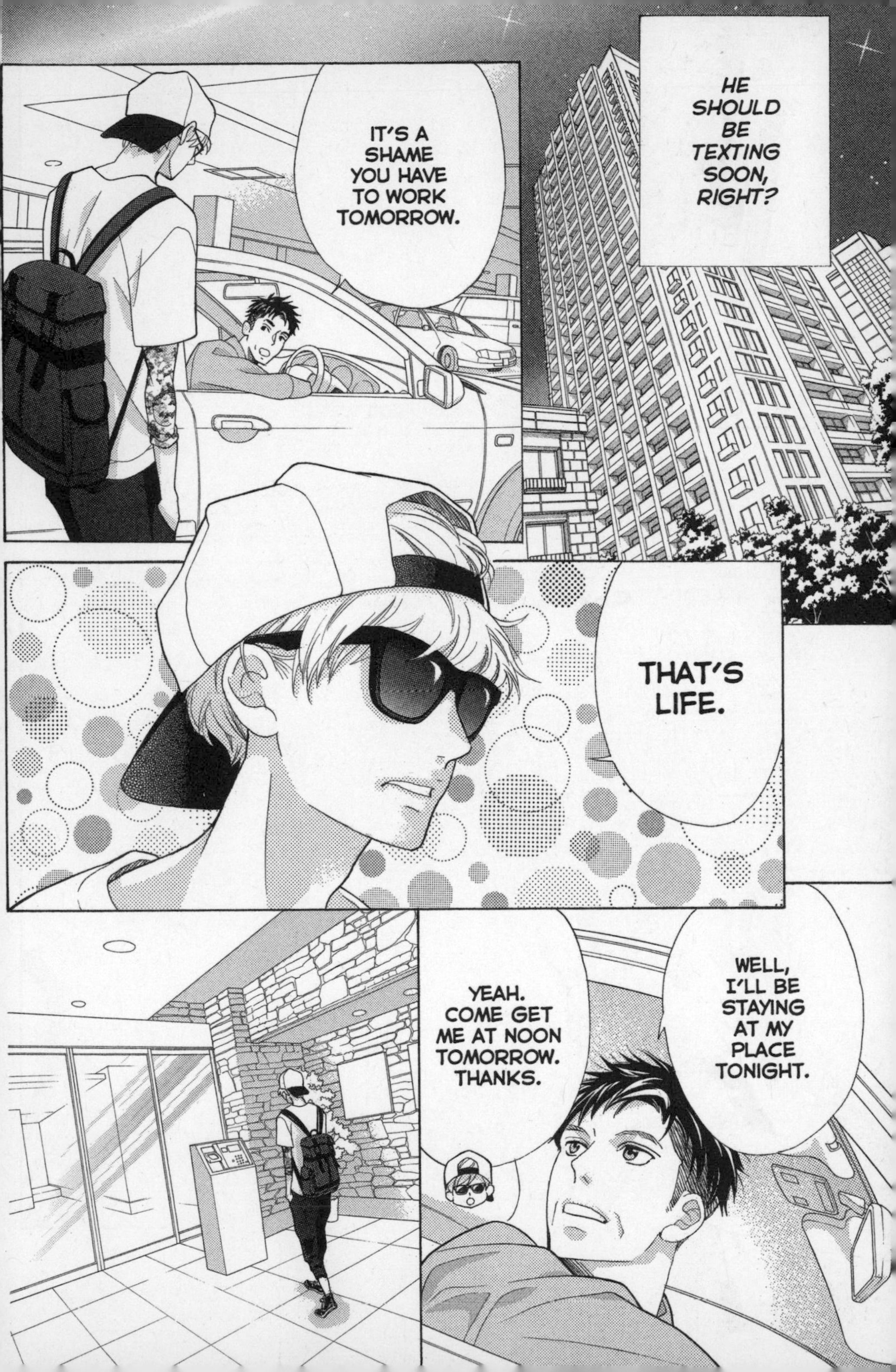
HE SHOULD BE TEXTING SOON, RIGHT?
IT'S A SHAME YOU HAVE TO WORK TOMORROW.
THAT'S LIFE.
WELL, I'LL BE STAYING AT MY PLACE TONIGHT.
YEAH. COME GET ME AT NOON TOMORROW. THANKS.

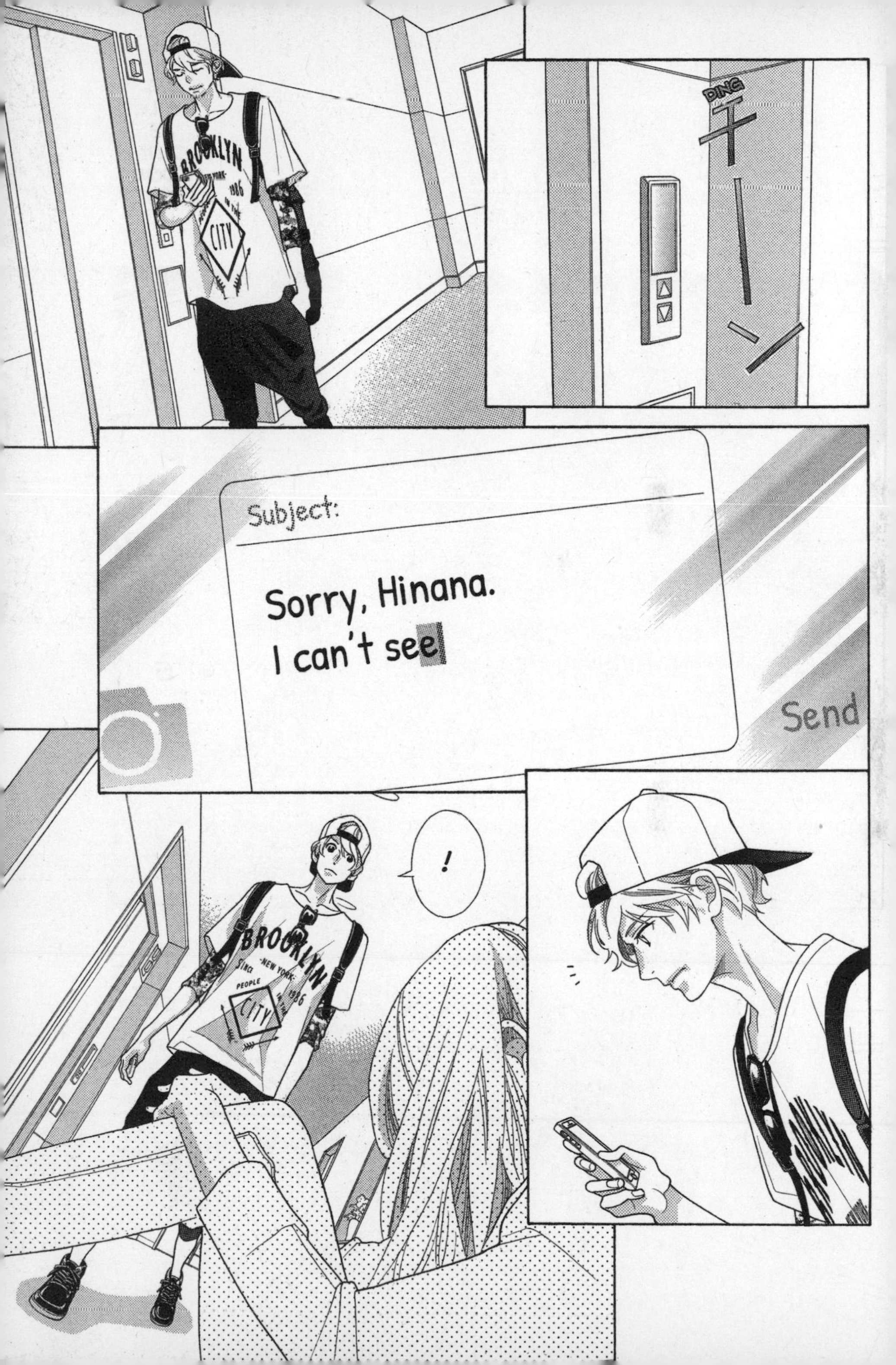
DING
Subject:
Sorry, Hinana.
I can't see
Send
!

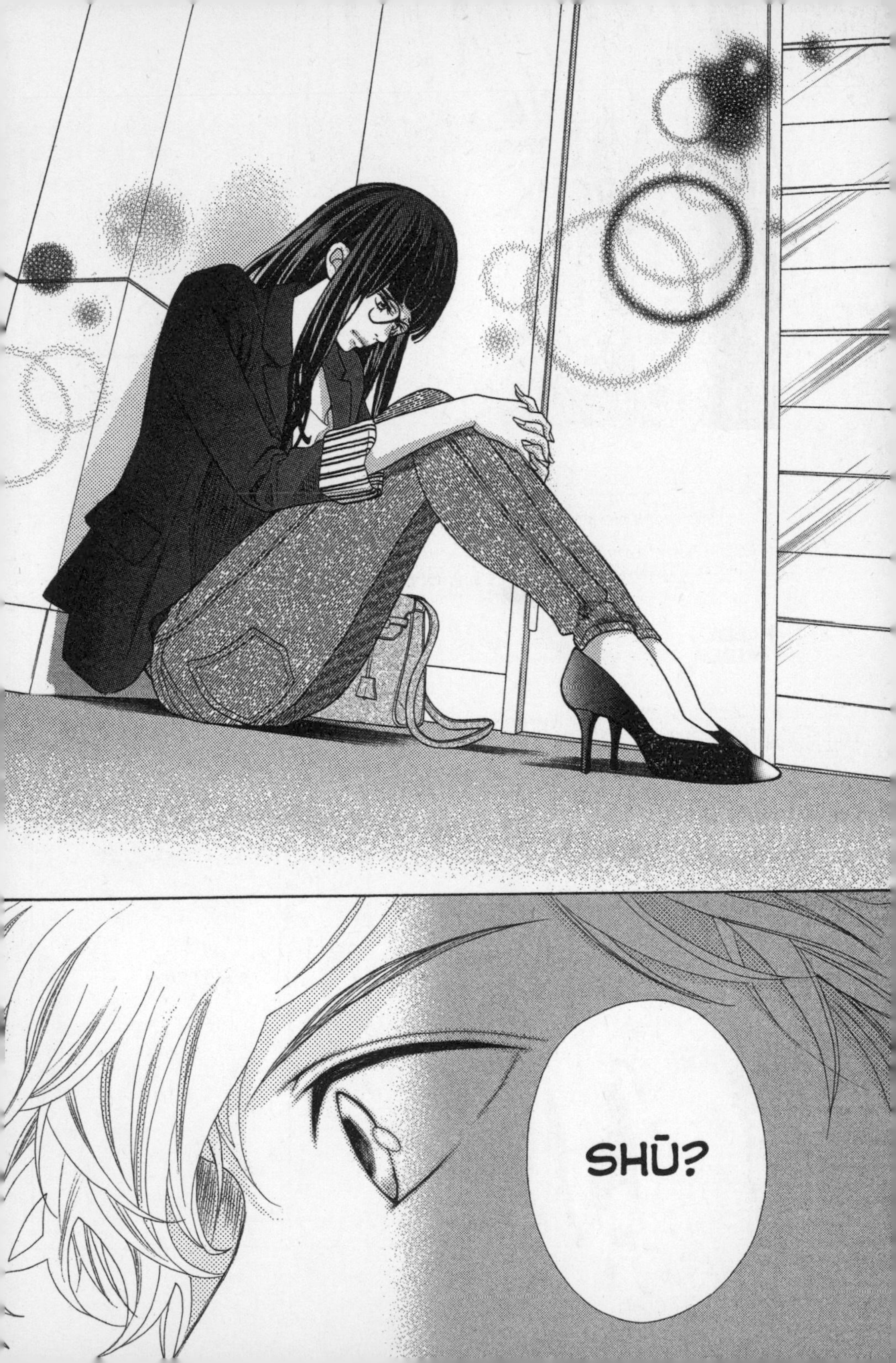
SHŪ?

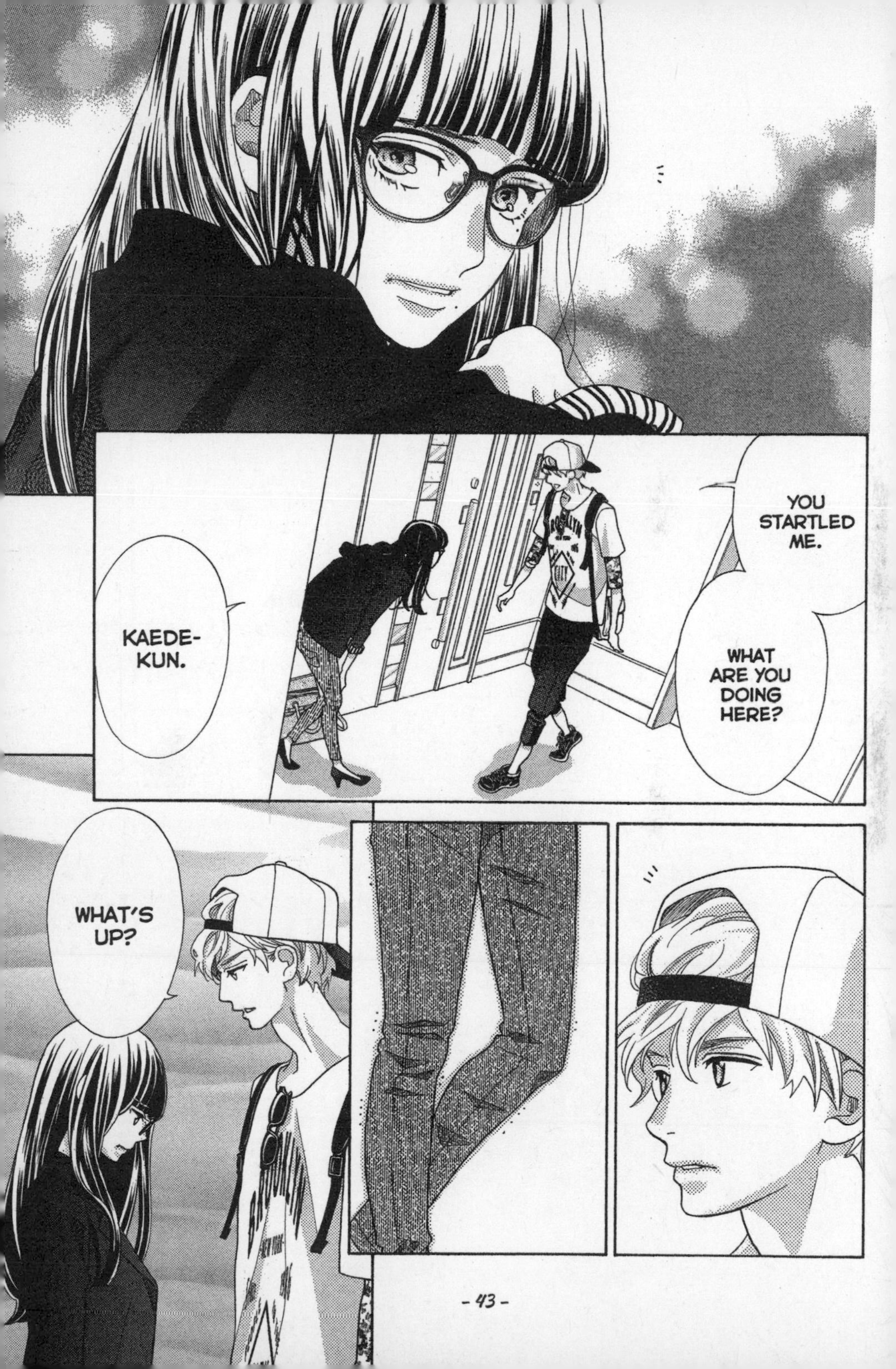
YOU STARTLED ME.
WHAT ARE YOU DOING HERE?
KAEDE-KUN.
WHAT'S UP?

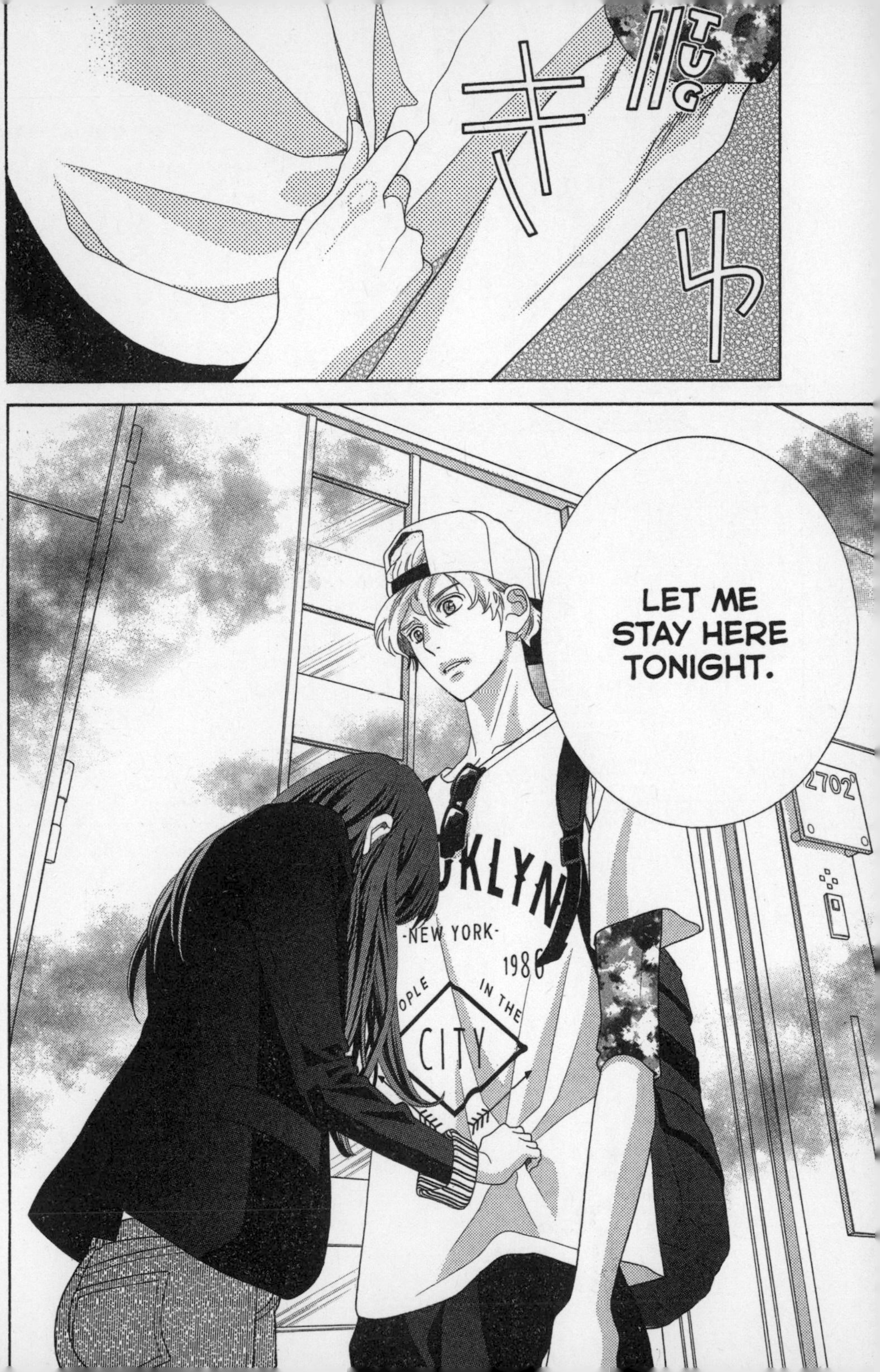
TUG
LET ME STAY HERE TONIGHT.

Kiss Me
at
the Stroke of
Midnight

Kiss Me
at
the Stroke of
Midnight

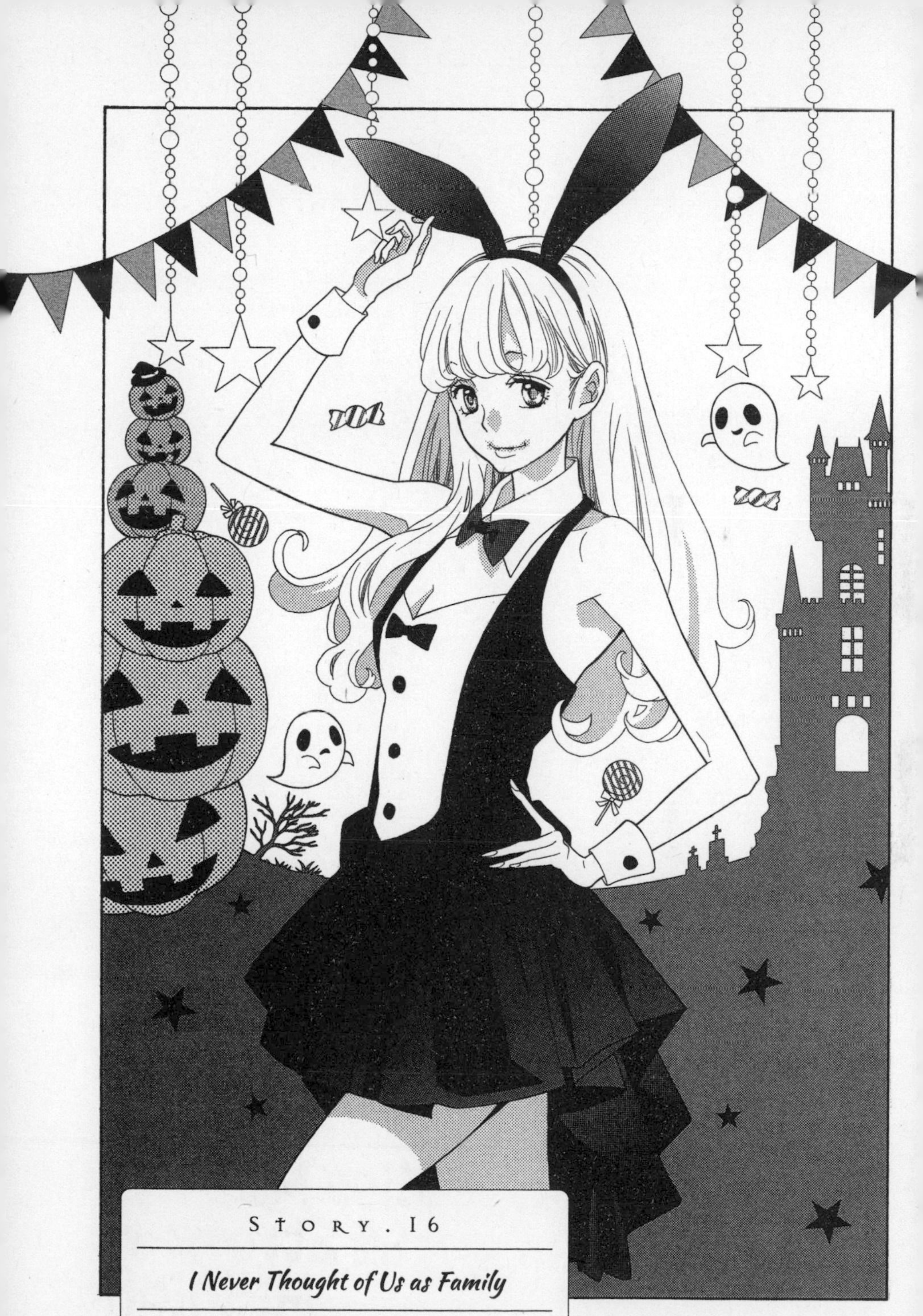

STORY. 16

I Never Thought of Us as Family

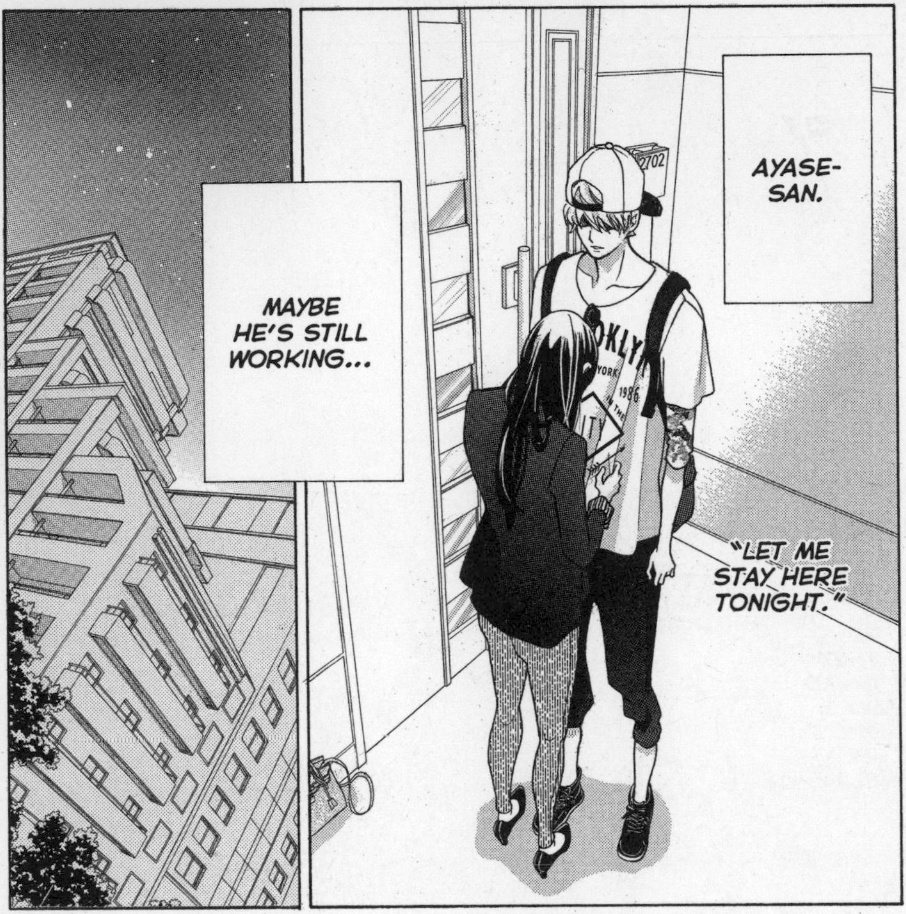
AYASE-SAN.
"LET ME STAY HERE TONIGHT."
MAYBE HE'S STILL WORKING...

Kiss Me at the Stroke of Midnight

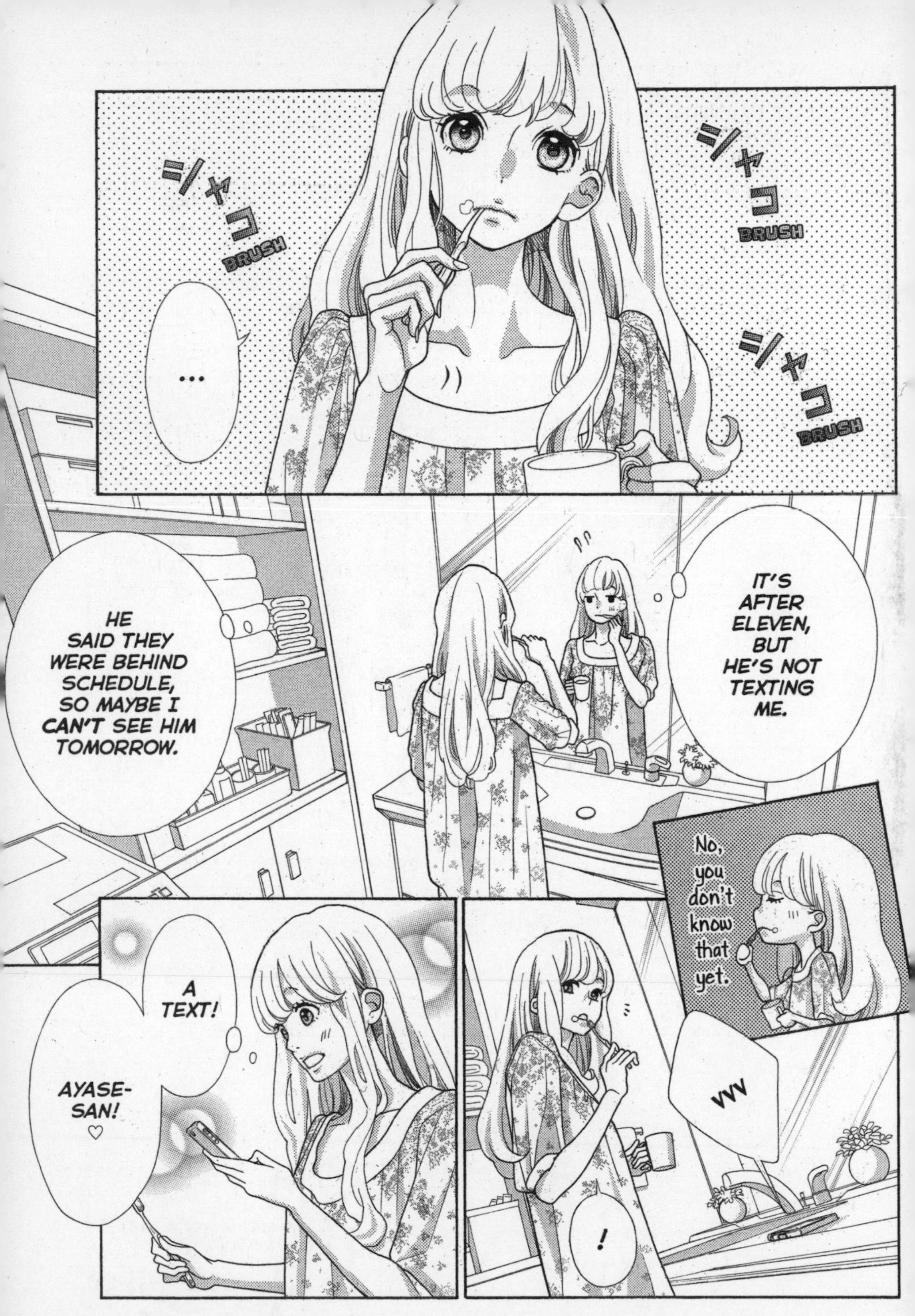
シャコ
BRUSH
シャコ
BRUSH
シャコ
BRUSH
...
IT'S AFTER ELEVEN, BUT HE'S NOT TEXTING ME.
HE SAID THEY WERE BEHIND SCHEDULE, SO MAYBE I CAN'T SEE HIM TOMORROW.
No, you don't know that yet.
VVV
!
A TEXT!
AYASE-SAN! ♡

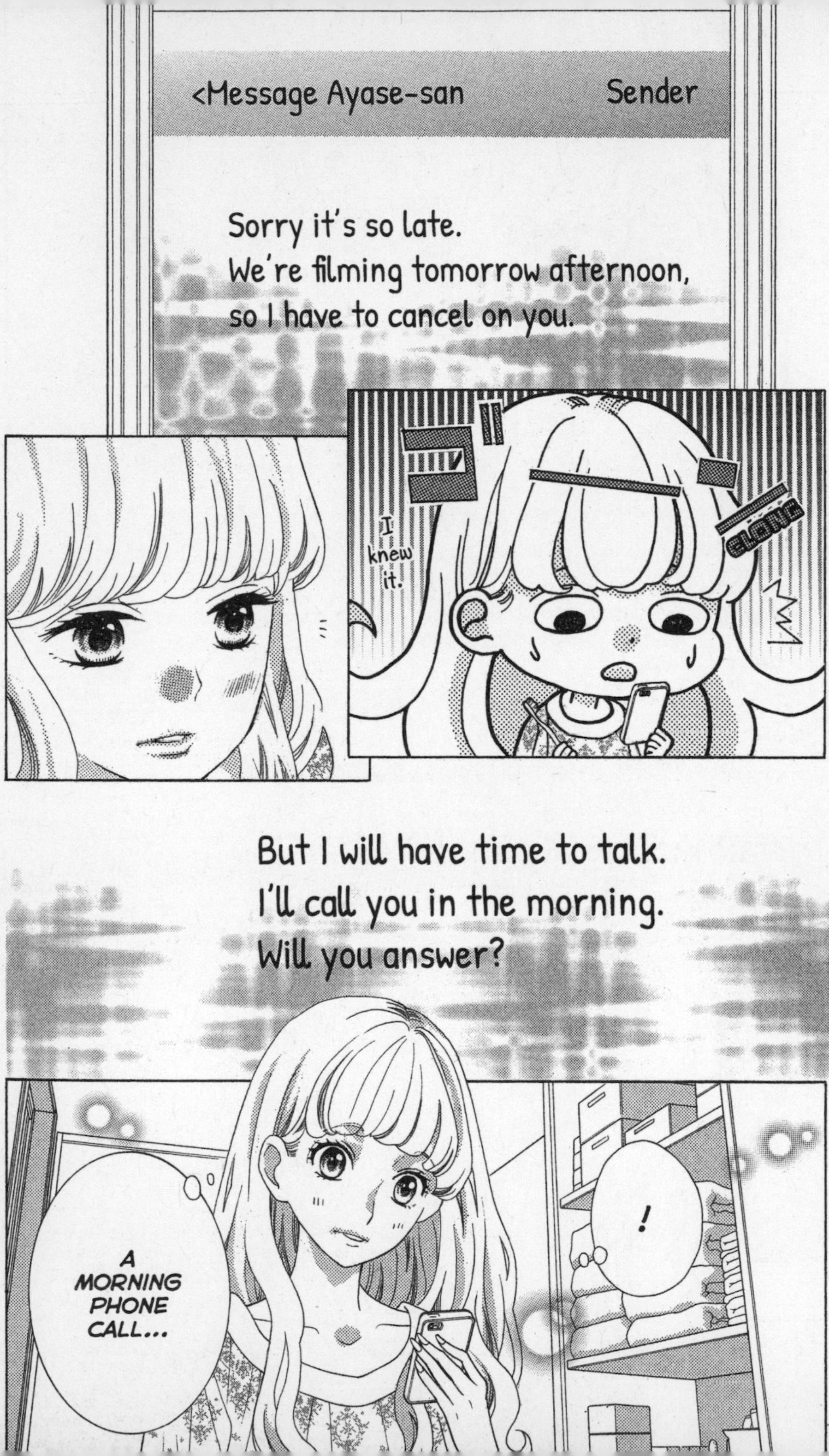

<Message Ayase-san Sender
Sorry it's so late.
We're filming tomorrow afternoon,
so I have to cancel on you.
I knew it.
But I will have time to talk.
I'll call you in the morning.
Will you answer?
!
A MORNING PHONE CALL...

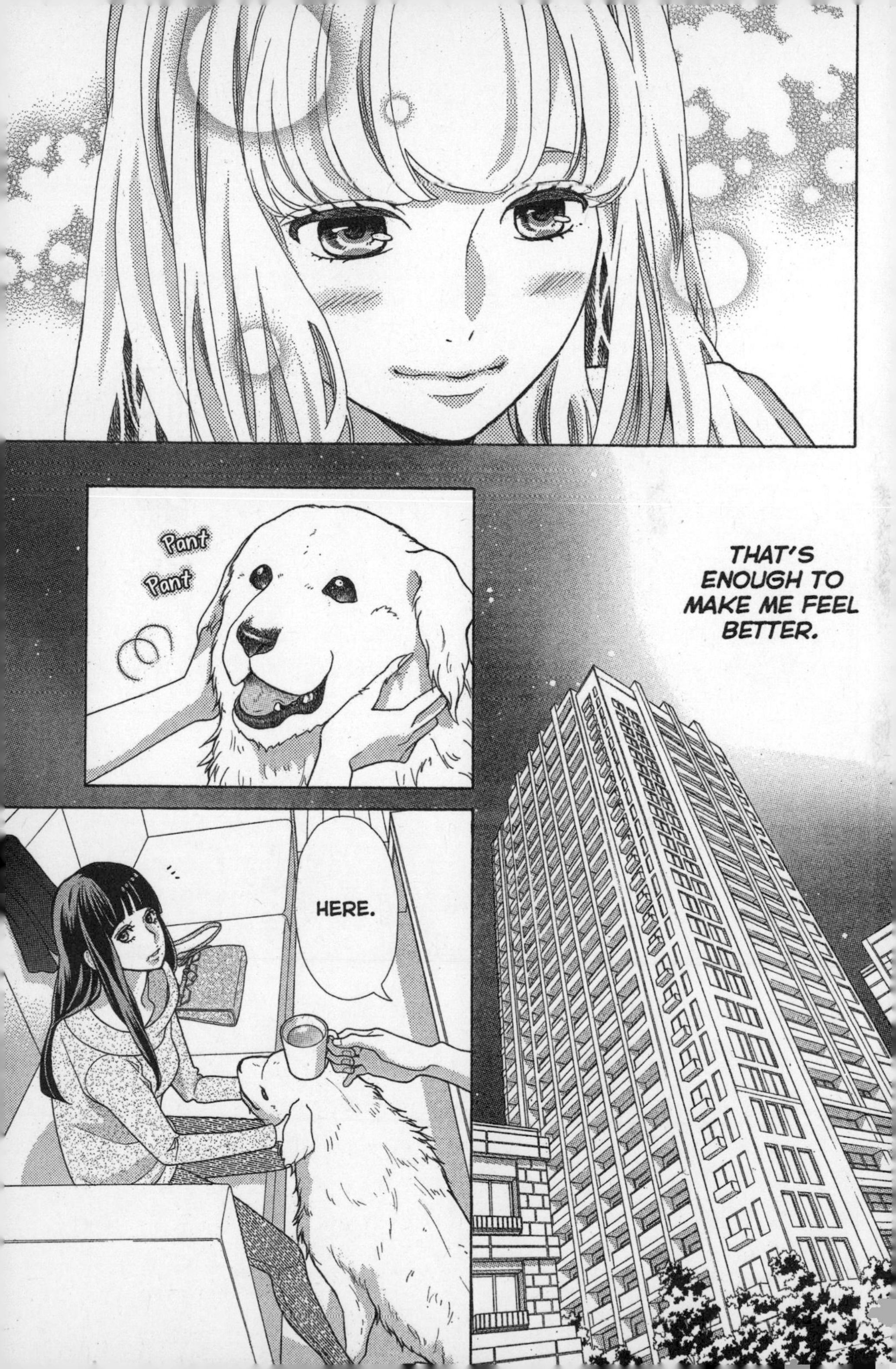
THAT'S ENOUGH TO MAKE ME FEEL BETTER.
Pant
Pant
HERE.

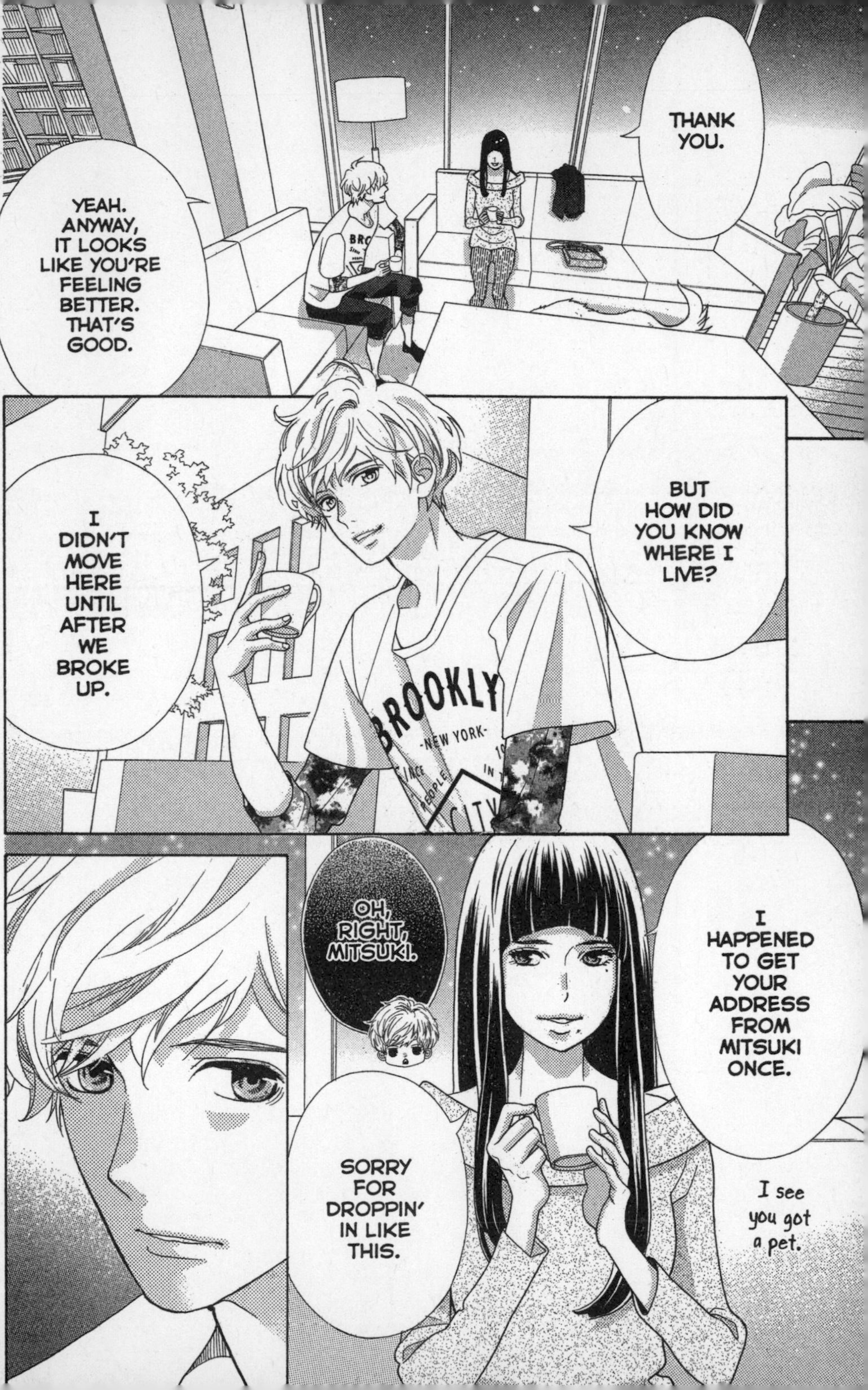
THANK YOU.
YEAH. ANYWAY, IT LOOKS LIKE YOU'RE FEELING BETTER. THAT'S GOOD.
BUT HOW DID YOU KNOW WHERE I LIVE?
I DIDN'T MOVE HERE UNTIL AFTER WE BROKE UP.
I HAPPENED TO GET YOUR ADDRESS FROM MITSUKI ONCE.
OH, RIGHT, MITSUKI.
I see you got a pet.
SORRY FOR DROPPIN' IN LIKE THIS.

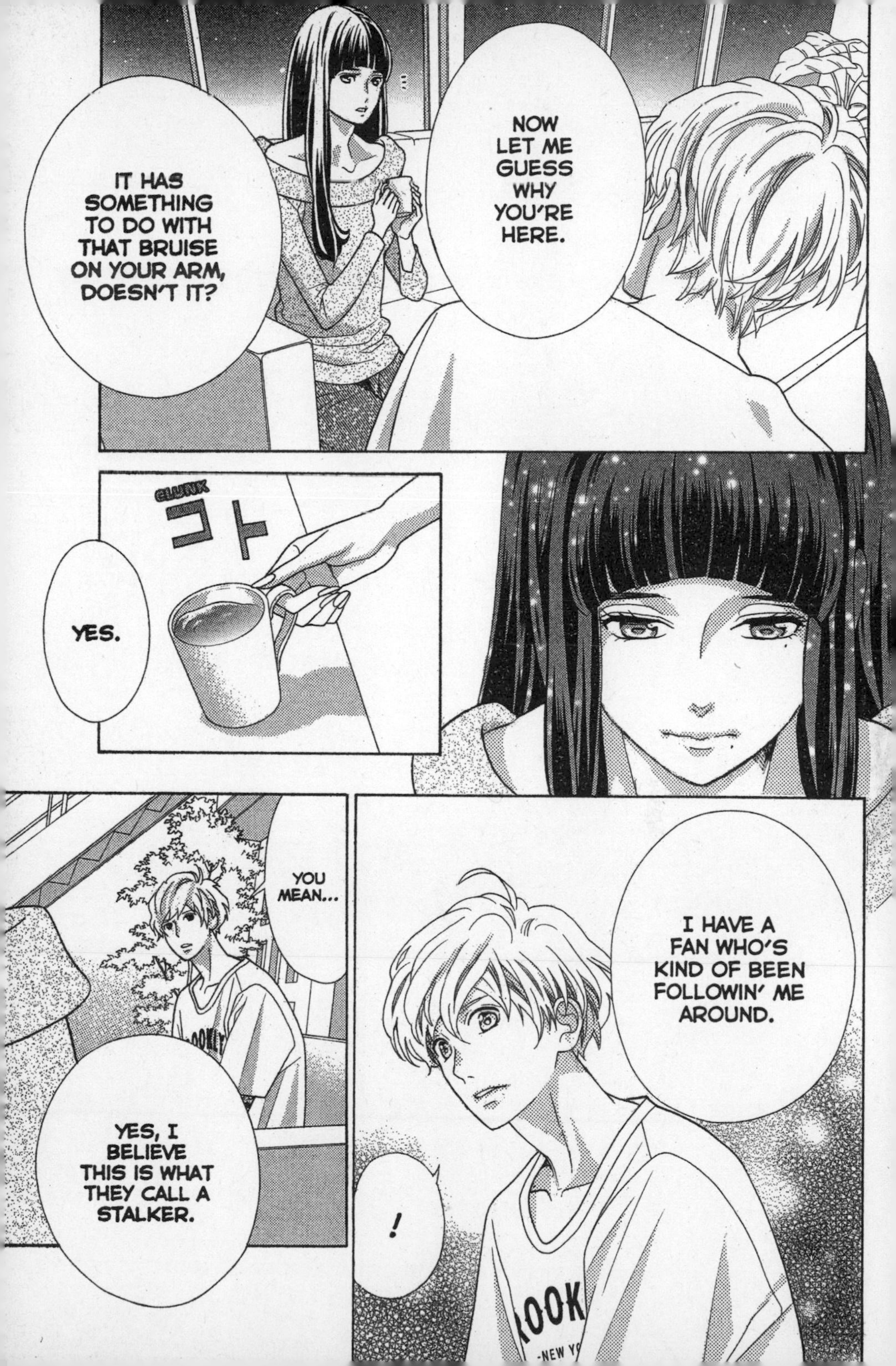
NOW LET ME GUESS WHY YOU'RE HERE.
IT HAS SOMETHING TO DO WITH THAT BRUISE ON YOUR ARM, DOESN'T IT?
CLUNK
コト
YES.
I HAVE A FAN WHO'S KIND OF BEEN FOLLOWIN' ME AROUND.
!
YOU MEAN...
YES, I BELIEVE THIS IS WHAT THEY CALL A STALKER.

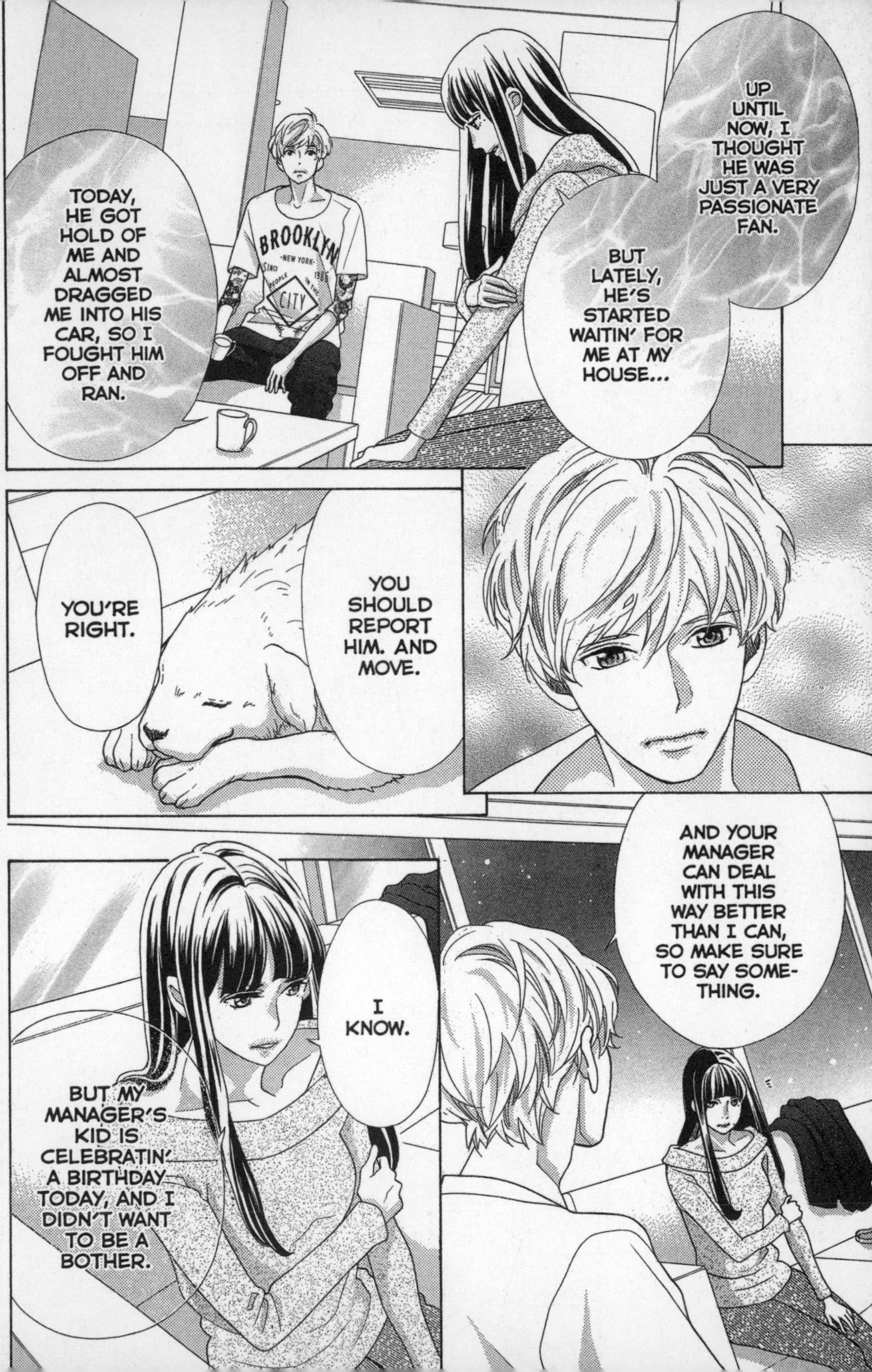
UP UNTIL NOW, I THOUGHT HE WAS JUST A VERY PASSIONATE FAN.
BUT LATELY, HE'S STARTED WAITIN' FOR ME AT MY HOUSE...
TODAY, HE GOT HOLD OF ME AND ALMOST DRAGGED ME INTO HIS CAR, SO I FOUGHT HIM OFF AND RAN.
YOU SHOULD REPORT HIM. AND MOVE.
YOU'RE RIGHT.
AND YOUR MANAGER CAN DEAL WITH THIS WAY BETTER THAN I CAN, SO MAKE SURE TO SAY SOME-THING.
I KNOW.
BUT MY MANAGER'S KID IS CELEBRATIN' A BIRTHDAY TODAY, AND I DIDN'T WANT TO BE A BOTHER.

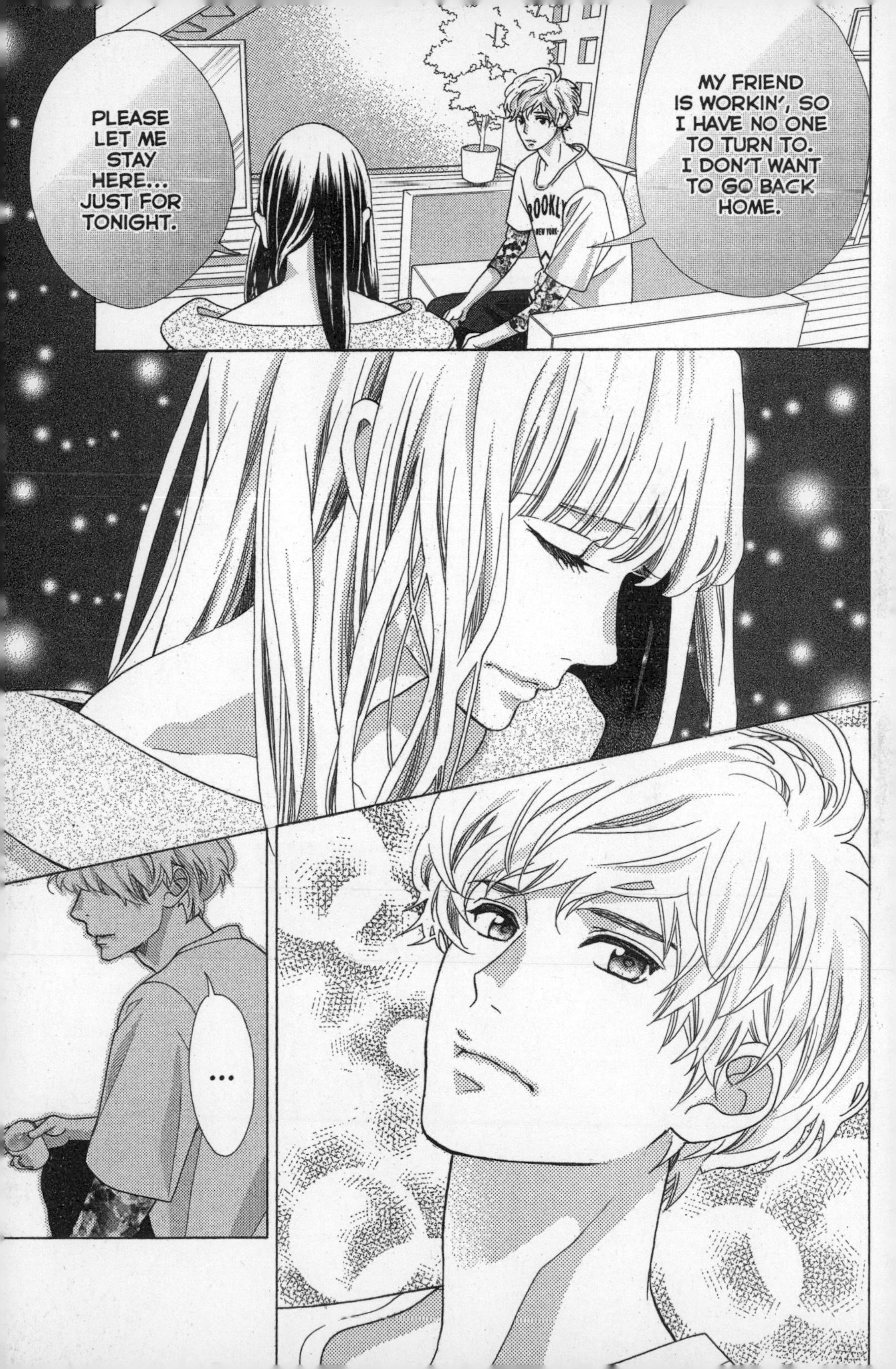
MY FRIEND IS WORKIN', SO I HAVE NO ONE TO TURN TO. I DON'T WANT TO GO BACK HOME.
PLEASE LET ME STAY HERE... JUST FOR TONIGHT.
...

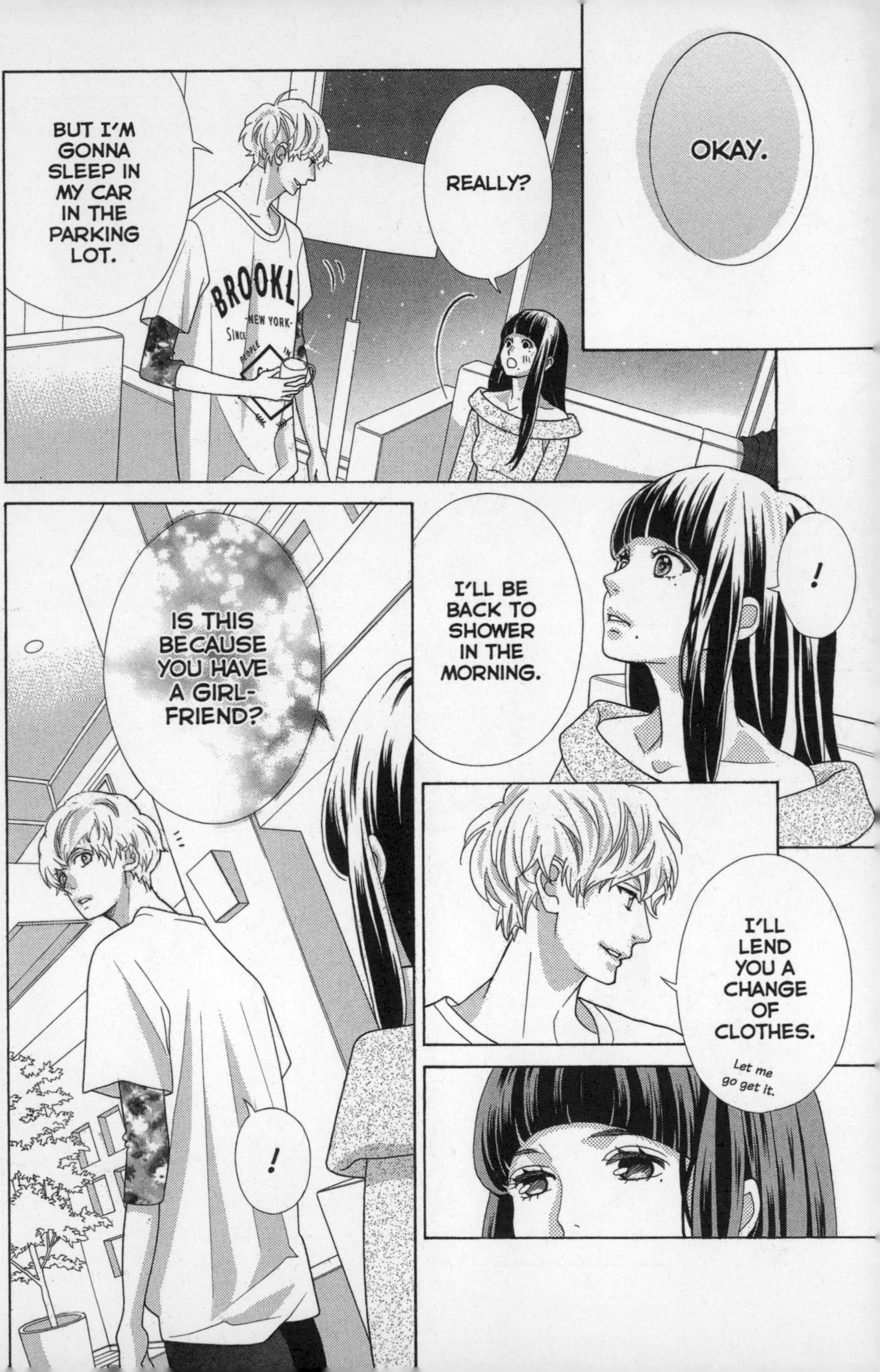
OKAY.
REALLY?
BUT I'M GONNA SLEEP IN MY CAR IN THE PARKING LOT.
BROOKL
-NEW YORK-
!
I'LL BE BACK TO SHOWER IN THE MORNING.
I'LL LEND YOU A CHANGE OF CLOTHES.
Let me go get it.
IS THIS BECAUSE YOU HAVE A GIRL-FRIEND?
!

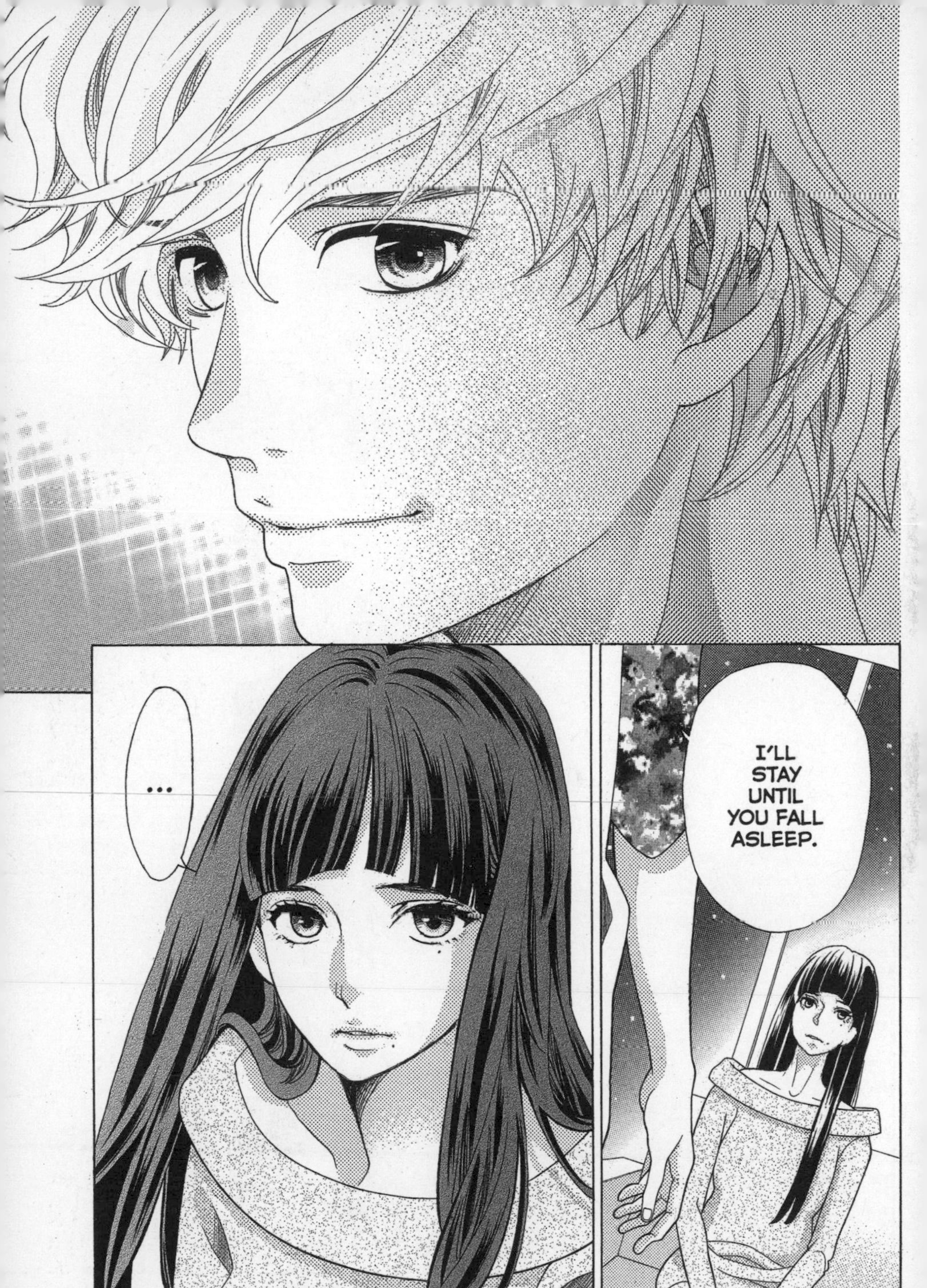
I'LL STAY UNTIL YOU FALL ASLEEP.
...

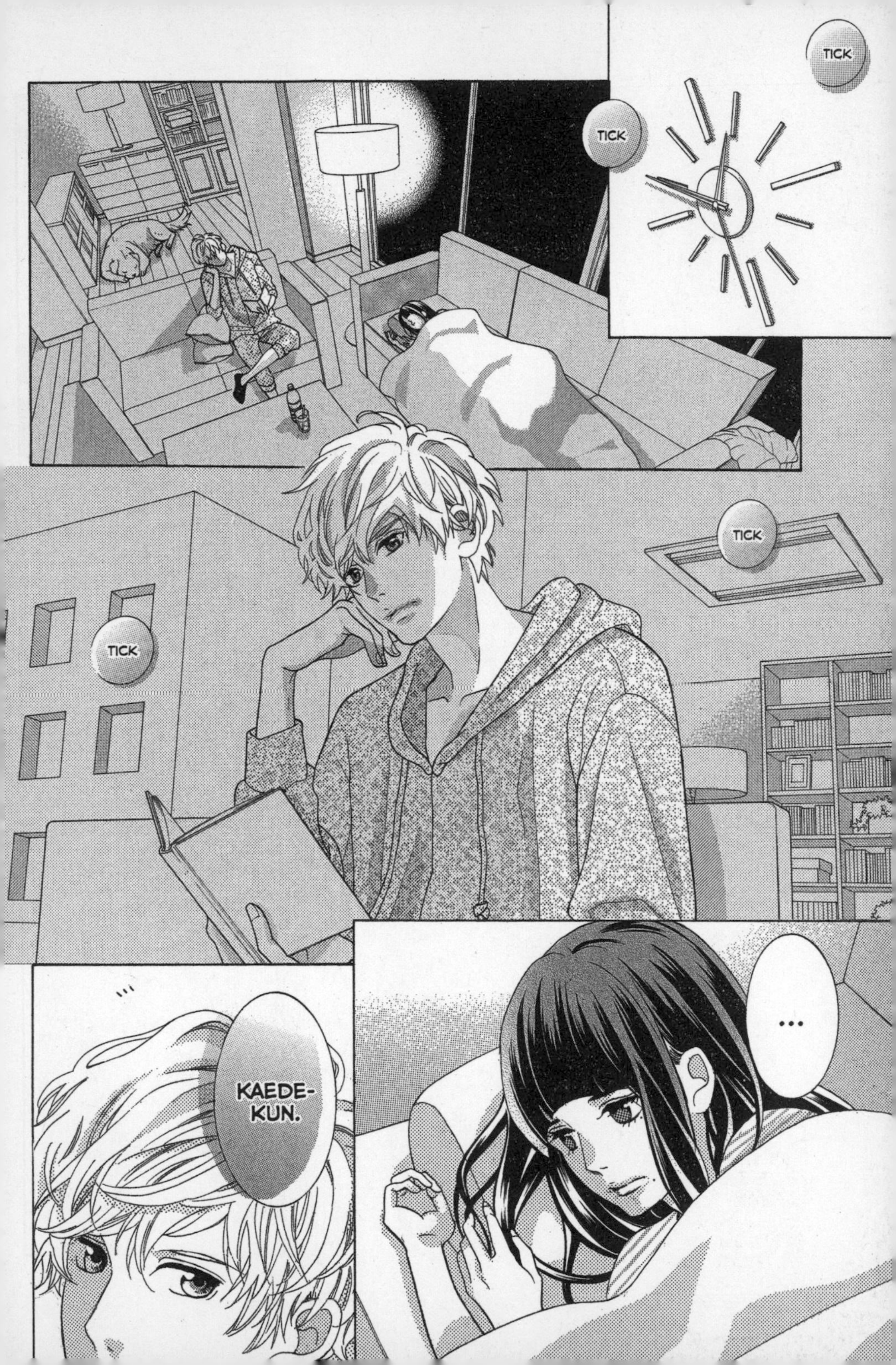
TICK
TICK
TICK
TICK
...
KAEDE-KUN.

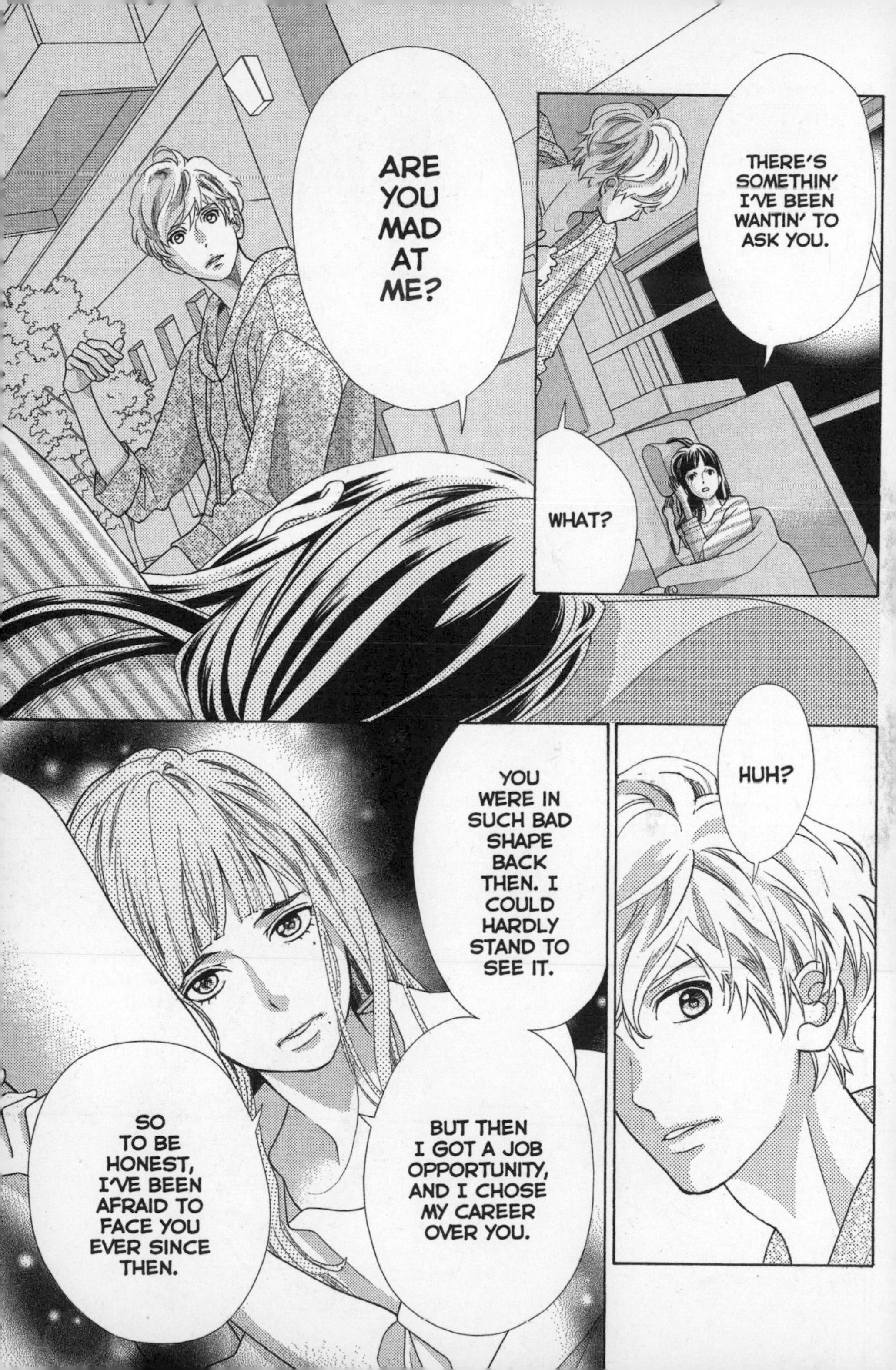
THERE'S SOMETHIN' I'VE BEEN WANTIN' TO ASK YOU.
WHAT?
ARE YOU MAD AT ME?
HUH?
YOU WERE IN SUCH BAD SHAPE BACK THEN. I COULD HARDLY STAND TO SEE IT.
BUT THEN I GOT A JOB OPPORTUNITY, AND I CHOSE MY CAREER OVER YOU.
SO TO BE HONEST, I'VE BEEN AFRAID TO FACE YOU EVER SINCE THEN.

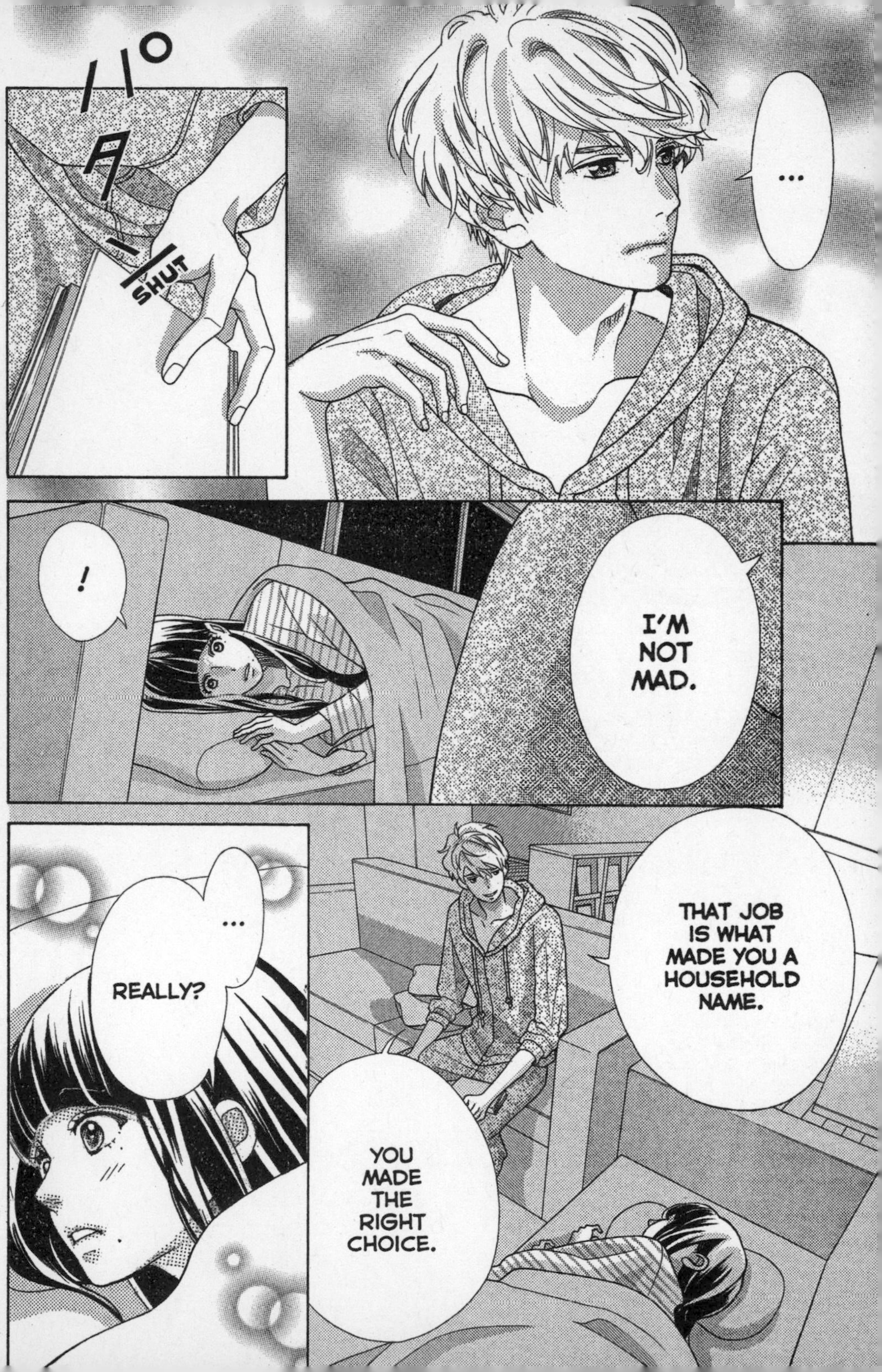
...
SHUT
I'M NOT MAD.
!
THAT JOB IS WHAT MADE YOU A HOUSEHOLD NAME.
YOU MADE THE RIGHT CHOICE.
...
REALLY?

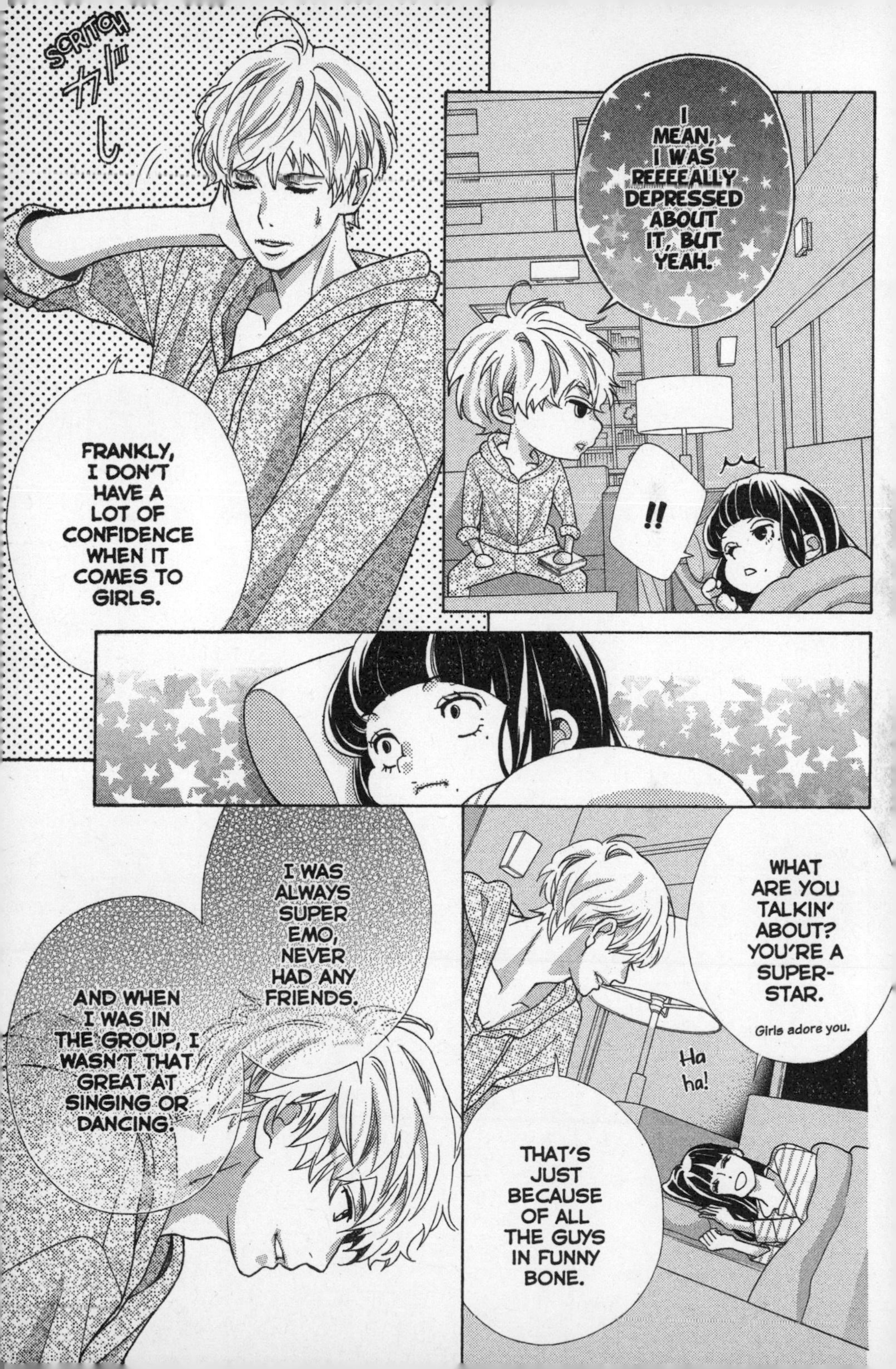
I MEAN, I WAS REEEEALLY DEPRESSED ABOUT IT, BUT YEAH.
!!
SCRITCH
FRANKLY, I DON'T HAVE A LOT OF CONFIDENCE WHEN IT COMES TO GIRLS.
WHAT ARE YOU TALKIN' ABOUT? YOU'RE A SUPER-STAR.
Girls adore you.
Ha ha!
THAT'S JUST BECAUSE OF ALL THE GUYS IN FUNNY BONE.
I WAS ALWAYS SUPER EMO, NEVER HAD ANY FRIENDS.
AND WHEN I WAS IN THE GROUP, I WASN'T THAT GREAT AT SINGING OR DANCING.

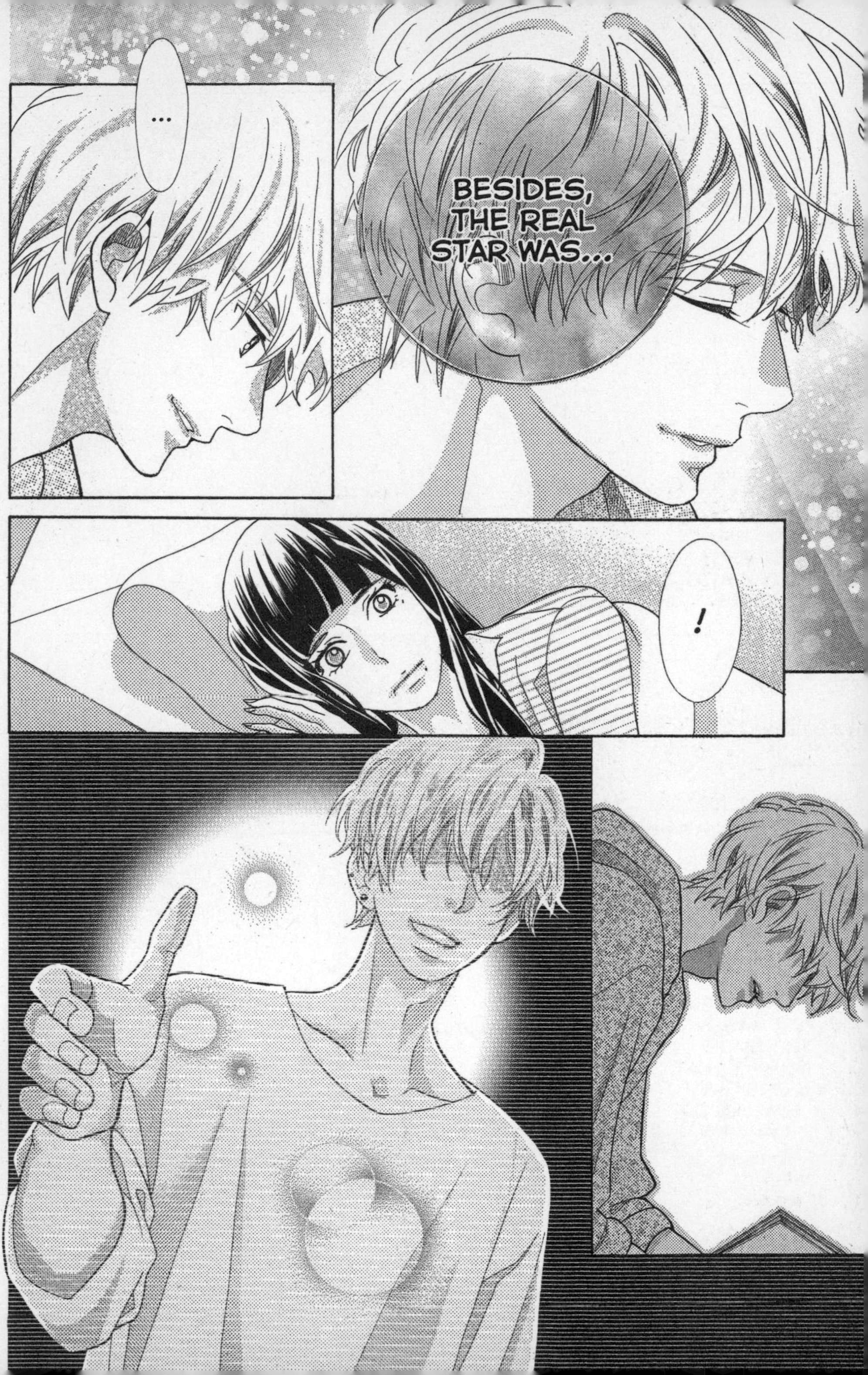
BESIDES, THE REAL STAR WAS...
...
!

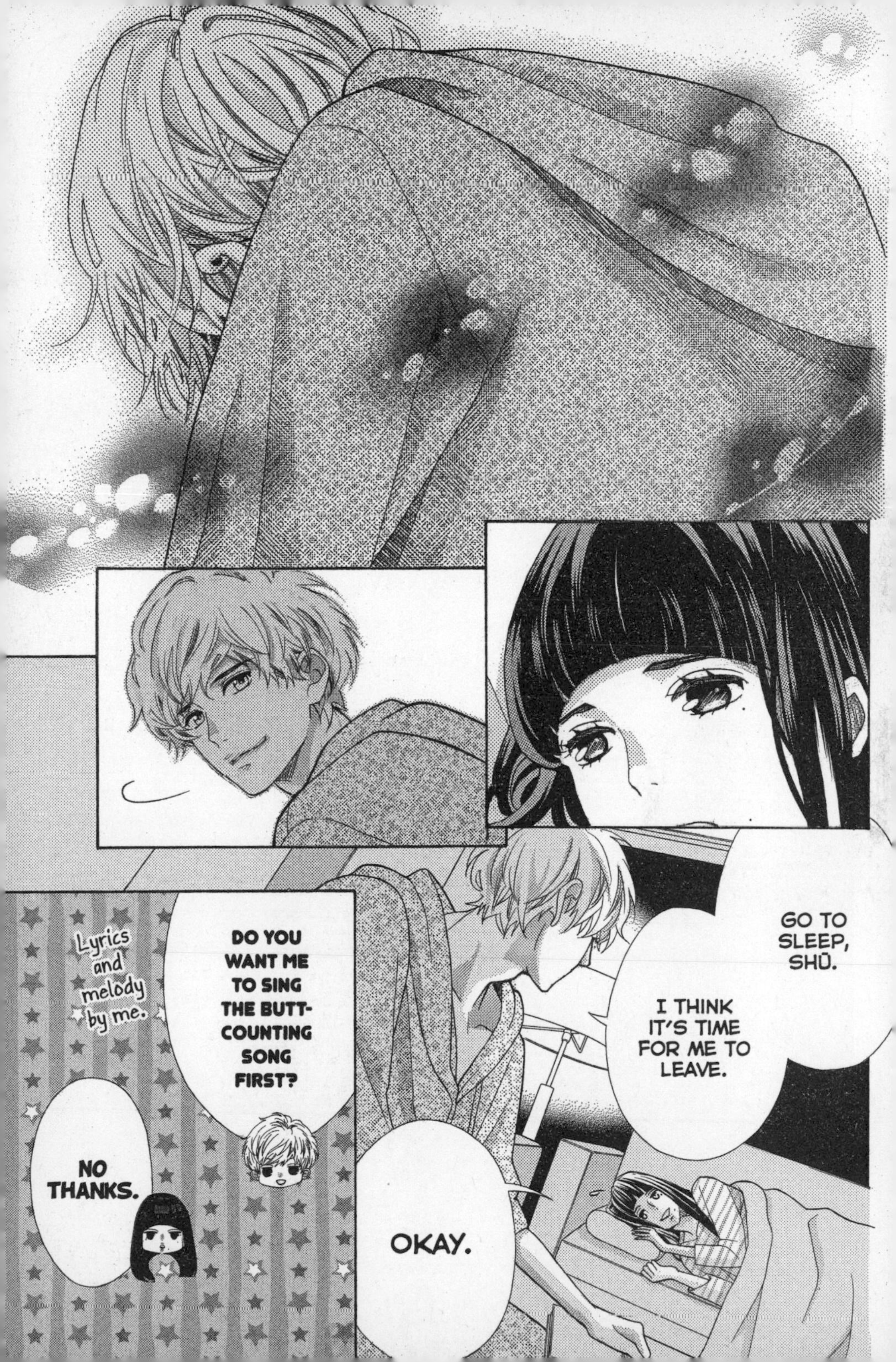
GO TO SLEEP, SHŪ.
I THINK IT'S TIME FOR ME TO LEAVE.
OKAY.
DO YOU WANT ME TO SING THE BUTT-COUNTING SONG FIRST?
Lyrics and melody by me.
NO THANKS.

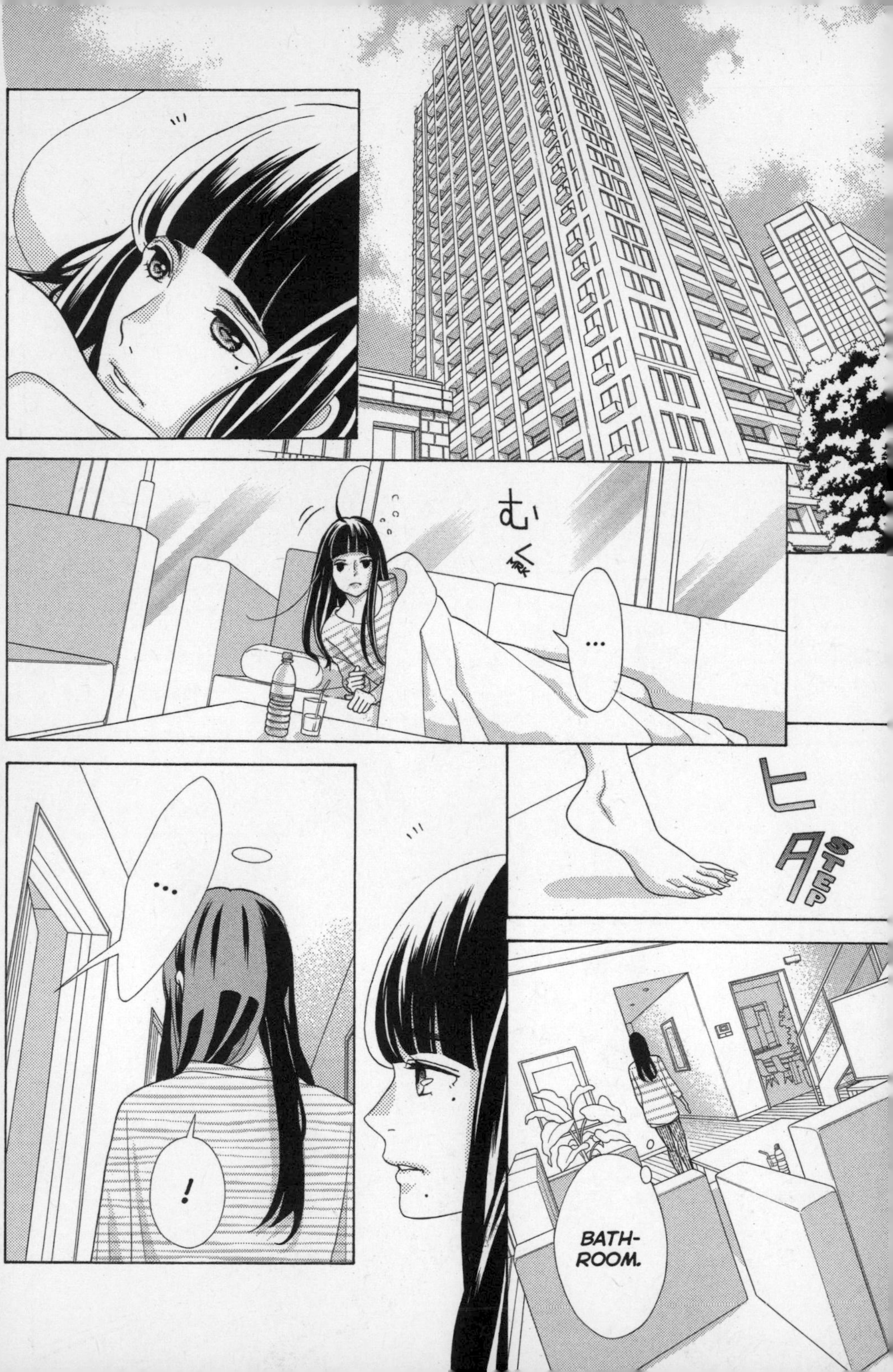
むく
MRK
...
ヒタ
STEP
BATH-ROOM.
...
!

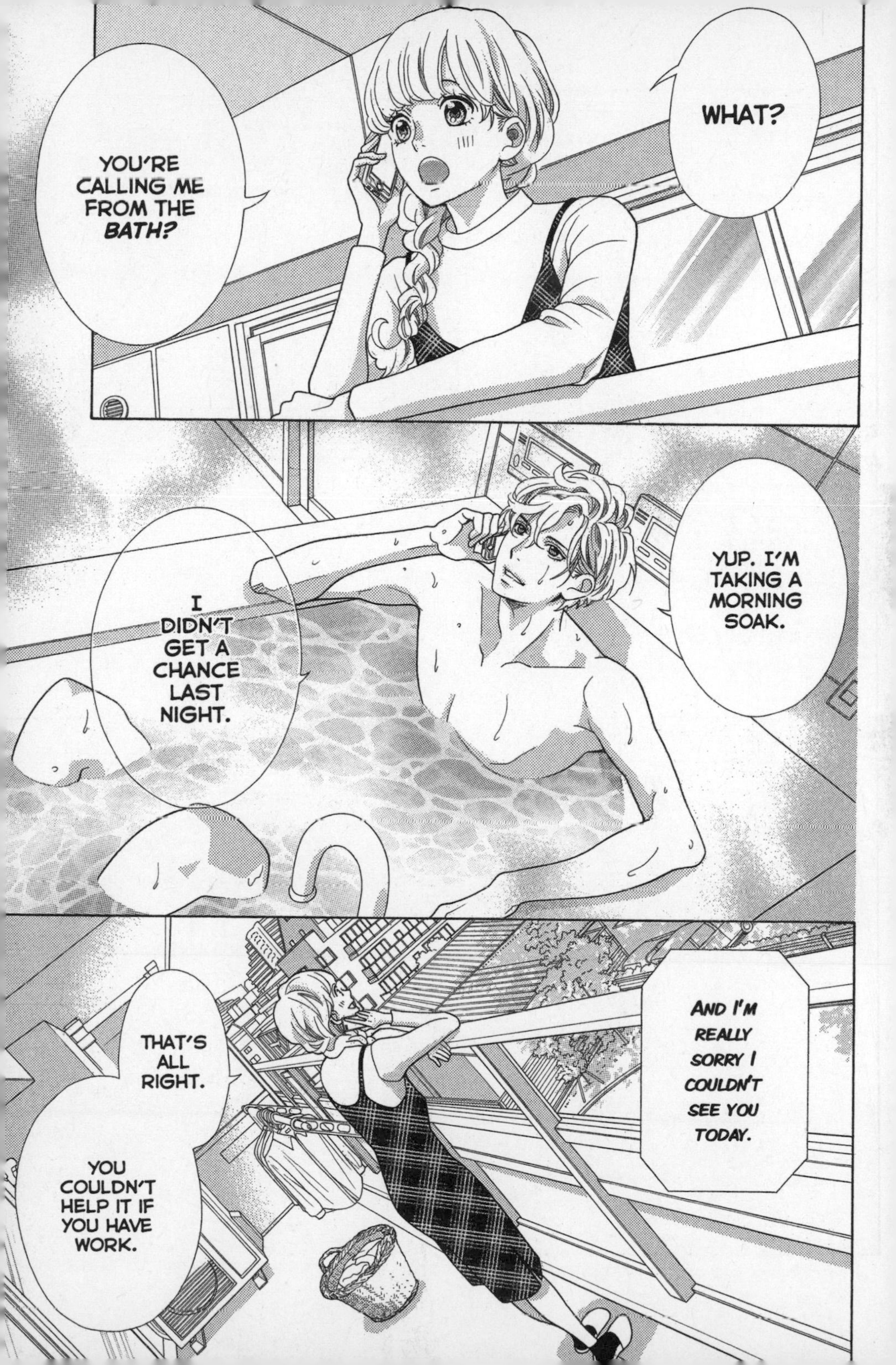
WHAT?
YOU'RE CALLING ME FROM THE *BATH?*
YUP. I'M TAKING A MORNING SOAK.
I DIDN'T GET A CHANCE LAST NIGHT.
AND I'M REALLY SORRY I COULDN'T SEE YOU TODAY.
THAT'S ALL RIGHT.
YOU COULDN'T HELP IT IF YOU HAVE WORK.

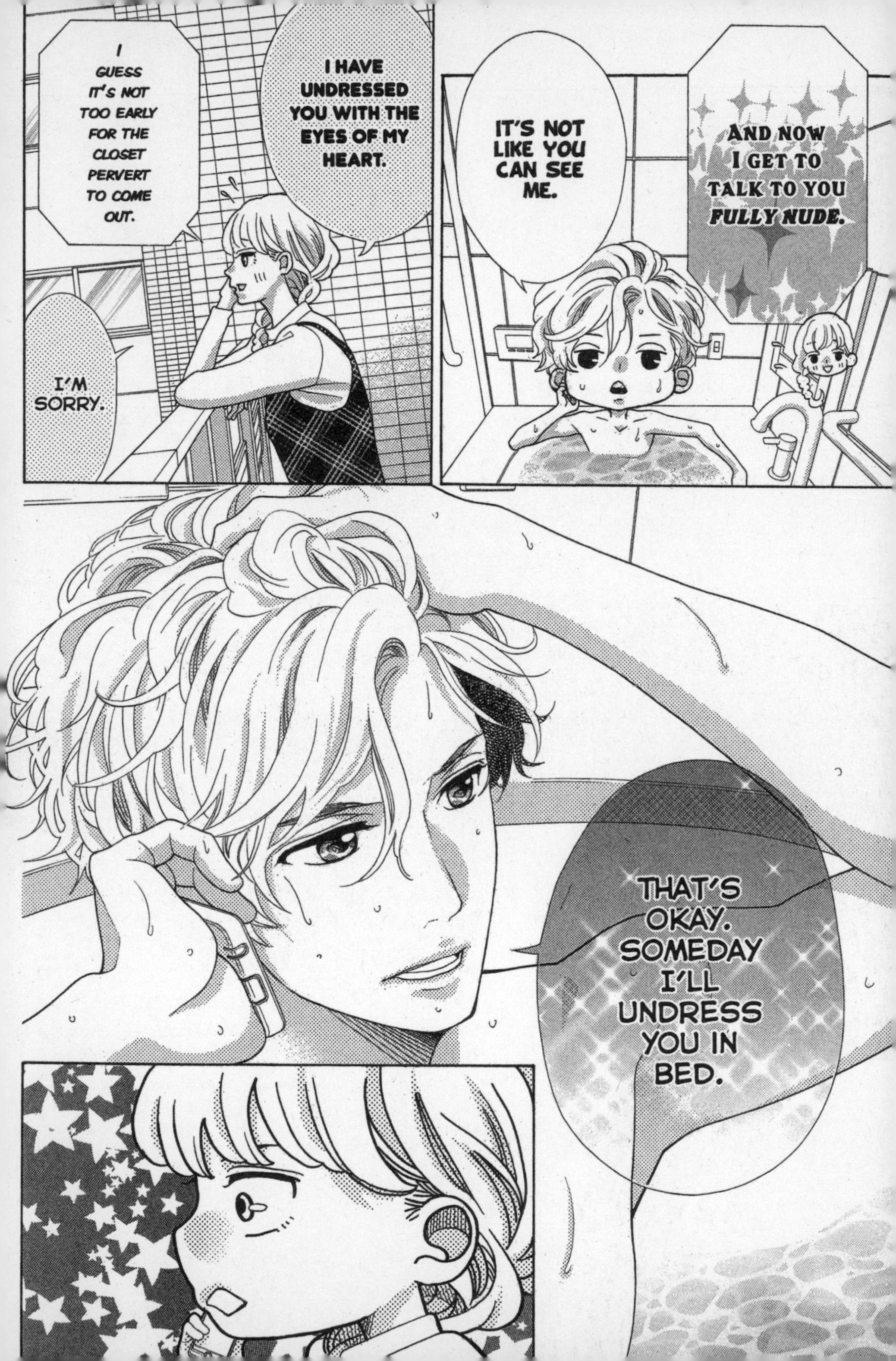
AND NOW I GET TO TALK TO YOU *FULLY NUDE*.
IT'S NOT LIKE YOU CAN SEE ME.
I HAVE UNDRESSED YOU WITH THE EYES OF MY HEART.
I GUESS IT'S NOT TOO EARLY FOR THE CLOSET PERVERT TO COME OUT.
I'M SORRY.
THAT'S OKAY. SOMEDAY I'LL UNDRESS YOU IN BED.

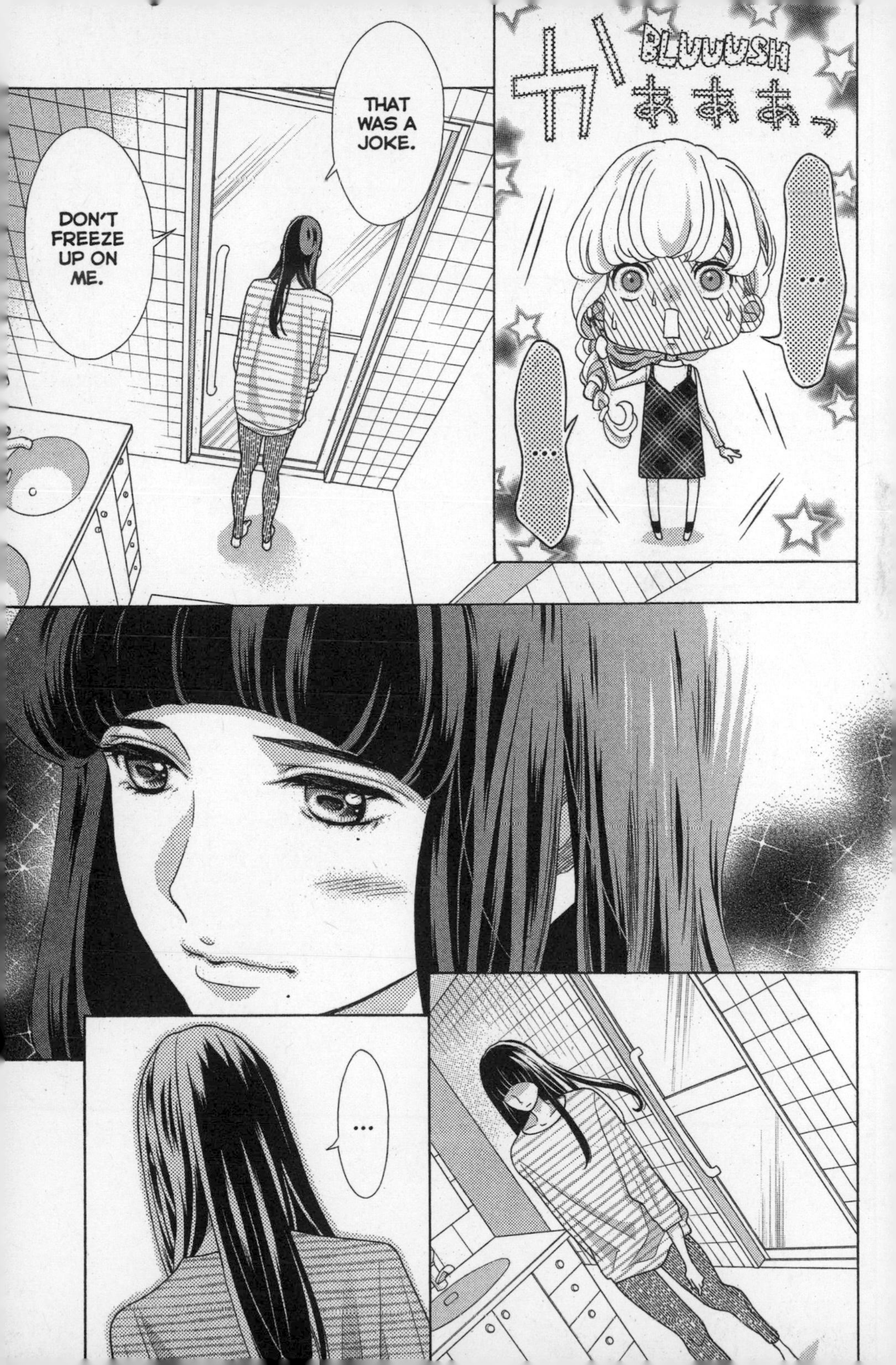
BLUUUSH
あああっ
...
...
THAT WAS A JOKE.
DON'T FREEZE UP ON ME.
...

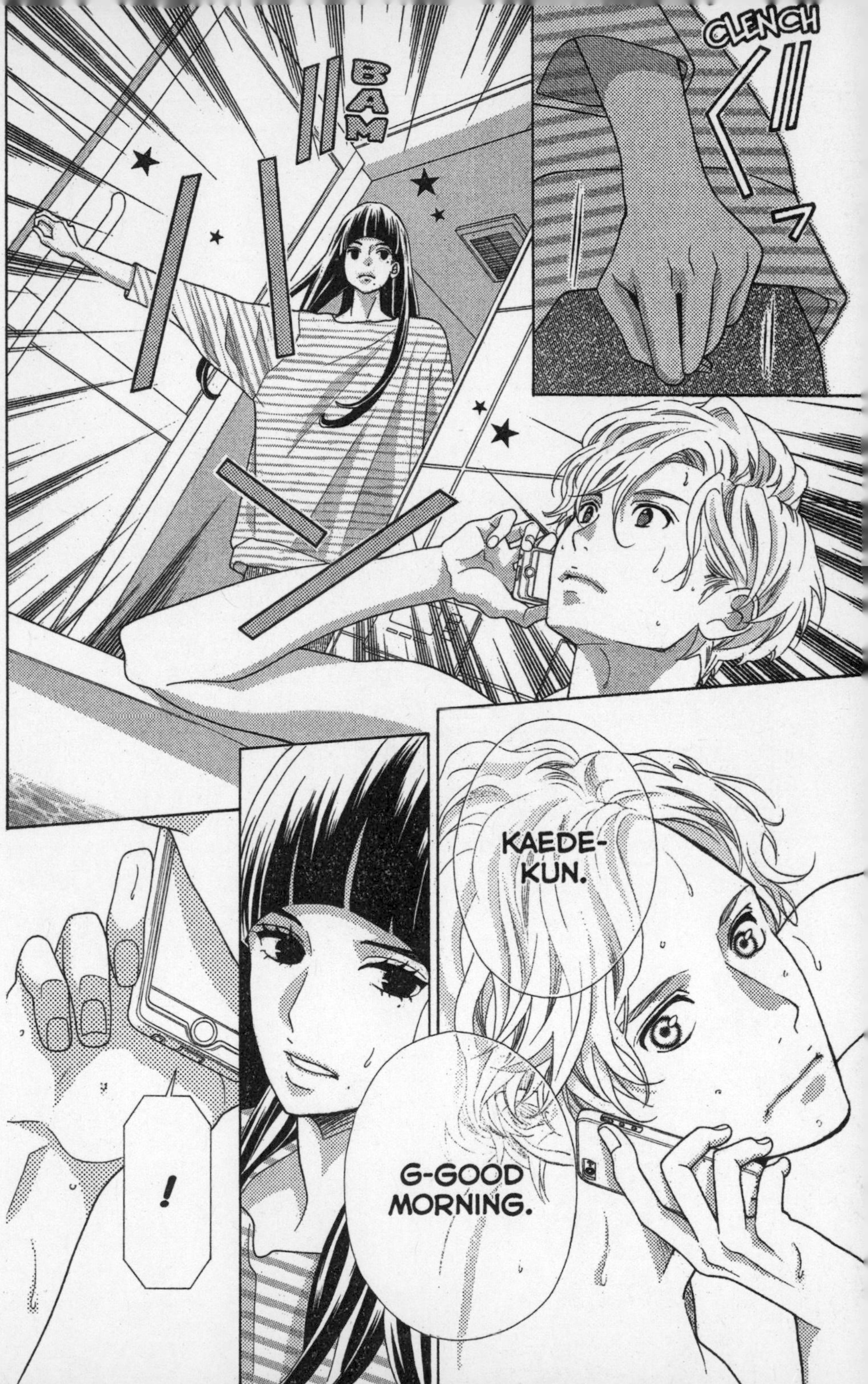
CLENCH
BAM
KAEDE-KUN.
G-GOOD MORNING.
!

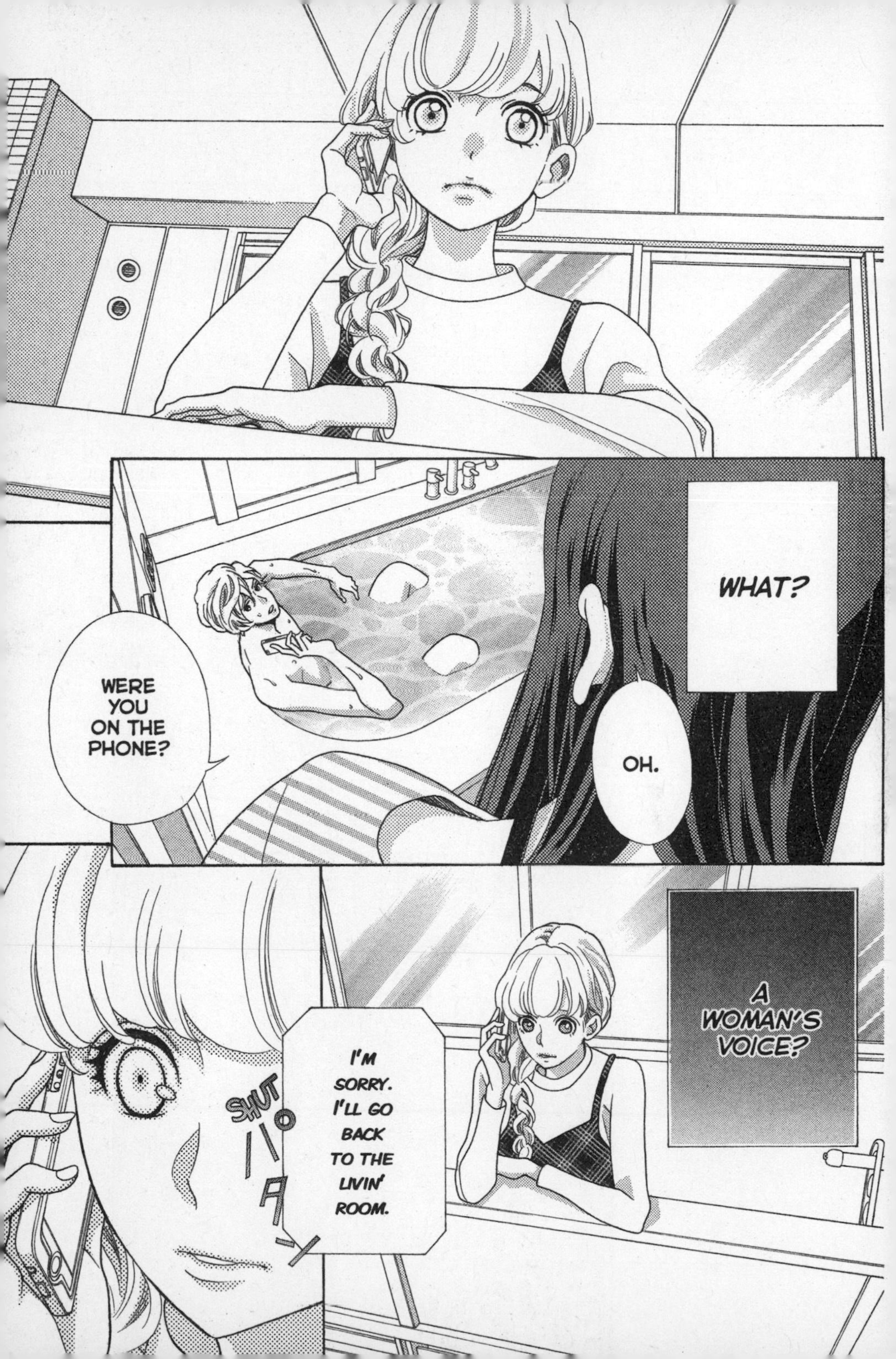
WHAT?
OH.
WERE YOU ON THE PHONE?
A WOMAN'S VOICE?
I'M SORRY. I'LL GO BACK TO THE LIVIN' ROOM.
SHUT

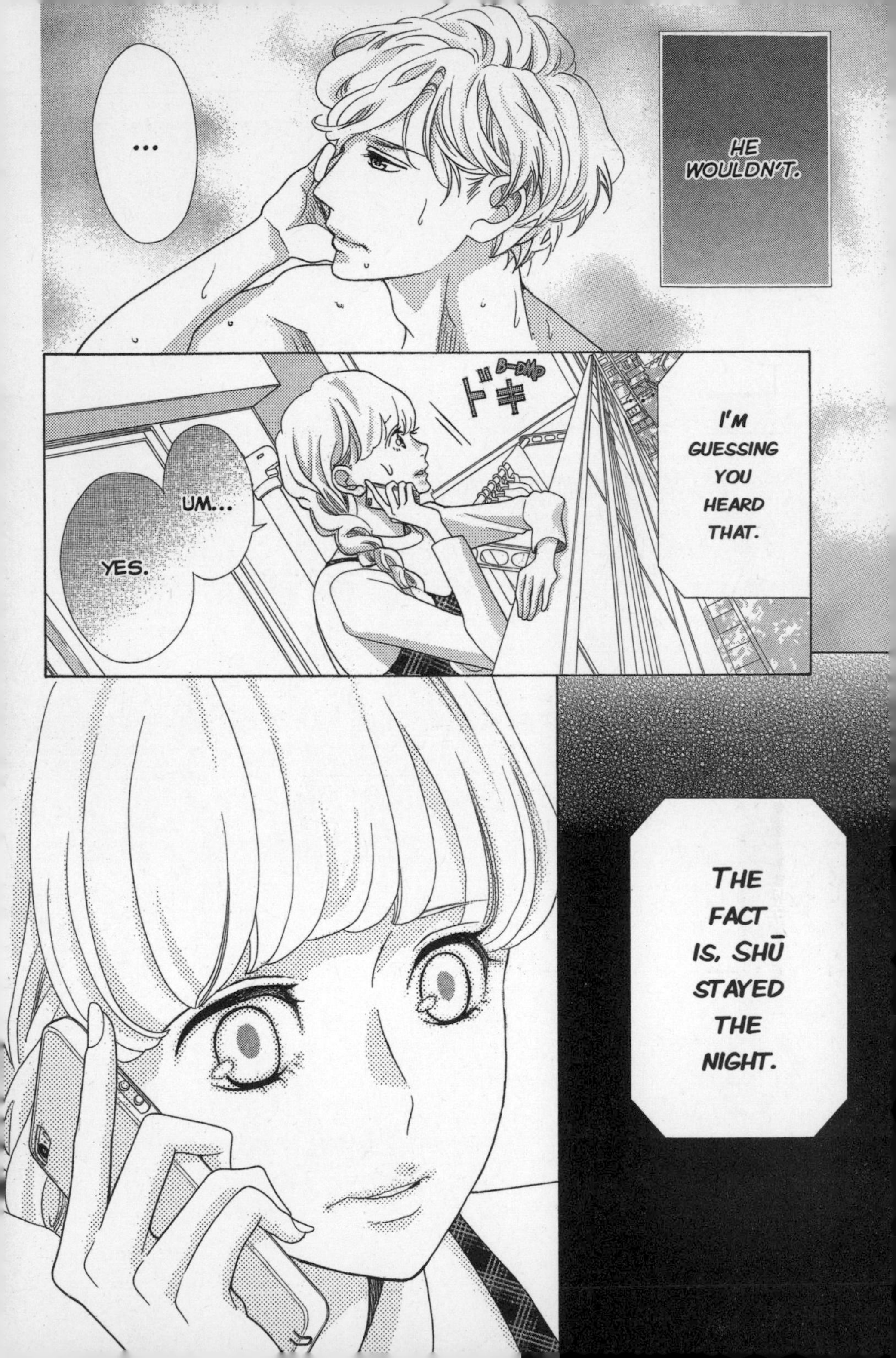
HE WOULDN'T.
...
I'M GUESSING YOU HEARD THAT.
ドキ B-DMP
UM... YES.
THE FACT IS, SHŪ STAYED THE NIGHT.

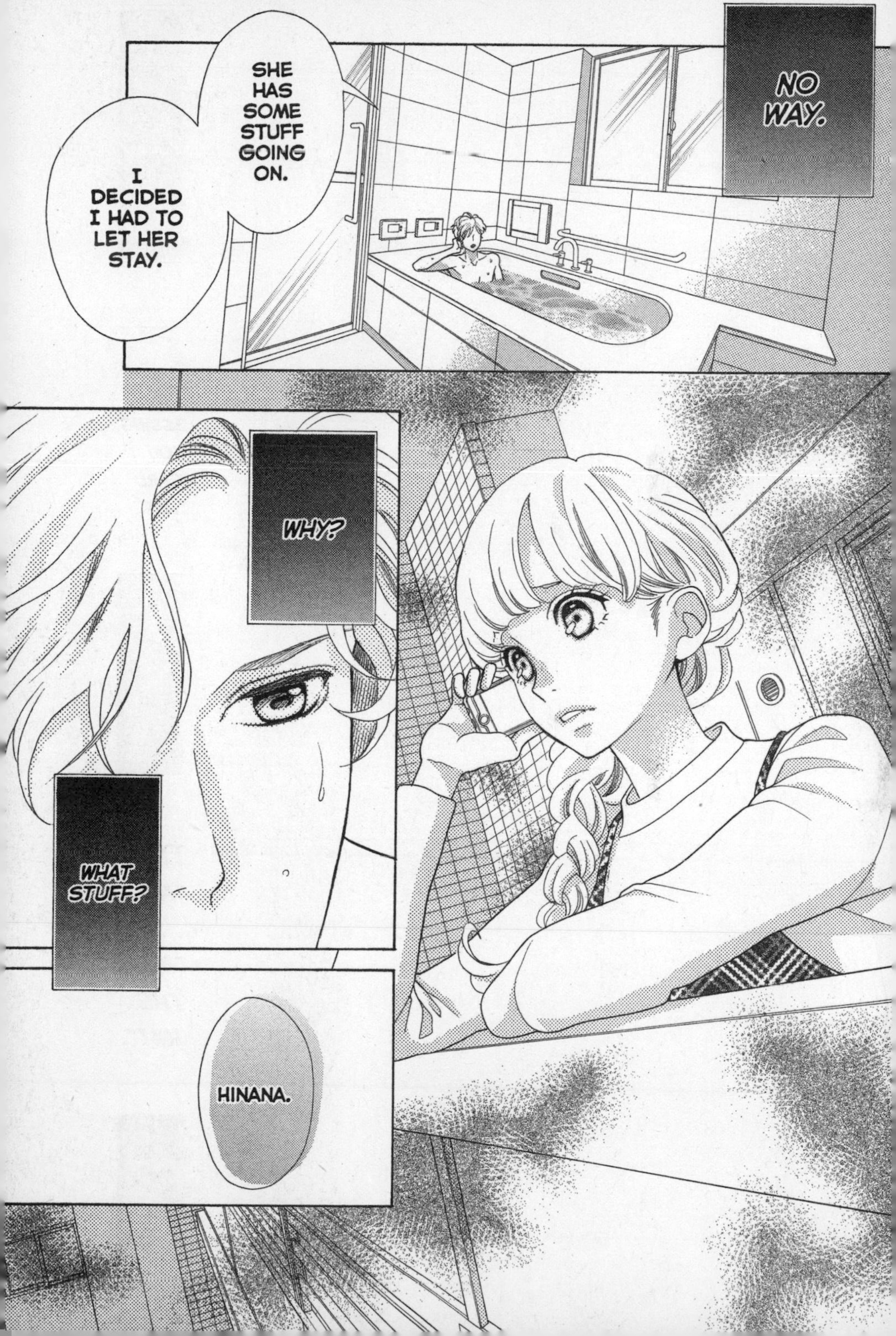
NO WAY.
SHE HAS SOME STUFF GOING ON.
I DECIDED I HAD TO LET HER STAY.
WHY?
WHAT STUFF?
HINANA.

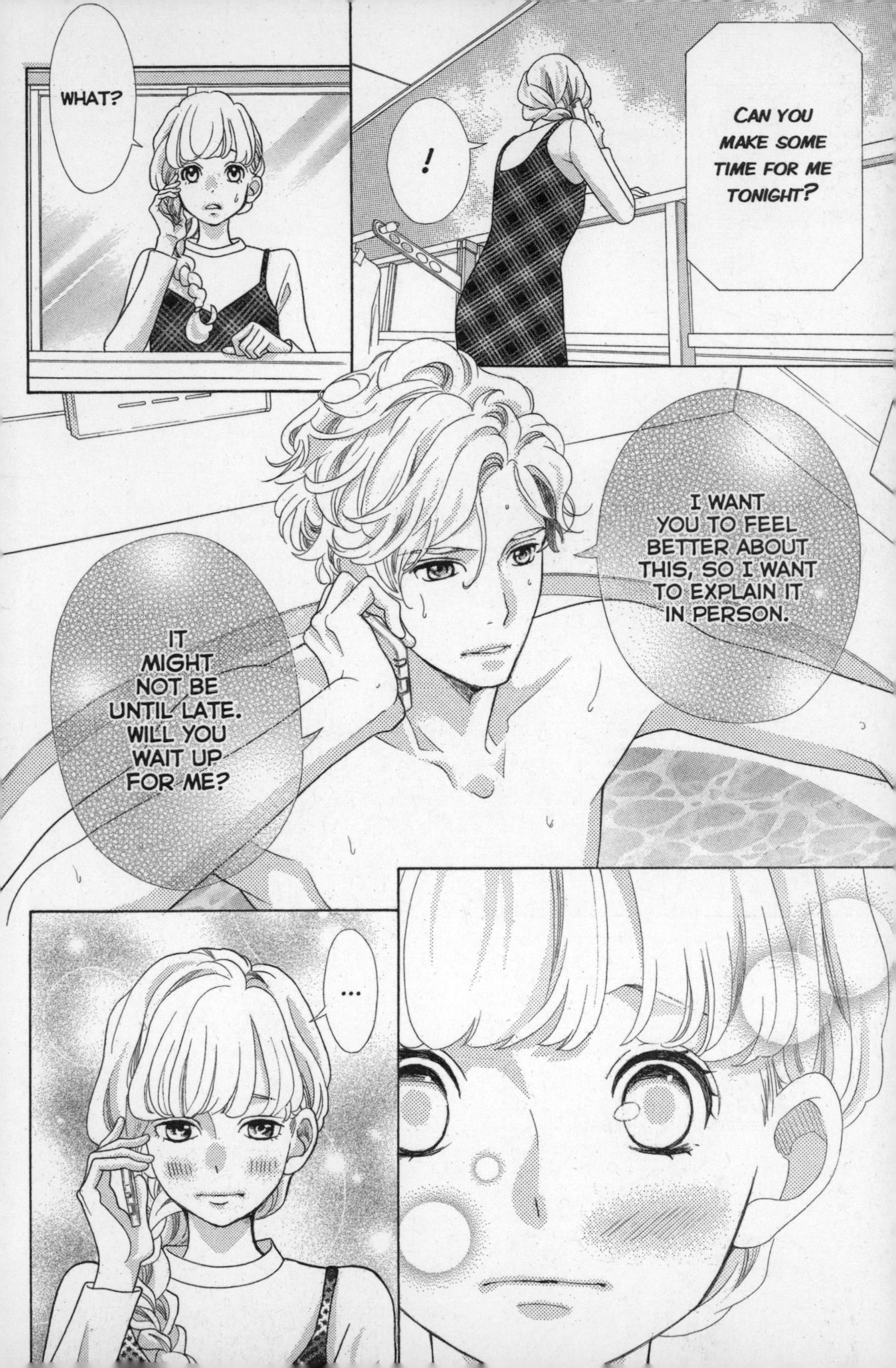
CAN YOU MAKE SOME TIME FOR ME TONIGHT?
!
WHAT?
I WANT YOU TO FEEL BETTER ABOUT THIS, SO I WANT TO EXPLAIN IT IN PERSON.
IT MIGHT NOT BE UNTIL LATE. WILL YOU WAIT UP FOR ME?
...

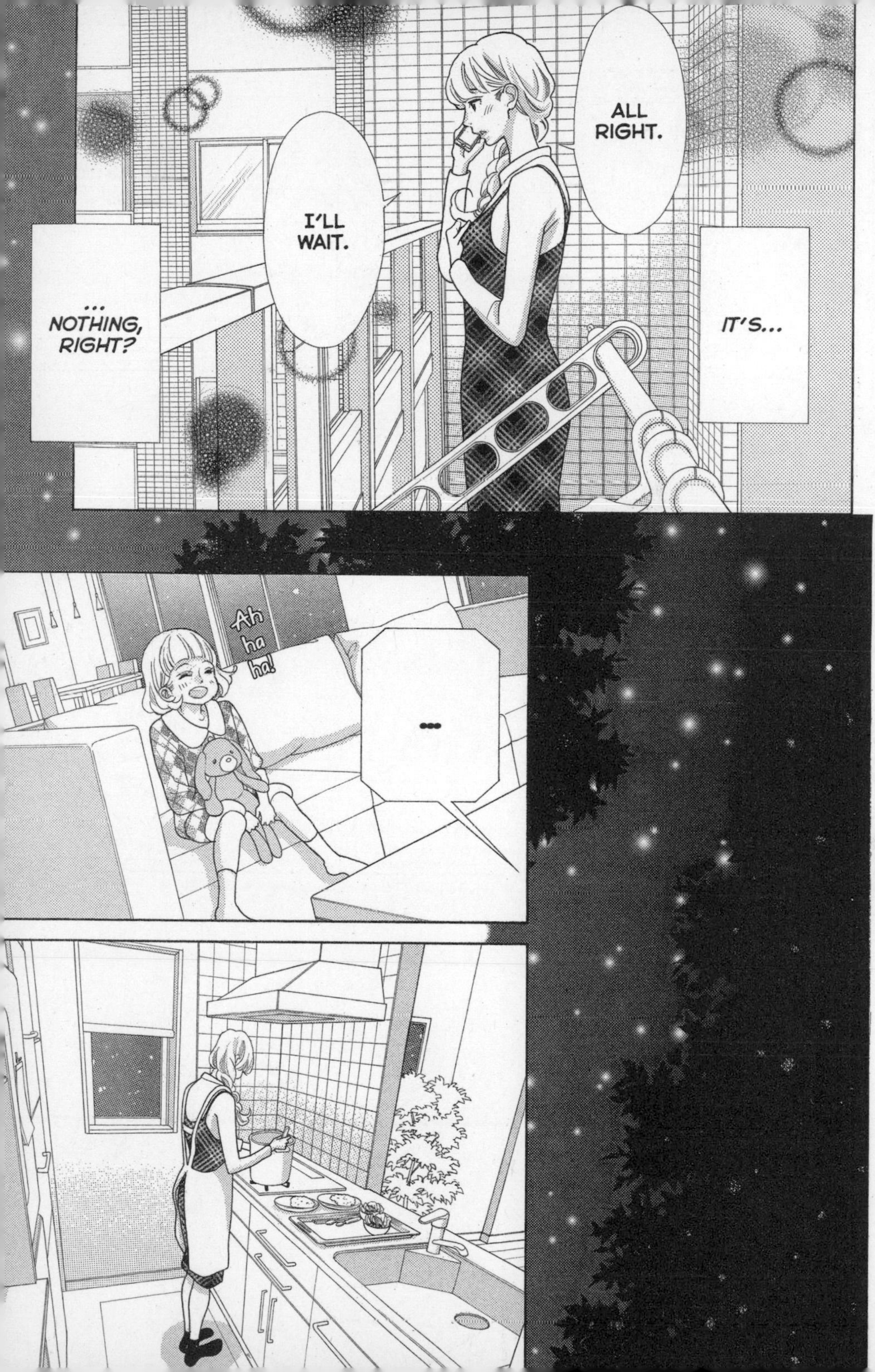
IT'S...
ALL RIGHT.
I'LL WAIT.
... NOTHING, RIGHT?
...
Ah ha ha!

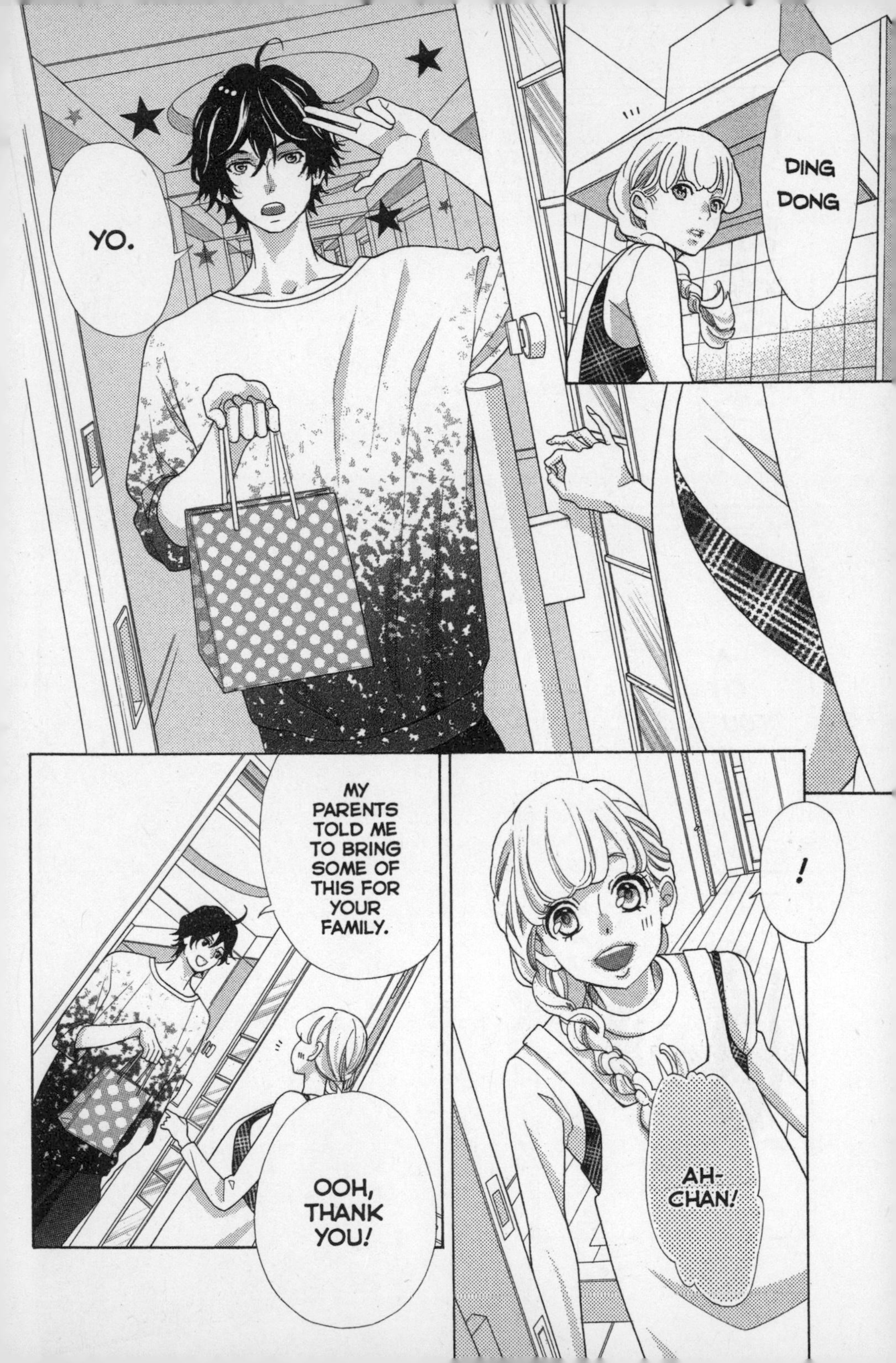
DING DONG
YO.
!
AH-CHAN!
MY PARENTS TOLD ME TO BRING SOME OF THIS FOR YOUR FAMILY.
OOH, THANK YOU!

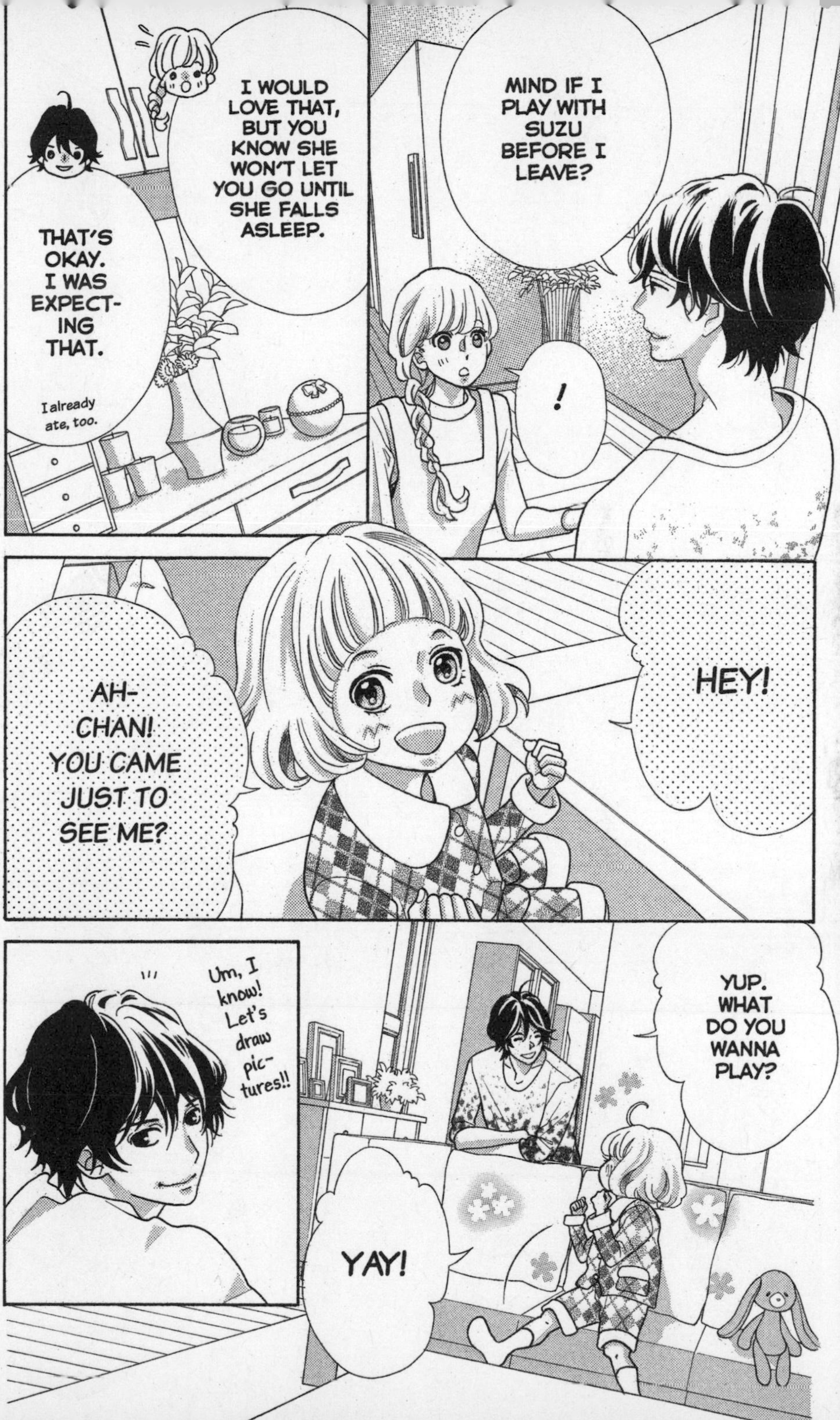
MIND IF I PLAY WITH SUZU BEFORE I LEAVE?
!
I WOULD LOVE THAT, BUT YOU KNOW SHE WON'T LET YOU GO UNTIL SHE FALLS ASLEEP.
THAT'S OKAY. I WAS EXPECTING THAT.
I already ate, too.
HEY!
AH-CHAN! YOU CAME JUST TO SEE ME?
YUP. WHAT DO YOU WANNA PLAY?
YAY!
Um, I know! Let's draw pictures!!

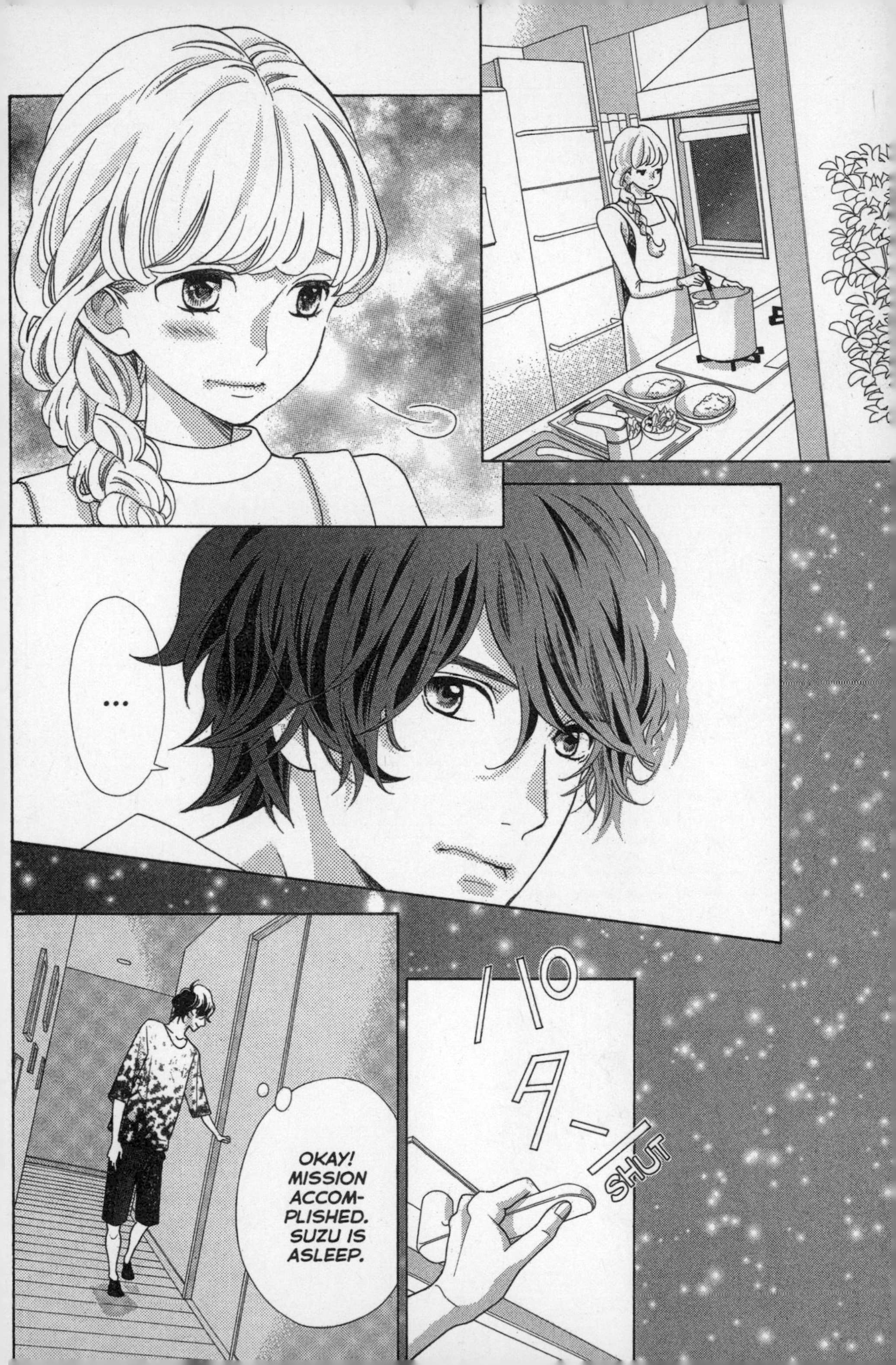
...
SHUT
OKAY! MISSION ACCOMPLISHED. SUZU IS ASLEEP.

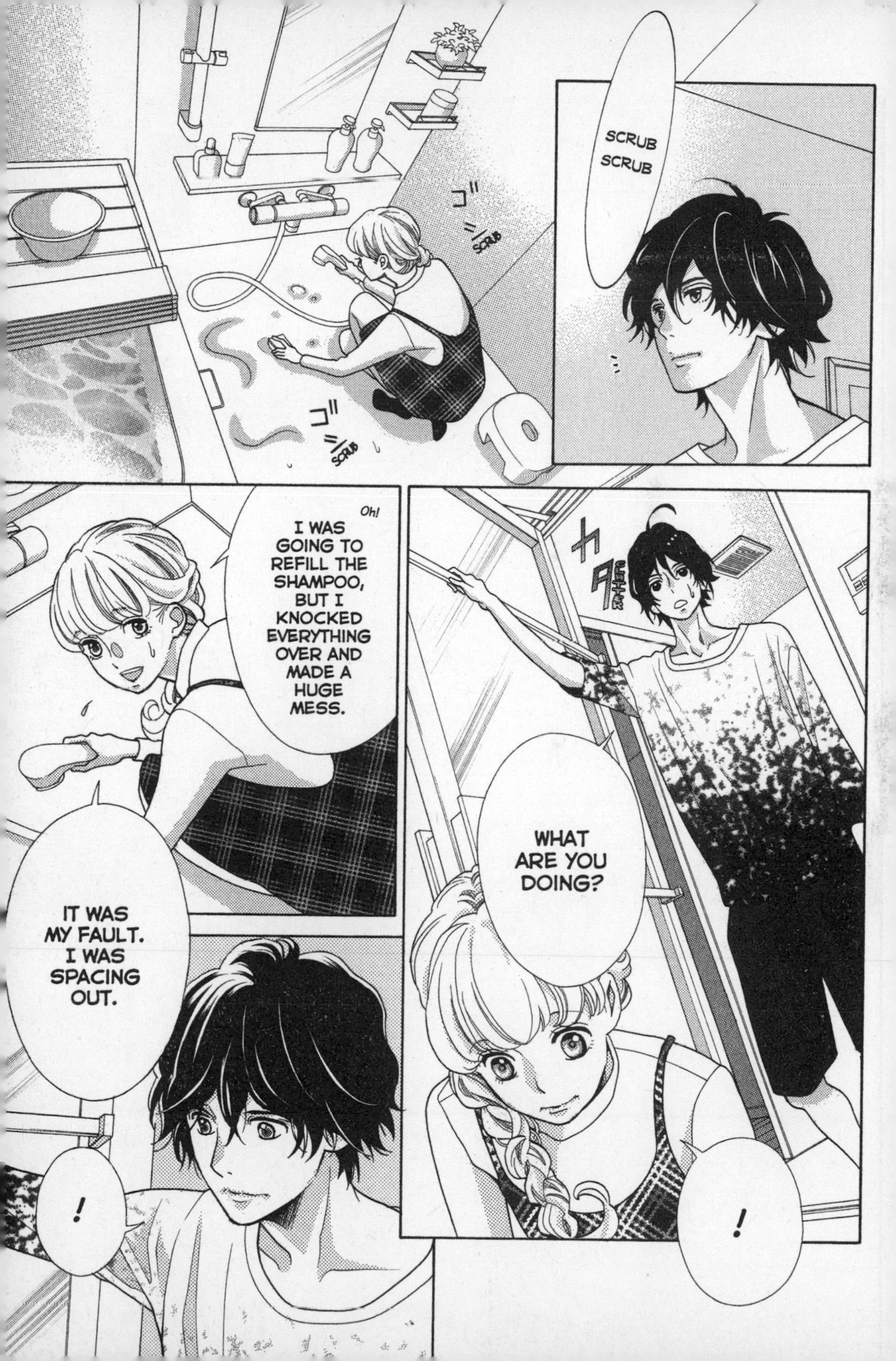
SCRUB SCRUB
ゴシ SCRUB
ゴシ SCRUB
カタ CLATTER
WHAT ARE YOU DOING?
!
Oh!
I WAS GOING TO REFILL THE SHAMPOO, BUT I KNOCKED EVERYTHING OVER AND MADE A HUGE MESS.
IT WAS MY FAULT. I WAS SPACING OUT.
!

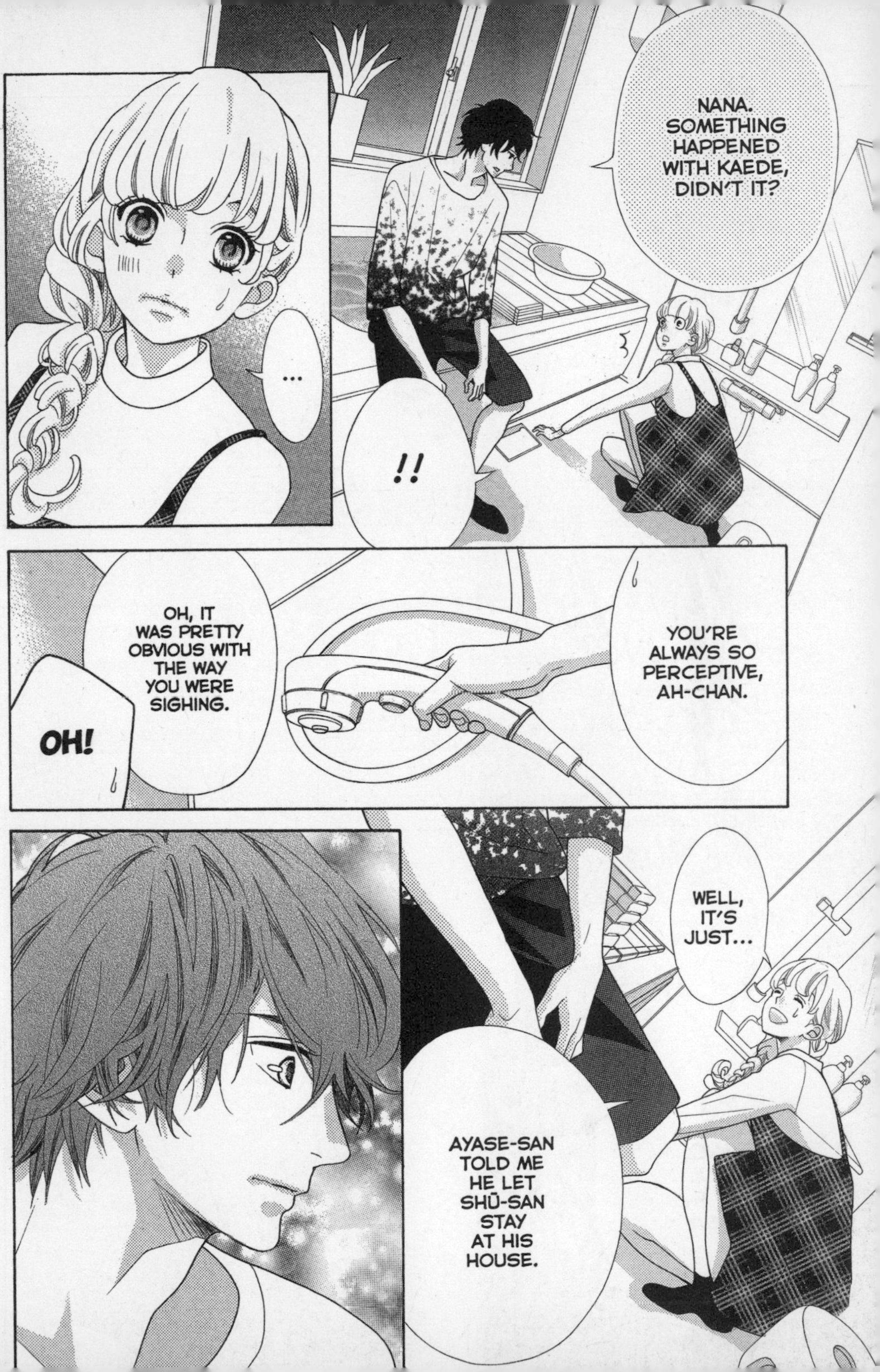
NANA. SOMETHING HAPPENED WITH KAEDE, DIDN'T IT?
!!
...
YOU'RE ALWAYS SO PERCEPTIVE, AH-CHAN.
OH, IT WAS PRETTY OBVIOUS WITH THE WAY YOU WERE SIGHING.
OH!
WELL, IT'S JUST...
AYASE-SAN TOLD ME HE LET SHŪ-SAN STAY AT HIS HOUSE.

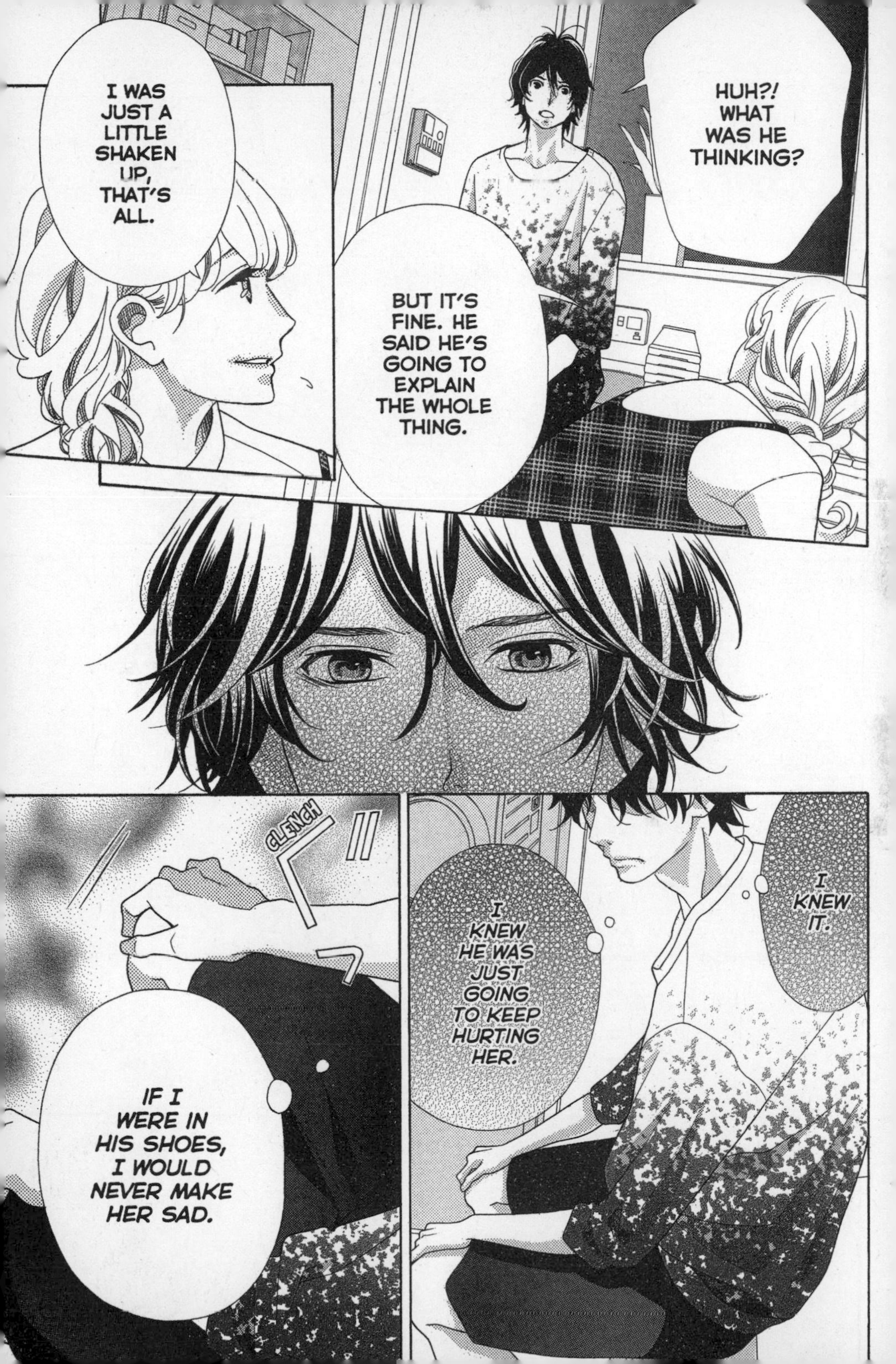
HUH?! WHAT WAS HE THINKING?
I WAS JUST A LITTLE SHAKEN UP, THAT'S ALL.
BUT IT'S FINE. HE SAID HE'S GOING TO EXPLAIN THE WHOLE THING.
I KNEW IT.
I KNEW HE WAS JUST GOING TO KEEP HURTING HER.
CLENCH
IF I WERE IN HIS SHOES, I WOULD NEVER MAKE HER SAD.

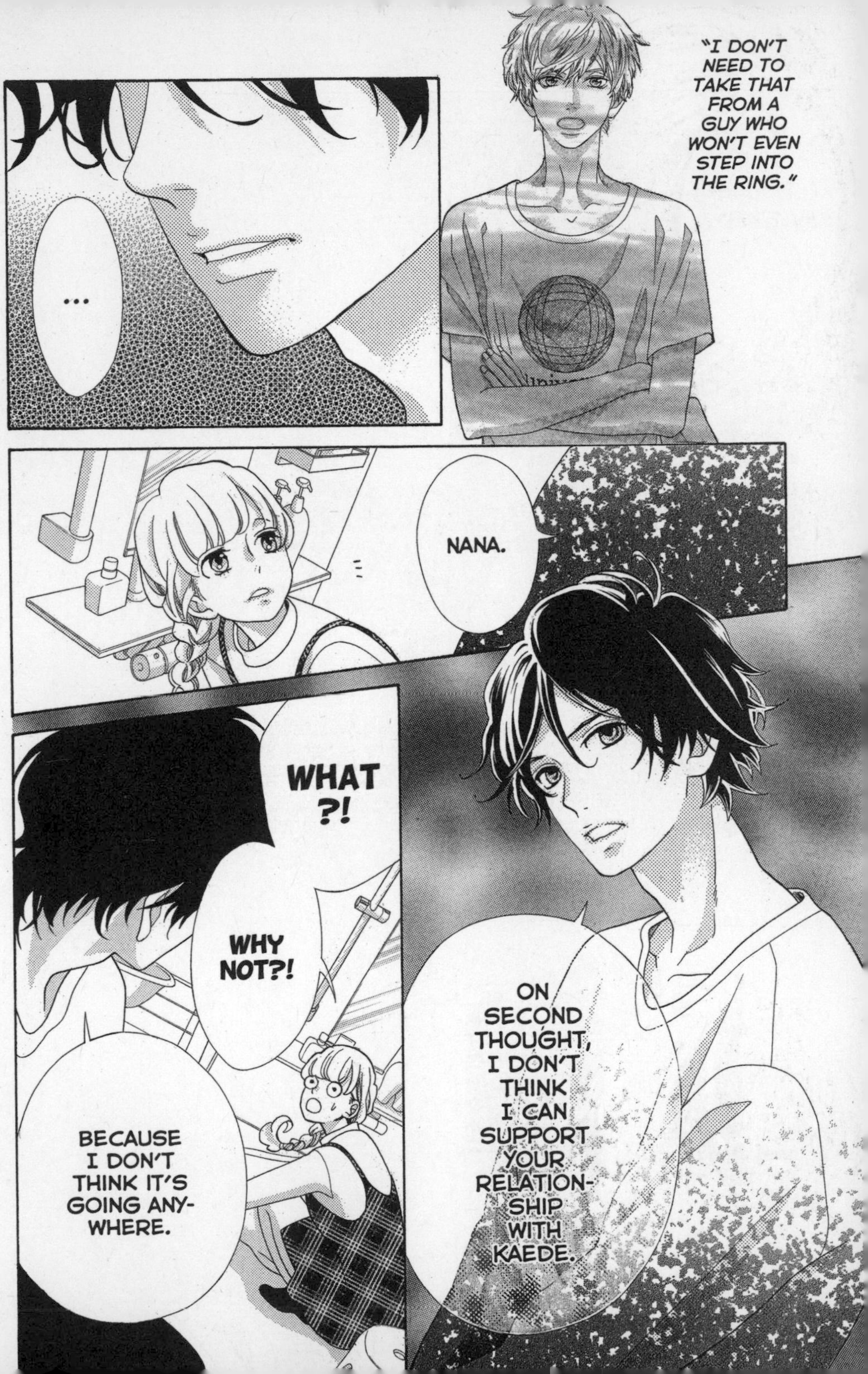
"I DON'T NEED TO TAKE THAT FROM A GUY WHO WON'T EVEN STEP INTO THE RING."
...
NANA.
ON SECOND THOUGHT, I DON'T THINK I CAN SUPPORT YOUR RELATION-SHIP WITH KAEDE.
WHAT ?!
WHY NOT?!
BECAUSE I DON'T THINK IT'S GOING ANY-WHERE.

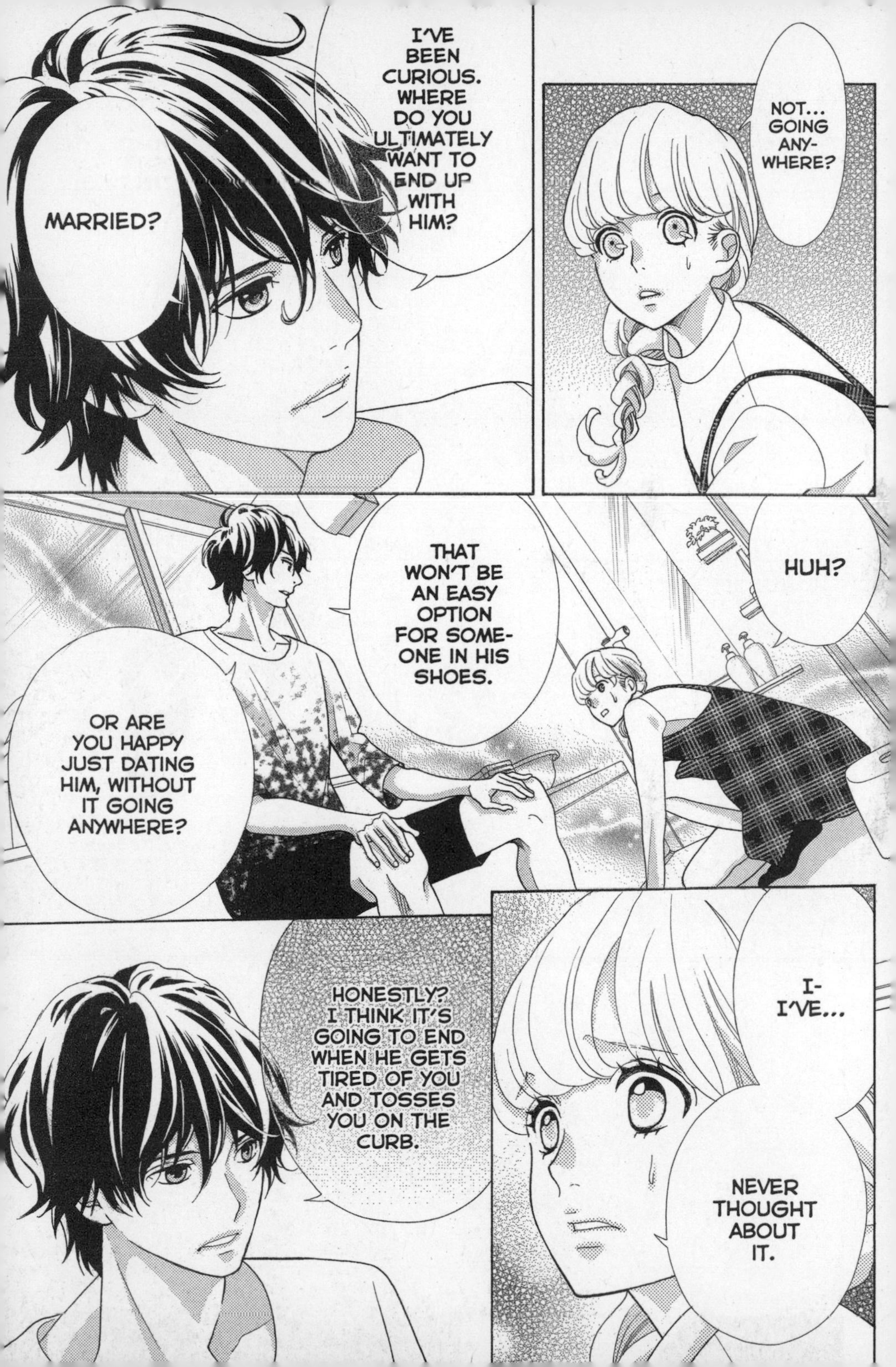
NOT... GOING ANY-WHERE?
I'VE BEEN CURIOUS. WHERE DO YOU ULTIMATELY WANT TO END UP WITH HIM?
MARRIED?
HUH?
THAT WON'T BE AN EASY OPTION FOR SOME-ONE IN HIS SHOES.
OR ARE YOU HAPPY JUST DATING HIM, WITHOUT IT GOING ANYWHERE?
I- I'VE...
NEVER THOUGHT ABOUT IT.
HONESTLY? I THINK IT'S GOING TO END WHEN HE GETS TIRED OF YOU AND TOSSES YOU ON THE CURB.

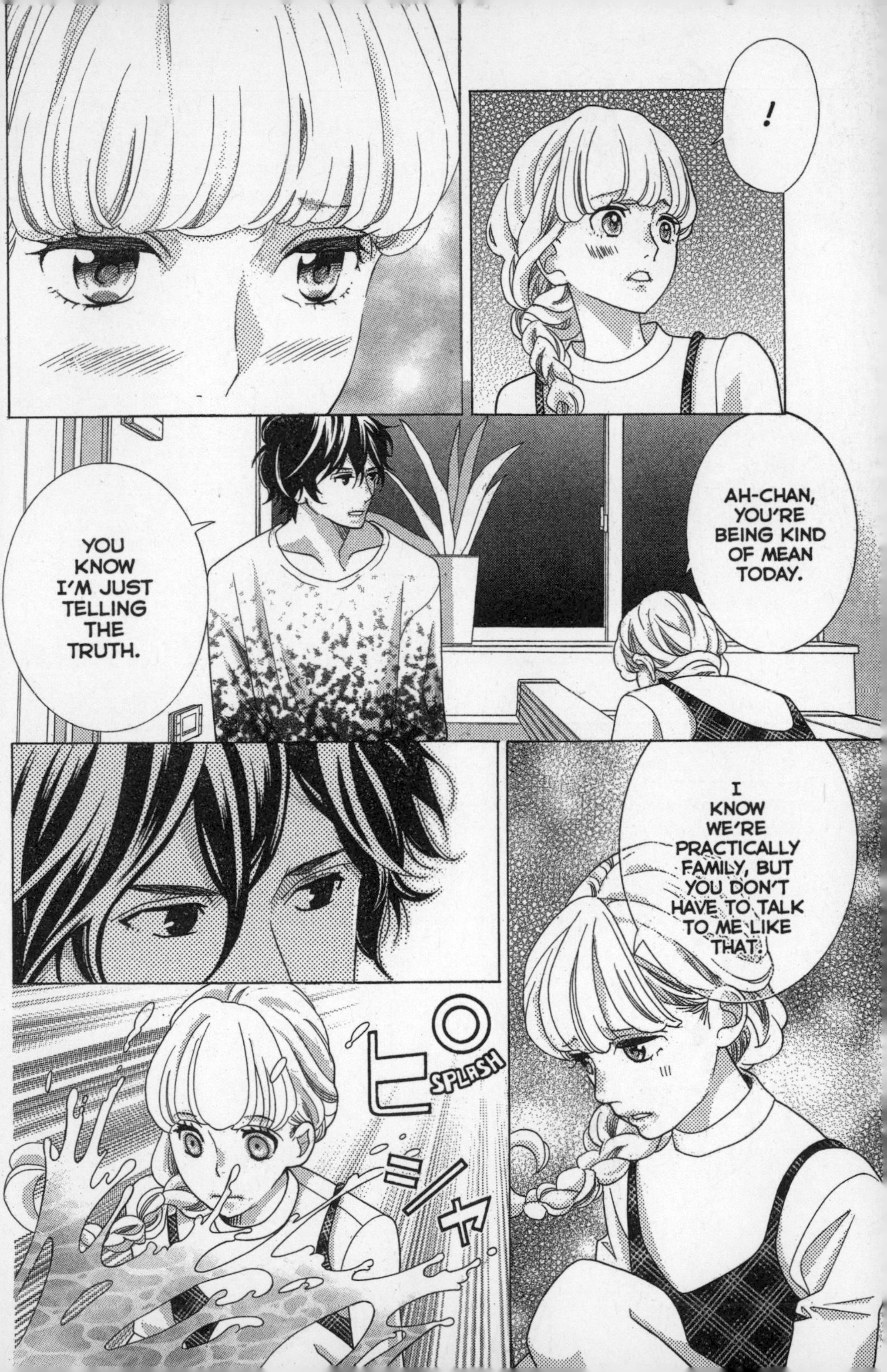
!
AH-CHAN, YOU'RE BEING KIND OF MEAN TODAY.
YOU KNOW I'M JUST TELLING THE TRUTH.
I KNOW WE'RE PRACTICALLY FAMILY, BUT YOU DON'T HAVE TO TALK TO ME LIKE THAT.
SPLASH

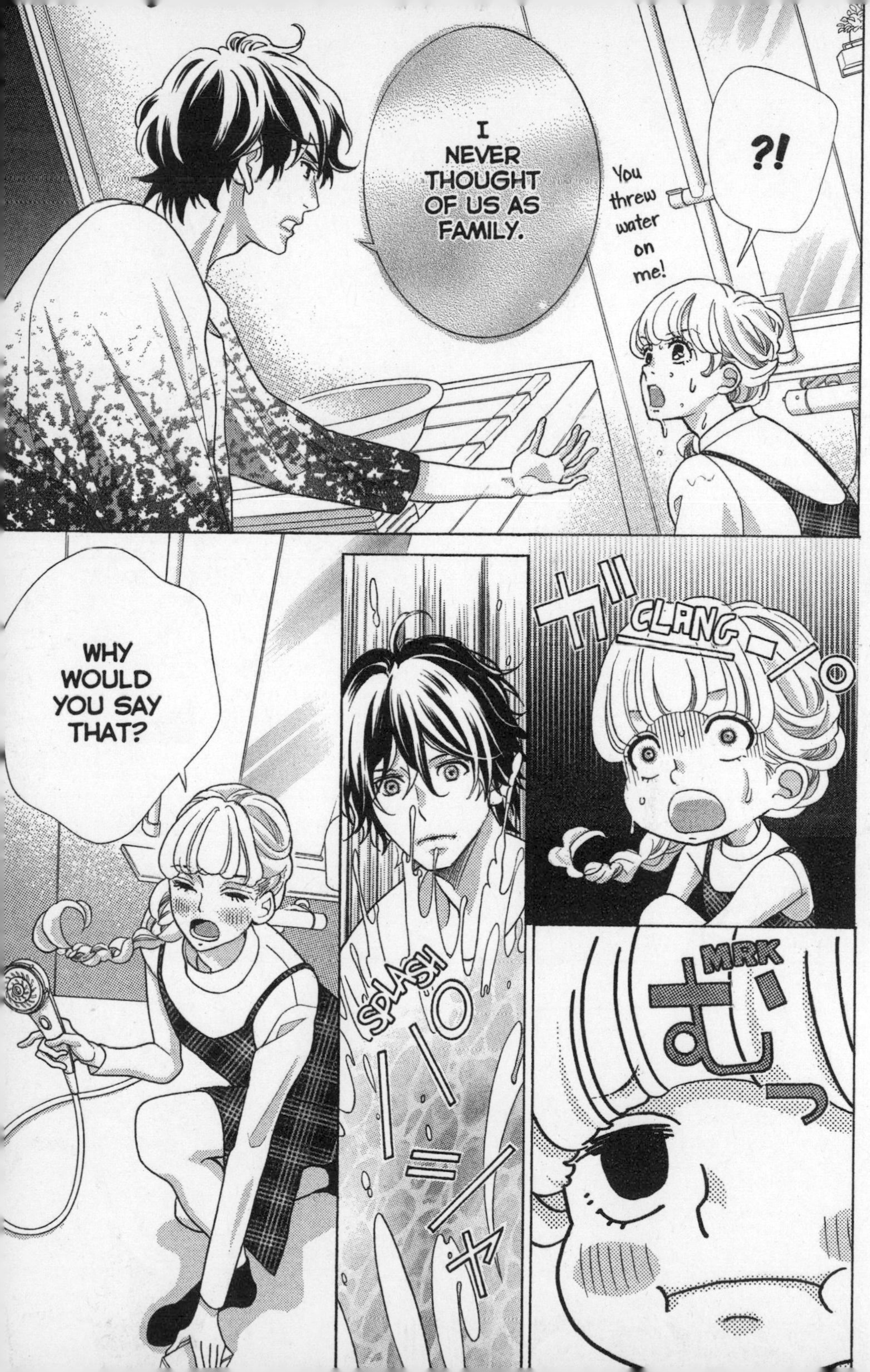
?!
You threw water on me!
I NEVER THOUGHT OF US AS FAMILY.
CLANG
MRK
SPLASH!
WHY WOULD YOU SAY THAT?

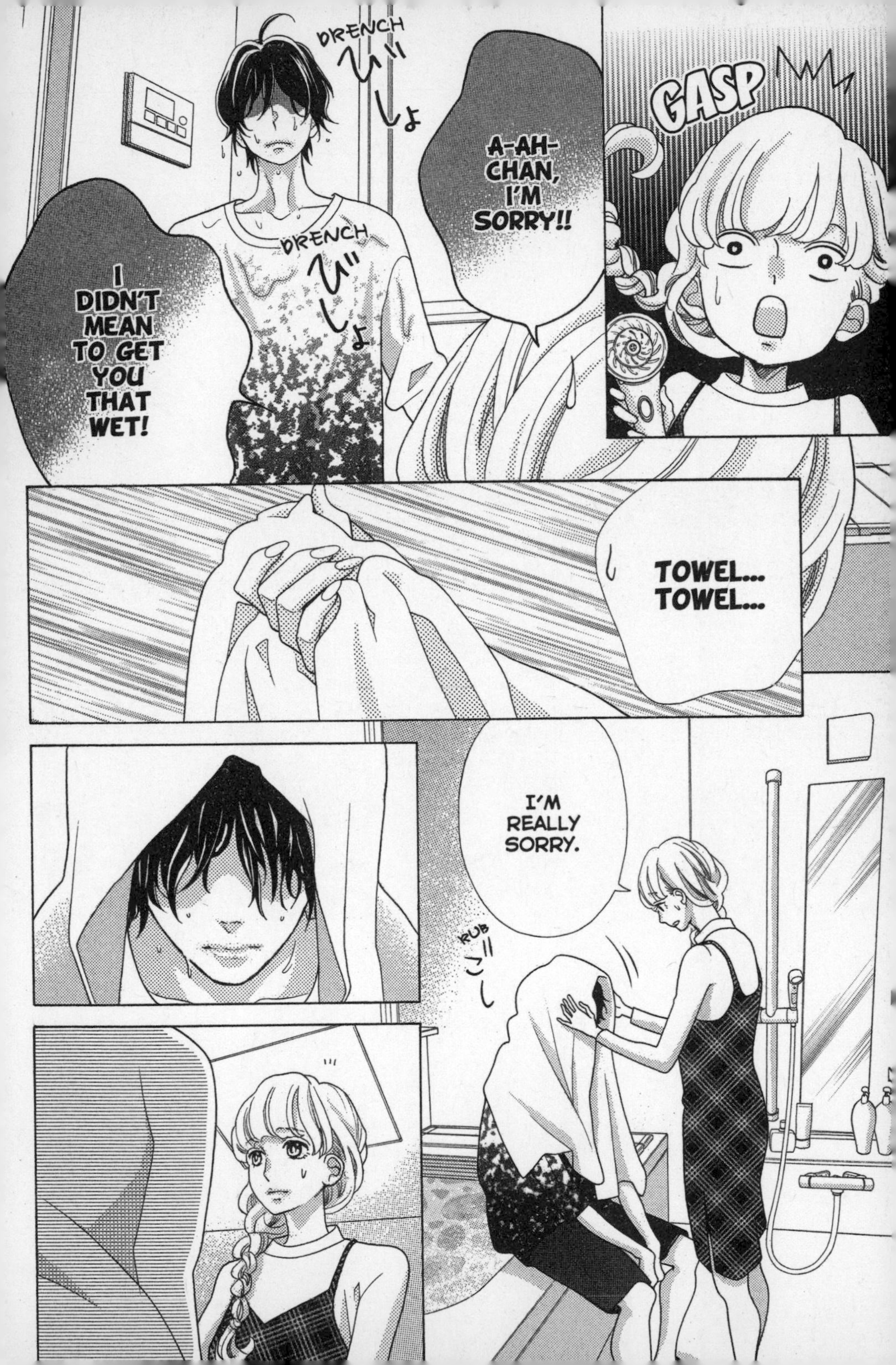
GASP
A-AH-CHAN, I'M SORRY!!
DRENCH
びしょ
DRENCH
びしょ
I DIDN'T MEAN TO GET YOU THAT WET!
TOWEL... TOWEL...
I'M REALLY SORRY.
RUB
ごし

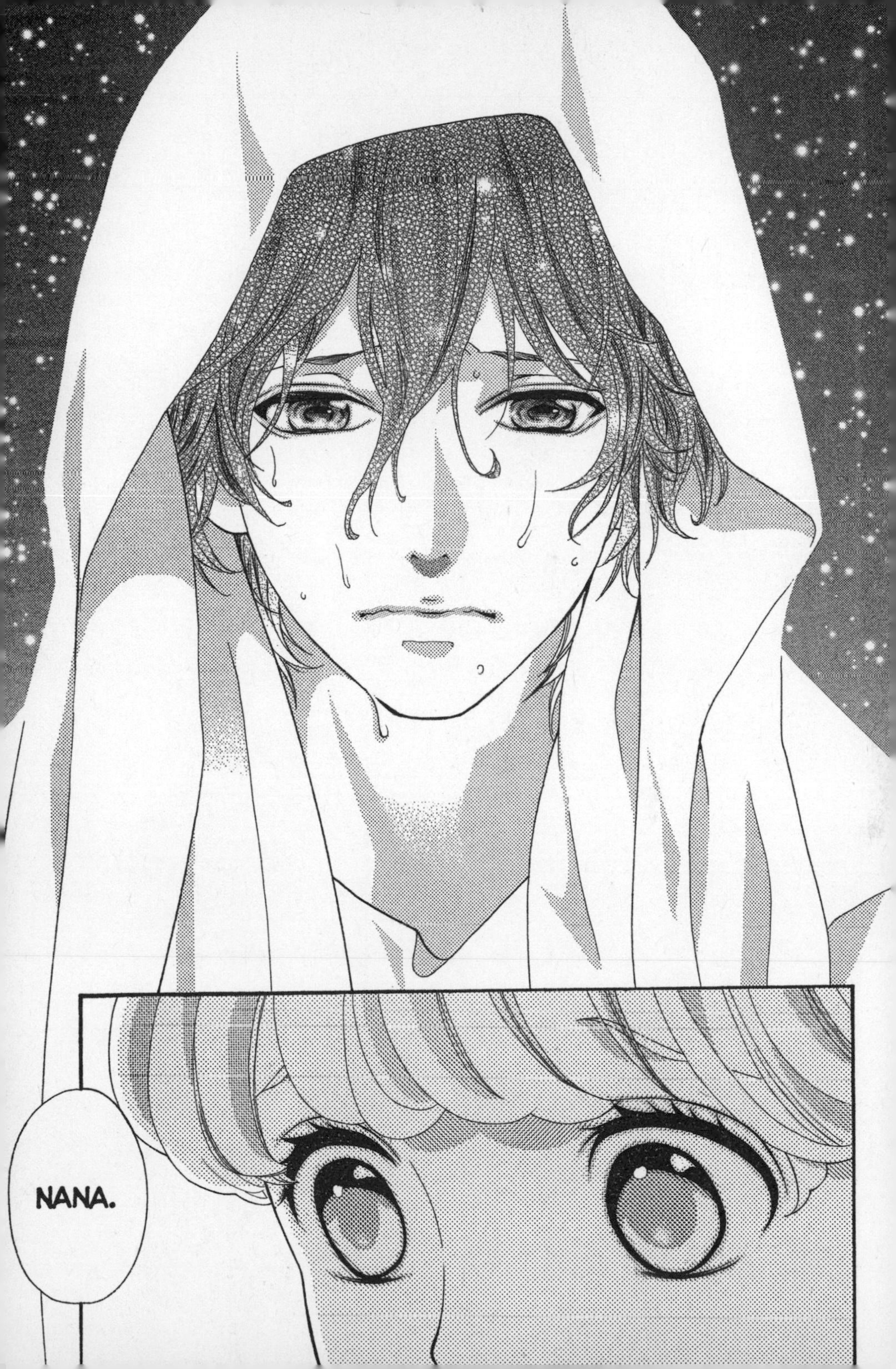
NANA.

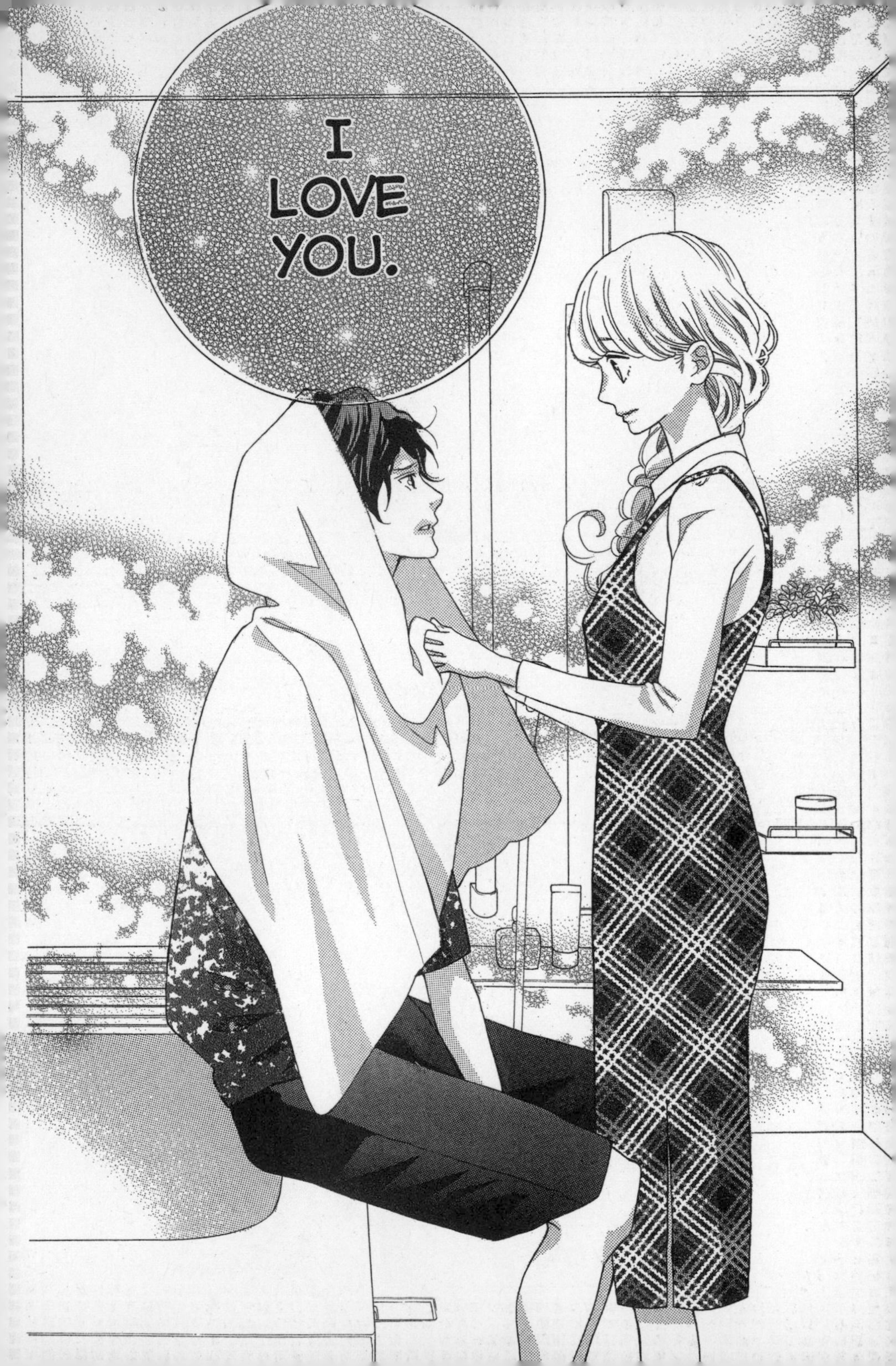
I LOVE YOU.

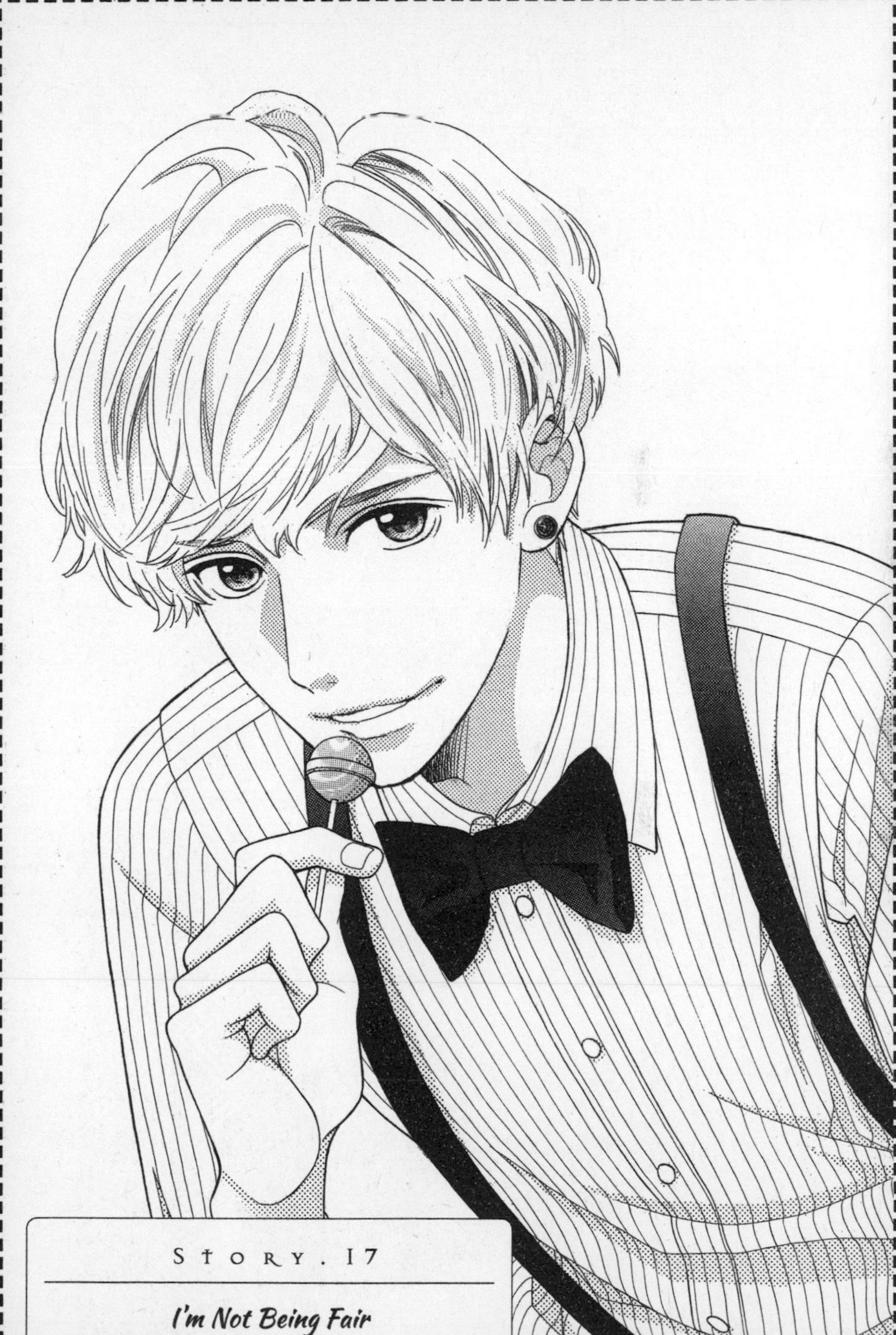

Story. 17

I'm Not Being Fair

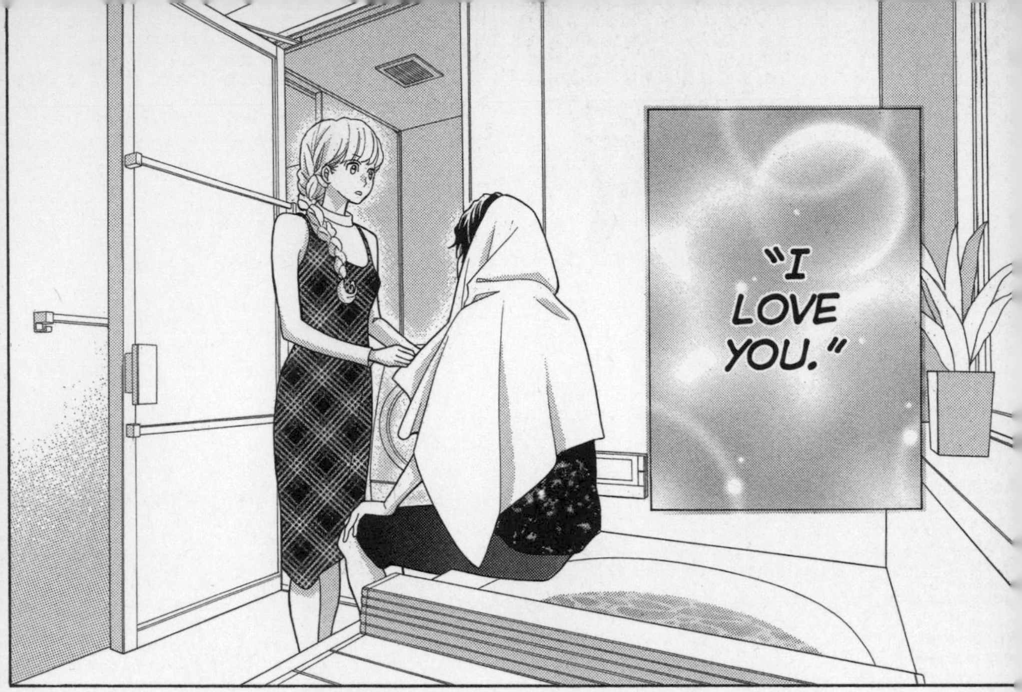
"I LOVE YOU."
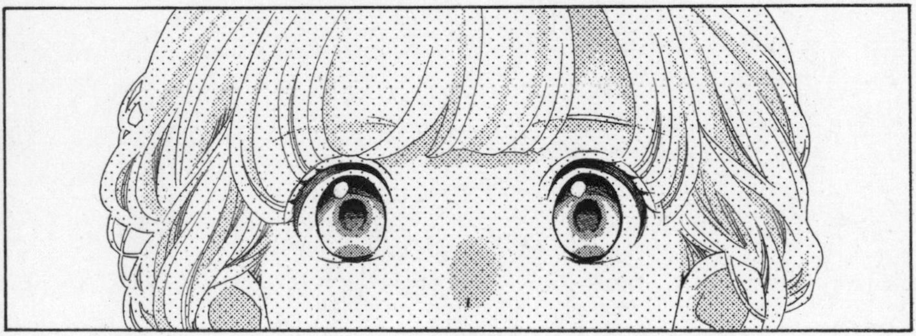

Kiss Me at the Stroke of Midnight

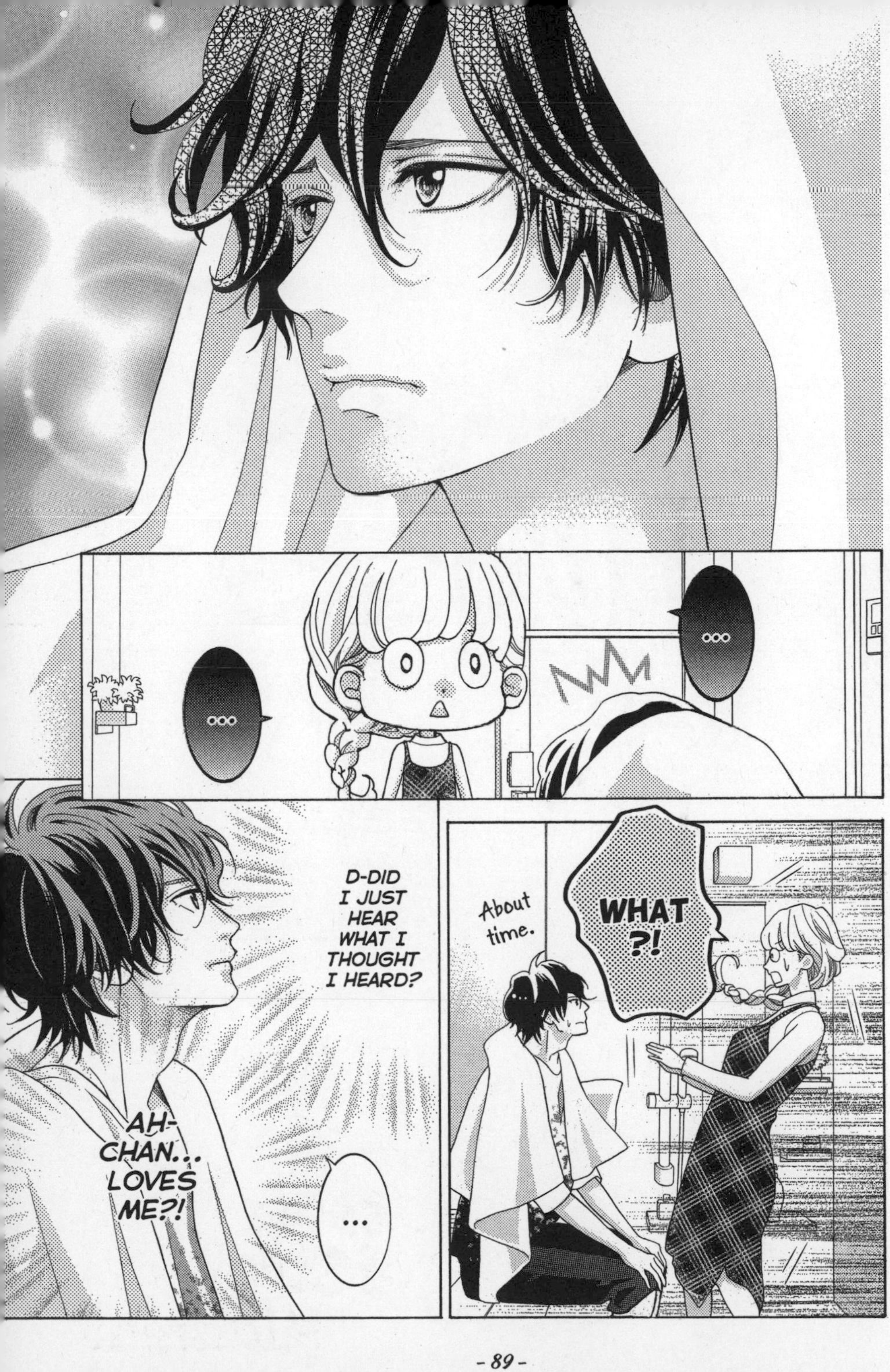
...
...
WHAT ?!
About time.
D-DID I JUST HEAR WHAT I THOUGHT I HEARD?
AH-CHAN... LOVES ME?!
...

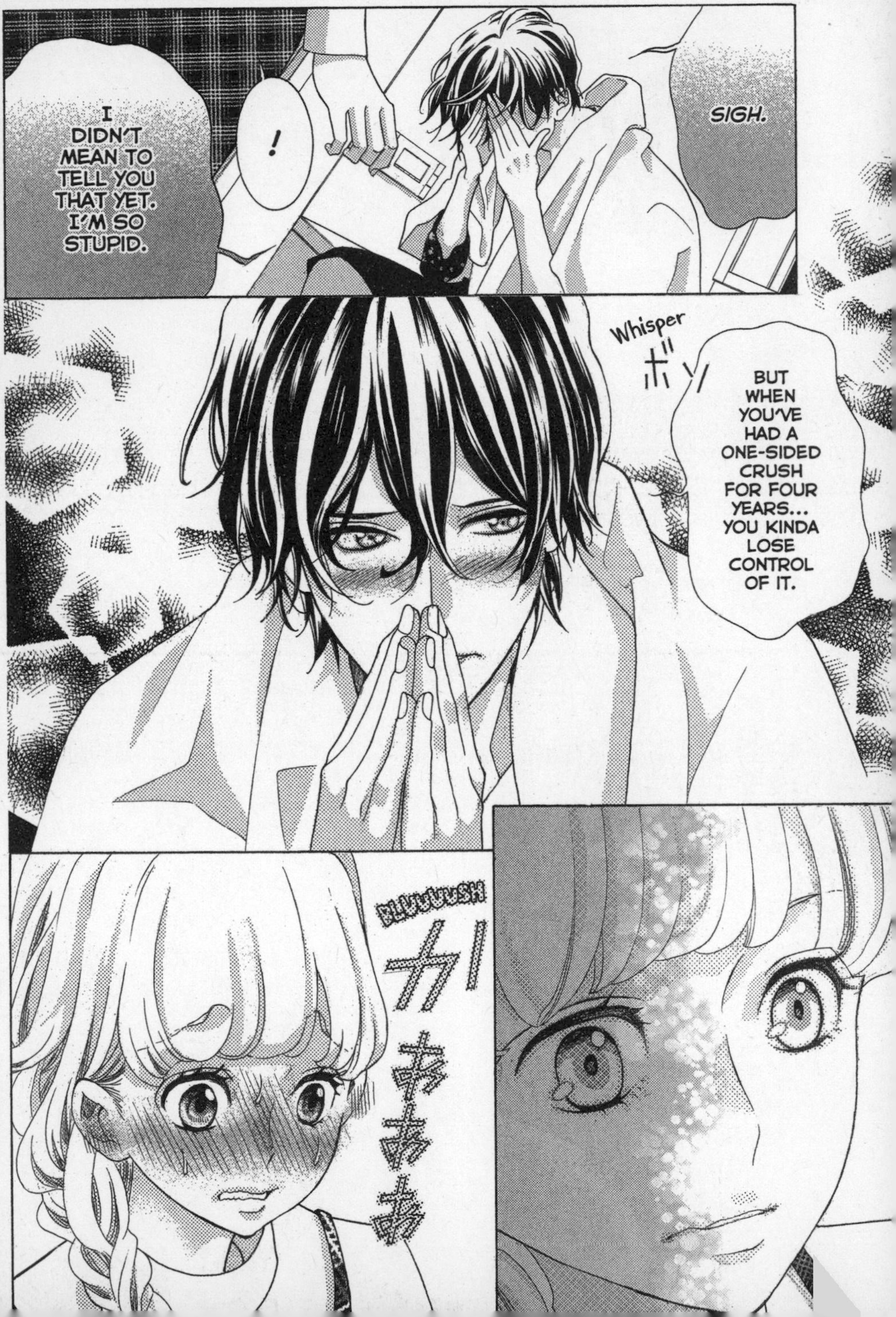
SIGH.
!
I DIDN'T MEAN TO TELL YOU THAT YET. I'M SO STUPID.
Whisper
ボソ
BUT WHEN YOU'VE HAD A ONE-SIDED CRUSH FOR FOUR YEARS... YOU KINDA LOSE CONTROL OF IT.
BLUUUUSH

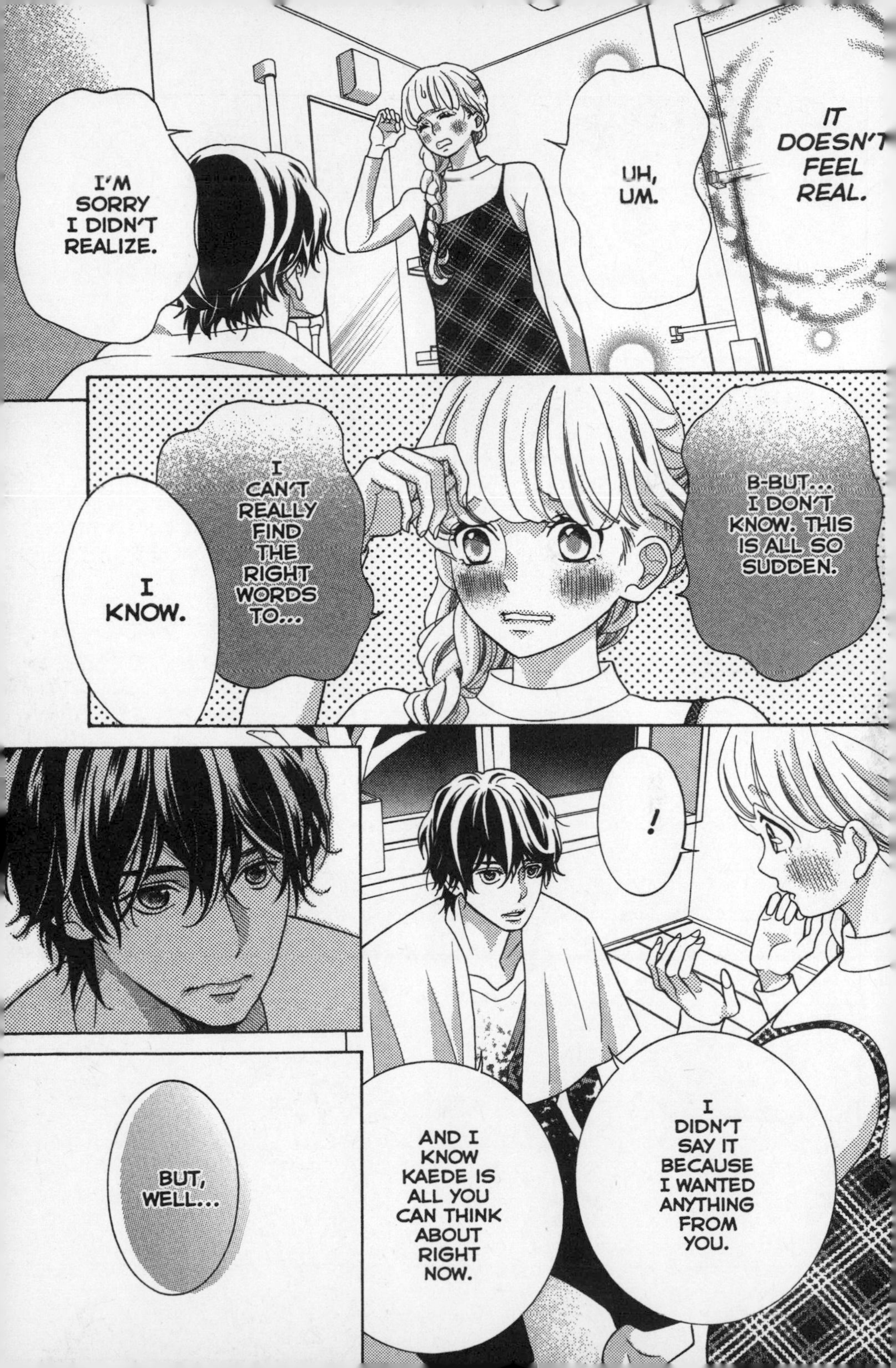
IT DOESN'T FEEL REAL.
UH, UM.
I'M SORRY I DIDN'T REALIZE.
B-BUT... I DON'T KNOW. THIS IS ALL SO SUDDEN.
I CAN'T REALLY FIND THE RIGHT WORDS TO...
I KNOW.
!
I DIDN'T SAY IT BECAUSE I WANTED ANYTHING FROM YOU.
AND I KNOW KAEDE IS ALL YOU CAN THINK ABOUT RIGHT NOW.
BUT, WELL...

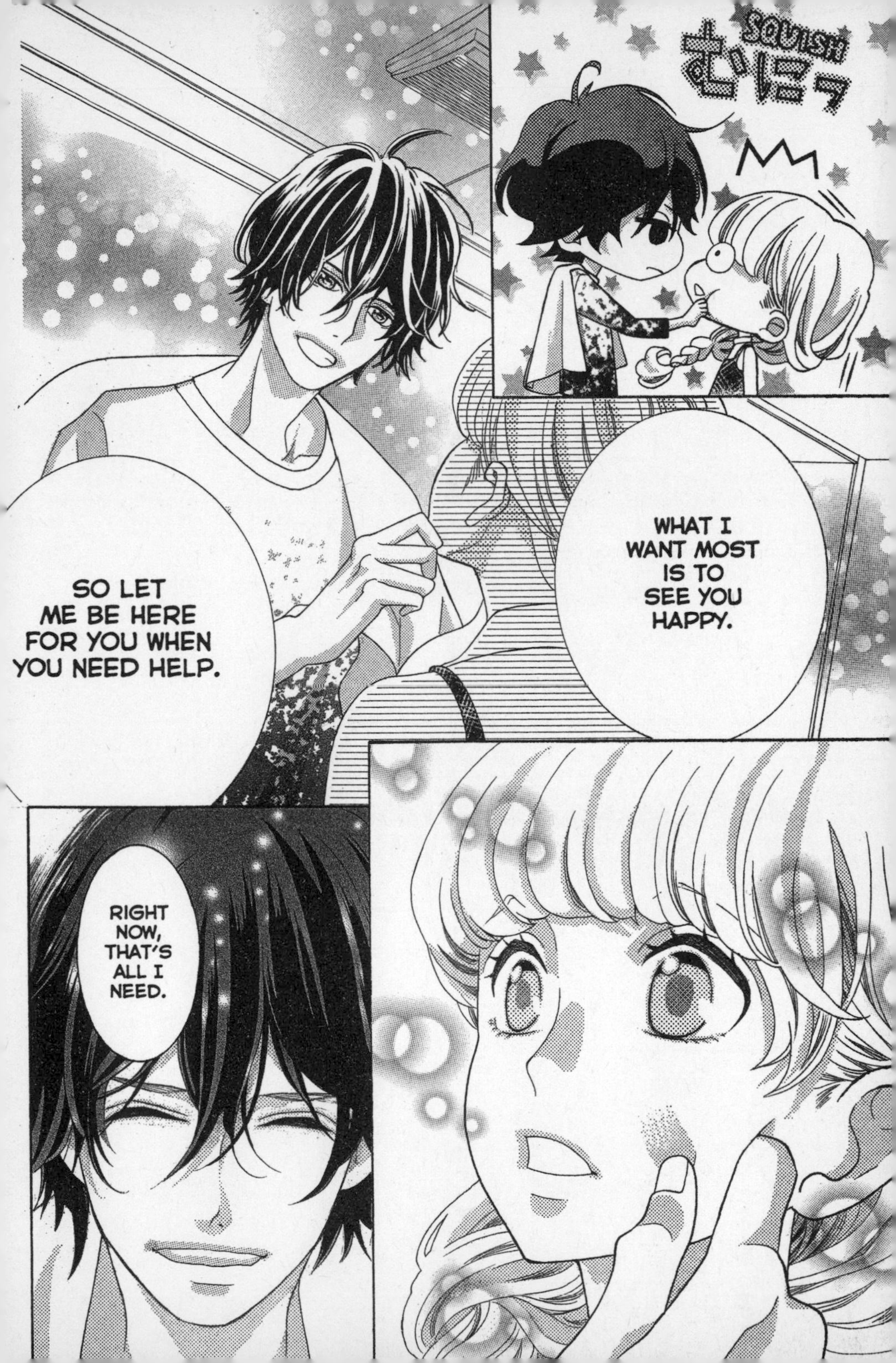
SQUISH
WHAT I WANT MOST IS TO SEE YOU HAPPY.
SO LET ME BE HERE FOR YOU WHEN YOU NEED HELP.
RIGHT NOW, THAT'S ALL I NEED.

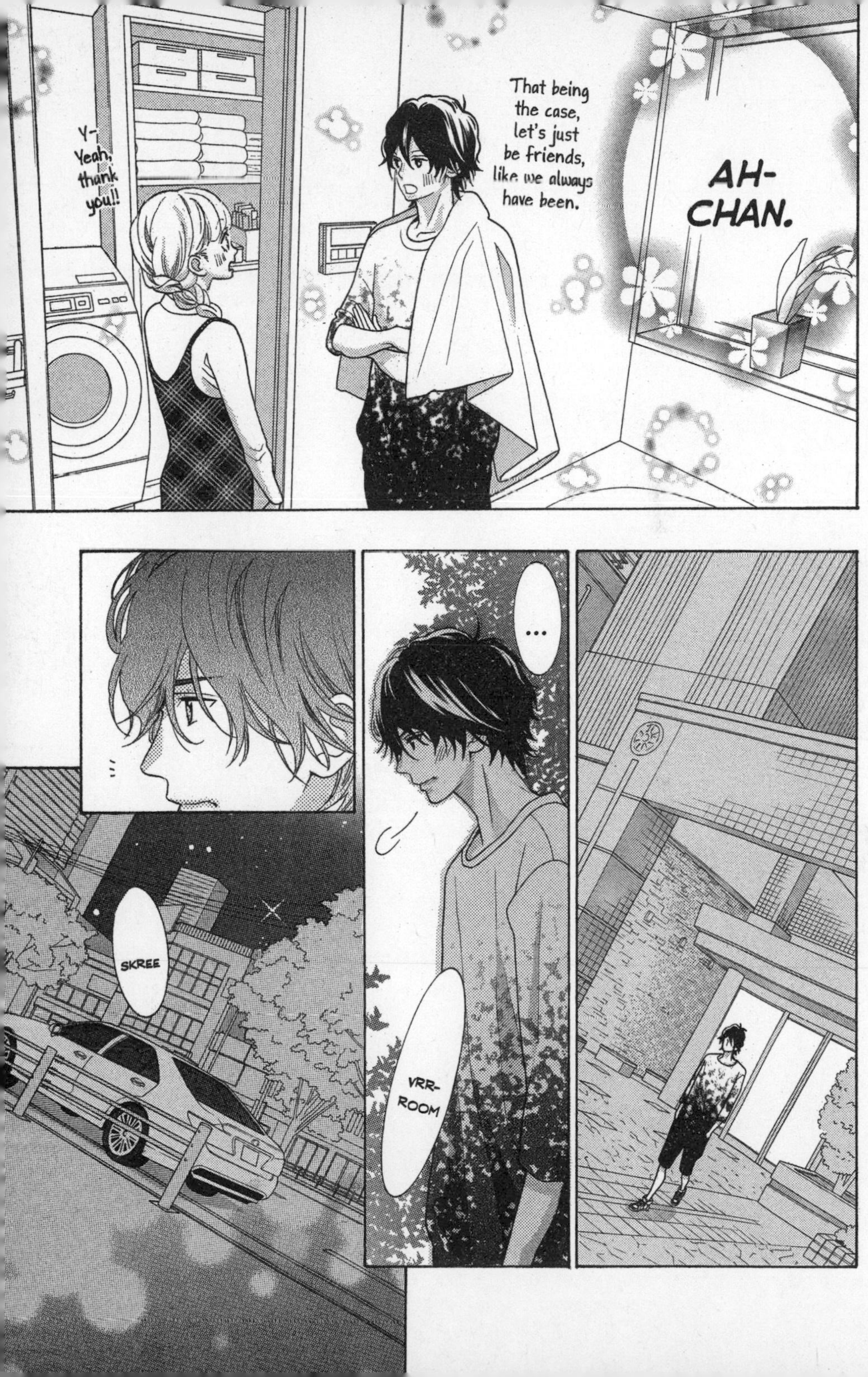
AH-CHAN.
That being the case, let's just be friends, like we always have been.
Y- Yeah, thank you!!
...
VRR-ROOM
SKREE

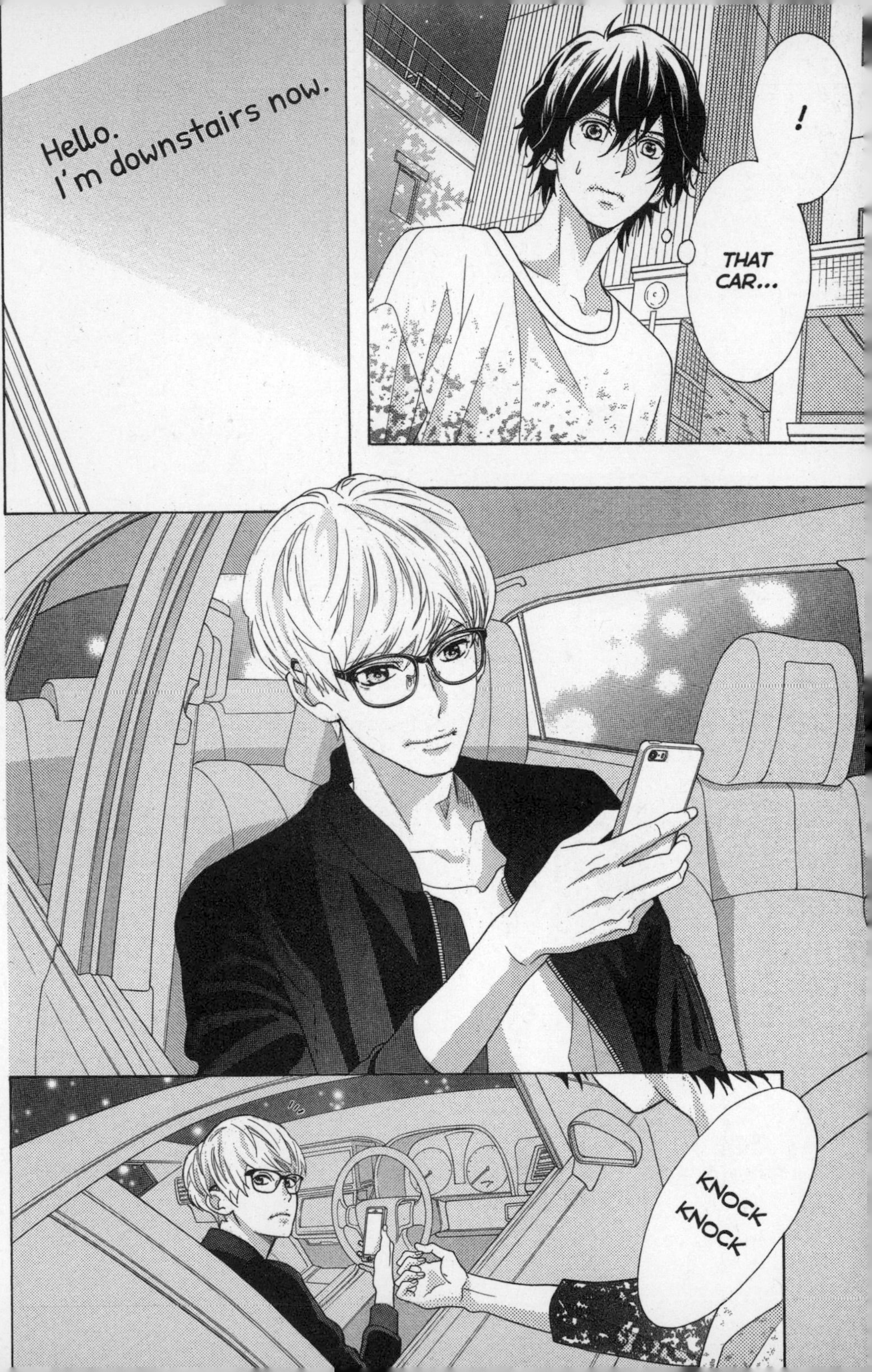
!
THAT CAR...
Hello.
I'm downstairs now.
KNOCK KNOCK

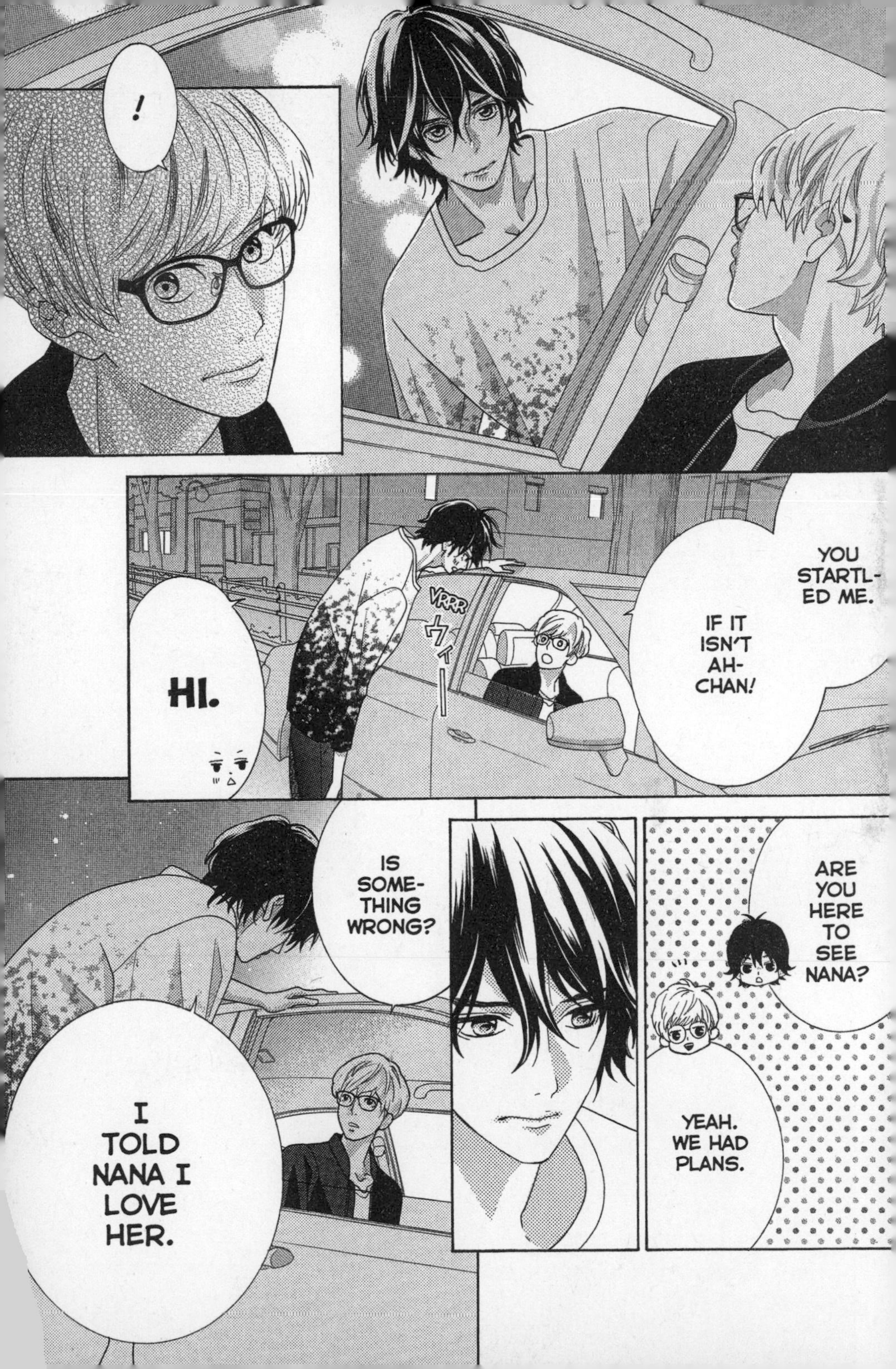
!
YOU STARTLED ME.
IF IT ISN'T AH-CHAN!
VRRR
ウィー
HI.
ARE YOU HERE TO SEE NANA?
YEAH. WE HAD PLANS.
IS SOMETHING WRONG?
I TOLD NANA I LOVE HER.

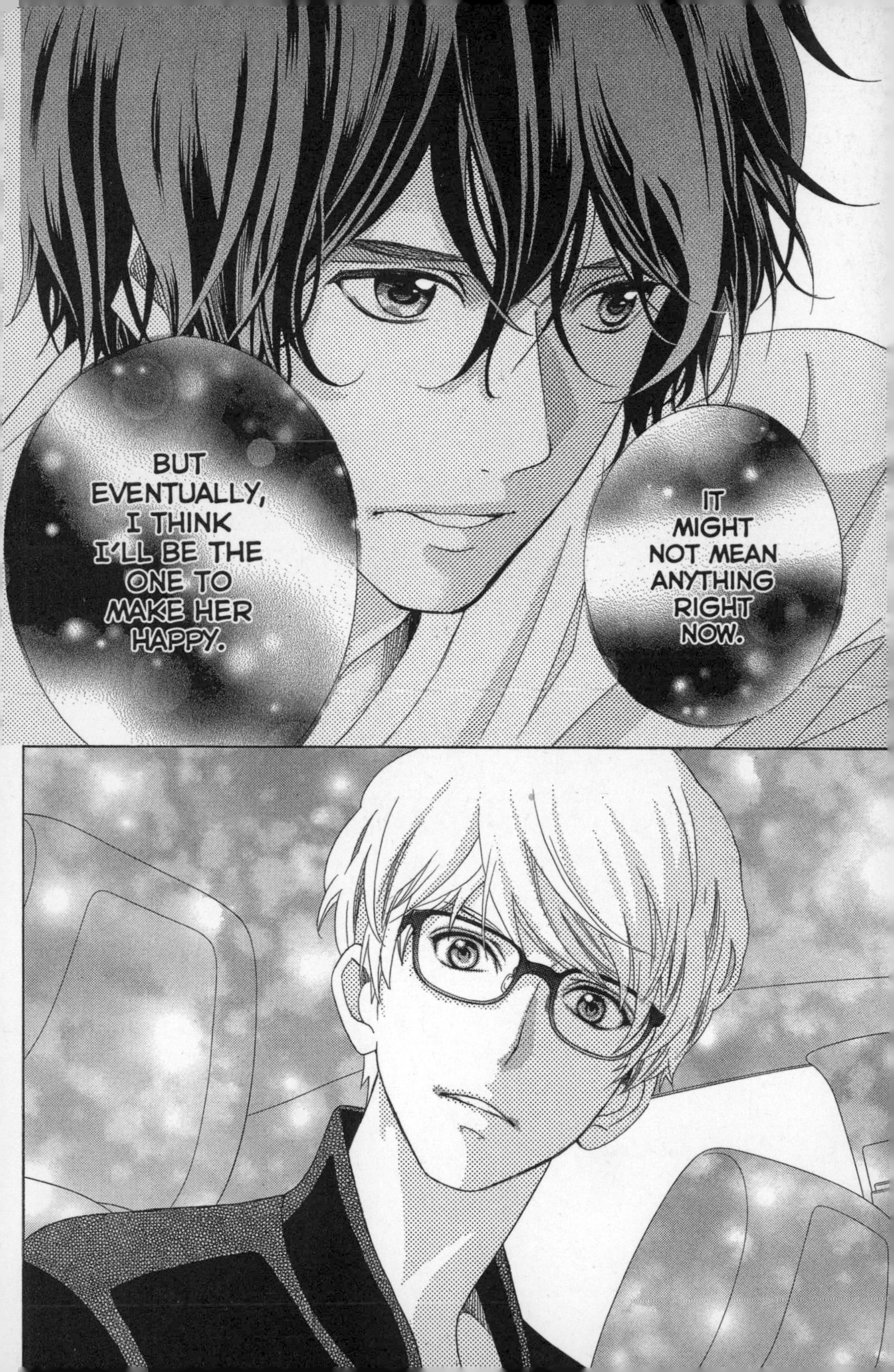
IT MIGHT NOT MEAN ANYTHING RIGHT NOW.
BUT EVENTUALLY, I THINK I'LL BE THE ONE TO MAKE HER HAPPY.

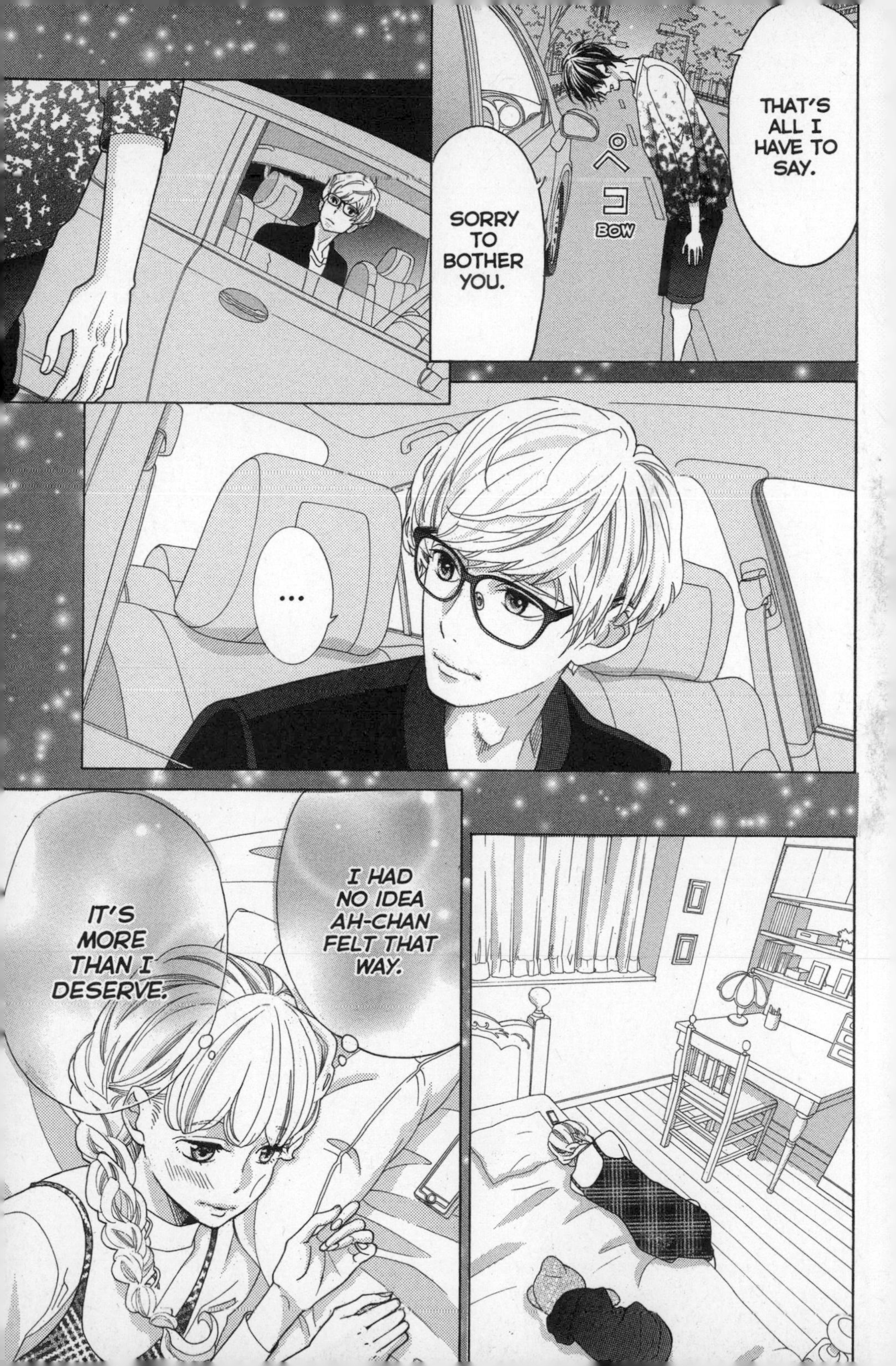
THAT'S ALL I HAVE TO SAY.
ペコ
BOW
SORRY TO BOTHER YOU.
...
I HAD NO IDEA AH-CHAN FELT THAT WAY.
IT'S MORE THAN I DESERVE.

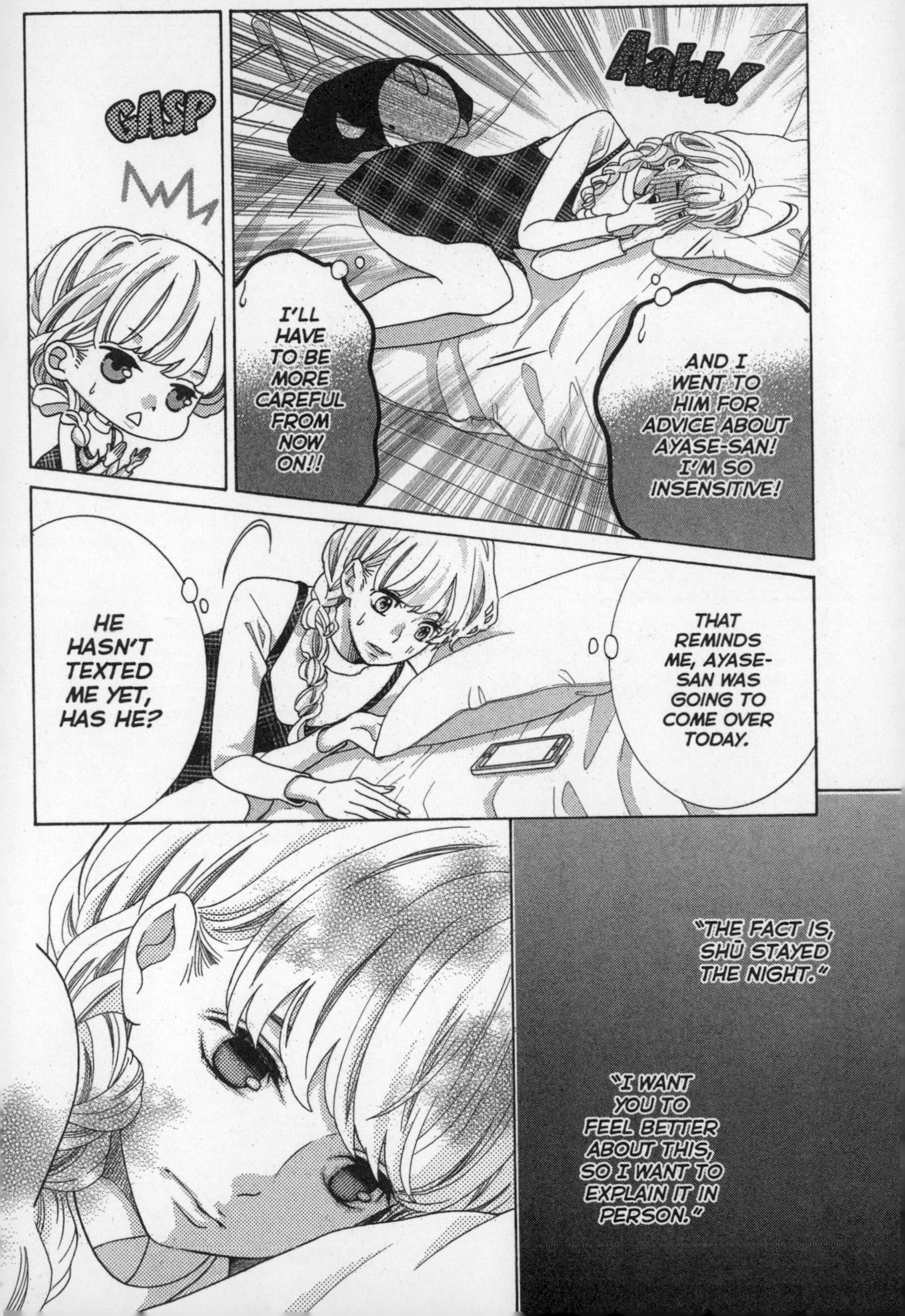
Aahh!
AND I WENT TO HIM FOR ADVICE ABOUT AYASE-SAN! I'M SO INSENSITIVE!
I'LL HAVE TO BE MORE CAREFUL FROM NOW ON!!
GASP
THAT REMINDS ME, AYASE-SAN WAS GOING TO COME OVER TODAY.
HE HASN'T TEXTED ME YET, HAS HE?
"THE FACT IS, SHŪ STAYED THE NIGHT."
"I WANT YOU TO FEEL BETTER ABOUT THIS, SO I WANT TO EXPLAIN IT IN PERSON."

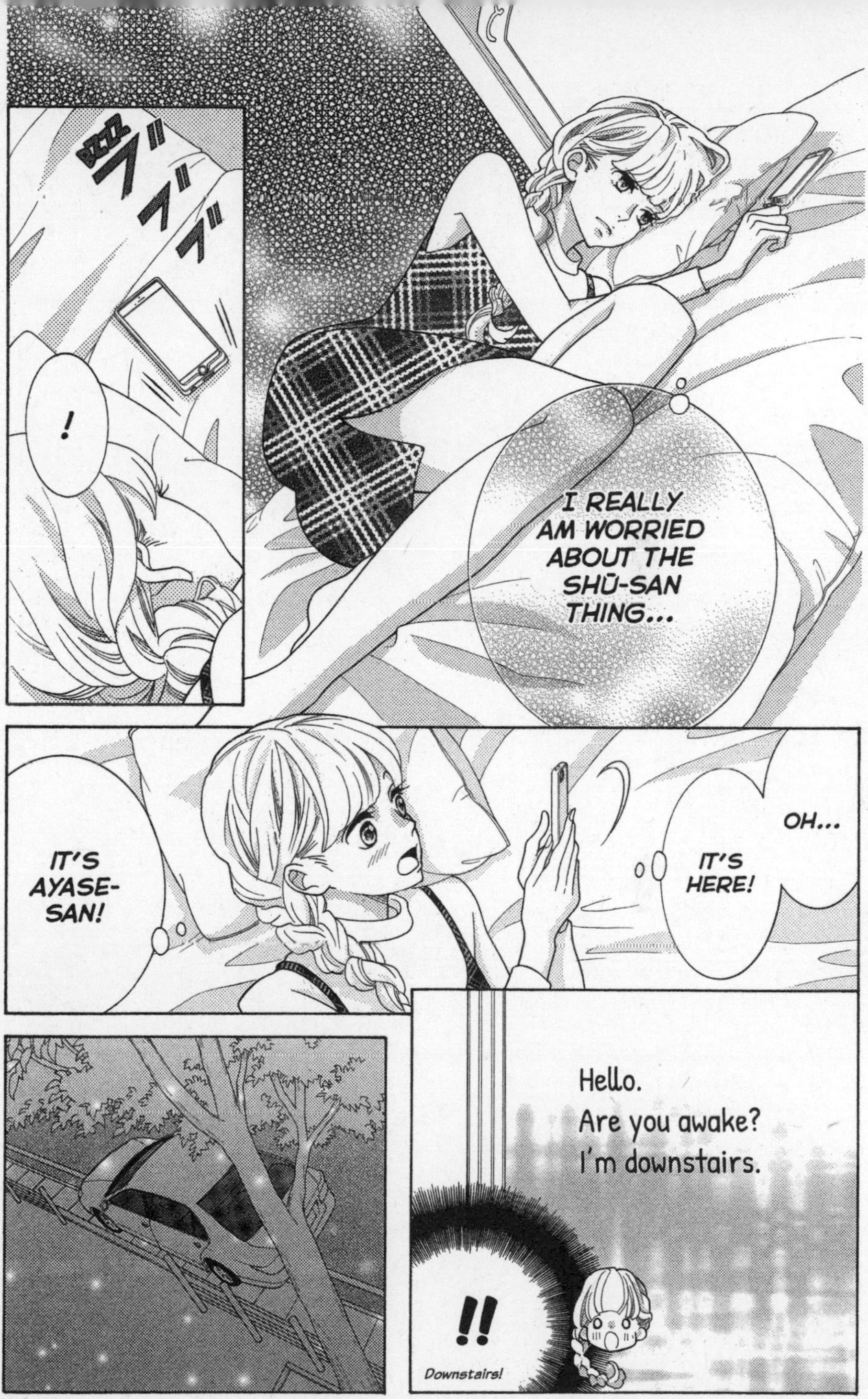
I REALLY AM WORRIED ABOUT THE SHŪ-SAN THING...
ブブブ
!
OH... IT'S HERE!
IT'S AYASE-SAN!
Hello.
Are you awake?
I'm downstairs.
!!
Downstairs!

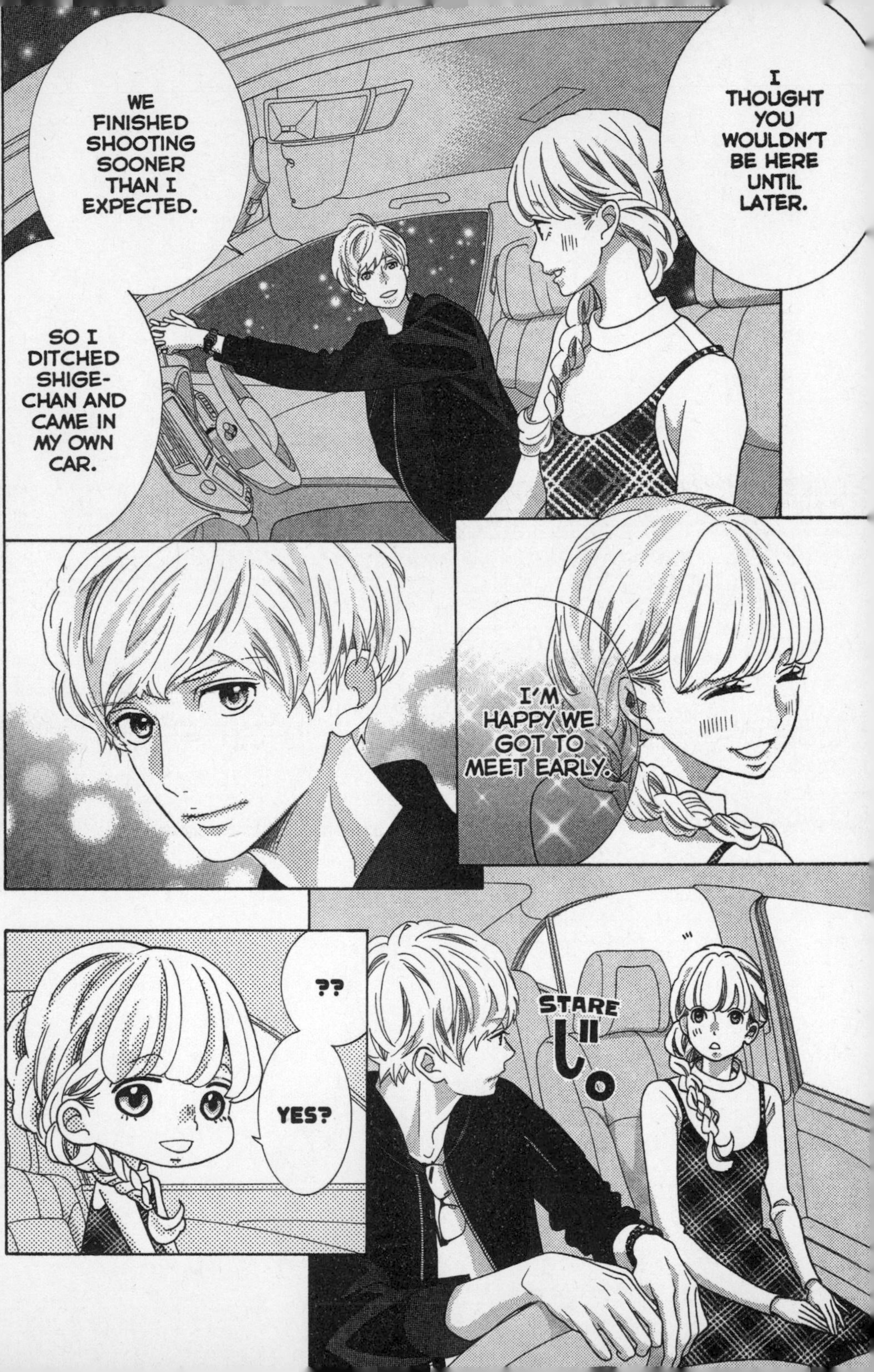
I THOUGHT YOU WOULDN'T BE HERE UNTIL LATER.
WE FINISHED SHOOTING SOONER THAN I EXPECTED.
SO I DITCHED SHIGE-CHAN AND CAME IN MY OWN CAR.
I'M HAPPY WE GOT TO MEET EARLY.
STARE
??
YES?

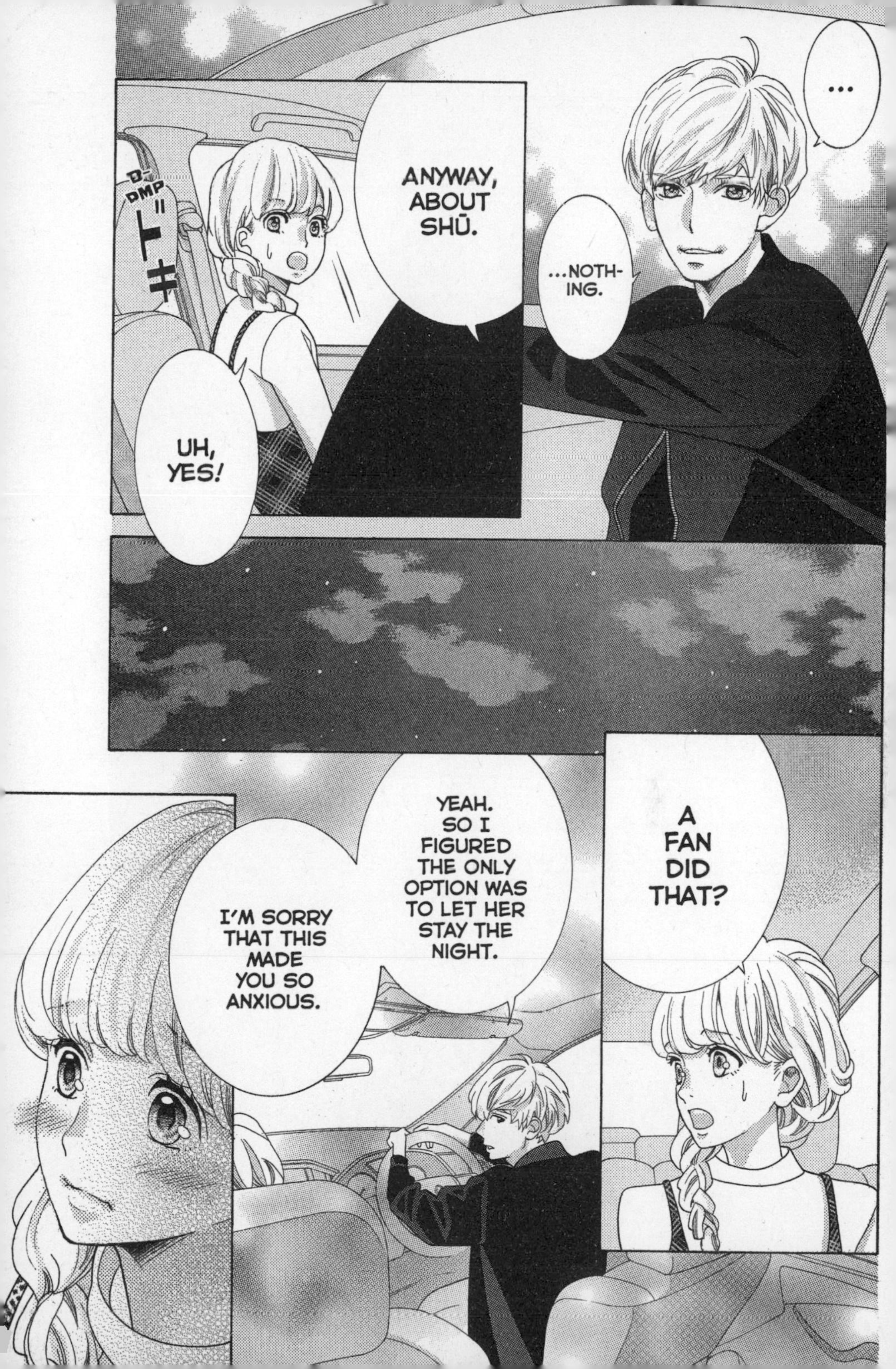
...
...NOTHING.
ANYWAY, ABOUT SHŪ.
B-DMP
ドキ
UH, YES!
A FAN DID THAT?
YEAH. SO I FIGURED THE ONLY OPTION WAS TO LET HER STAY THE NIGHT.
I'M SORRY THAT THIS MADE YOU SO ANXIOUS.

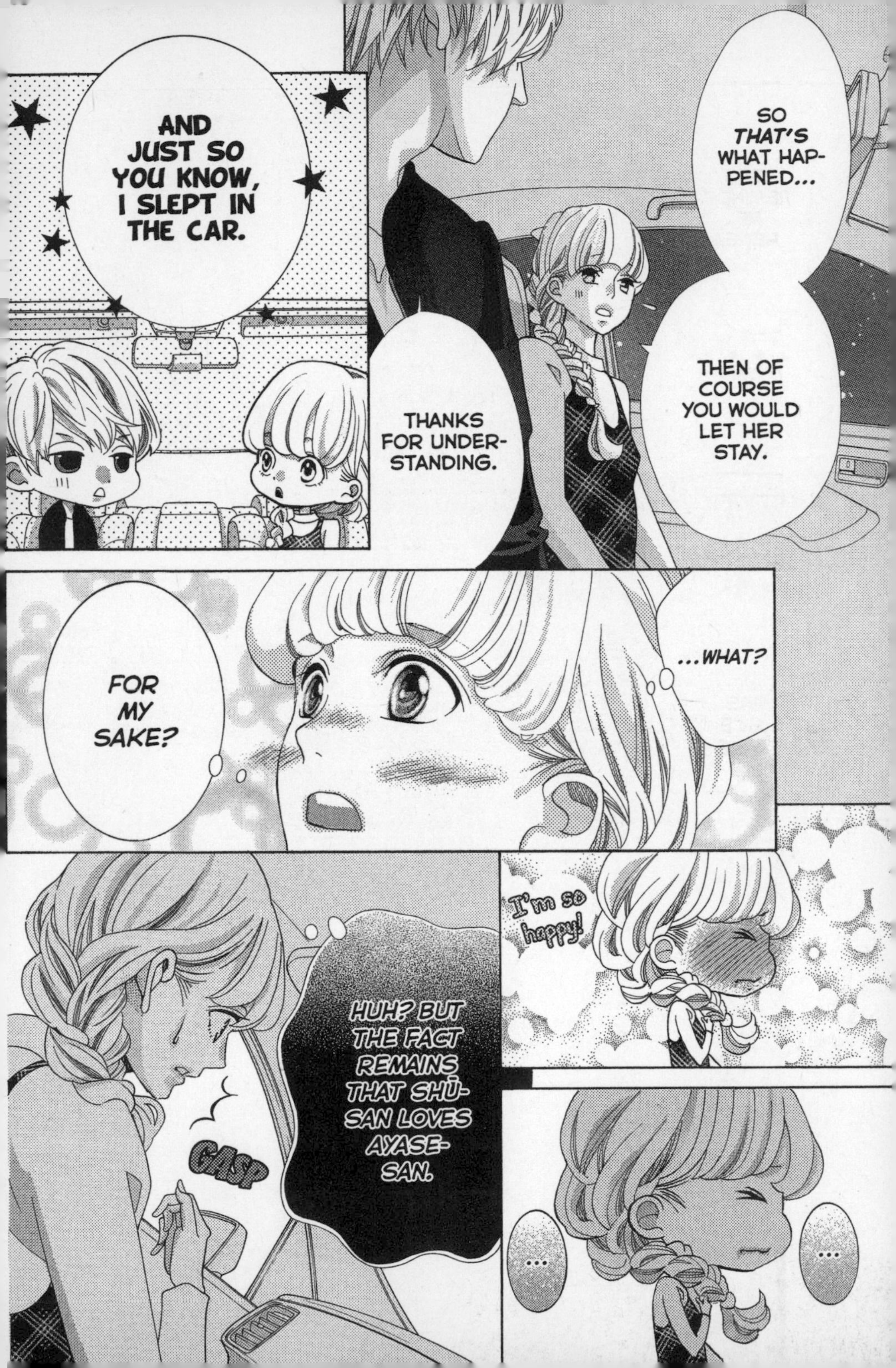
SO THAT'S WHAT HAP-PENED...
THEN OF COURSE YOU WOULD LET HER STAY.
THANKS FOR UNDER-STANDING.
AND JUST SO YOU KNOW, I SLEPT IN THE CAR.
...WHAT?
FOR MY SAKE?
I'm so happy!
...
...
HUH? BUT THE FACT REMAINS THAT SHŪ-SAN LOVES AYASE-SAN.
GASP

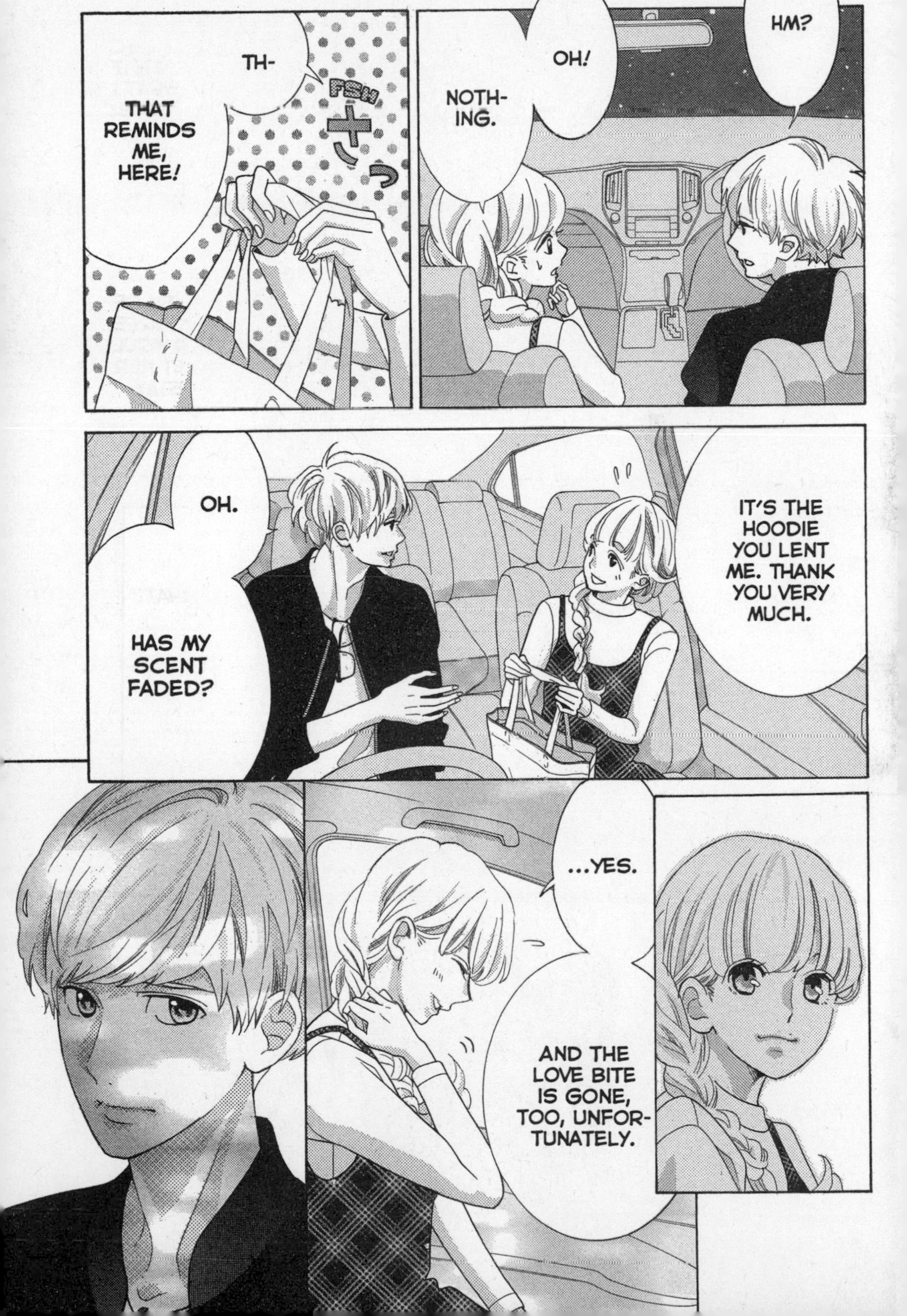
HM?
OH!
NOTHING.
TH-
FSH
THAT REMINDS ME, HERE!
IT'S THE HOODIE YOU LENT ME. THANK YOU VERY MUCH.
OH.
HAS MY SCENT FADED?
...YES.
AND THE LOVE BITE IS GONE, TOO, UNFORTUNATELY.

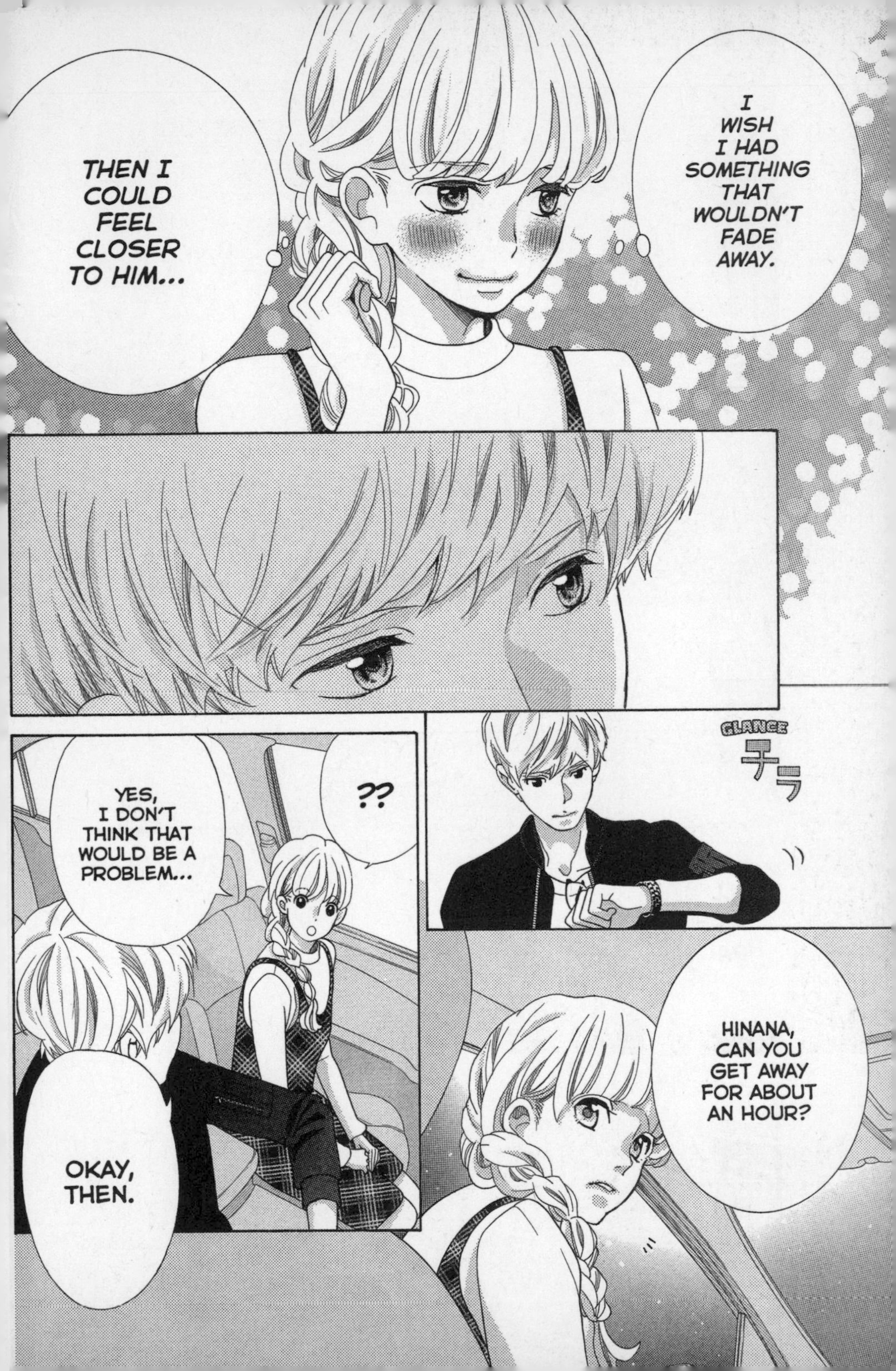
I WISH I HAD SOMETHING THAT WOULDN'T FADE AWAY.
THEN I COULD FEEL CLOSER TO HIM...
GLANCE
チラ
HINANA, CAN YOU GET AWAY FOR ABOUT AN HOUR?
??
YES, I DON'T THINK THAT WOULD BE A PROBLEM...
OKAY, THEN.

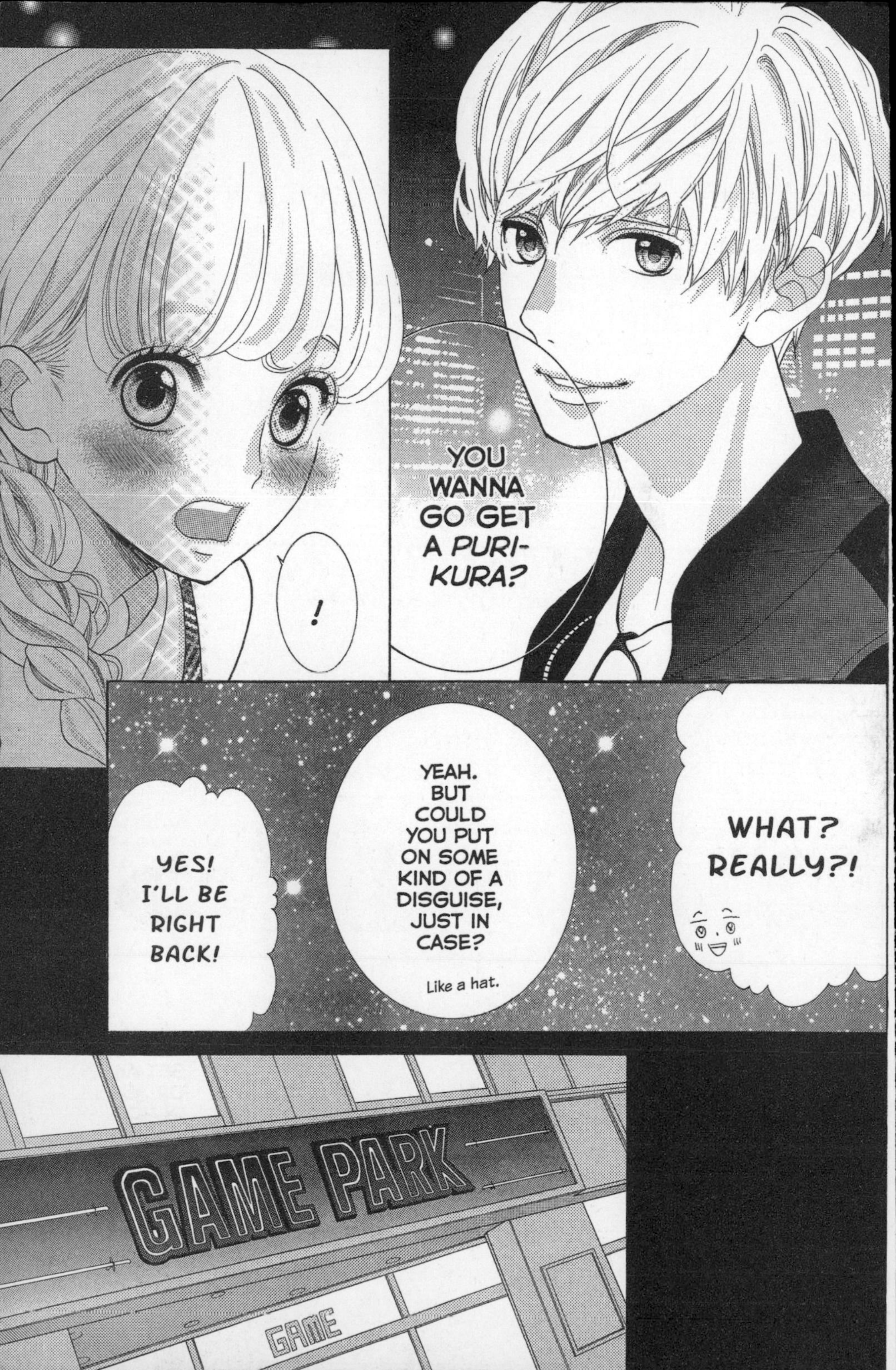
YOU WANNA GO GET A *PURI-KURA*?
!
WHAT? REALLY?!
YEAH. BUT COULD YOU PUT ON SOME KIND OF A DISGUISE, JUST IN CASE?
Like a hat.
YES! I'LL BE RIGHT BACK!
GAME PARK
GAME

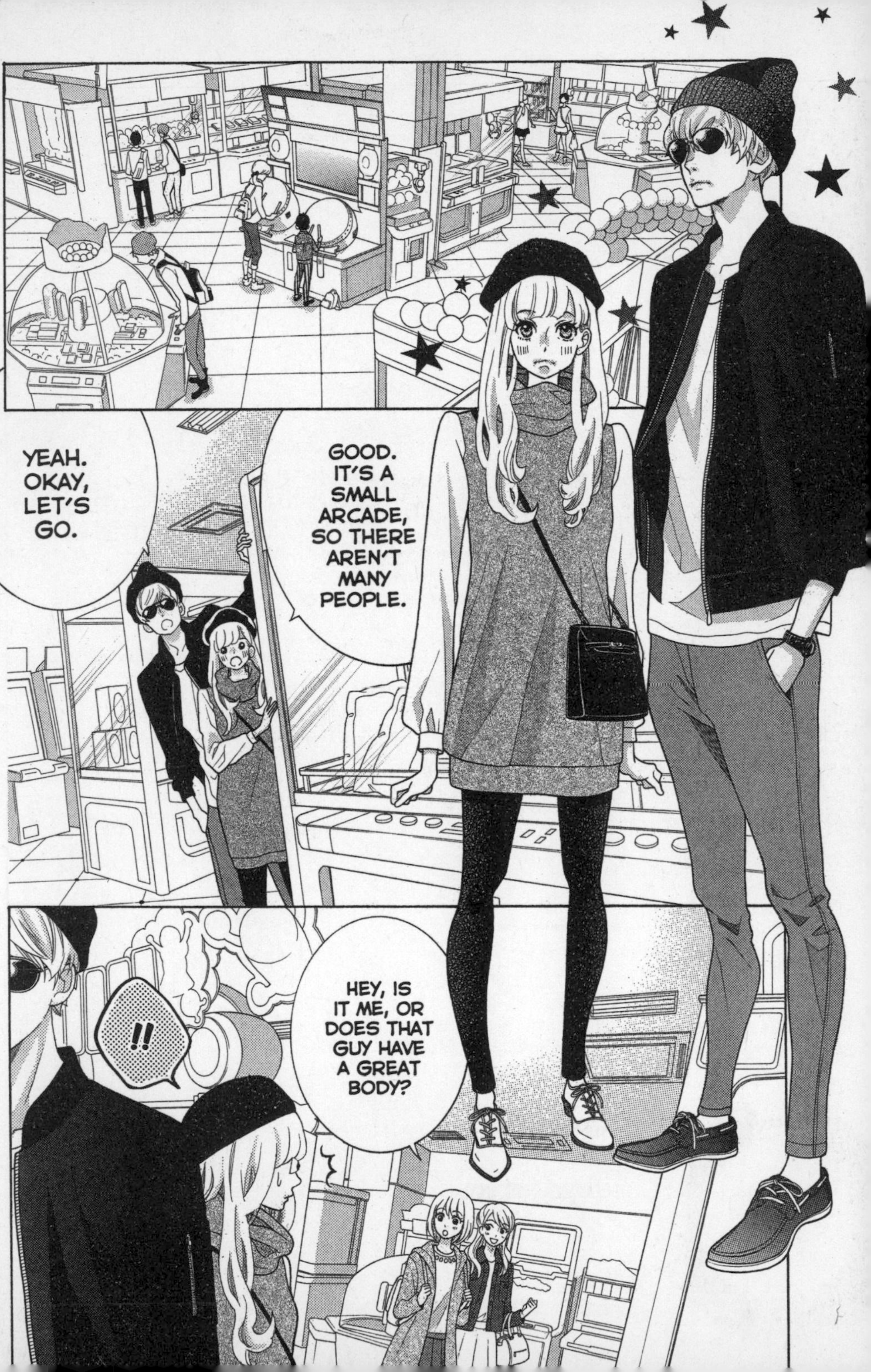
GOOD. IT'S A SMALL ARCADE, SO THERE AREN'T MANY PEOPLE.
YEAH. OKAY, LET'S GO.
HEY, IS IT ME, OR DOES THAT GUY HAVE A GREAT BODY?
!!

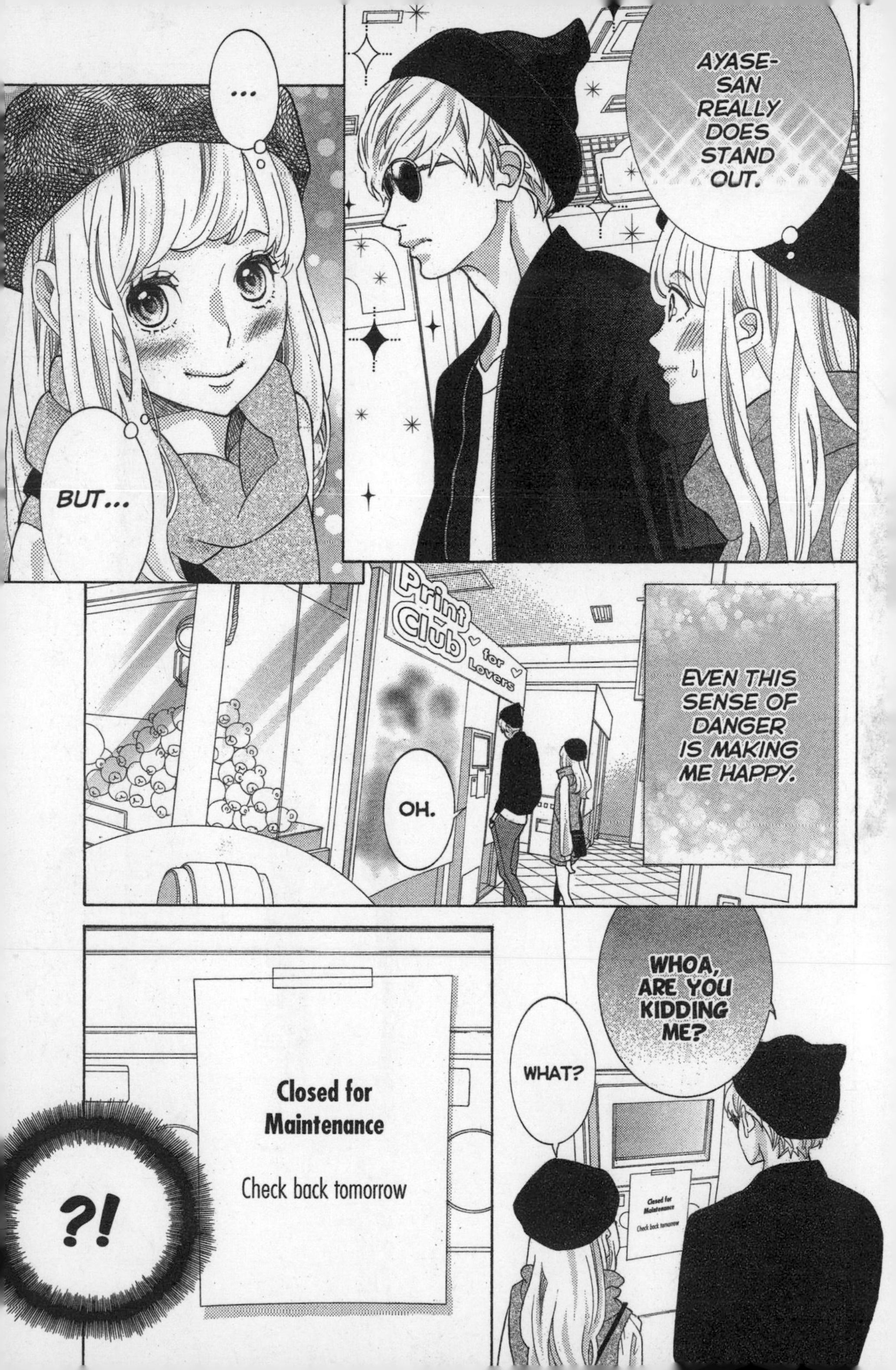
AYASE-SAN REALLY DOES STAND OUT.
...
BUT...
Print Club for Lovers
EVEN THIS SENSE OF DANGER IS MAKING ME HAPPY.
OH.
WHOA, ARE YOU KIDDING ME?
WHAT?
Closed for Maintenance
Check back tomorrow
?!

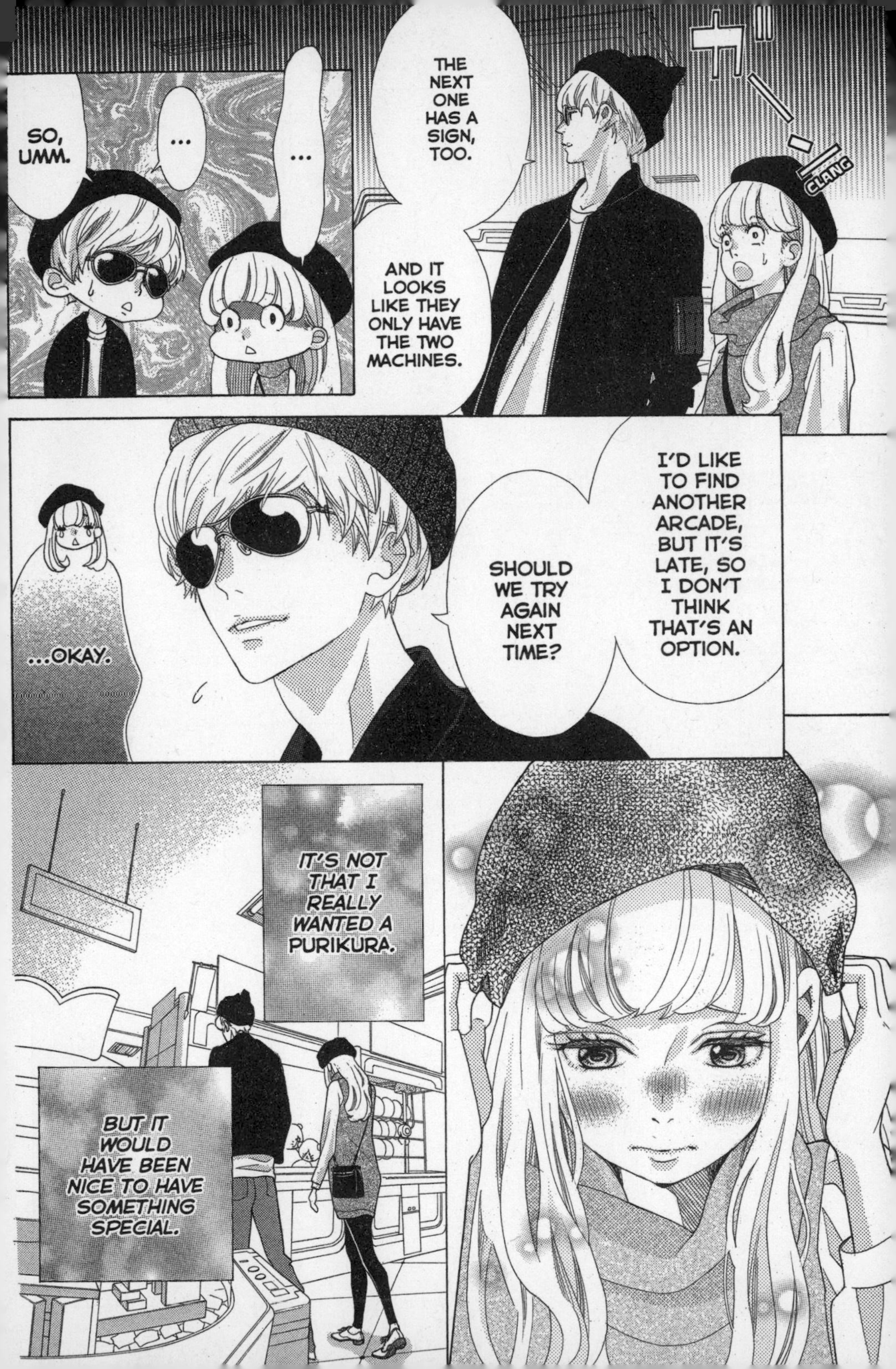
CLANG
THE NEXT ONE HAS A SIGN, TOO.
AND IT LOOKS LIKE THEY ONLY HAVE THE TWO MACHINES.
...
...
SO, UMM.
I'D LIKE TO FIND ANOTHER ARCADE, BUT IT'S LATE, SO I DON'T THINK THAT'S AN OPTION.
SHOULD WE TRY AGAIN NEXT TIME?
...OKAY.
IT'S NOT THAT I REALLY WANTED A PURIKURA.
BUT IT WOULD HAVE BEEN NICE TO HAVE SOMETHING SPECIAL.

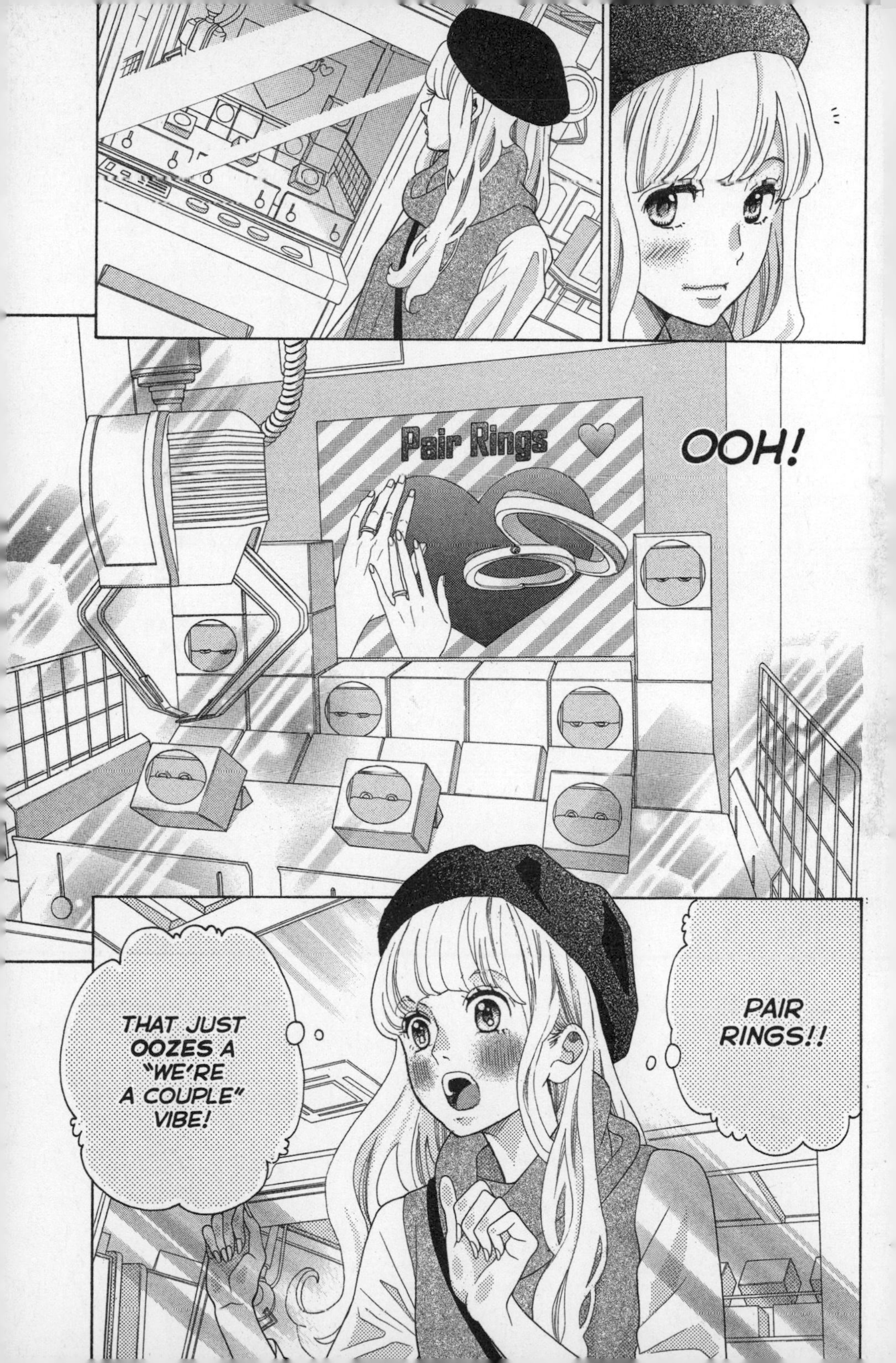
Pair Rings
OOH!
PAIR RINGS!!
THAT JUST OOZES A "WE'RE A COUPLE" VIBE!

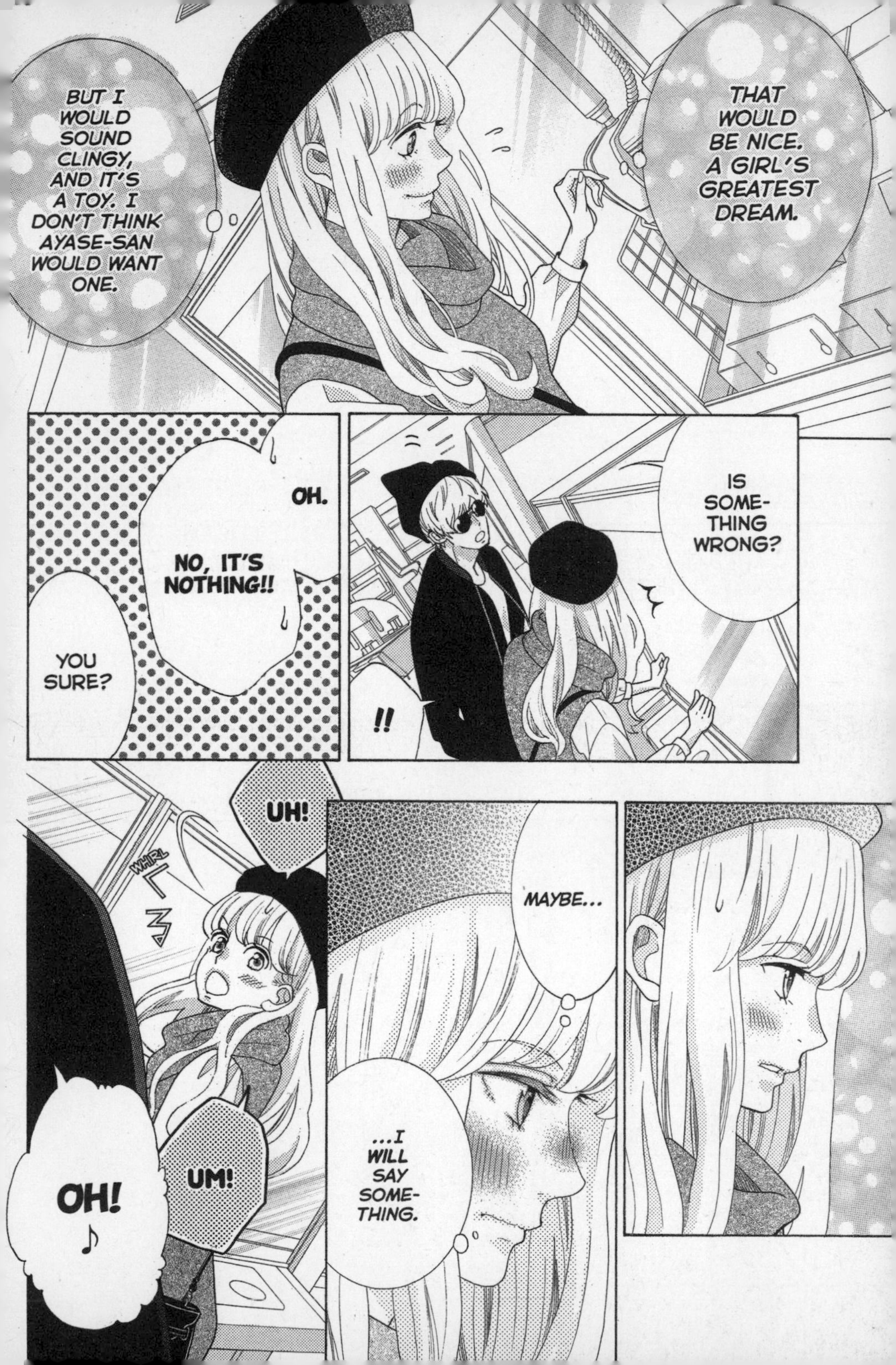
THAT WOULD BE NICE. A GIRL'S GREATEST DREAM.
BUT I WOULD SOUND CLINGY, AND IT'S A TOY. I DON'T THINK AYASE-SAN WOULD WANT ONE.
IS SOMETHING WRONG?
!!
OH.
NO, IT'S NOTHING!!
YOU SURE?
MAYBE...
...I WILL SAY SOMETHING.
UH!
WHIRL
UM!
OH! ♪

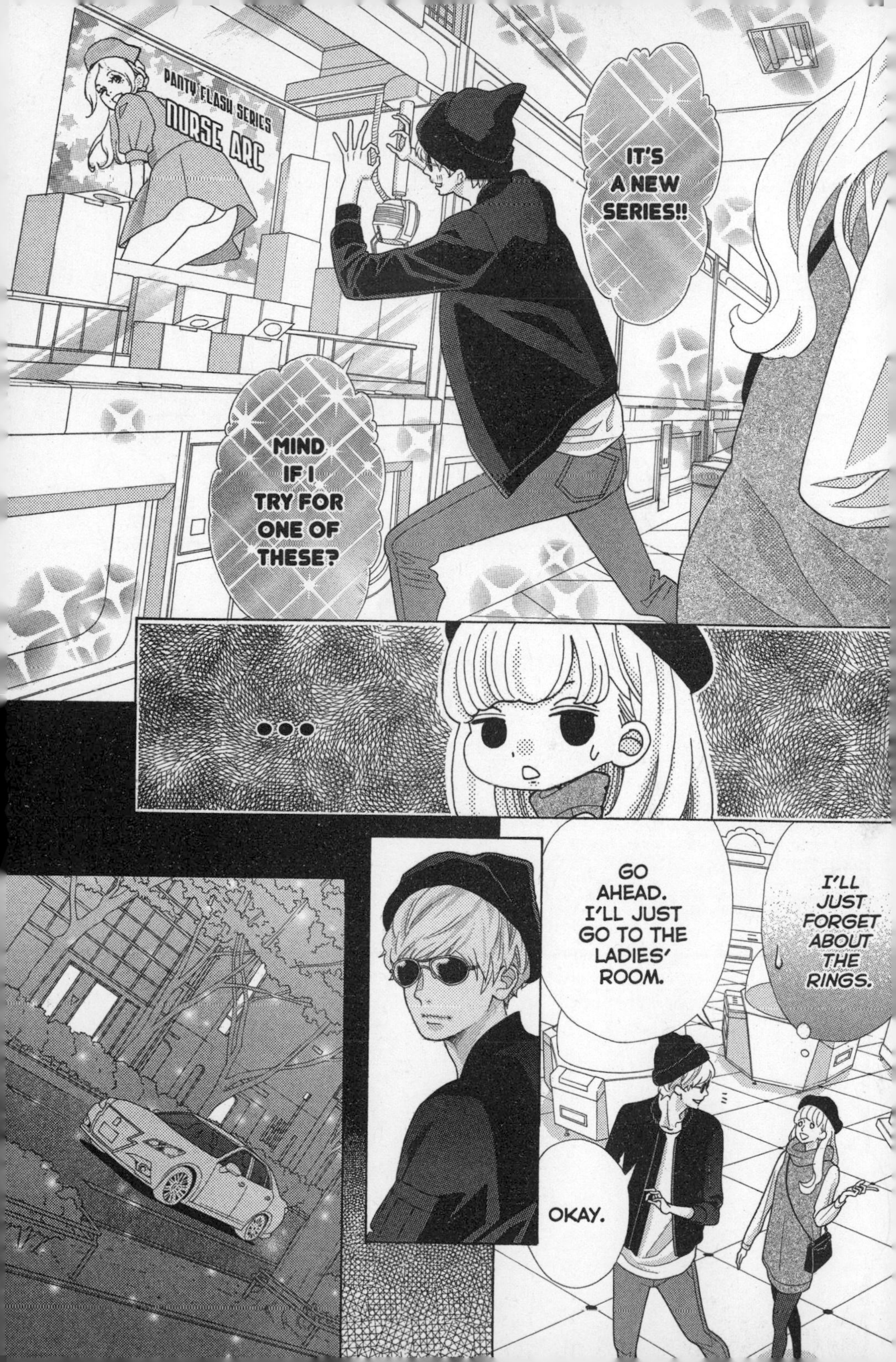
IT'S A NEW SERIES!!
PANTY FLASH SERIES
NURSE ARC
MIND IF I TRY FOR ONE OF THESE?
...
I'LL JUST FORGET ABOUT THE RINGS.
GO AHEAD. I'LL JUST GO TO THE LADIES' ROOM.
OKAY.

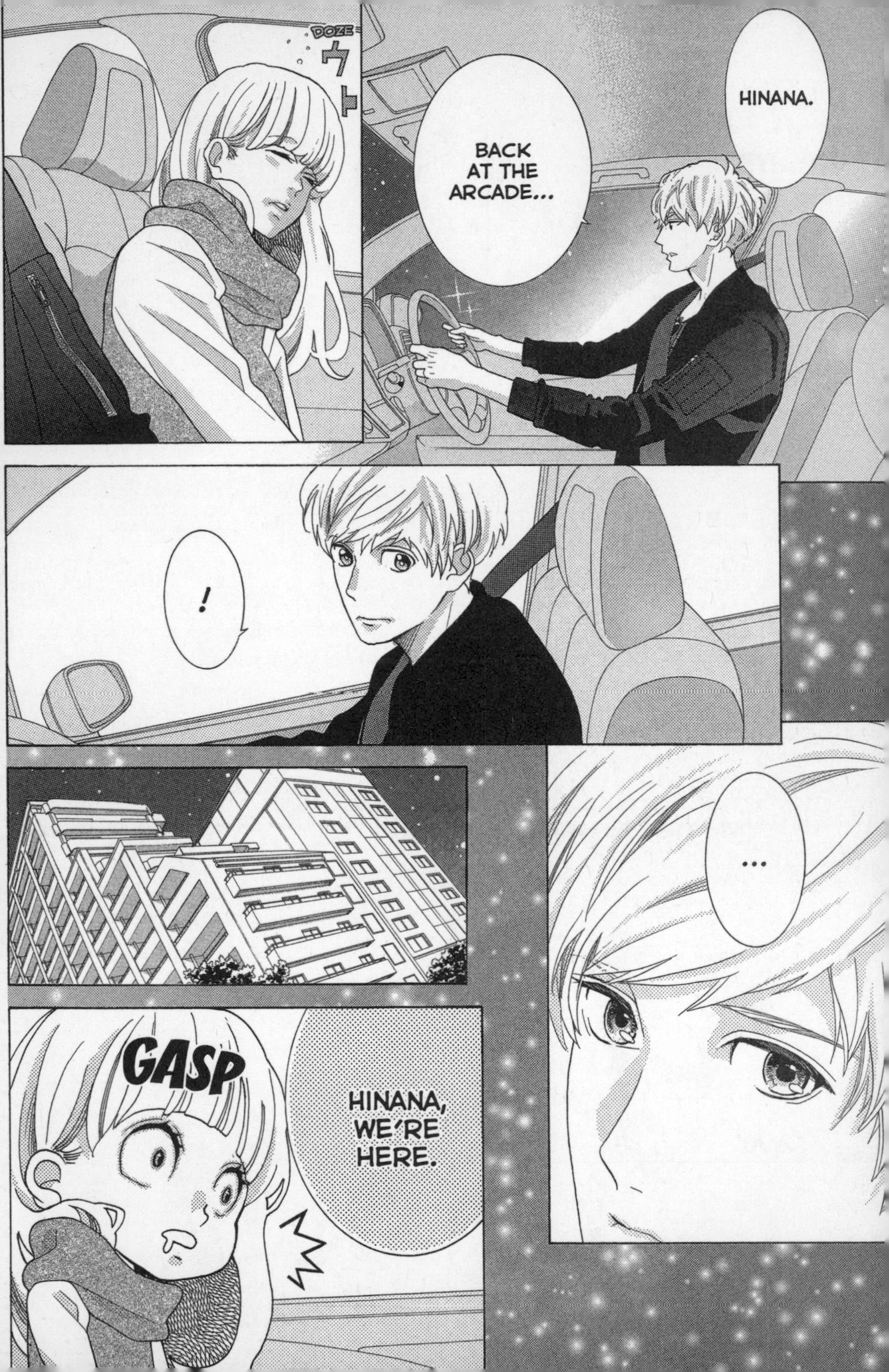
HINANA.
BACK AT THE ARCADE...
DOZE
ウト
!
...
HINANA, WE'RE HERE.
GASP

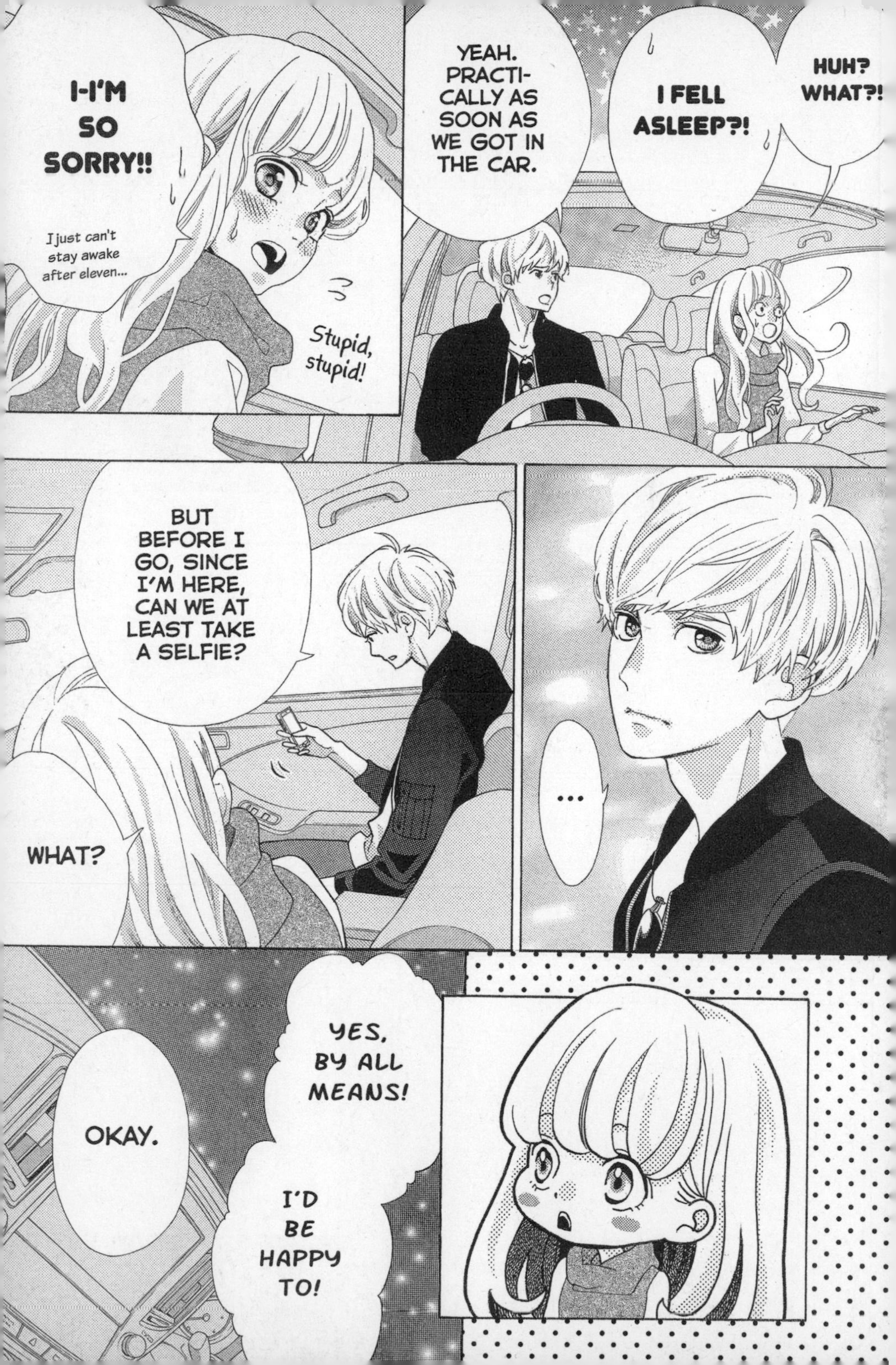
HUH? WHAT?!
I FELL ASLEEP?!
YEAH. PRACTI-CALLY AS SOON AS WE GOT IN THE CAR.
I-I'M SO SORRY!!
I just can't stay awake after eleven...
Stupid, stupid!
...
BUT BEFORE I GO, SINCE I'M HERE, CAN WE AT LEAST TAKE A SELFIE?
WHAT?
YES. BY ALL MEANS!
OKAY.
I'D BE HAPPY TO!

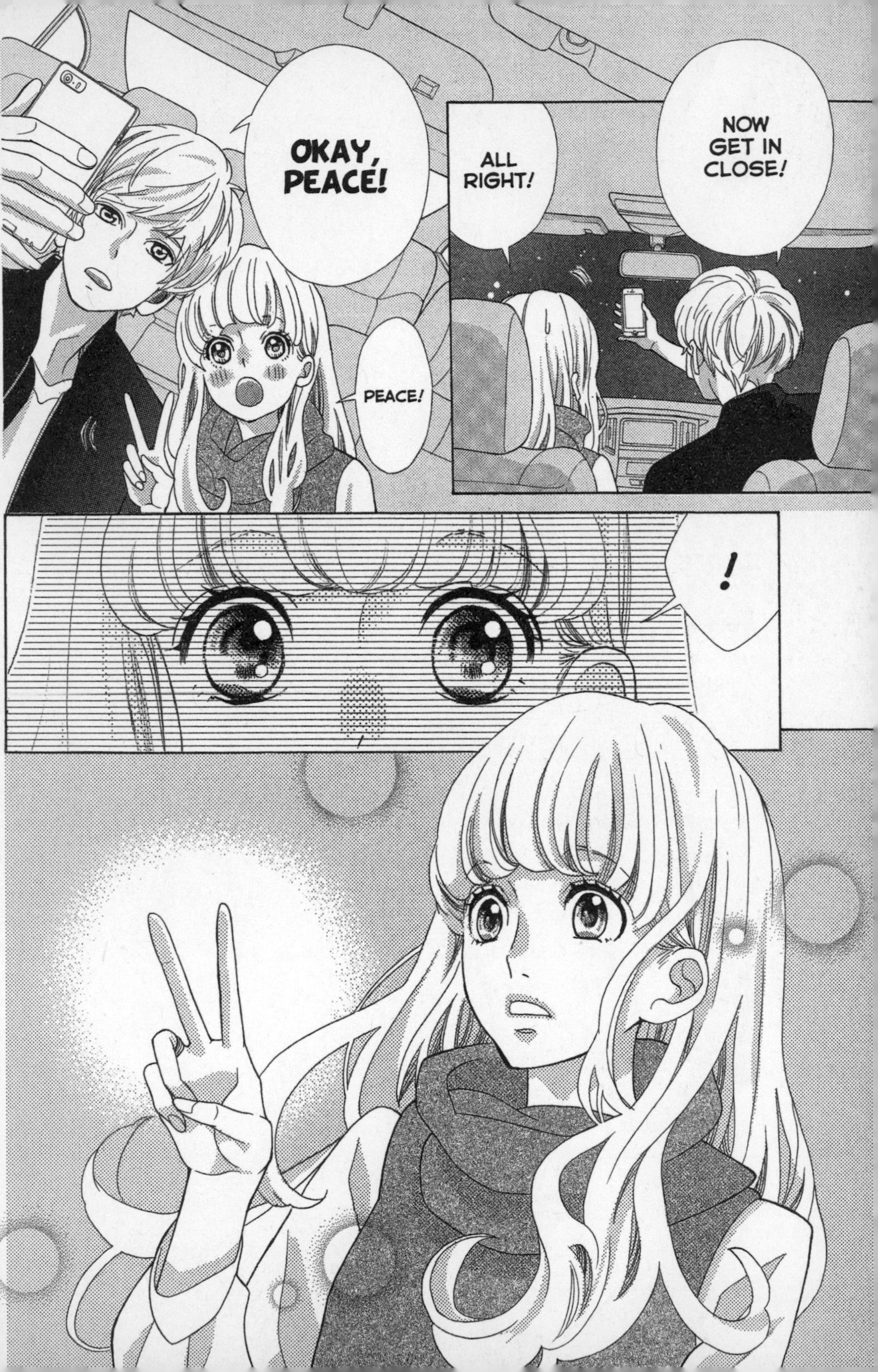

NOW GET IN CLOSE!
ALL RIGHT!
OKAY, PEACE!
PEACE!
!

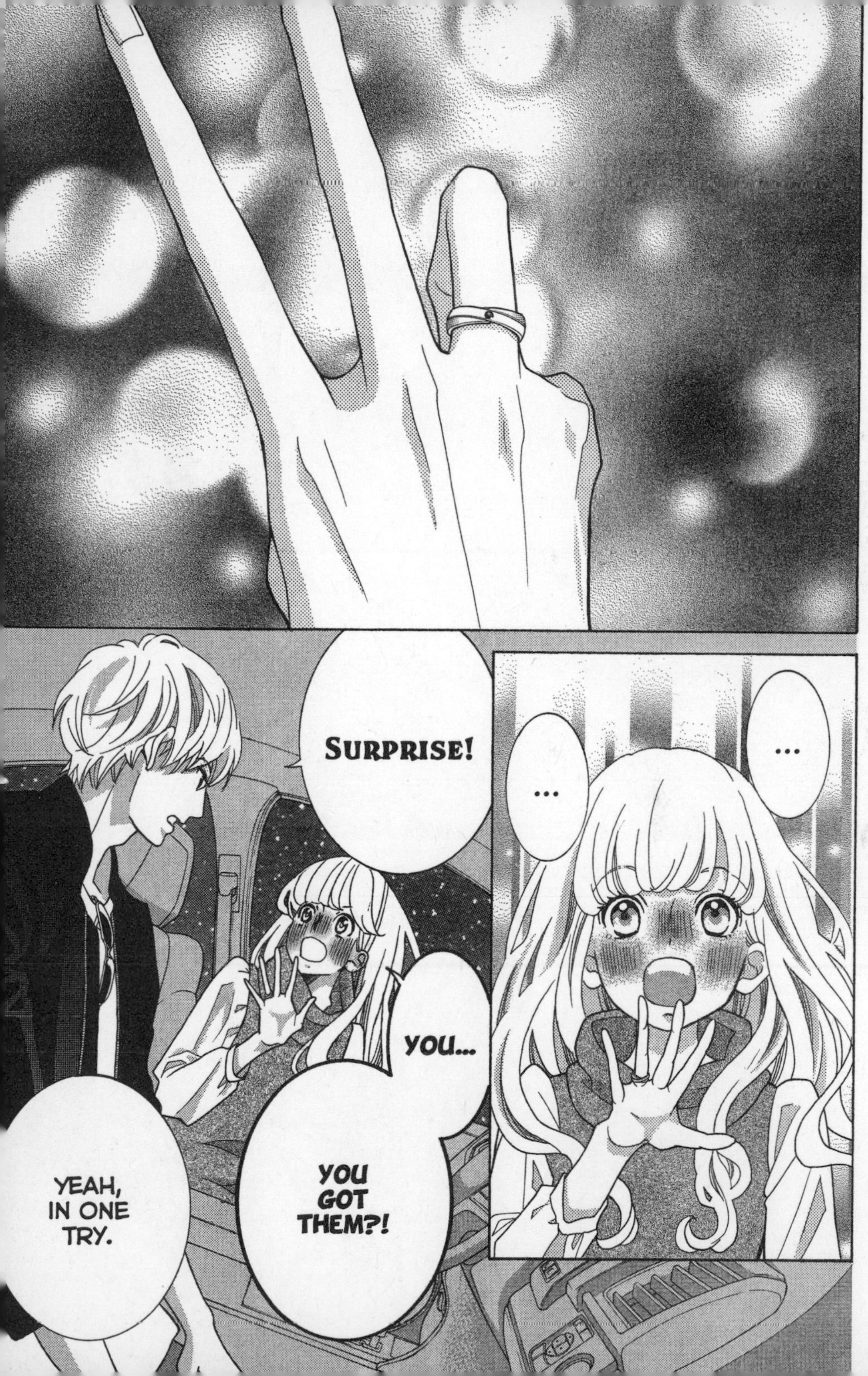
...
...
SURPRISE!
YOU...
YOU GOT THEM?!
YEAH, IN ONE TRY.

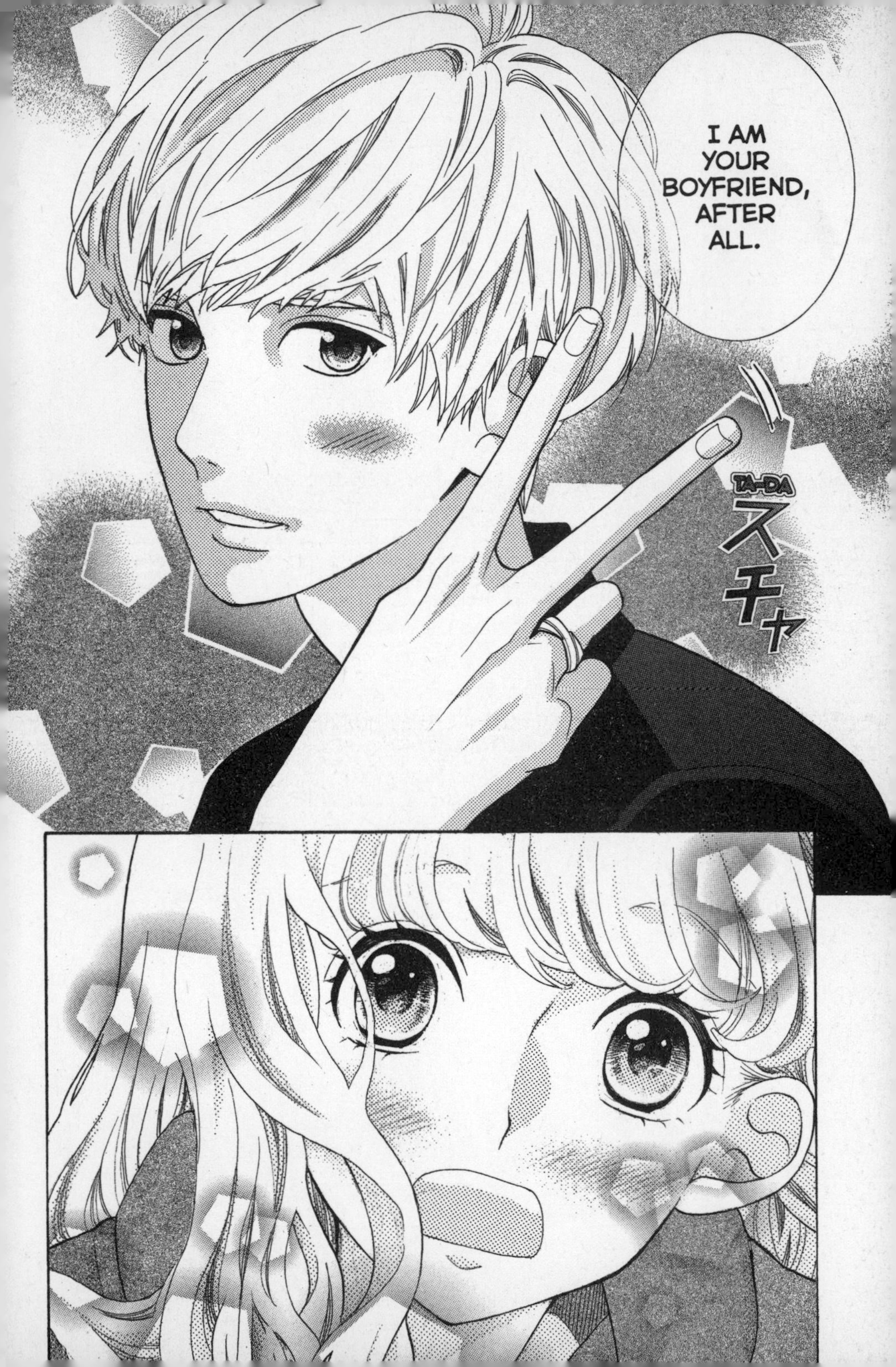
I AM YOUR BOYFRIEND, AFTER ALL.
TA-DA
スチャ

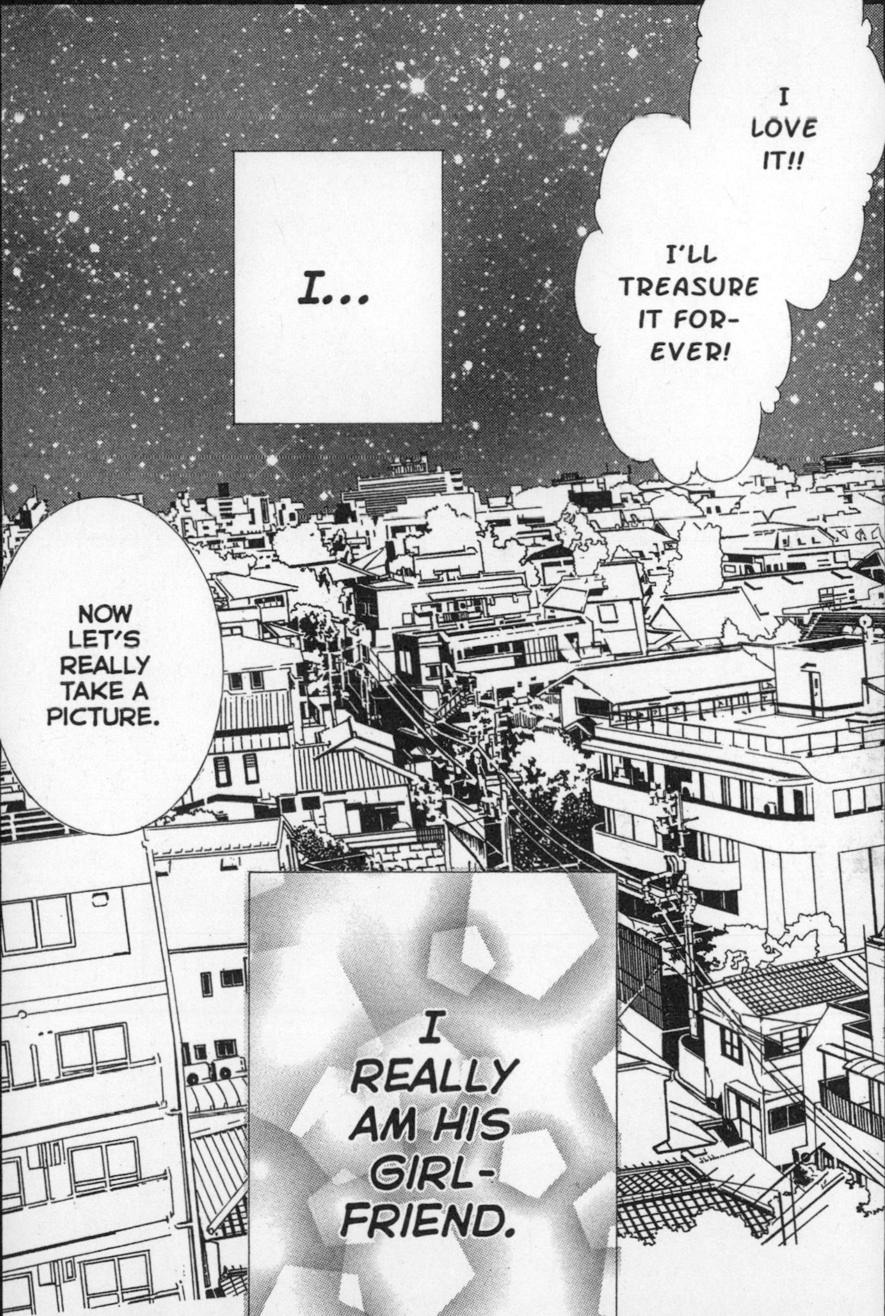
I LOVE IT!!
I'LL TREASURE IT FOR-EVER!
I...
NOW LET'S REALLY TAKE A PICTURE.
I REALLY AM HIS GIRL-FRIEND.

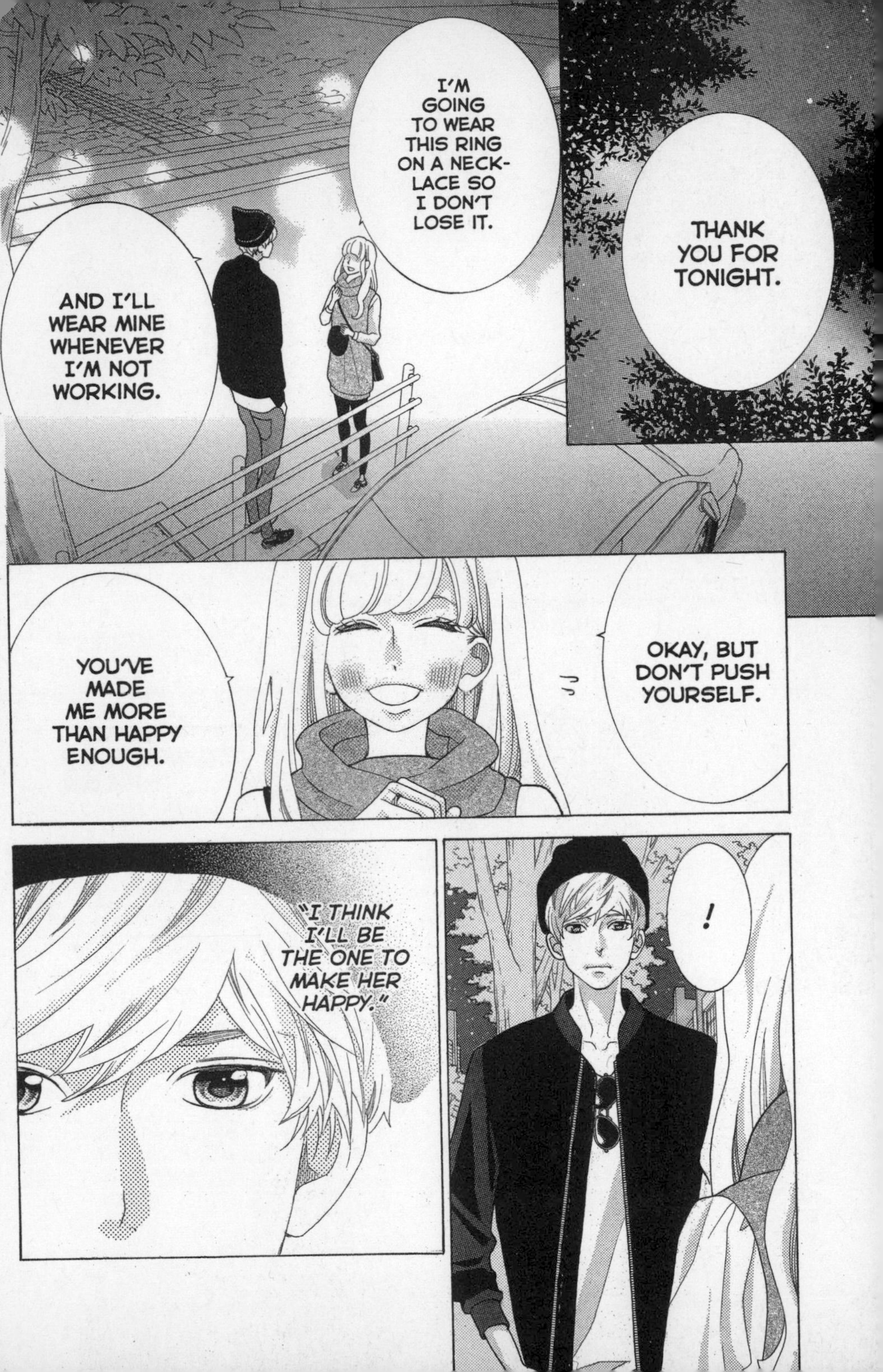
THANK YOU FOR TONIGHT.
I'M GOING TO WEAR THIS RING ON A NECKLACE SO I DON'T LOSE IT.
AND I'LL WEAR MINE WHENEVER I'M NOT WORKING.
OKAY, BUT DON'T PUSH YOURSELF.
YOU'VE MADE ME MORE THAN HAPPY ENOUGH.
!
"I THINK I'LL BE THE ONE TO MAKE HER HAPPY."

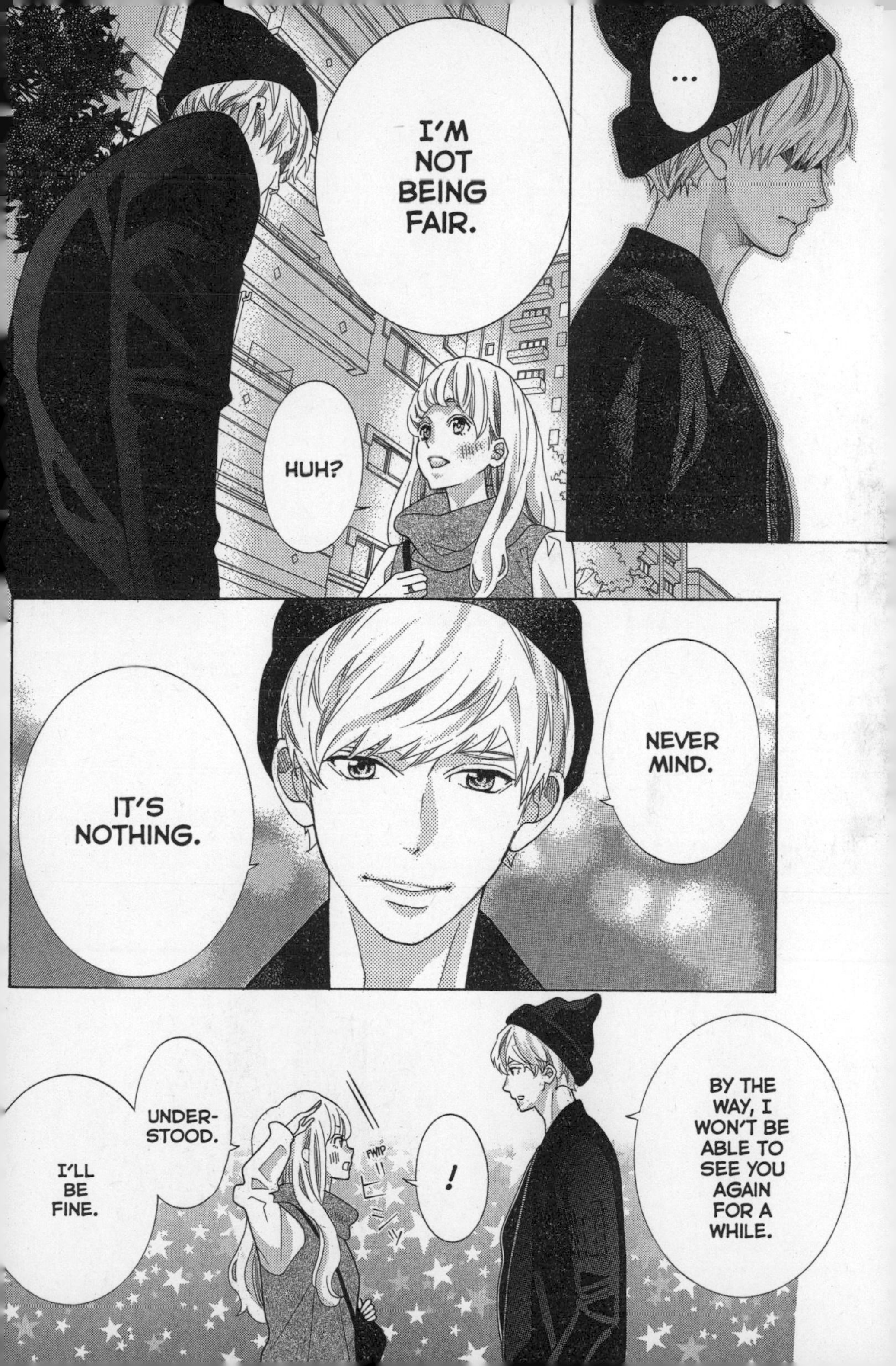
...
I'M NOT BEING FAIR.
HUH?
NEVER MIND.
IT'S NOTHING.
BY THE WAY, I WON'T BE ABLE TO SEE YOU AGAIN FOR A WHILE.
!
FWIP
UNDER-STOOD.
I'LL BE FINE.

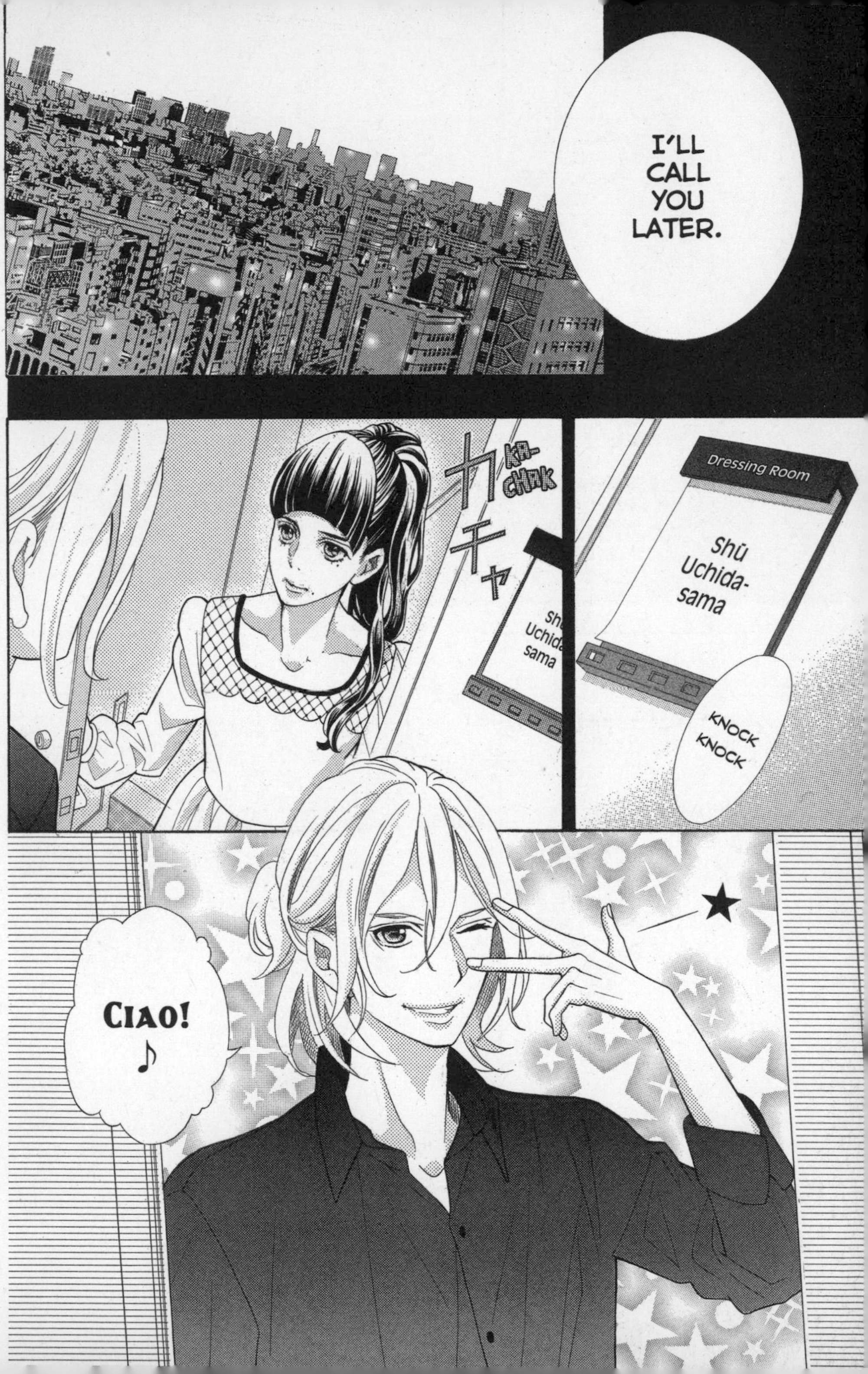
I'LL CALL YOU LATER.
Dressing Room
Shū Uchida-sama
KNOCK KNOCK
カチャ
KA-CHAK
Shū Uchida-sama
CIAO! ♪

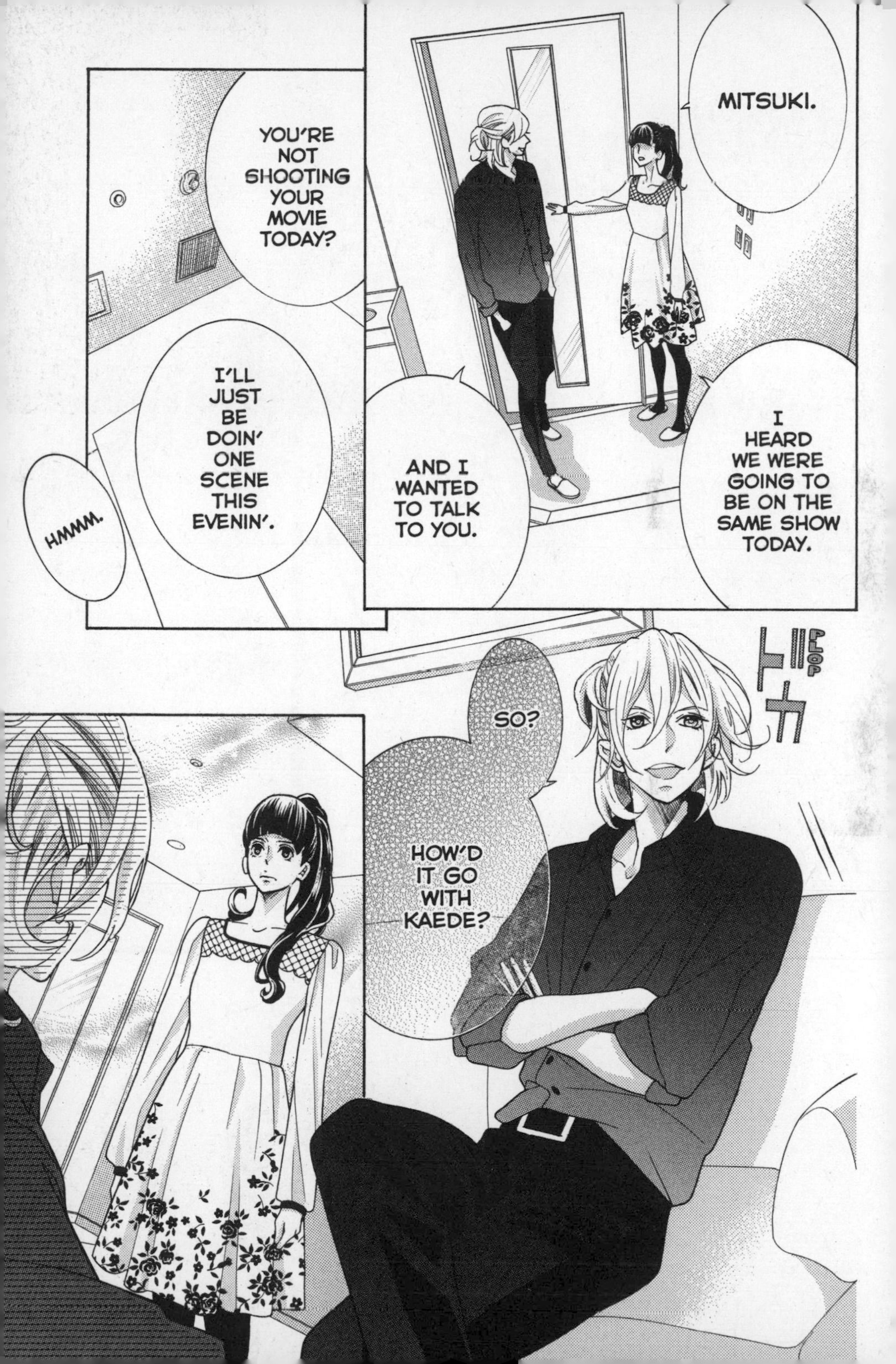
MITSUKI.
I HEARD WE WERE GOING TO BE ON THE SAME SHOW TODAY.
AND I WANTED TO TALK TO YOU.
YOU'RE NOT SHOOTING YOUR MOVIE TODAY?
I'LL JUST BE DOIN' ONE SCENE THIS EVENIN'.
HMMM.
ドカ
PLOP
SO?
HOW'D IT GO WITH KAEDE?

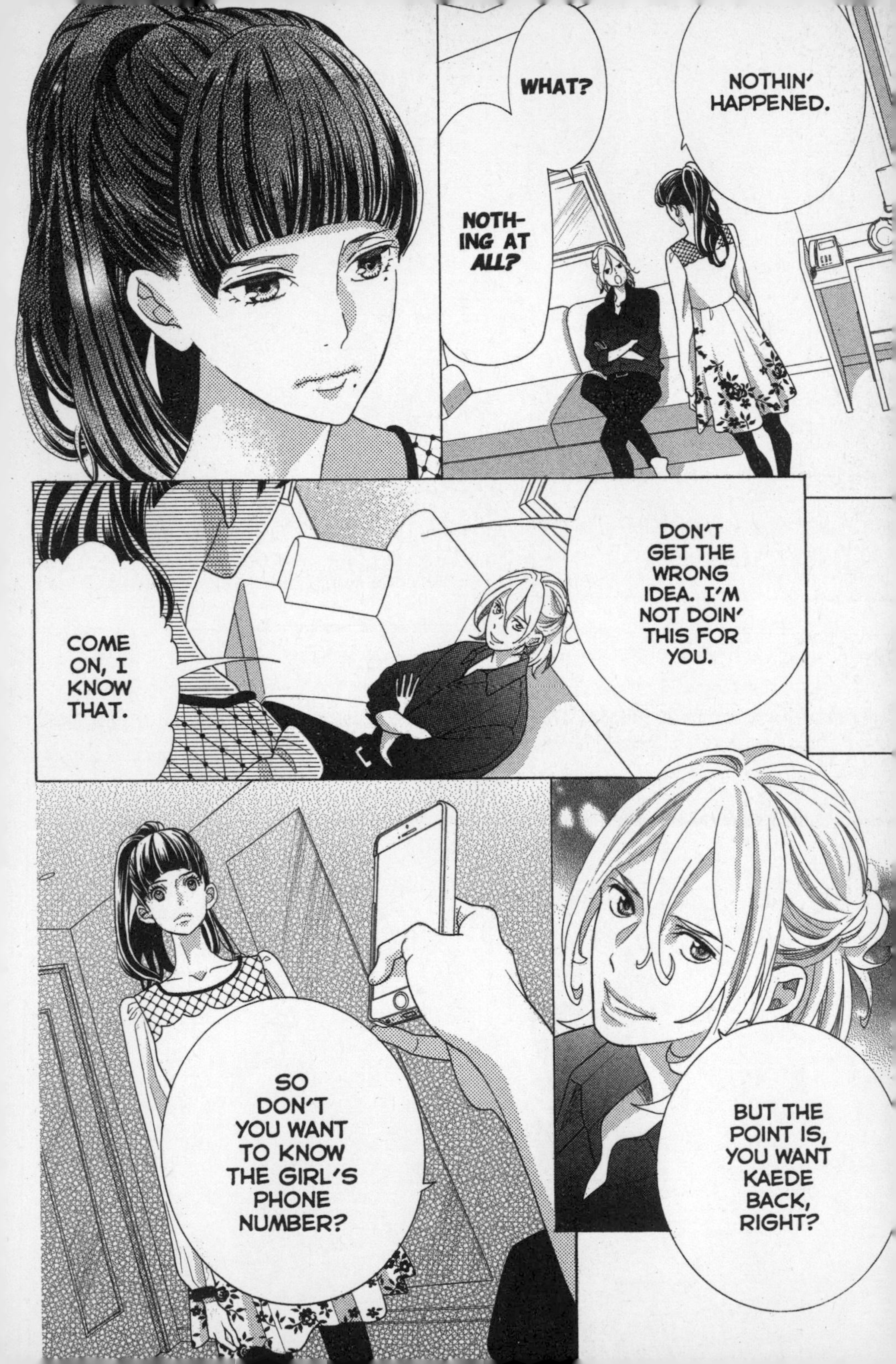
NOTHIN' HAPPENED.
WHAT?
NOTHING AT ALL?
DON'T GET THE WRONG IDEA. I'M NOT DOIN' THIS FOR YOU.
COME ON, I KNOW THAT.
BUT THE POINT IS, YOU WANT KAEDE BACK, RIGHT?
SO DON'T YOU WANT TO KNOW THE GIRL'S PHONE NUMBER?

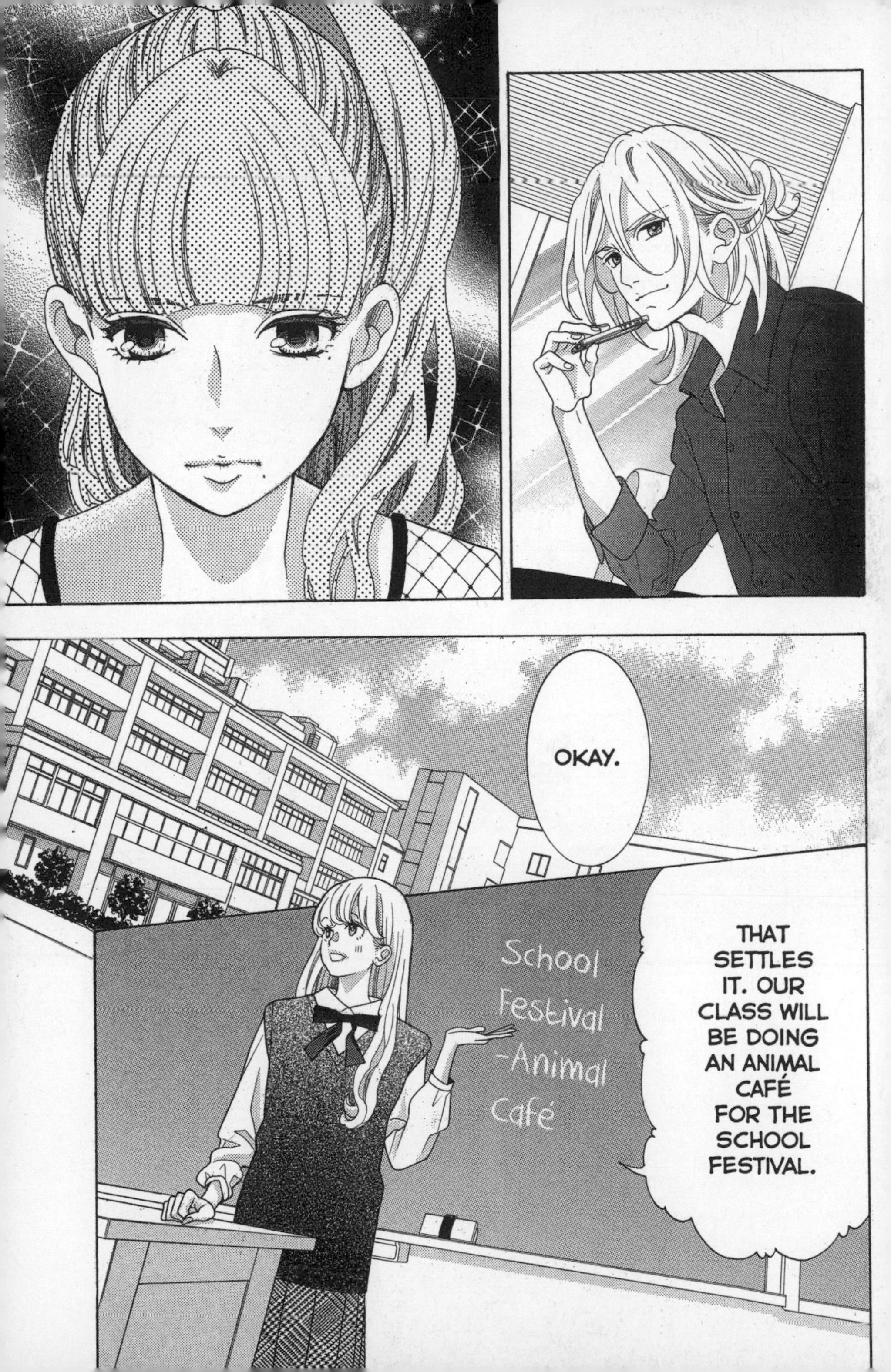
OKAY.
THAT SETTLES IT. OUR CLASS WILL BE DOING AN ANIMAL CAFÉ FOR THE SCHOOL FESTIVAL.
School Festival -Animal Café

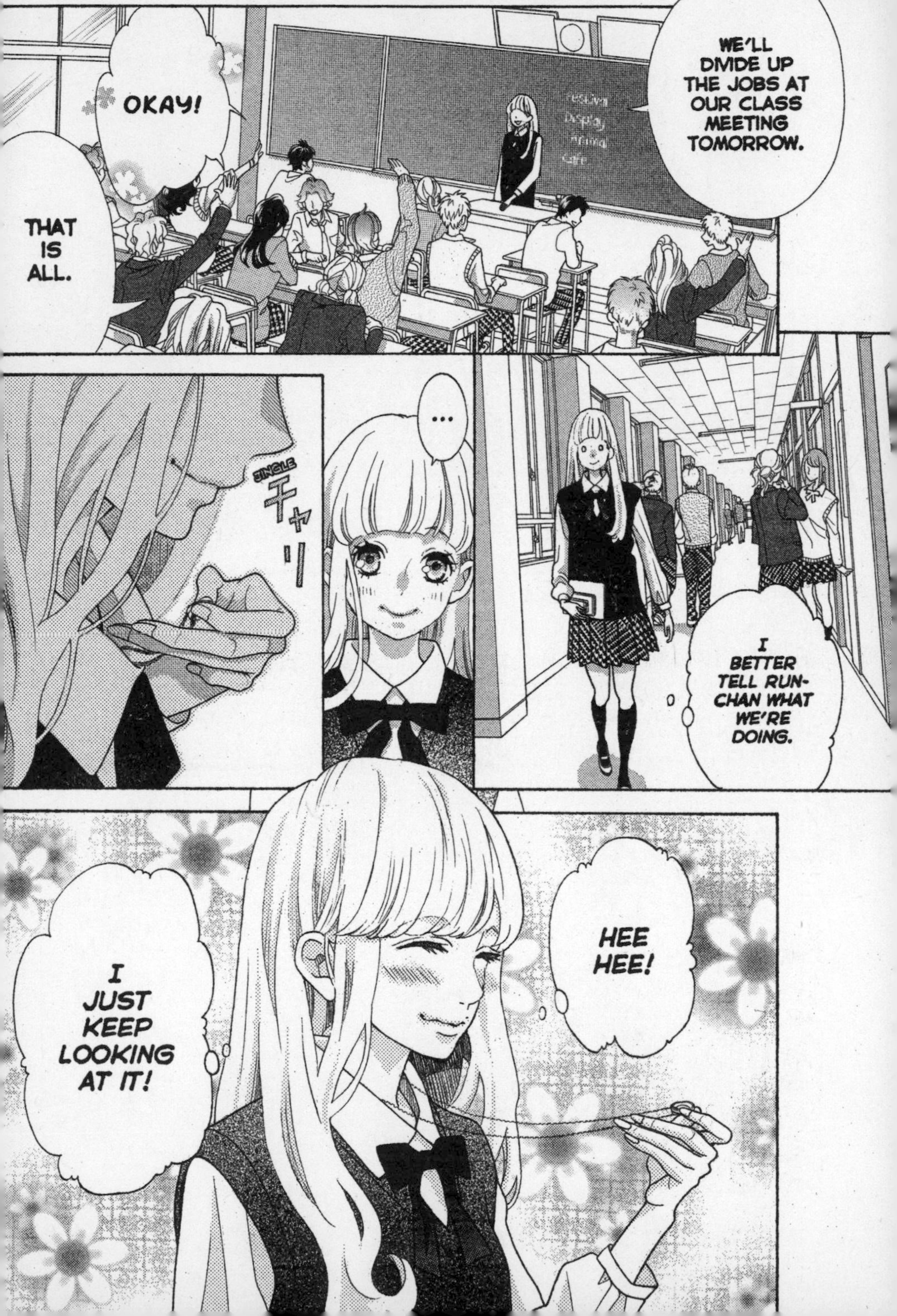
WE'LL DIVIDE UP THE JOBS AT OUR CLASS MEETING TOMORROW.
OKAY!
THAT IS ALL.
I BETTER TELL RUN-CHAN WHAT WE'RE DOING.
...
JINGLE
チャリ
HEE HEE!
I JUST KEEP LOOKING AT IT!

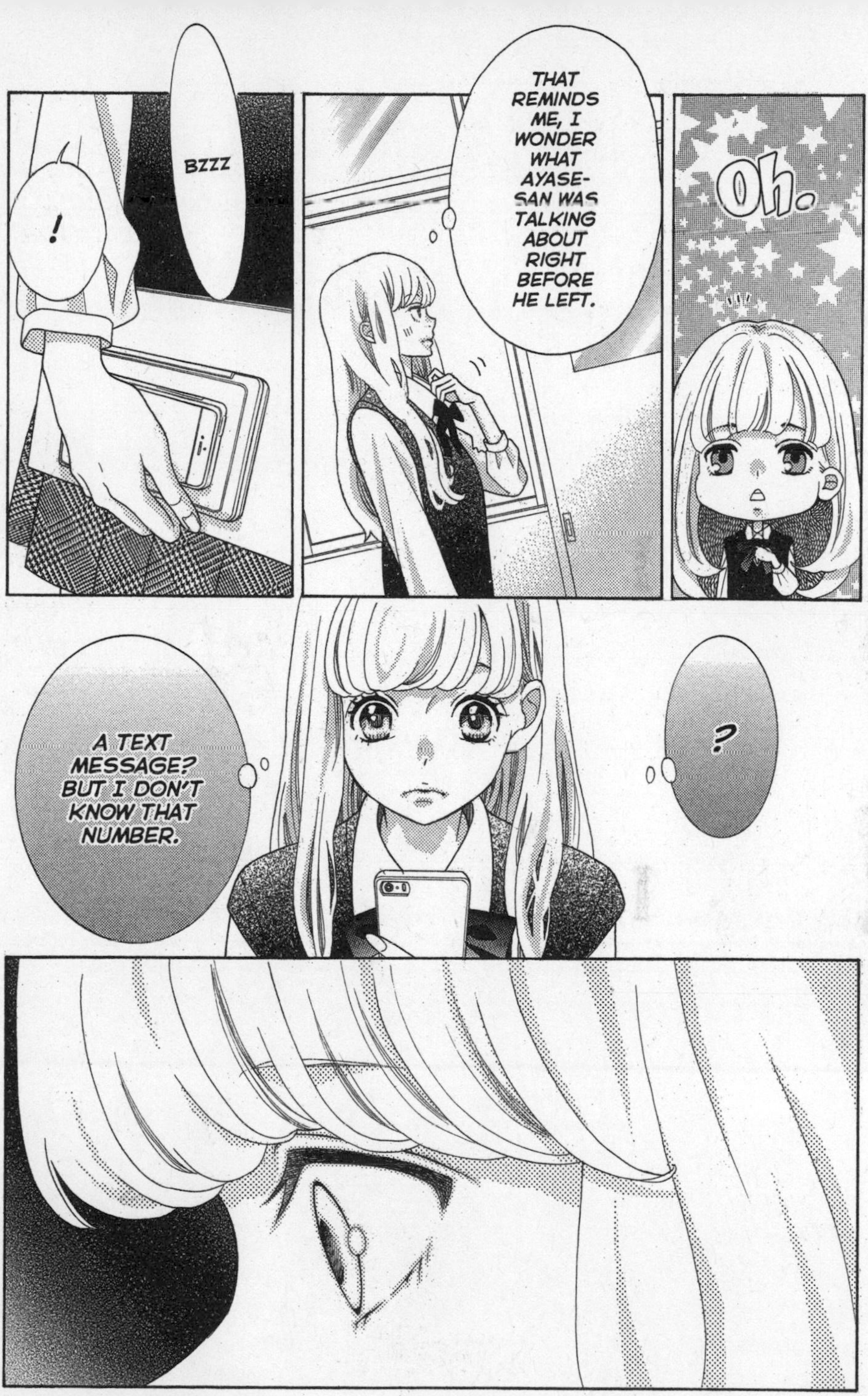
Oh.
THAT REMINDS ME, I WONDER WHAT AYASE-SAN WAS TALKING ABOUT RIGHT BEFORE HE LEFT.
BZZZ
!
?
A TEXT MESSAGE? BUT I DON'T KNOW THAT NUMBER.

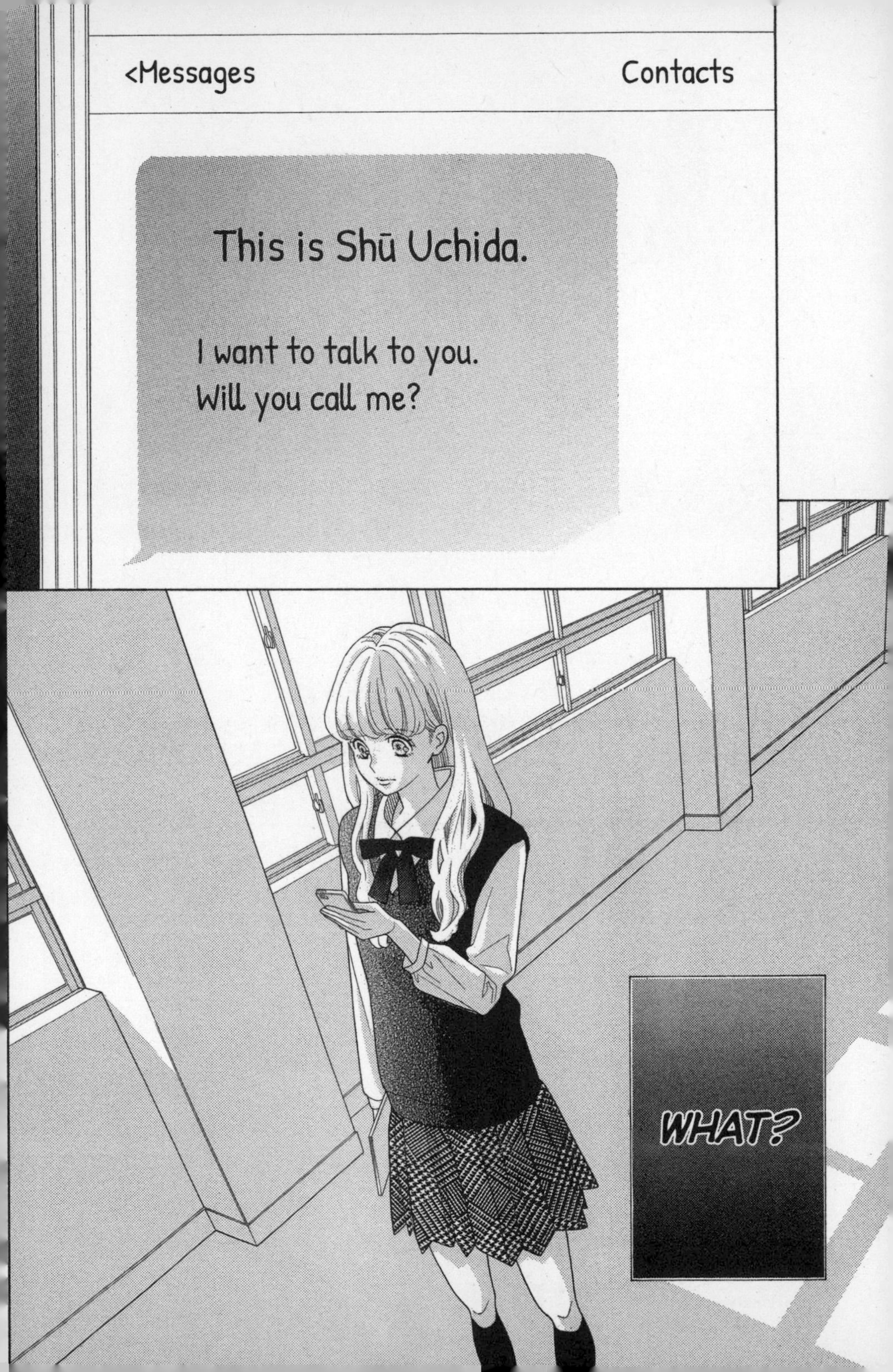

<Messages
Contacts
This is Shū Uchida.
I want to talk to you.
Will you call me?
WHAT?

Kiss Me at the Stroke of Midnight

Kiss Me at the Stroke of Midnight

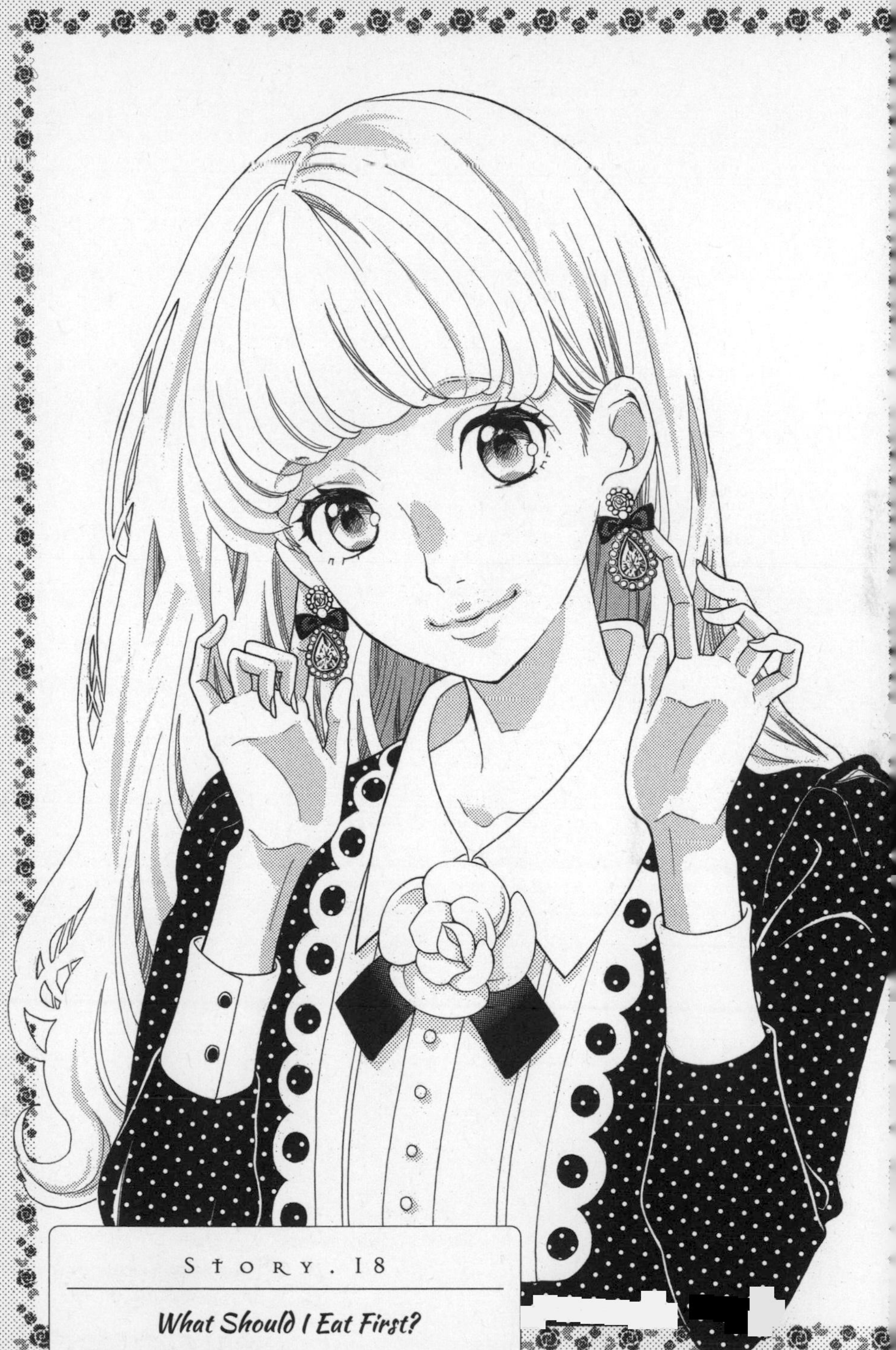
Story. 18
What Should I Eat First?

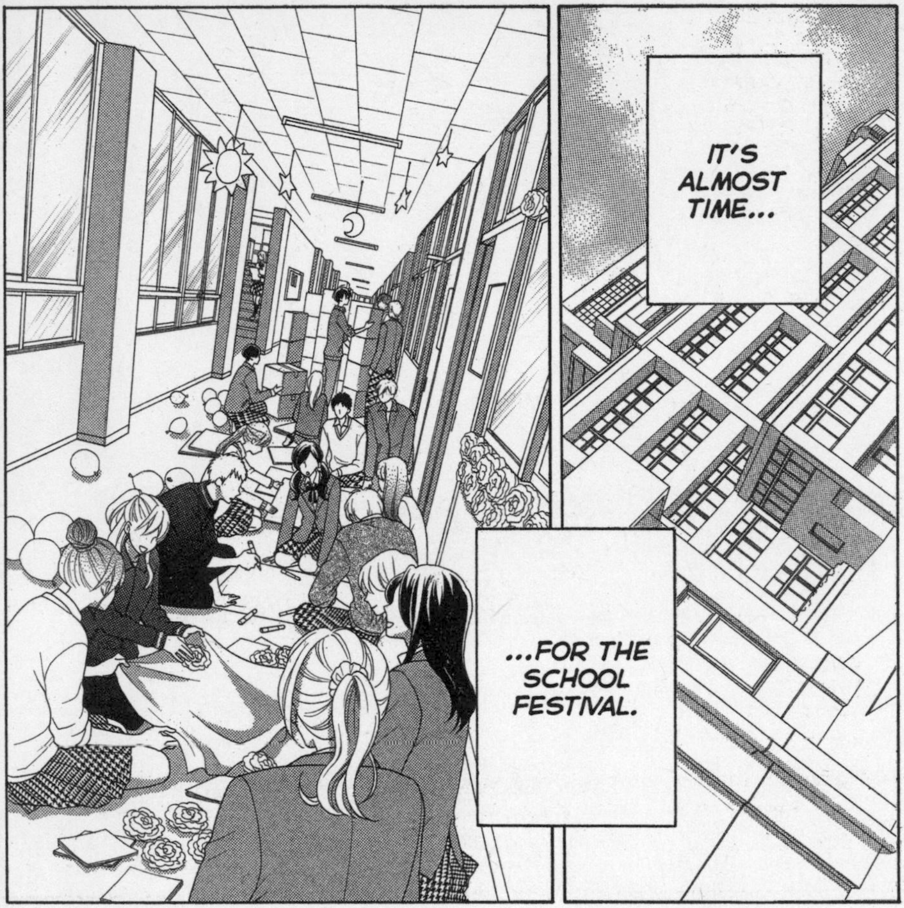
IT'S ALMOST TIME...
...FOR THE SCHOOL FESTIVAL.

Kiss Me at the Stroke of Midnight

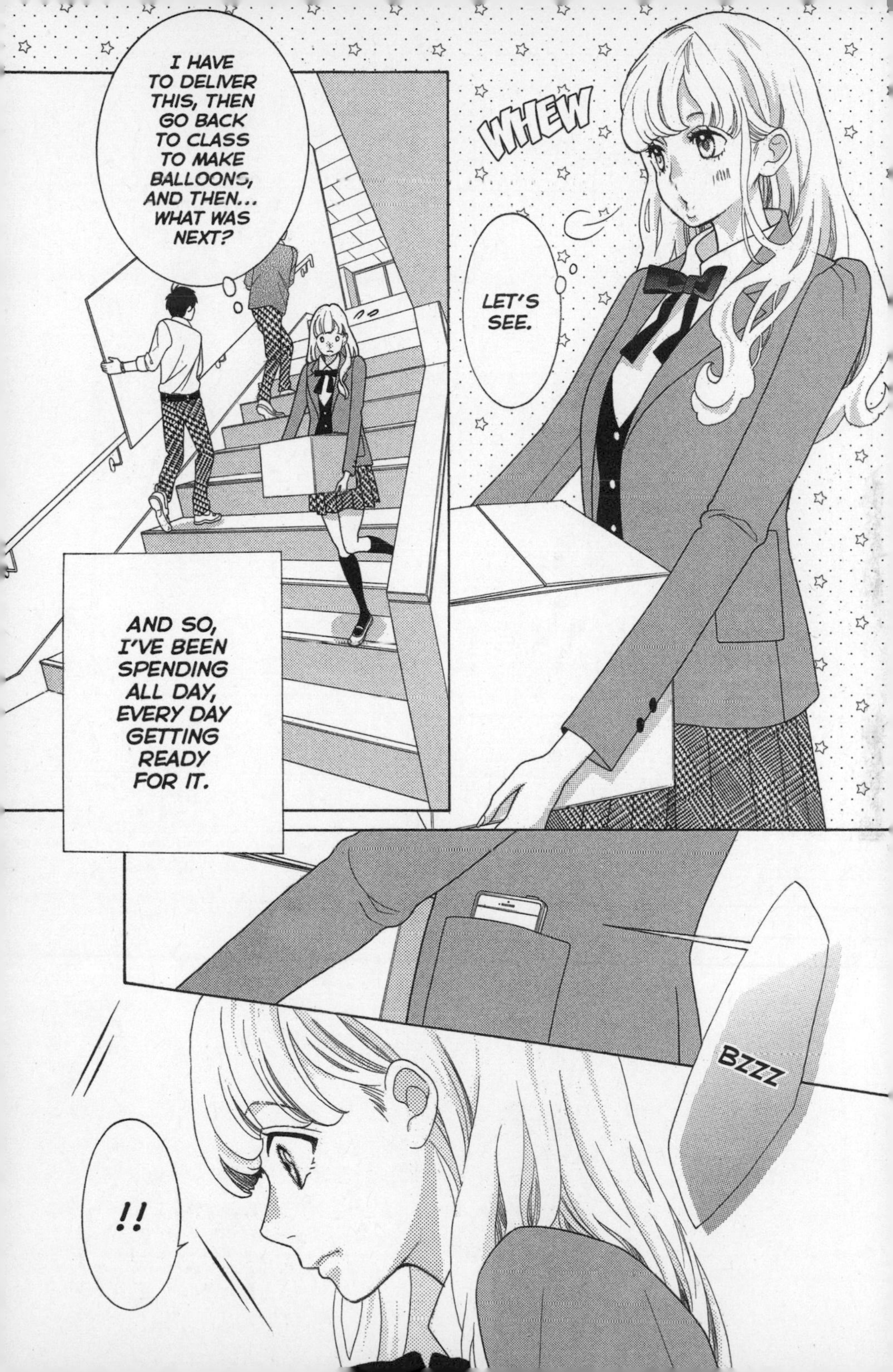
WHEW
LET'S SEE.
I HAVE TO DELIVER THIS, THEN GO BACK TO CLASS TO MAKE BALLOONS, AND THEN... WHAT WAS NEXT?
AND SO, I'VE BEEN SPENDING ALL DAY, EVERY DAY GETTING READY FOR IT.
BZZZ
!!

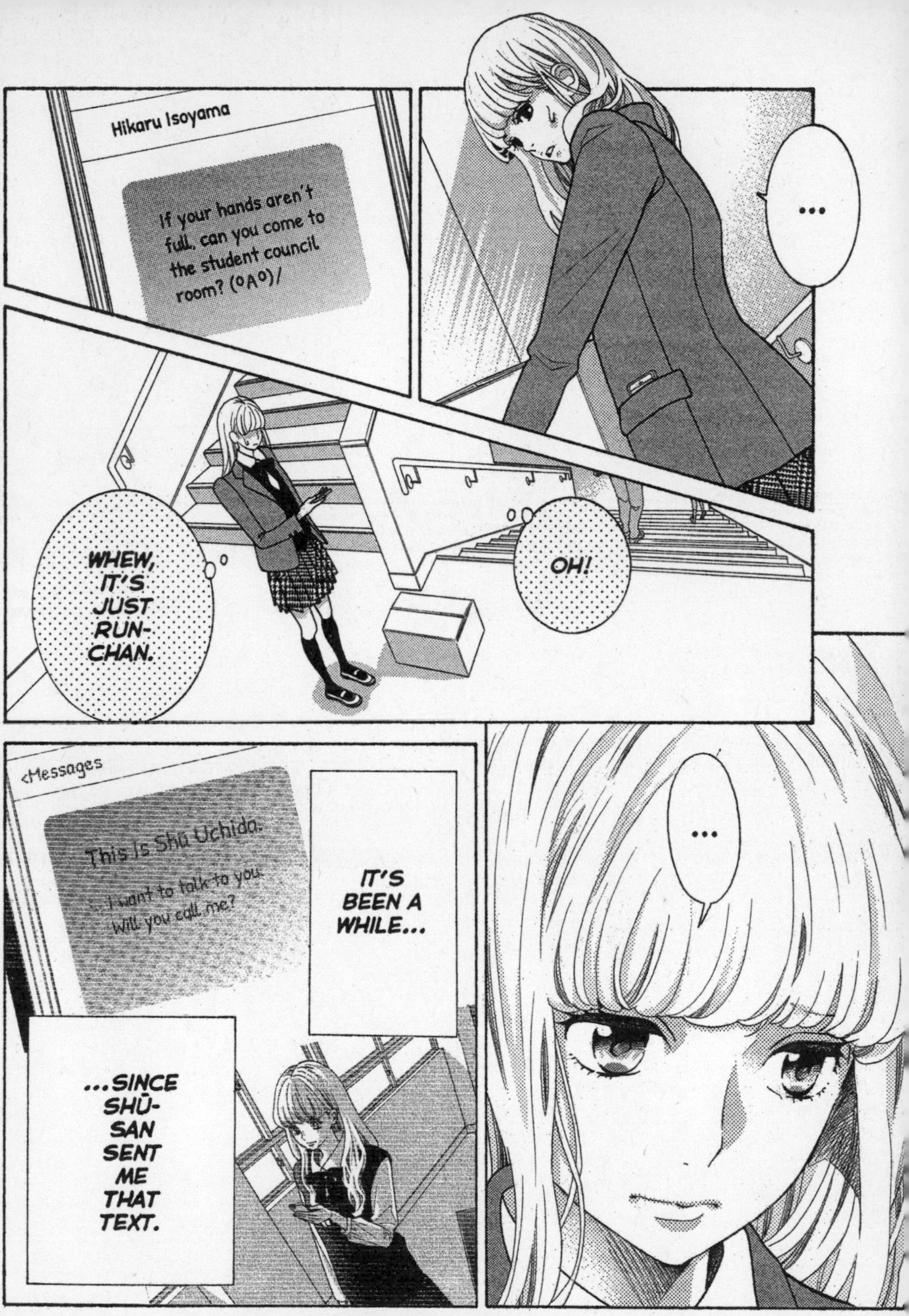
...
Hikaru Isoyama
If your hands aren't full, can you come to the student council room? (ºAº)/
OH!
WHEW, IT'S JUST RUN-CHAN.
...
<Messages
This is Shū Uchida.
...I want to talk to you. Will you call me?
IT'S BEEN A WHILE...
...SINCE SHŪ-SAN SENT ME THAT TEXT.

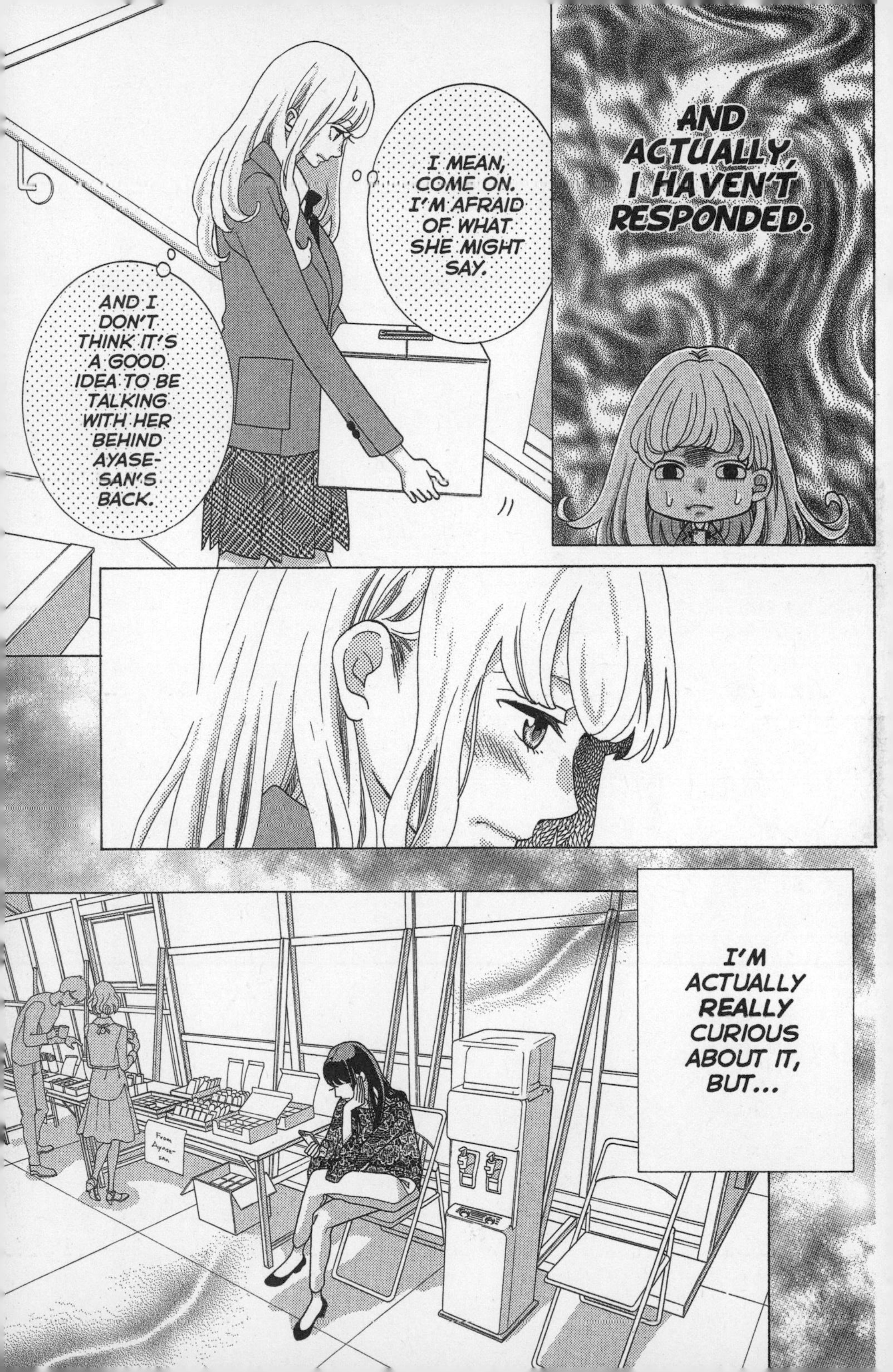
AND ACTUALLY, I HAVEN'T RESPONDED.
I MEAN, COME ON. I'M AFRAID OF WHAT SHE MIGHT SAY.
AND I DON'T THINK IT'S A GOOD IDEA TO BE TALKING WITH HER BEHIND AYASE-SAN'S BACK.
I'M ACTUALLY REALLY CURIOUS ABOUT IT, BUT...
From Ayase-san

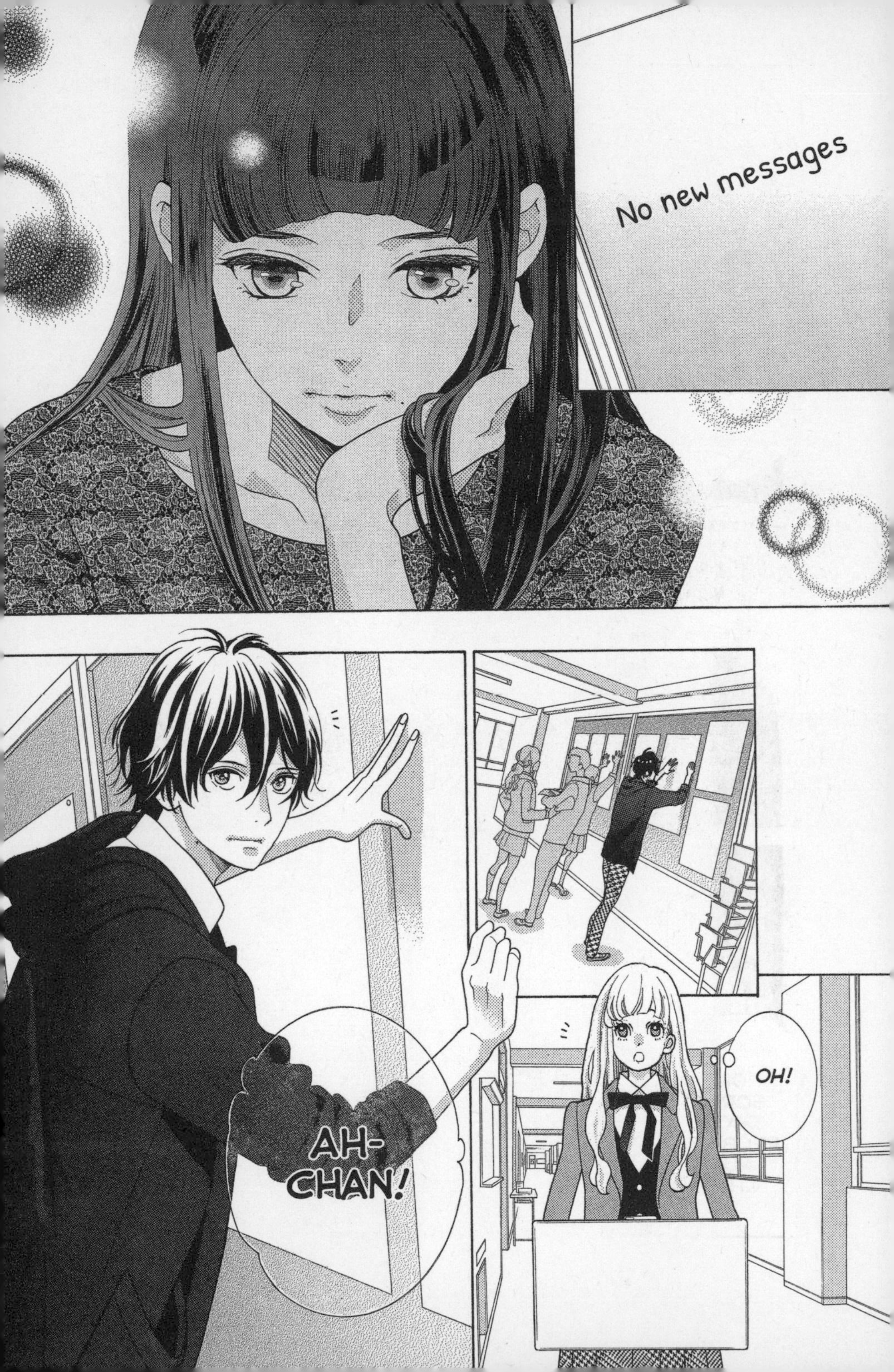
No new messages
OH!
AH-CHAN!

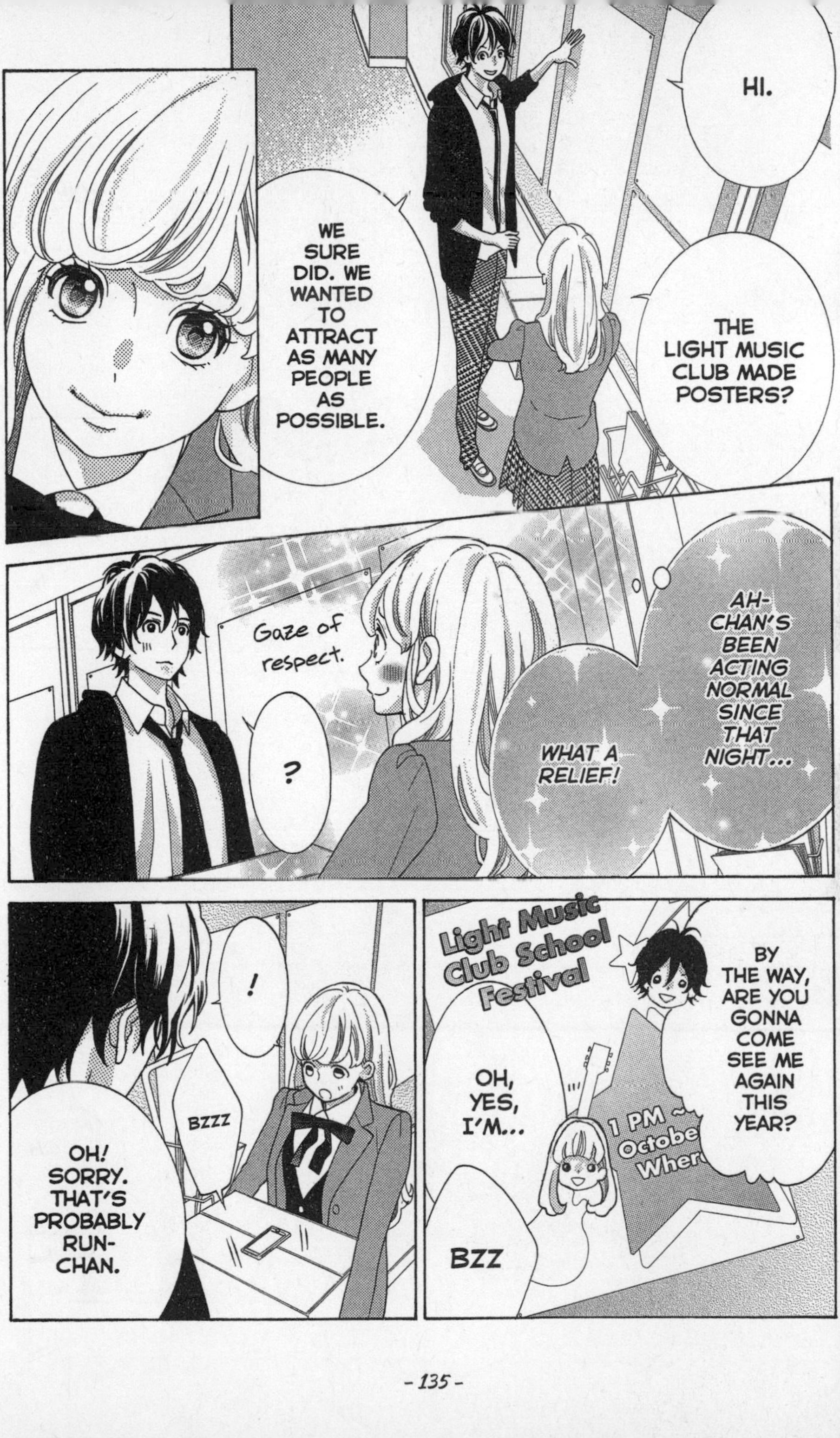
HI.
THE LIGHT MUSIC CLUB MADE POSTERS?
WE SURE DID. WE WANTED TO ATTRACT AS MANY PEOPLE AS POSSIBLE.
AH-CHAN'S BEEN ACTING NORMAL SINCE THAT NIGHT...
WHAT A RELIEF!
Gaze of respect.
?
Light Music Club School Festival
BY THE WAY, ARE YOU GONNA COME SEE ME AGAIN THIS YEAR?
OH, YES, I'M...
BZZ
!
BZZZ
OH! SORRY. THAT'S PROBABLY RUN-CHAN.

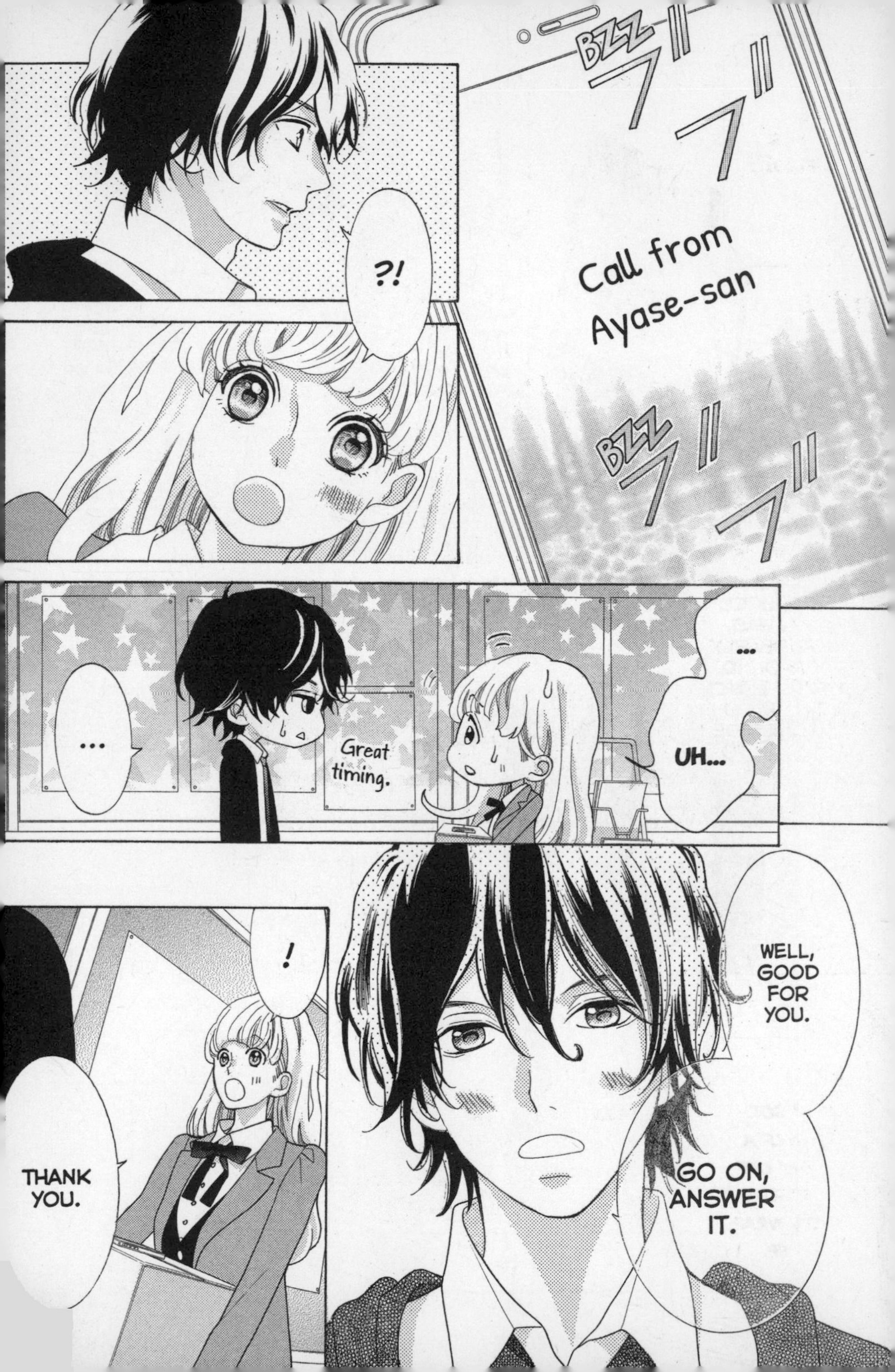
BZZ
Call from Ayase-san
BZZ
?!
...
UH...
Great timing.
...
WELL, GOOD FOR YOU.
GO ON, ANSWER IT.
!
THANK YOU.

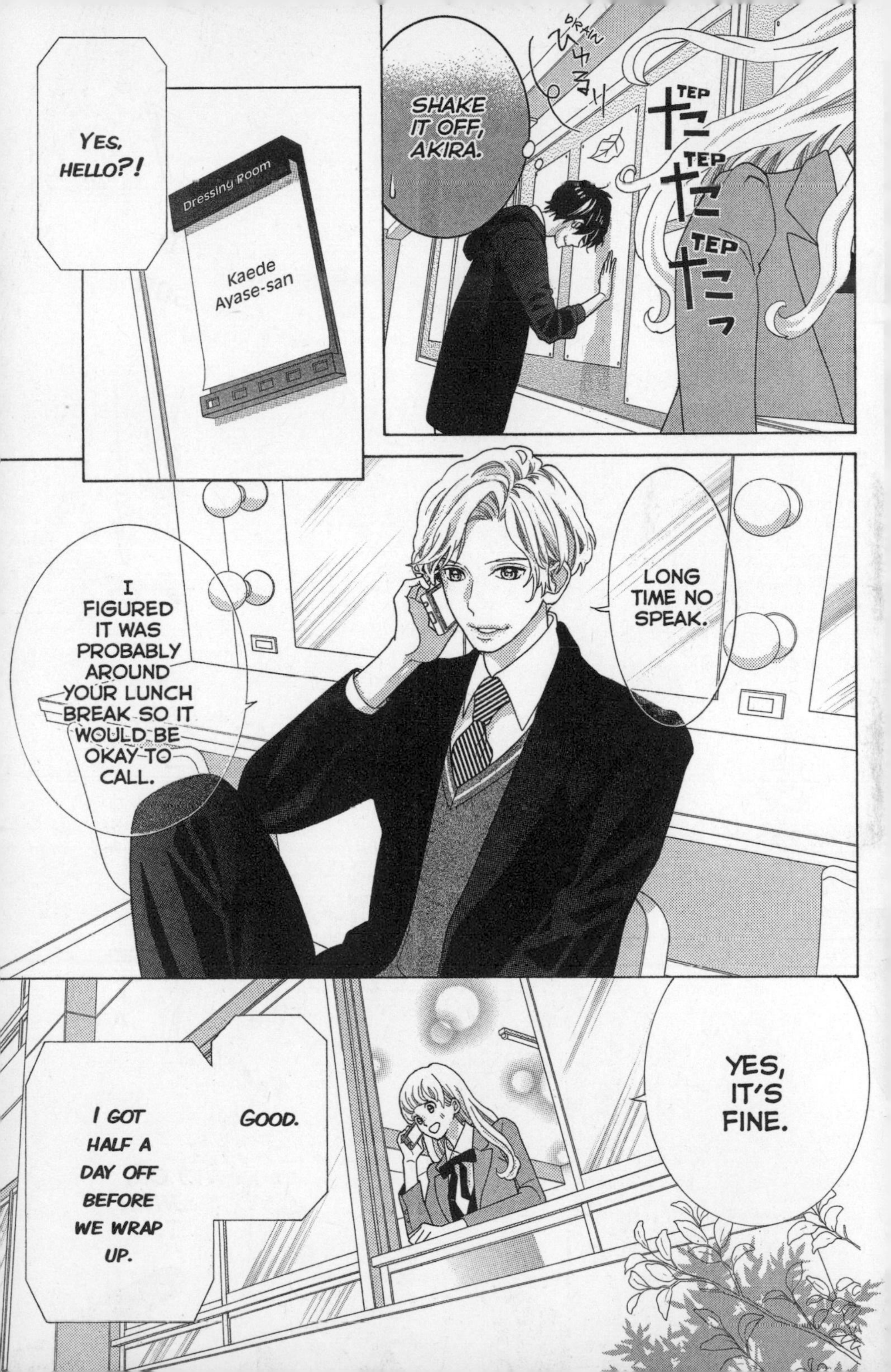
TEP
TEP
TEP
DRAIN
SHAKE IT OFF, AKIRA.
Dressing Room
Kaede Ayase-san
YES, HELLO?!
LONG TIME NO SPEAK.
I FIGURED IT WAS PROBABLY AROUND YOUR LUNCH BREAK SO IT WOULD BE OKAY TO CALL.
YES, IT'S FINE.
GOOD.
I GOT HALF A DAY OFF BEFORE WE WRAP UP.

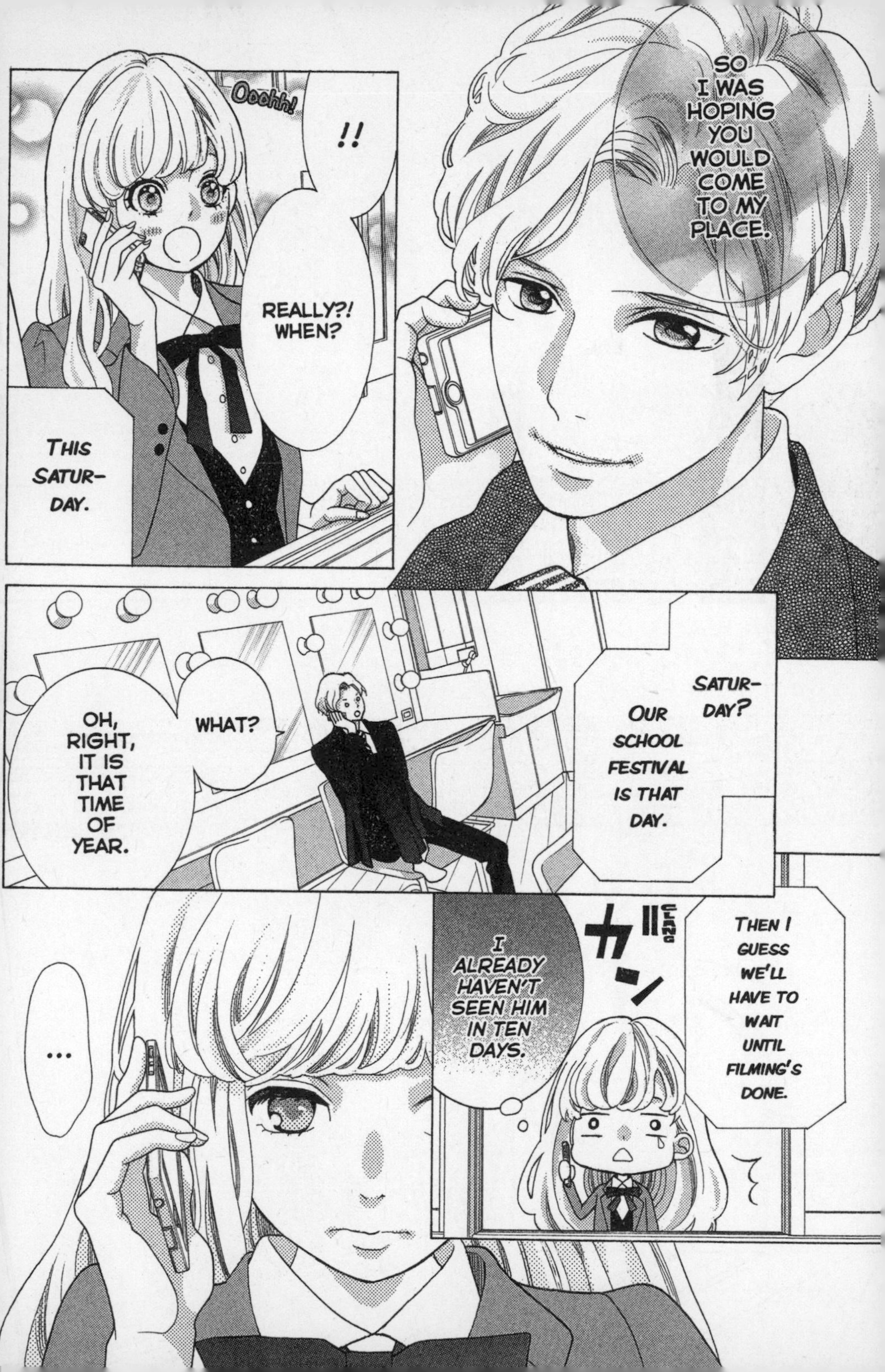
SO I WAS HOPING YOU WOULD COME TO MY PLACE.
Ooohh!
!!
REALLY?! WHEN?
THIS SATUR-DAY.
SATUR-DAY?
OUR SCHOOL FESTIVAL IS THAT DAY.
WHAT?
OH, RIGHT, IT IS THAT TIME OF YEAR.
THEN I GUESS WE'LL HAVE TO WAIT UNTIL FILMING'S DONE.
CLANG
I ALREADY HAVEN'T SEEN HIM IN TEN DAYS.
...

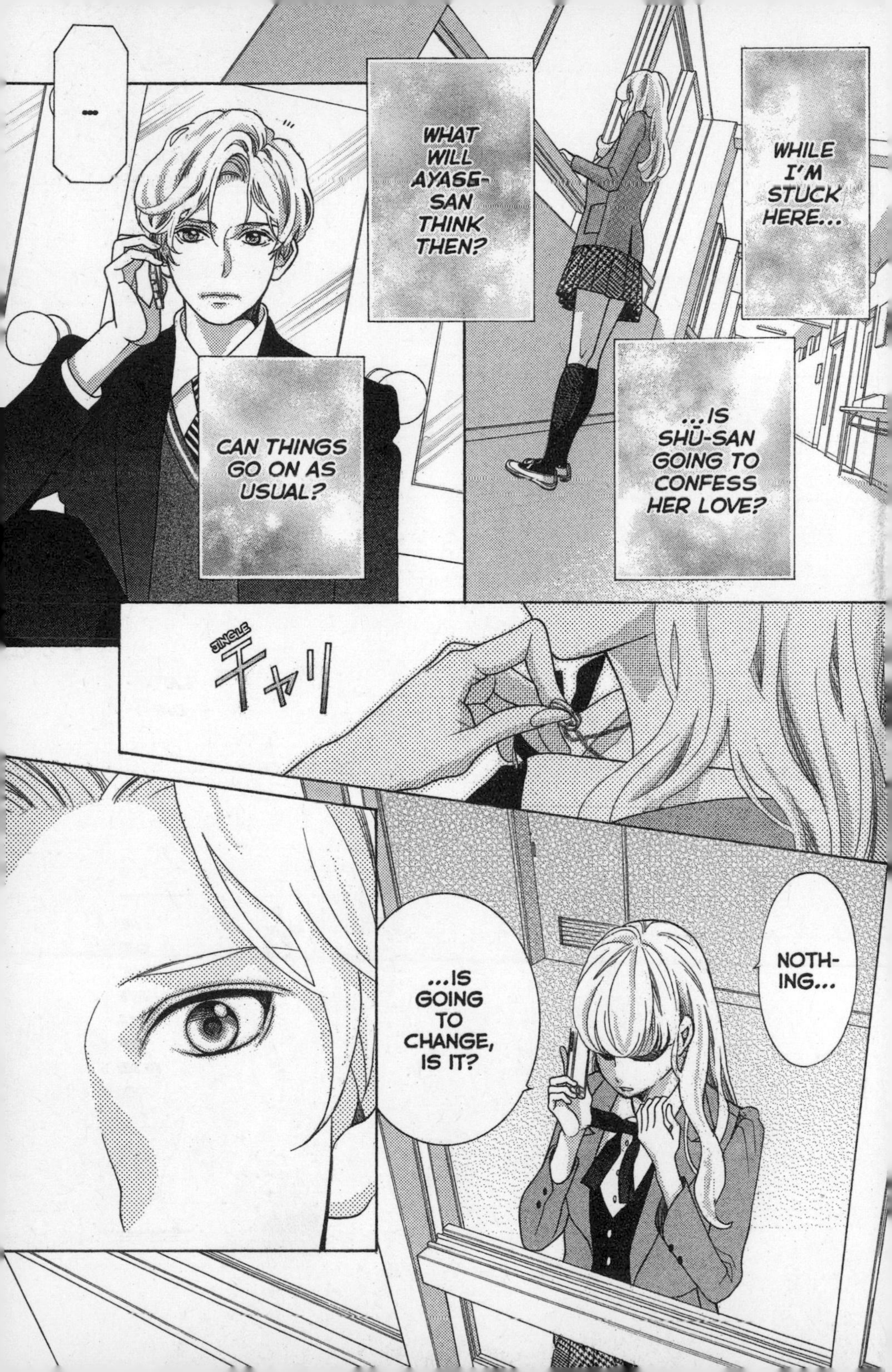
WHILE I'M STUCK HERE...
...IS SHŪ-SAN GOING TO CONFESS HER LOVE?
WHAT WILL AYASE-SAN THINK THEN?
...
CAN THINGS GO ON AS USUAL?
JINGLE
チャリ
NOTH-ING...
...IS GOING TO CHANGE, IS IT?

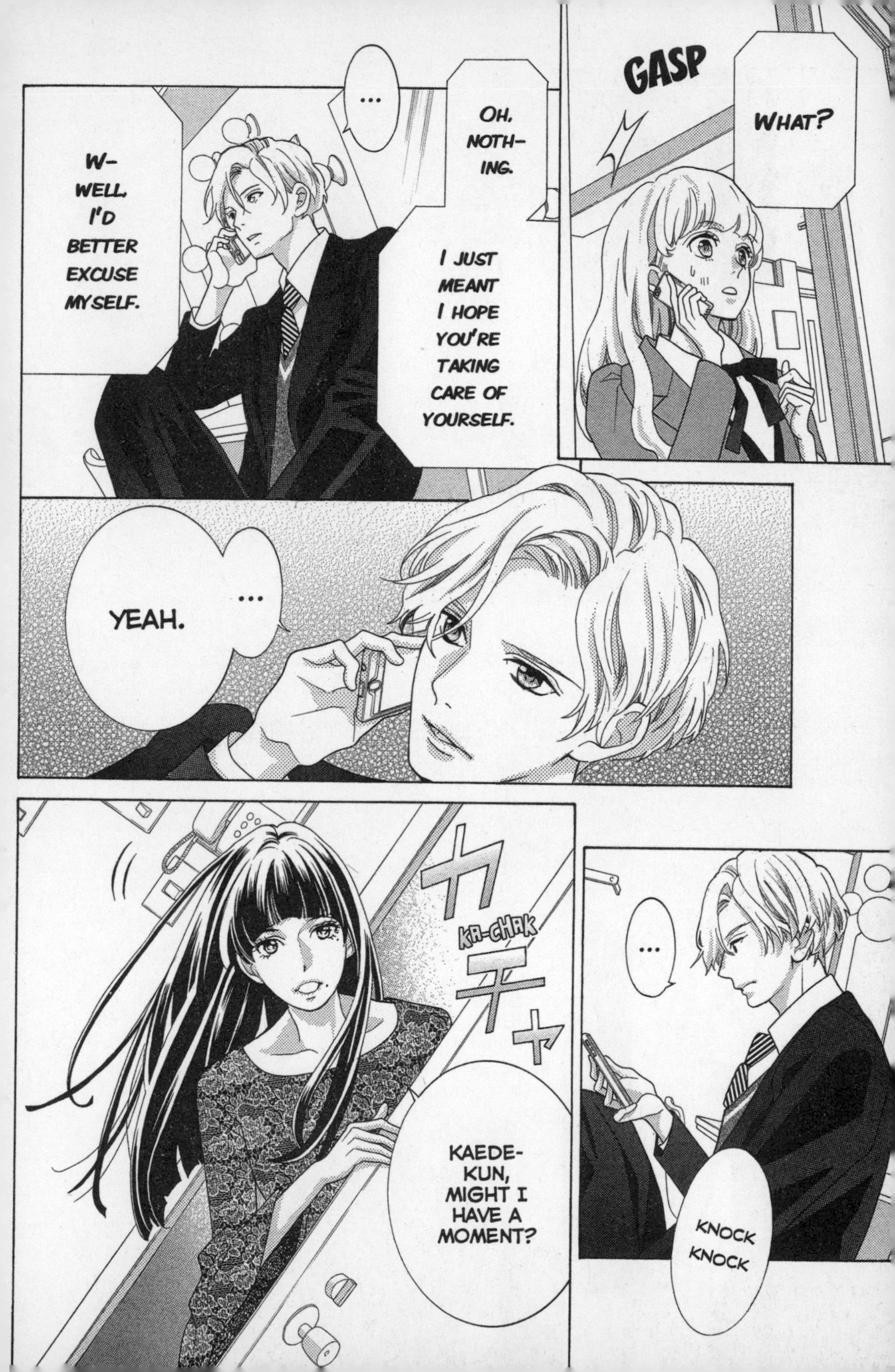
GASP
WHAT?
OH, NOTHING.
I JUST MEANT I HOPE YOU'RE TAKING CARE OF YOURSELF.
...
W-WELL, I'D BETTER EXCUSE MYSELF.
...
YEAH.
...
KNOCK KNOCK
カチャ
KA-CHAK
KAEDE-KUN, MIGHT I HAVE A MOMENT?

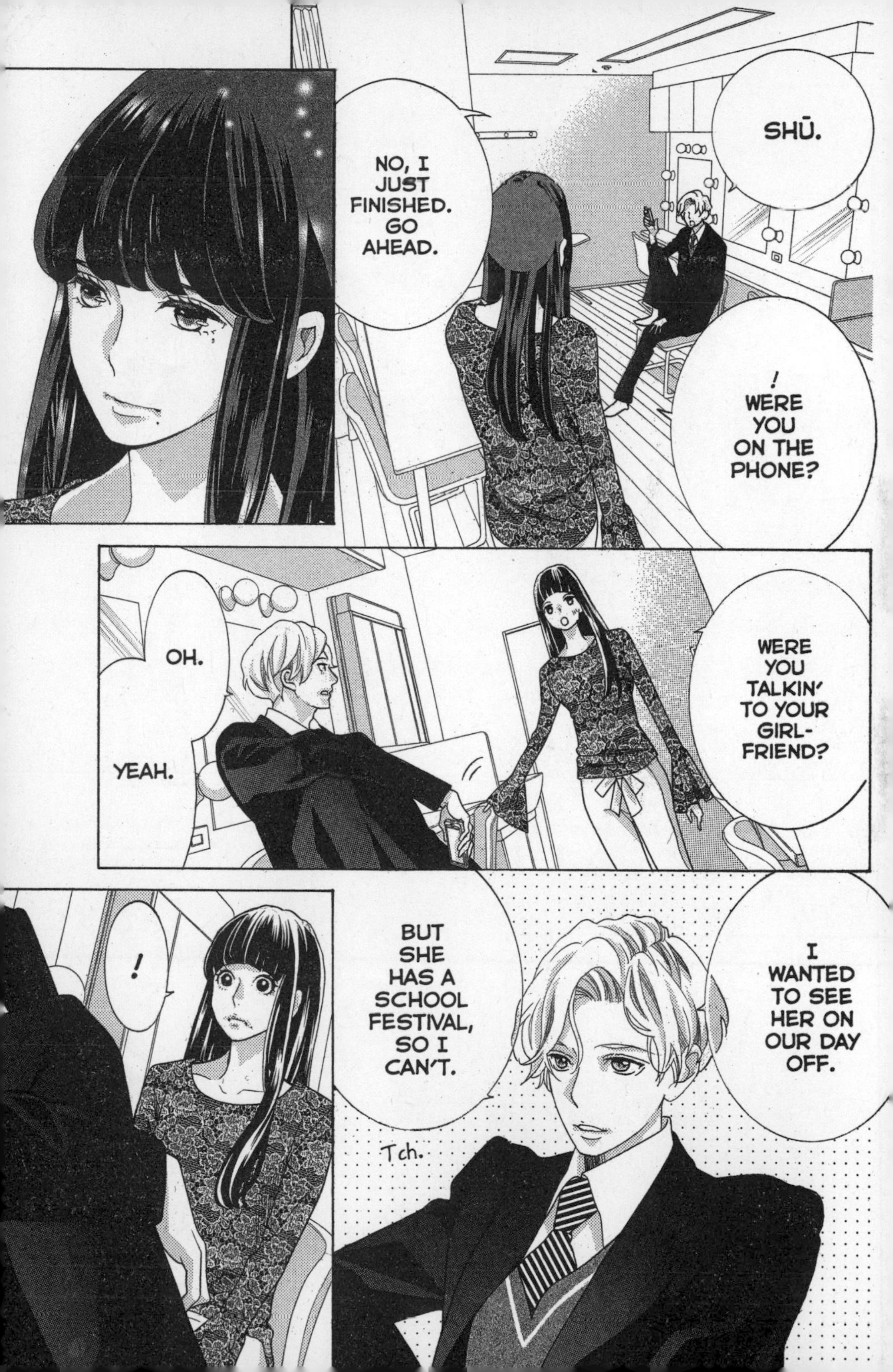
SHŪ.
! WERE YOU ON THE PHONE?
NO, I JUST FINISHED. GO AHEAD.
WERE YOU TALKIN' TO YOUR GIRL-FRIEND?
OH.
YEAH.
I WANTED TO SEE HER ON OUR DAY OFF.
BUT SHE HAS A SCHOOL FESTIVAL, SO I CAN'T.
Tch.
!

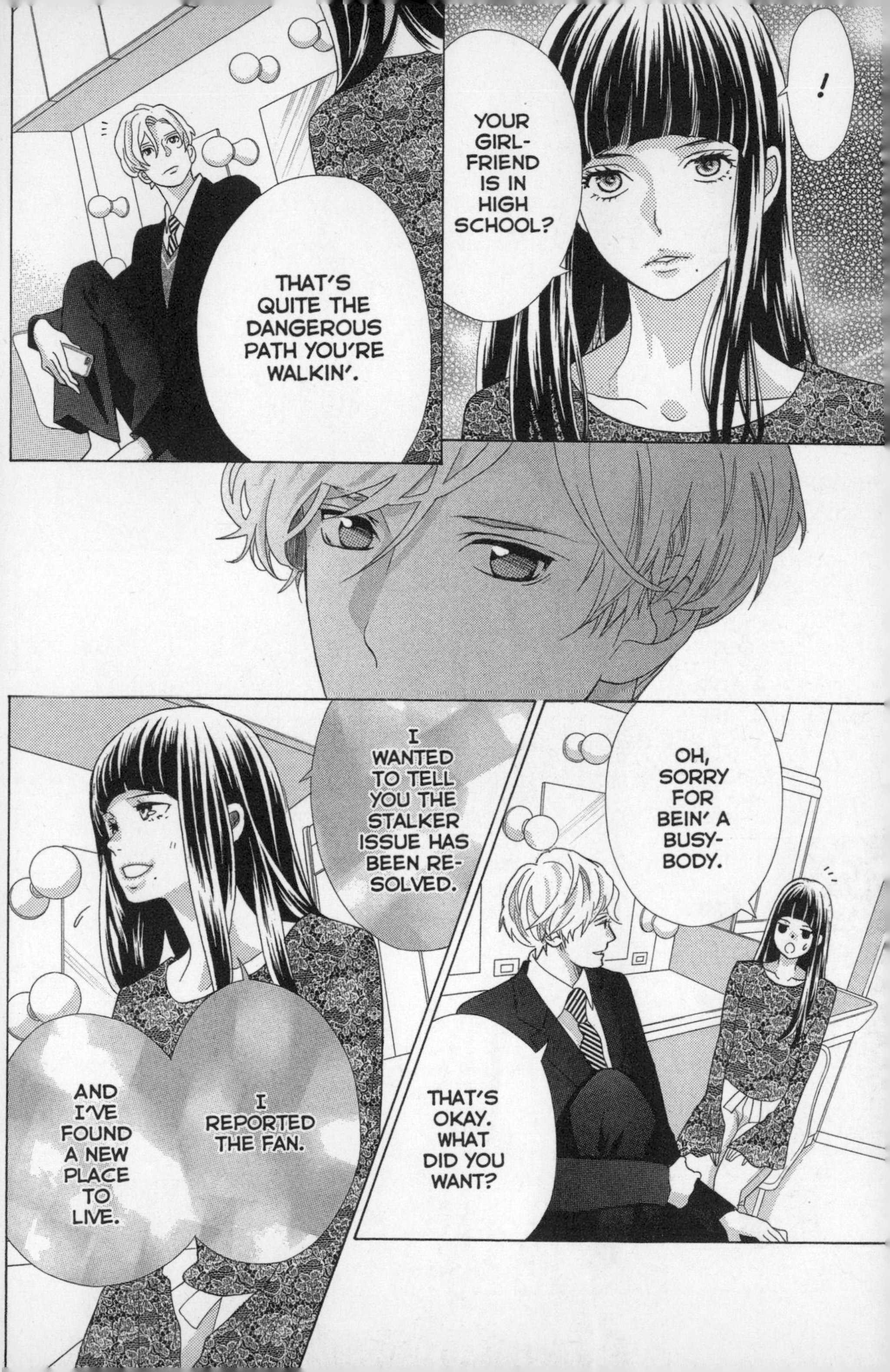
!
YOUR GIRL-FRIEND IS IN HIGH SCHOOL?
THAT'S QUITE THE DANGEROUS PATH YOU'RE WALKIN'.
OH, SORRY FOR BEIN' A BUSY-BODY.
THAT'S OKAY. WHAT DID YOU WANT?
I WANTED TO TELL YOU THE STALKER ISSUE HAS BEEN RE-SOLVED.
I REPORTED THE FAN.
AND I'VE FOUND A NEW PLACE TO LIVE.

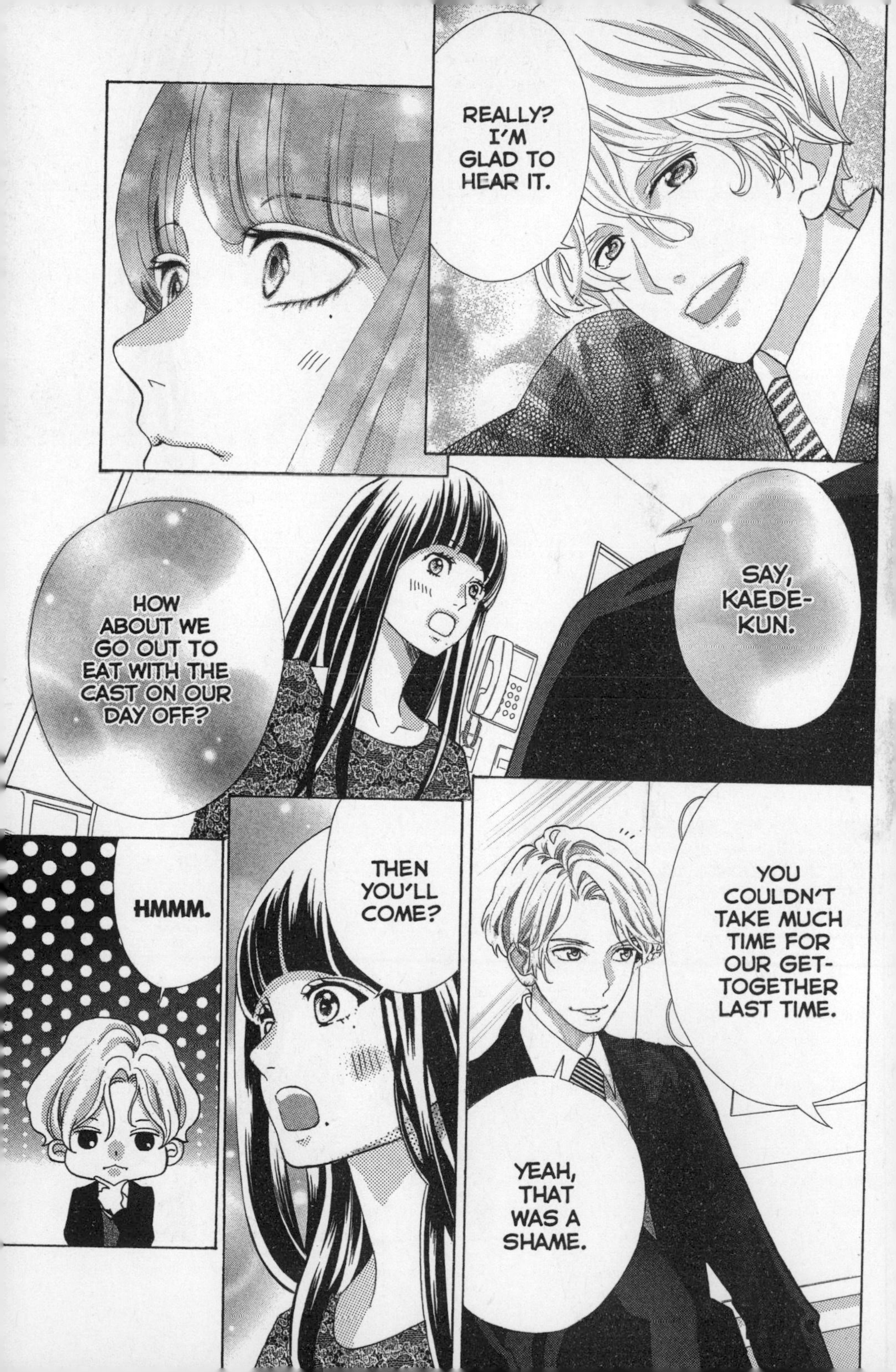
REALLY? I'M GLAD TO HEAR IT.
SAY, KAEDE-KUN.
HOW ABOUT WE GO OUT TO EAT WITH THE CAST ON OUR DAY OFF?
YOU COULDN'T TAKE MUCH TIME FOR OUR GET-TOGETHER LAST TIME.
YEAH, THAT WAS A SHAME.
THEN YOU'LL COME?
HMMM.

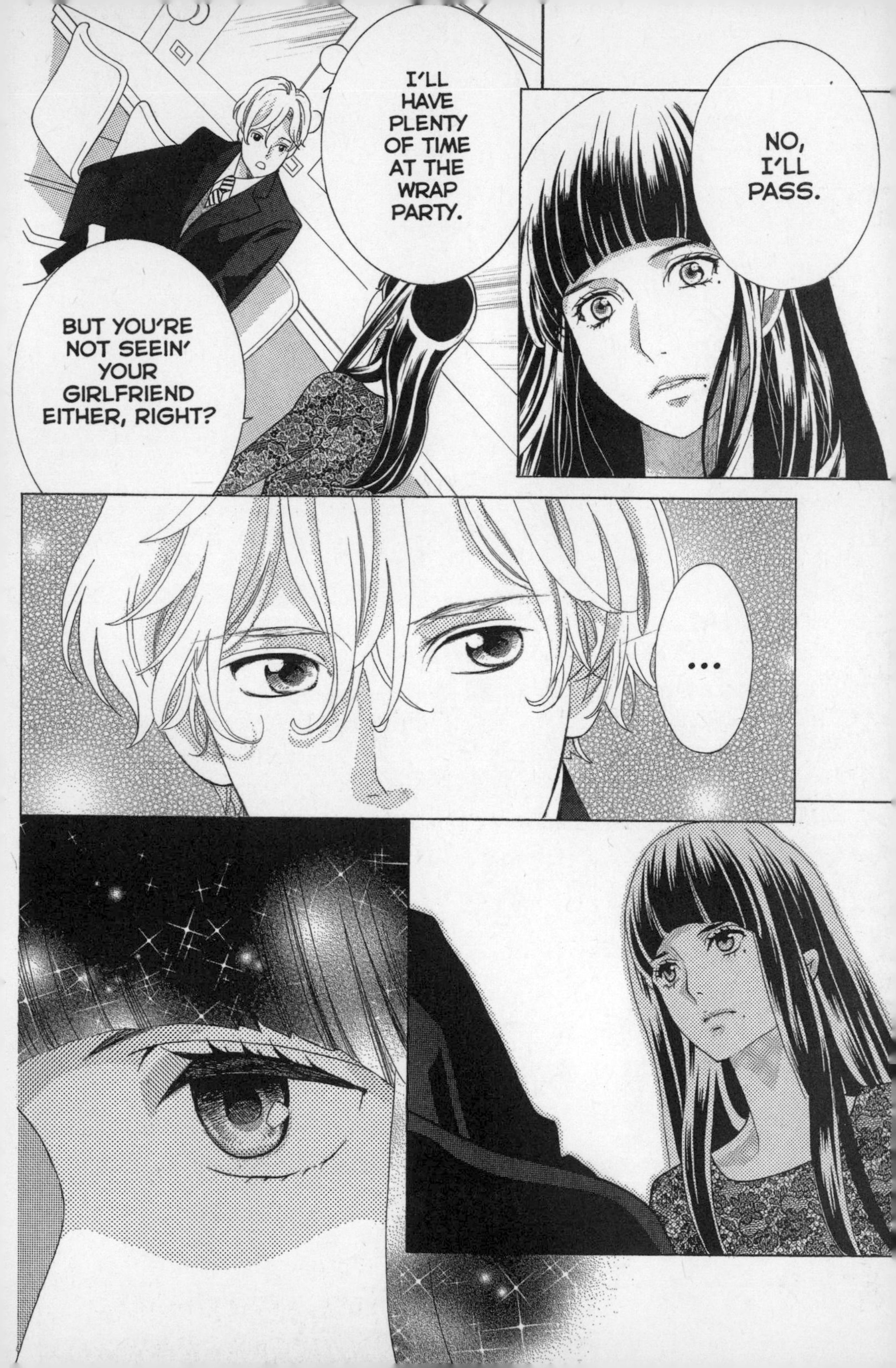
NO, I'LL PASS.
I'LL HAVE PLENTY OF TIME AT THE WRAP PARTY.
BUT YOU'RE NOT SEEIN' YOUR GIRLFRIEND EITHER, RIGHT?
...

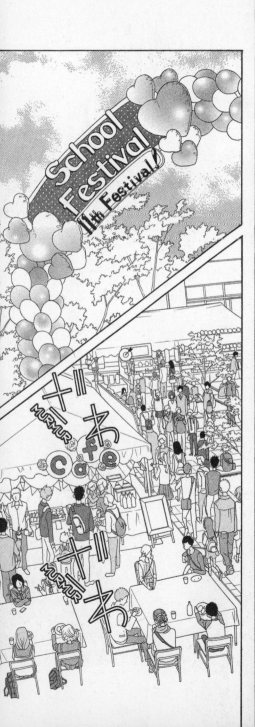

School Festival
11th Festival!

OF COURSE.

I UNDER-STAND.

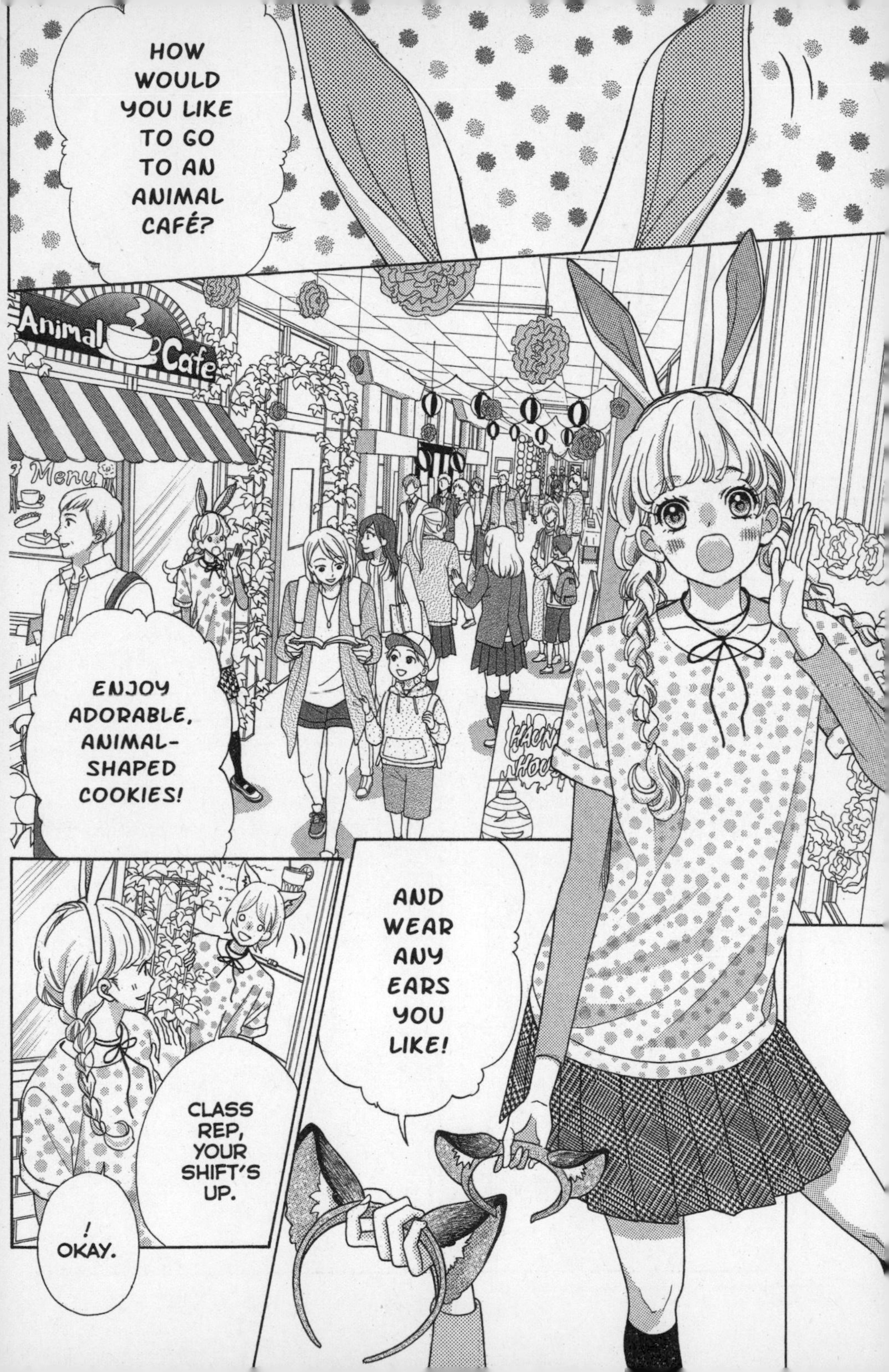
HOW WOULD YOU LIKE TO GO TO AN ANIMAL CAFÉ?
Animal Cafe
Menu
ENJOY ADORABLE, ANIMAL-SHAPED COOKIES!
AND WEAR ANY EARS YOU LIKE!
CLASS REP, YOUR SHIFT'S UP.
! OKAY.

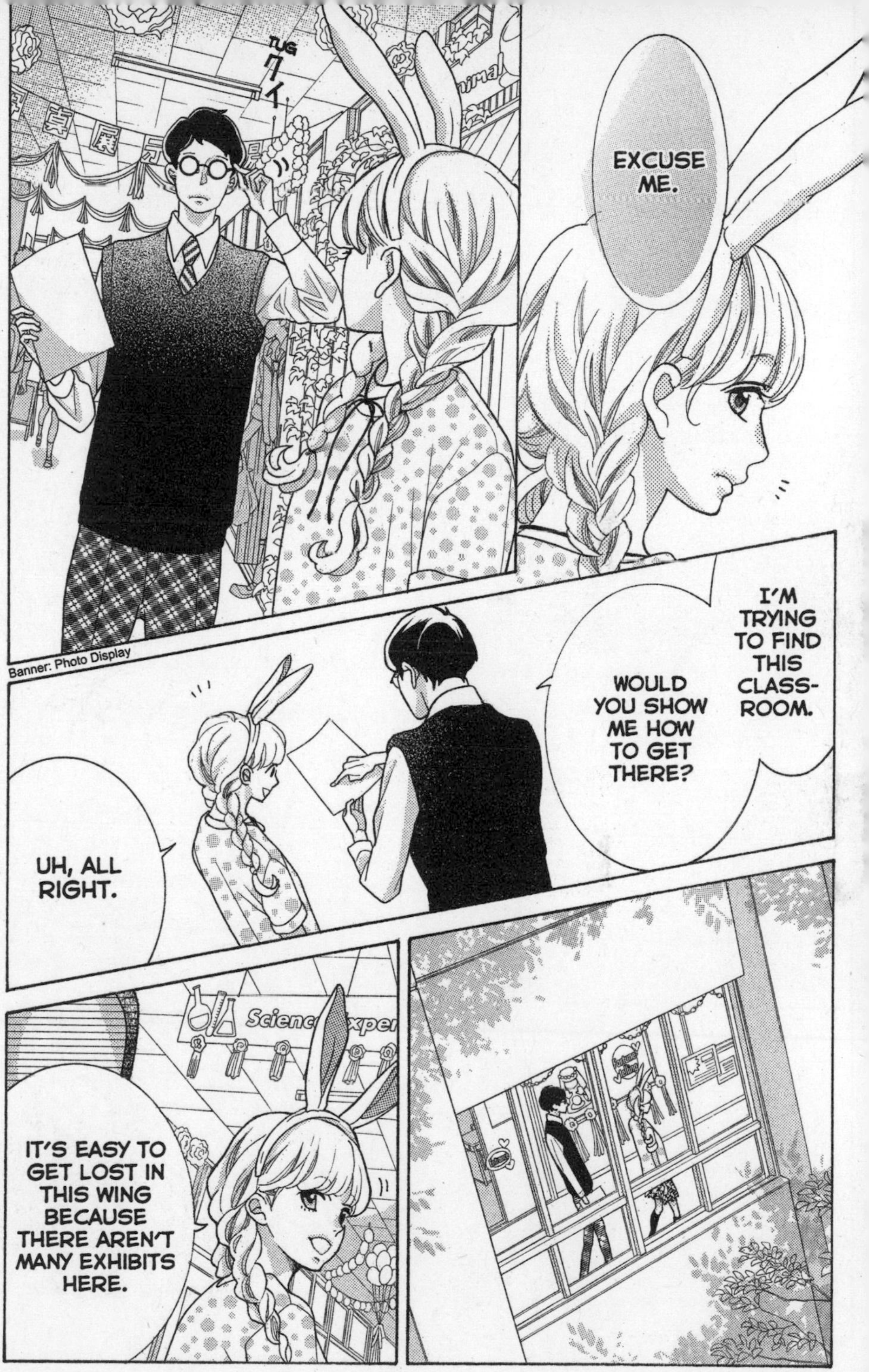
EXCUSE ME.
TUG
クイ
Banner: Photo Display
I'M TRYING TO FIND THIS CLASS-ROOM.
WOULD YOU SHOW ME HOW TO GET THERE?
UH, ALL RIGHT.
IT'S EASY TO GET LOST IN THIS WING BECAUSE THERE AREN'T MANY EXHIBITS HERE.

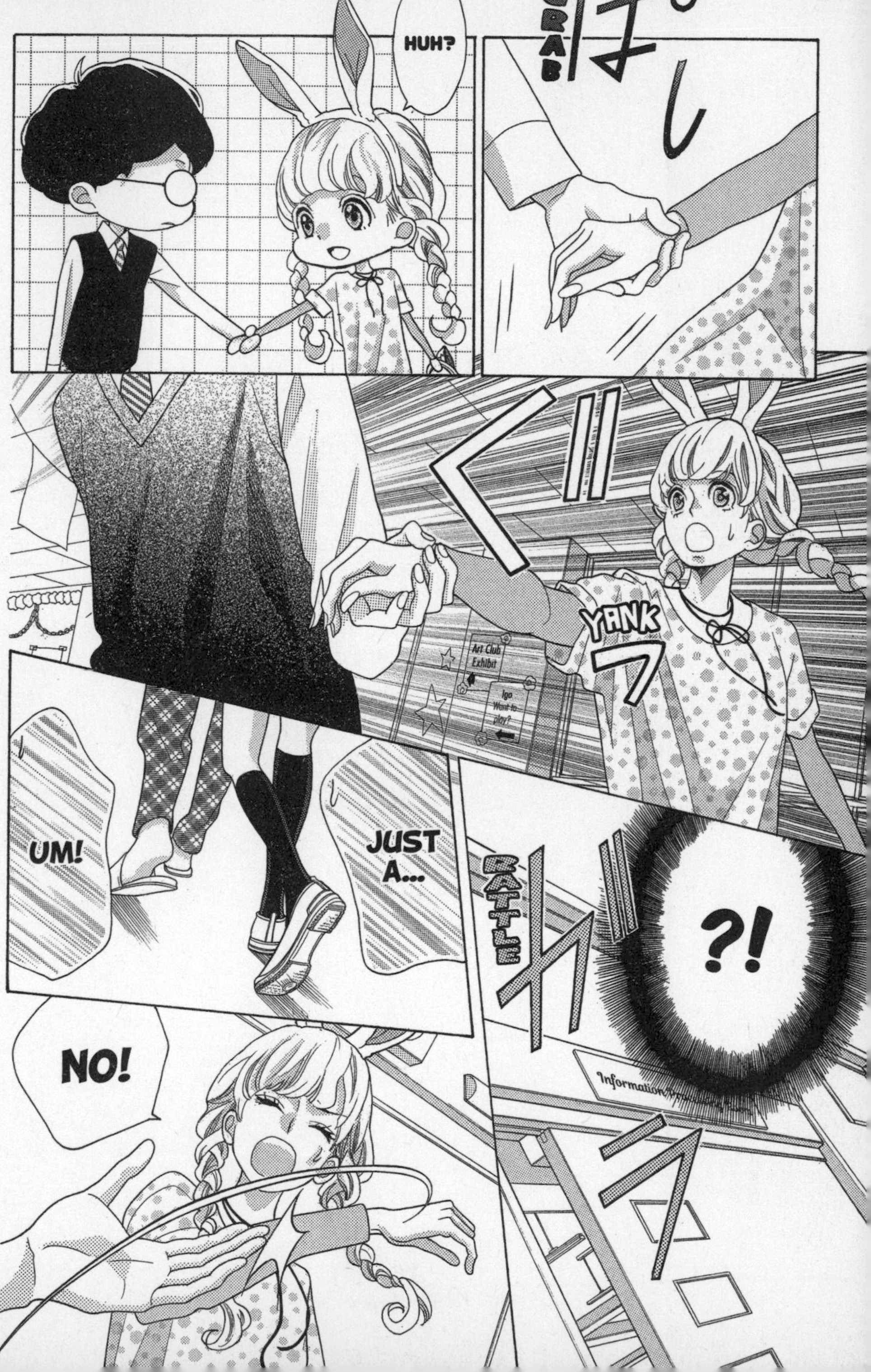
GRAB
ぱし
HUH?
YANK
Art Club Exhibit
Igo Want to play?
?!
RATTLE
JUST A...
UM!
Information
NO!

Banner: Photo Display

- 147 -

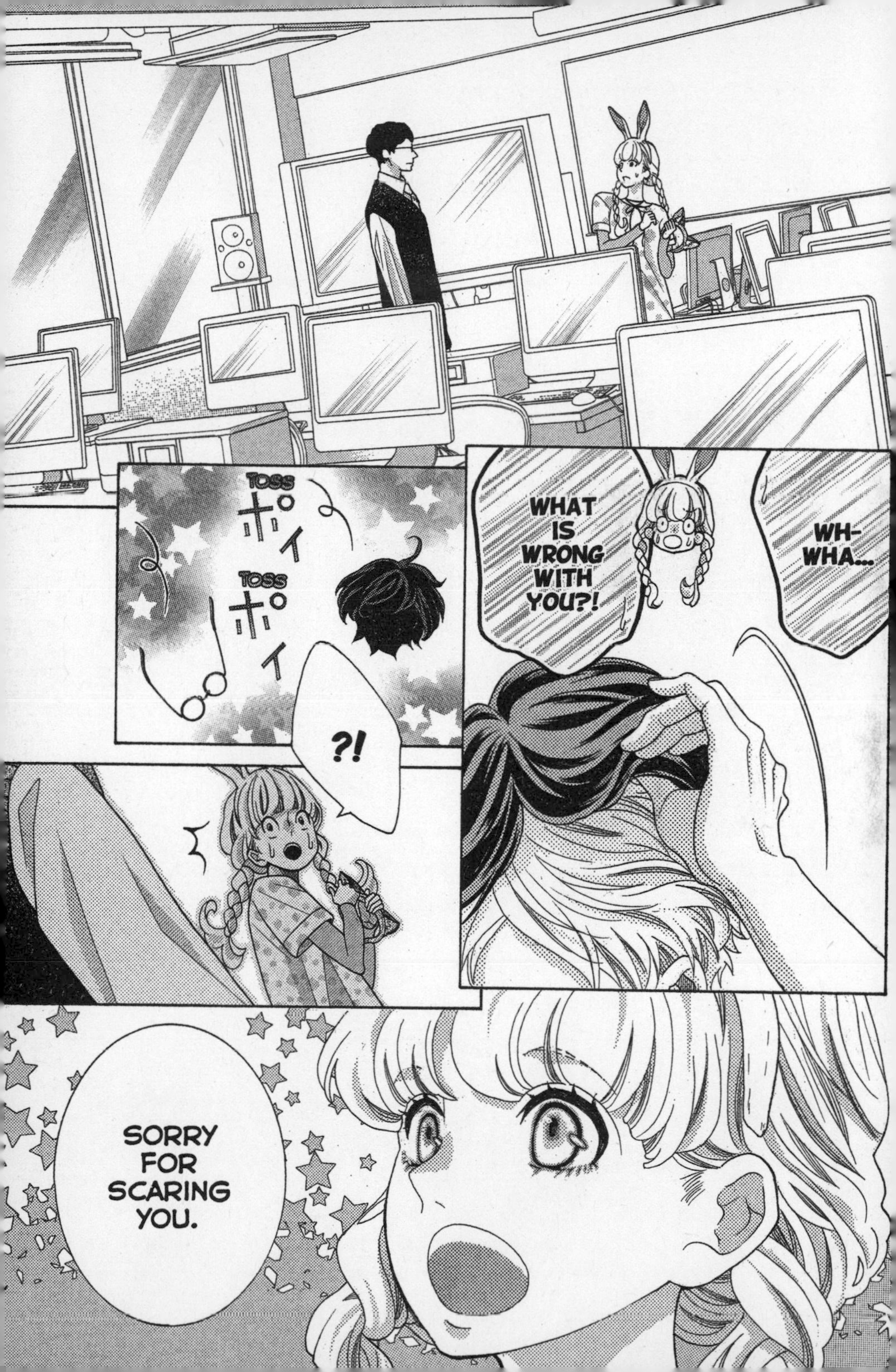
WH-WHA...
WHAT IS WRONG WITH YOU?!
TOSS ポイ
TOSS ポイ
?!
SORRY FOR SCARING YOU.

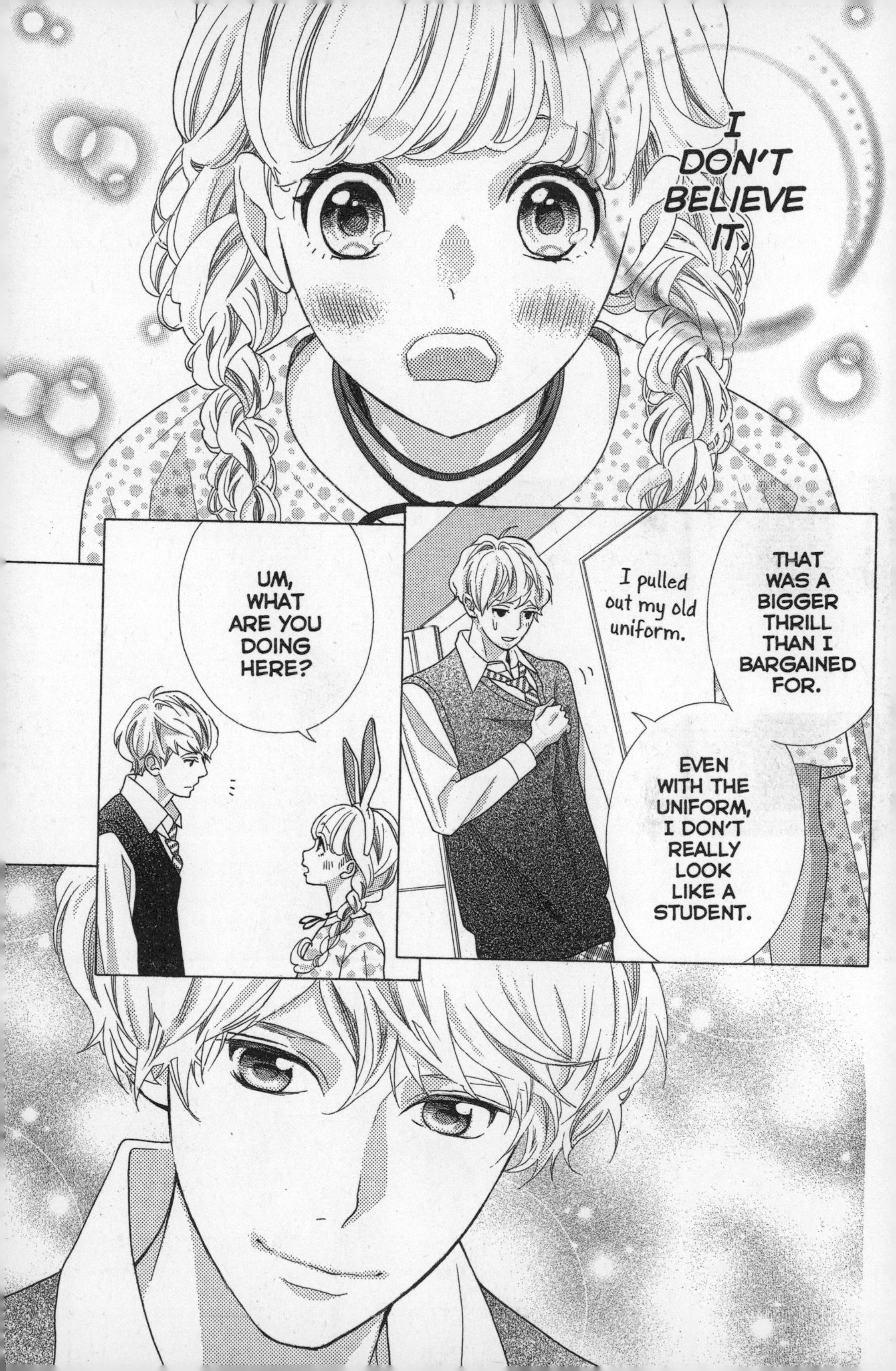
I DON'T BELIEVE IT.
THAT WAS A BIGGER THRILL THAN I BARGAINED FOR.
I pulled out my old uniform.
EVEN WITH THE UNIFORM, I DON'T REALLY LOOK LIKE A STUDENT.
UM, WHAT ARE YOU DOING HERE?

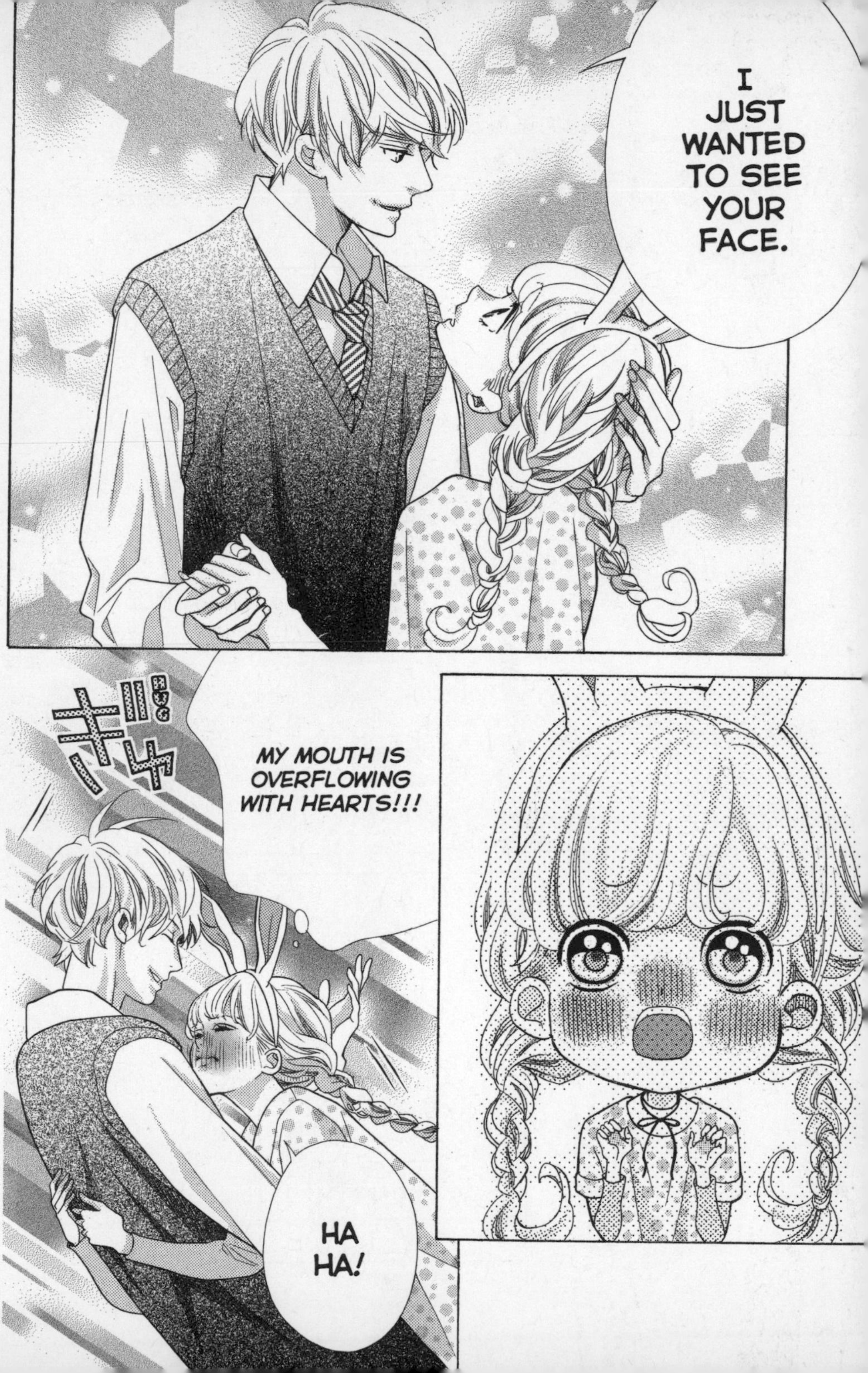
I JUST WANTED TO SEE YOUR FACE.
ギュッ
HUG
MY MOUTH IS OVERFLOWING WITH HEARTS!!!
HA HA!

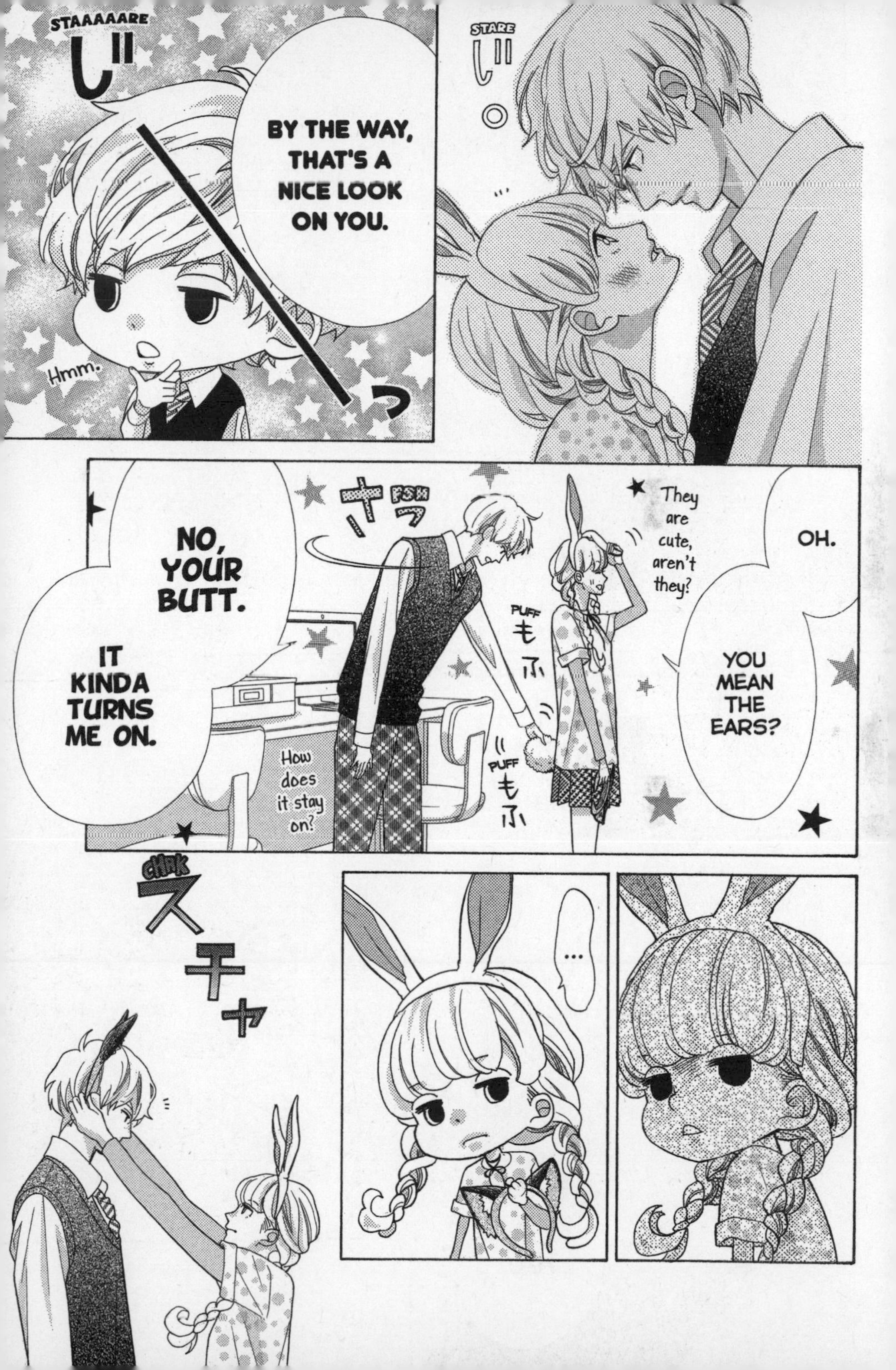

STARE
...
STAAAAARE
BY THE WAY, THAT'S A NICE LOOK ON YOU.
Hmm.
OH.
YOU MEAN THE EARS?
They are cute, aren't they?
FSH
PUFF もふ
PUFF もふ
NO, YOUR BUTT.
IT KINDA TURNS ME ON.
How does it stay on?
...
CHK スチャ

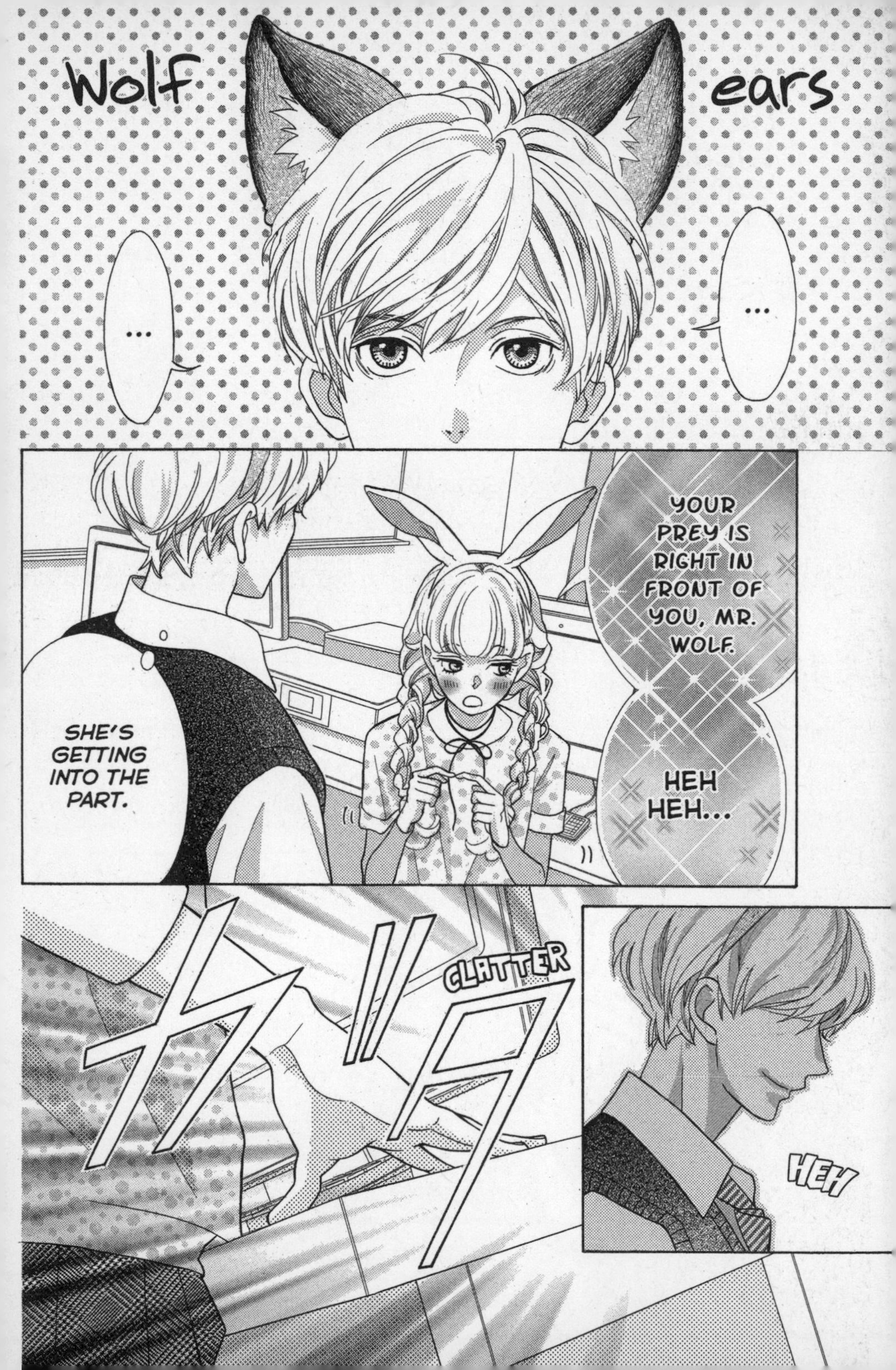
Wolf
ears
...
...
YOUR PREY IS RIGHT IN FRONT OF YOU, MR. WOLF.
HEH HEH...
SHE'S GETTING INTO THE PART.
HEH
CLATTER

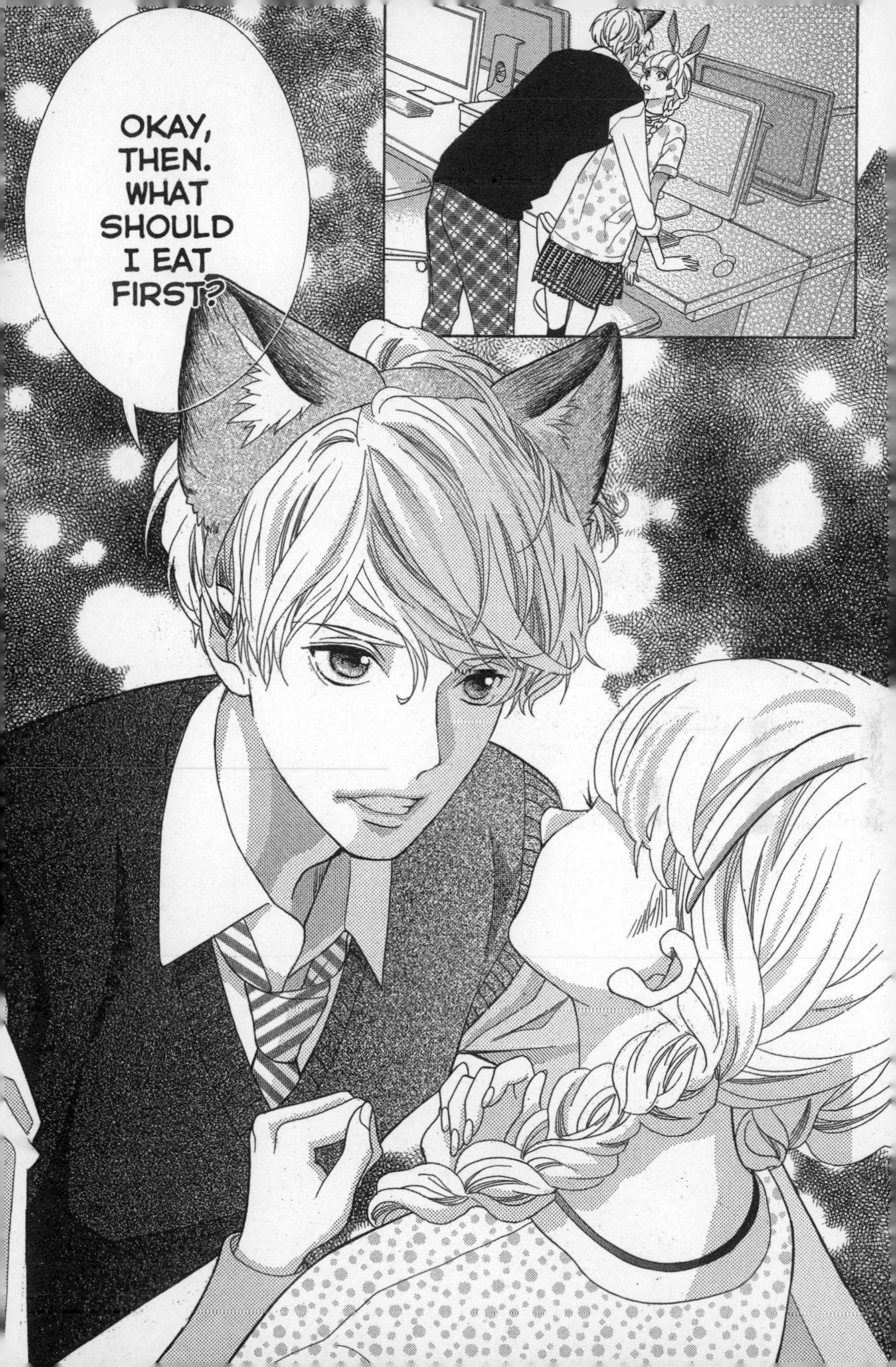
OKAY, THEN. WHAT SHOULD I EAT FIRST?

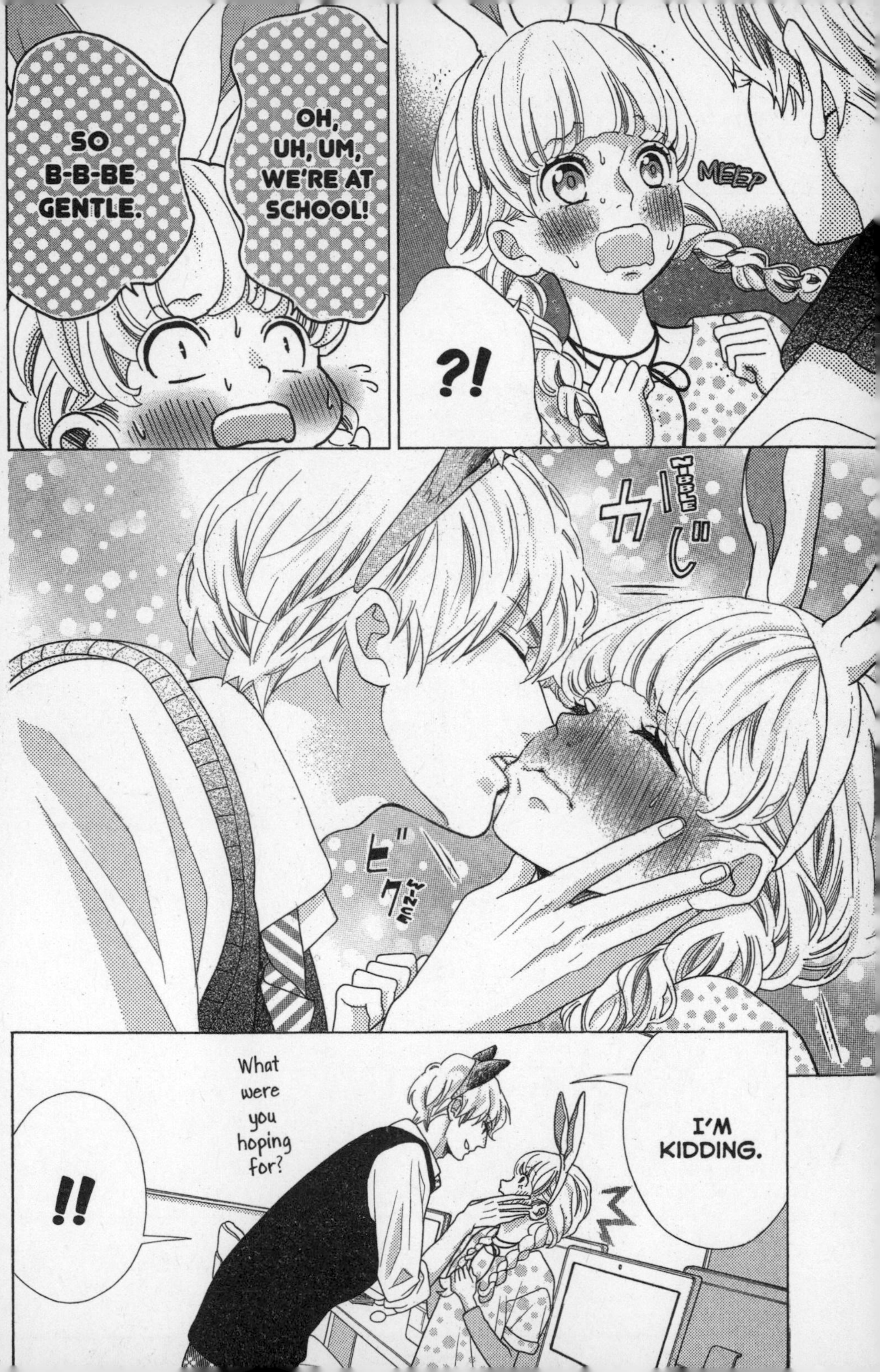
MEEP
?!
OH, UH, UM, WE'RE AT SCHOOL!
SO B-B-BE GENTLE.
NIBBLE
WINCE
I'M KIDDING.
What were you hoping for?
!!

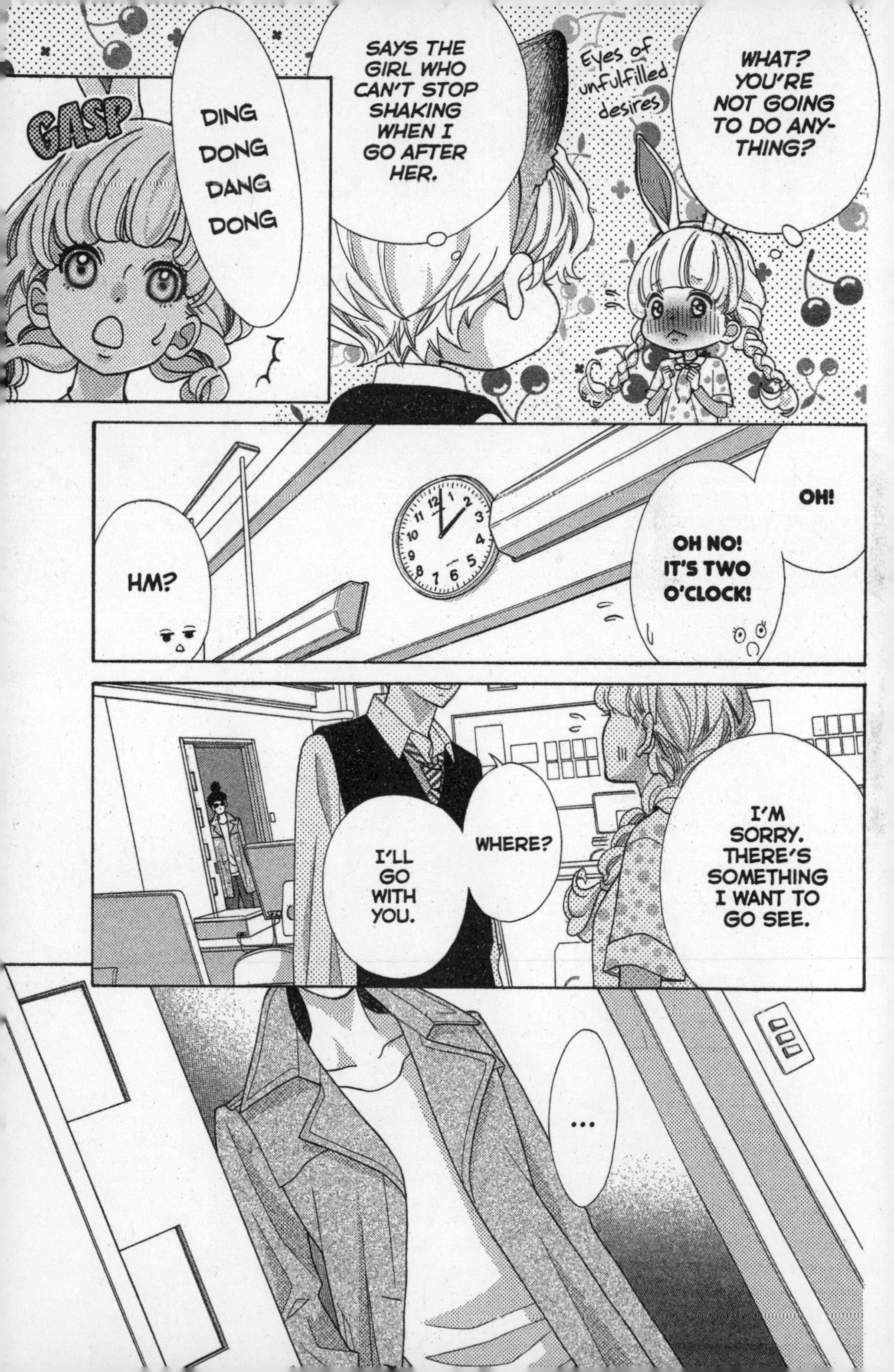
WHAT? YOU'RE NOT GOING TO DO ANYTHING?
Eyes of unfulfilled desires
SAYS THE GIRL WHO CAN'T STOP SHAKING WHEN I GO AFTER HER.
GASP
DING DONG DANG DONG
OH!
OH NO! IT'S TWO O'CLOCK!
HM?
I'M SORRY. THERE'S SOMETHING I WANT TO GO SEE.
WHERE?
I'LL GO WITH YOU.
...

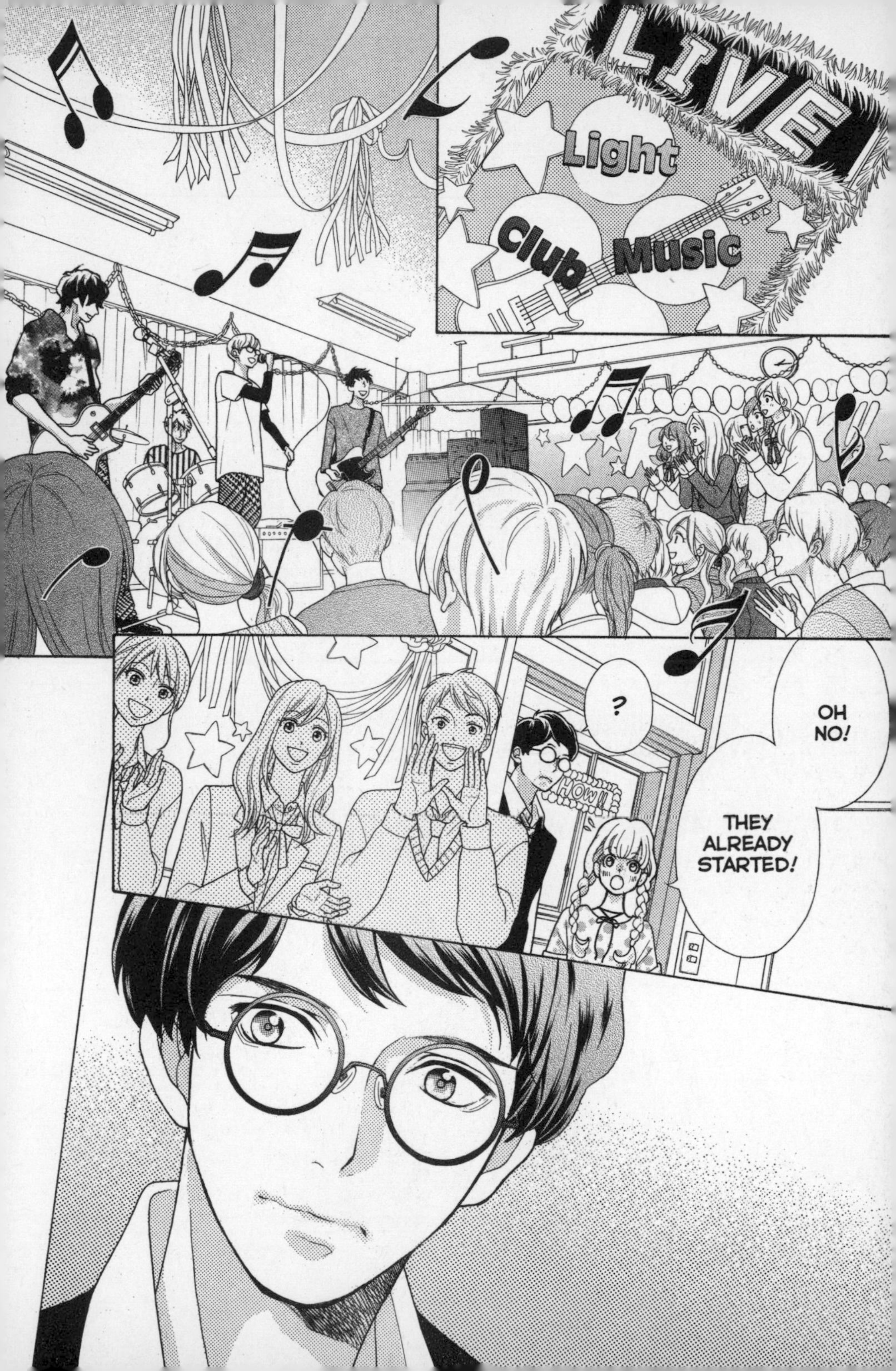
LIVE!
Light
Club
Music
OH NO!
THEY ALREADY STARTED!
?

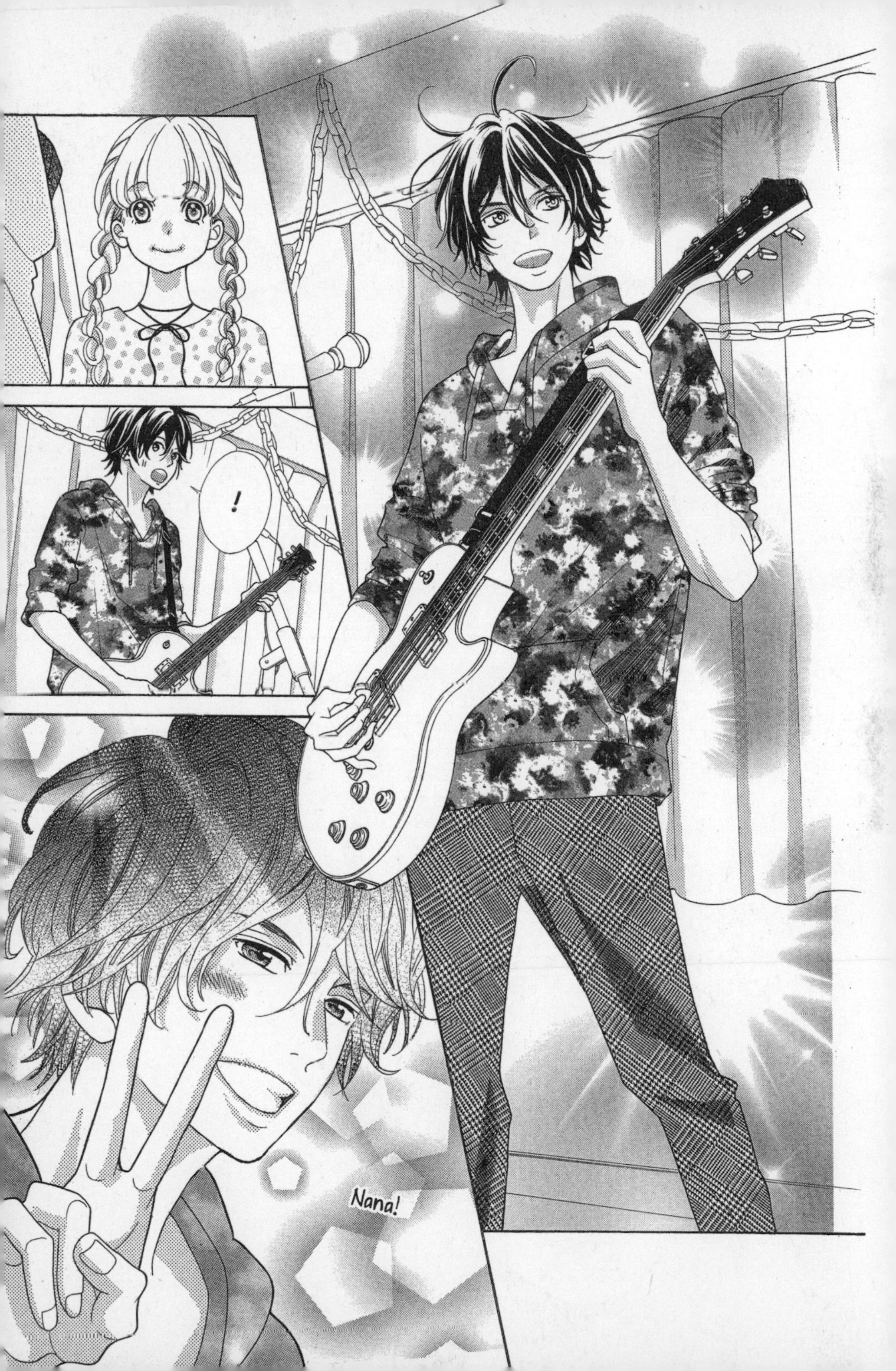
!
Nana!

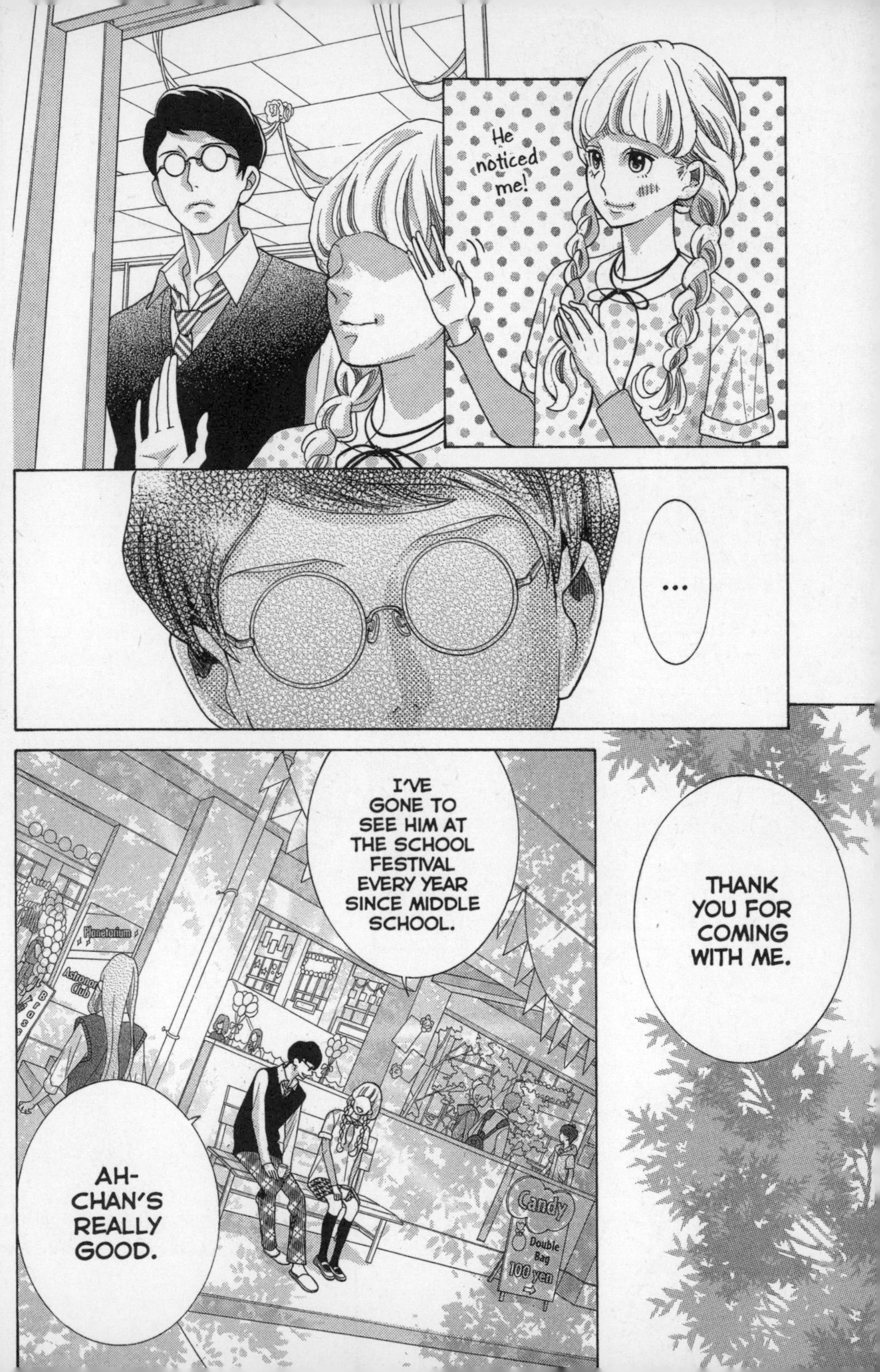
He noticed me!
...
THANK YOU FOR COMING WITH ME.
I'VE GONE TO SEE HIM AT THE SCHOOL FESTIVAL EVERY YEAR SINCE MIDDLE SCHOOL.
Planetarium
Candy
Double Bag
100 yen
AH-CHAN'S REALLY GOOD.

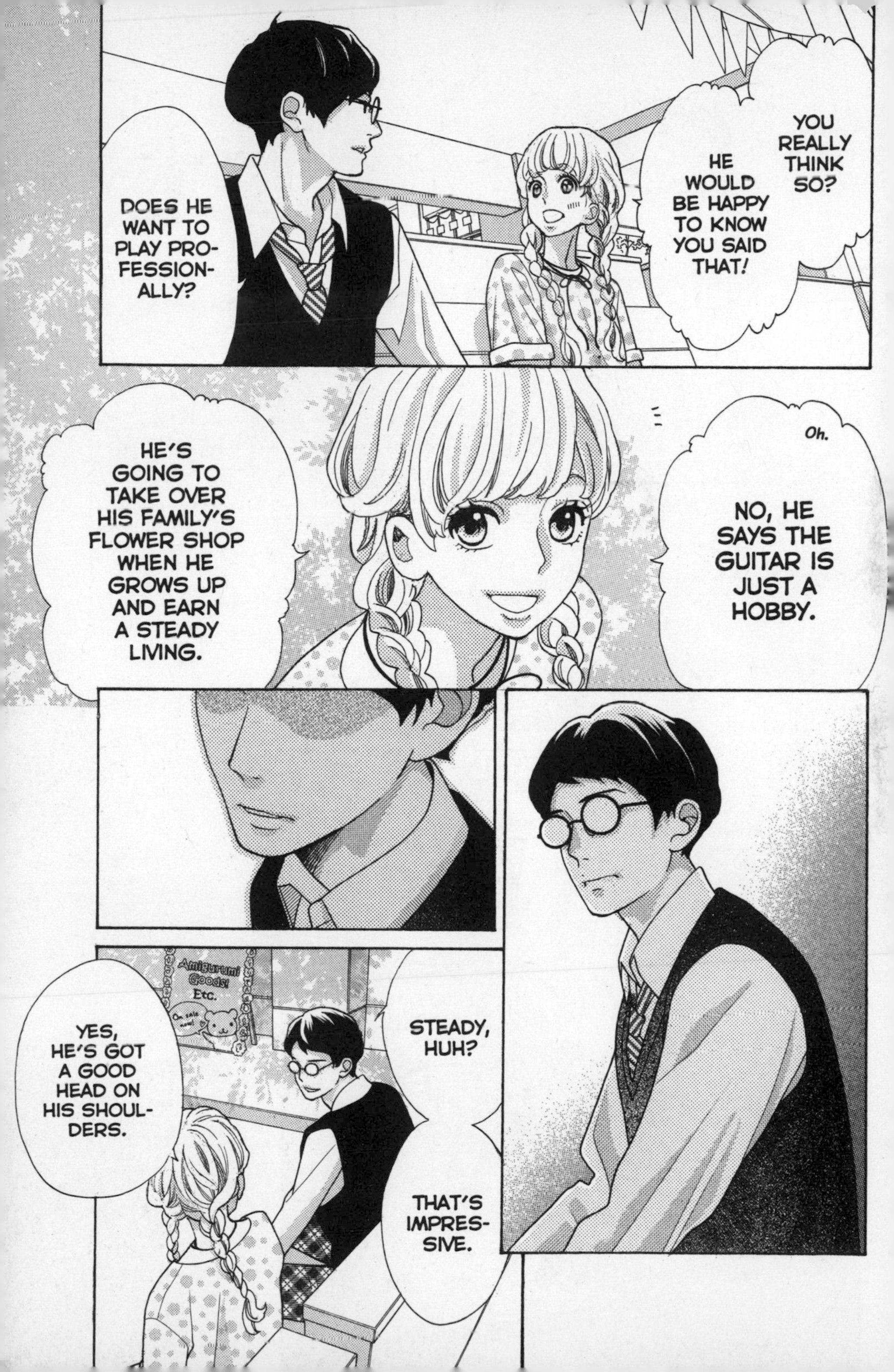
YOU REALLY THINK SO?
HE WOULD BE HAPPY TO KNOW YOU SAID THAT!
DOES HE WANT TO PLAY PRO-FESSION-ALLY?
Oh.
NO, HE SAYS THE GUITAR IS JUST A HOBBY.
HE'S GOING TO TAKE OVER HIS FAMILY'S FLOWER SHOP WHEN HE GROWS UP AND EARN A STEADY LIVING.
Amigurumi Goods! Etc.
STEADY, HUH?
THAT'S IMPRES-SIVE.
YES, HE'S GOT A GOOD HEAD ON HIS SHOUL-DERS.

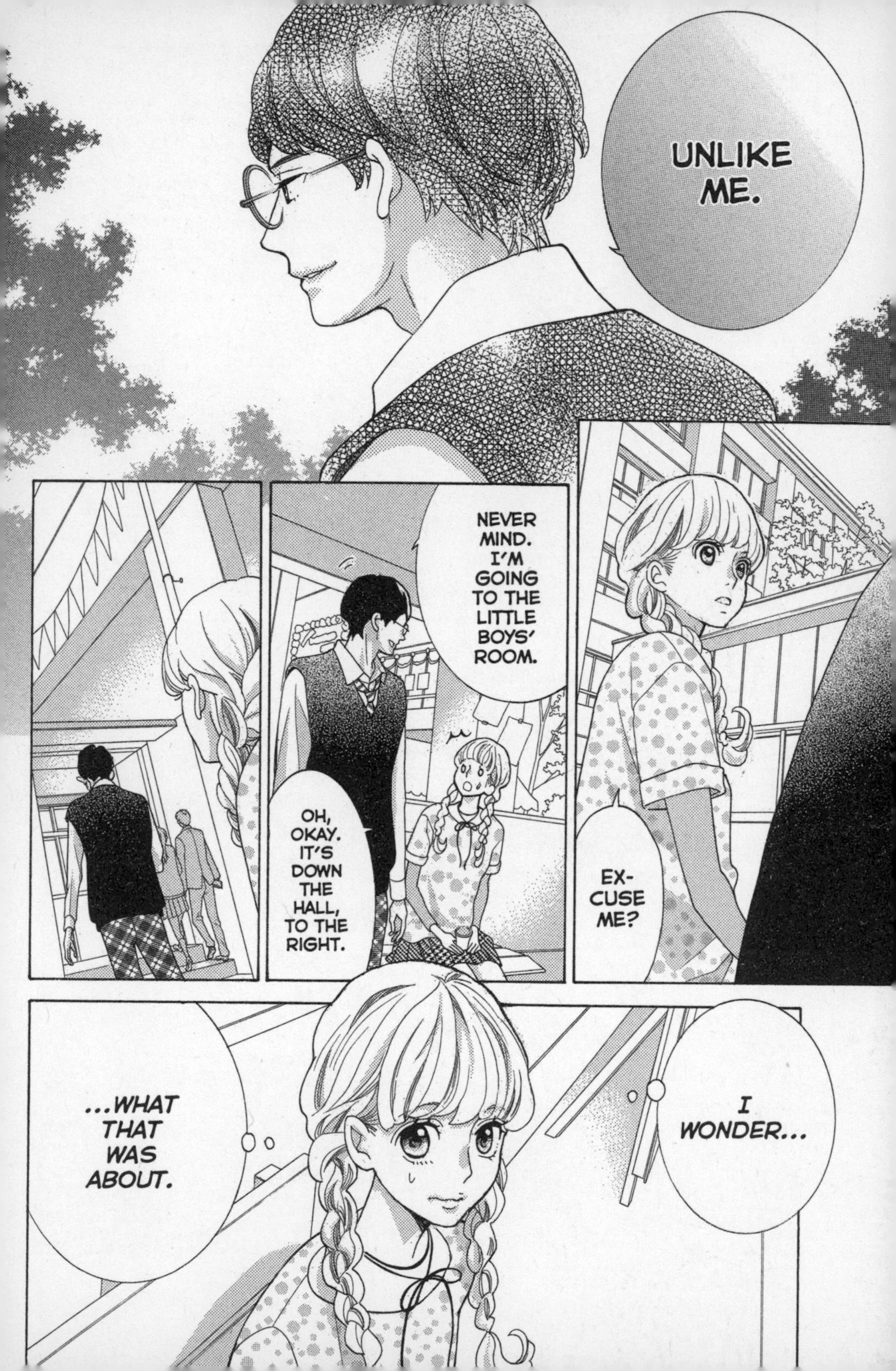
UNLIKE ME.
EX-CUSE ME?
NEVER MIND. I'M GOING TO THE LITTLE BOYS' ROOM.
OH, OKAY. IT'S DOWN THE HALL, TO THE RIGHT.
I WONDER...
...WHAT THAT WAS ABOUT.

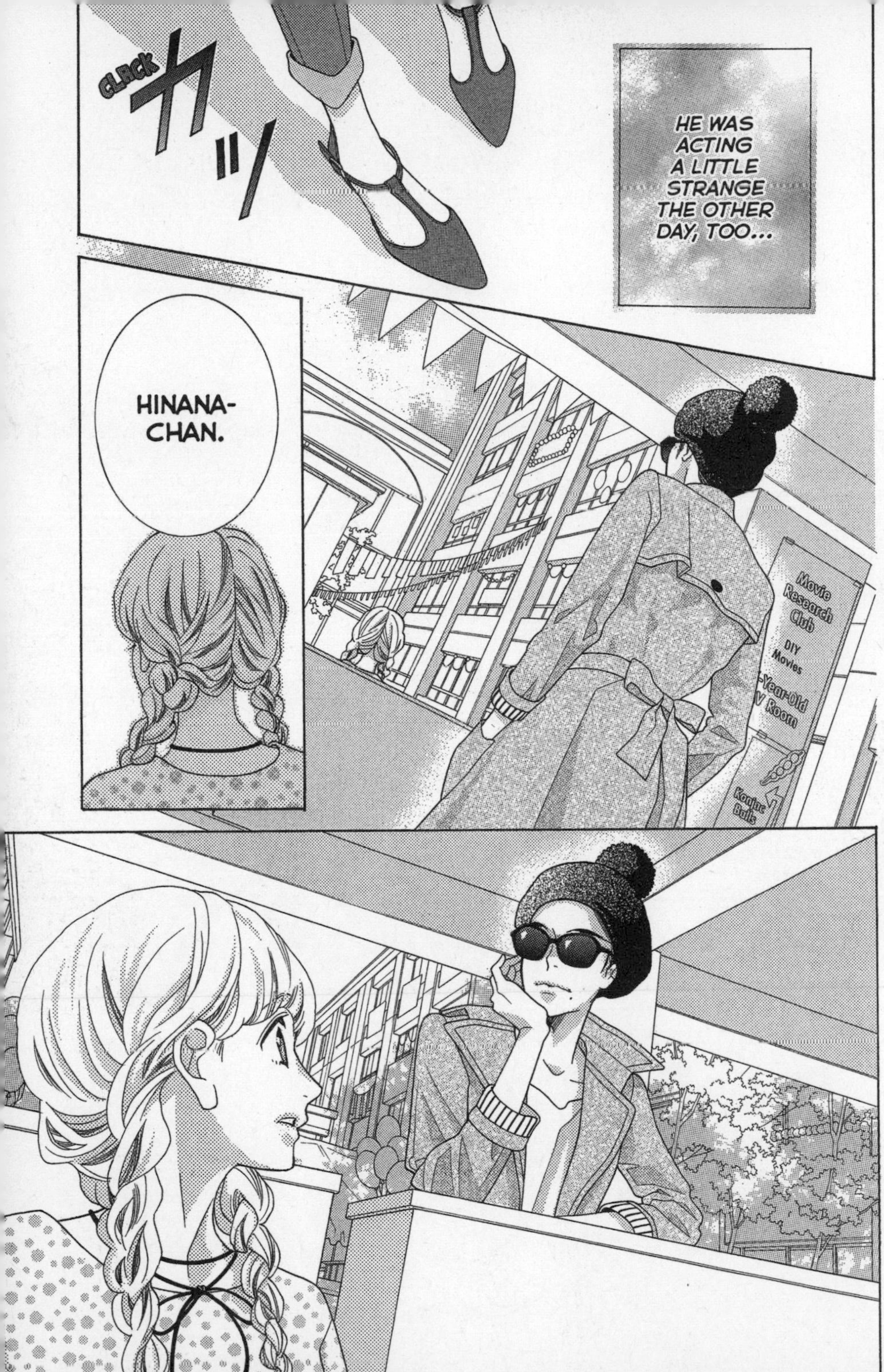
HE WAS ACTING A LITTLE STRANGE THE OTHER DAY, TOO...
CLACK
Movie Research Club
DIY Movies
Konjac Balls
HINANA-CHAN.

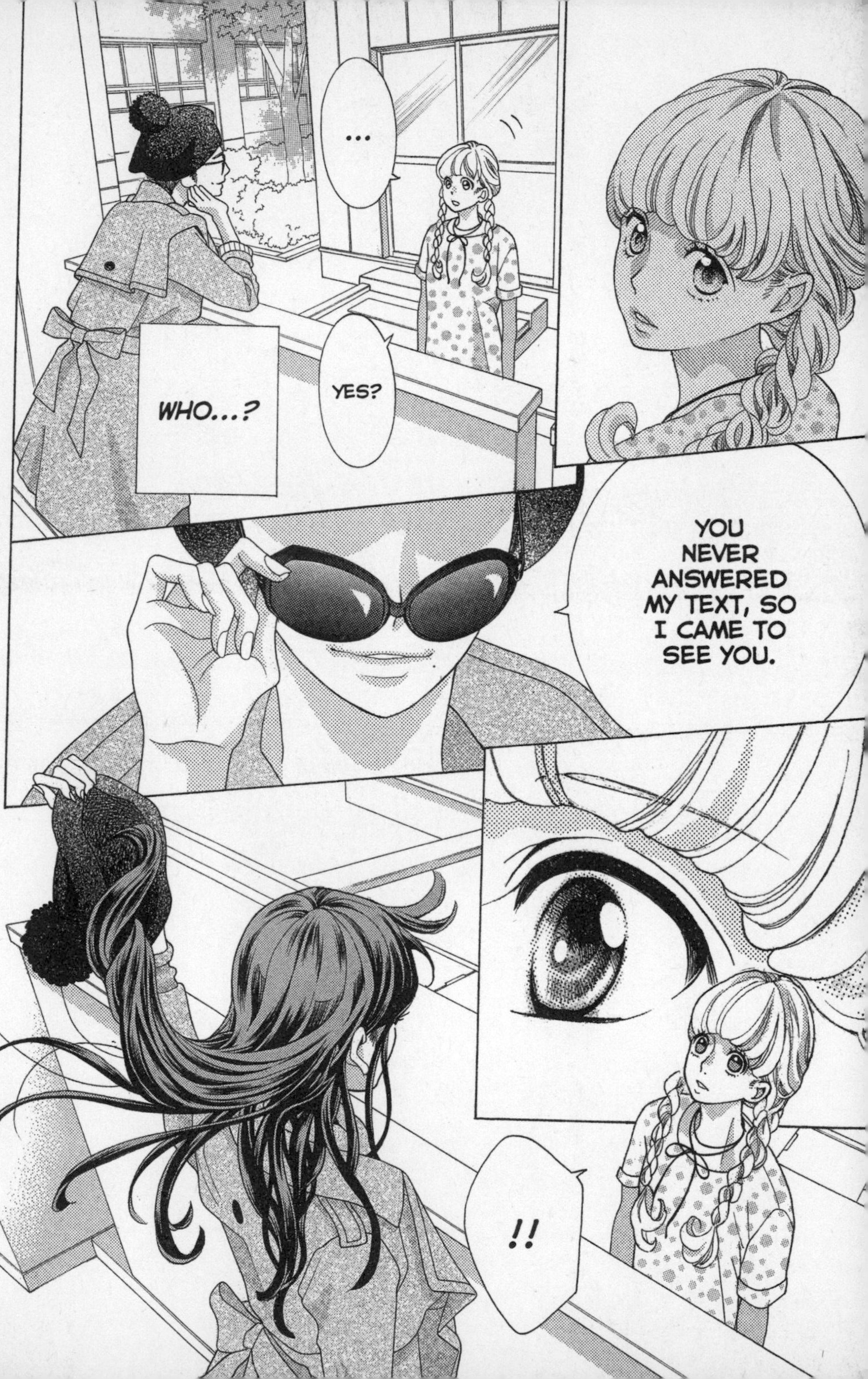

...
YES?
WHO...?
YOU NEVER ANSWERED MY TEXT, SO I CAME TO SEE YOU.
!!

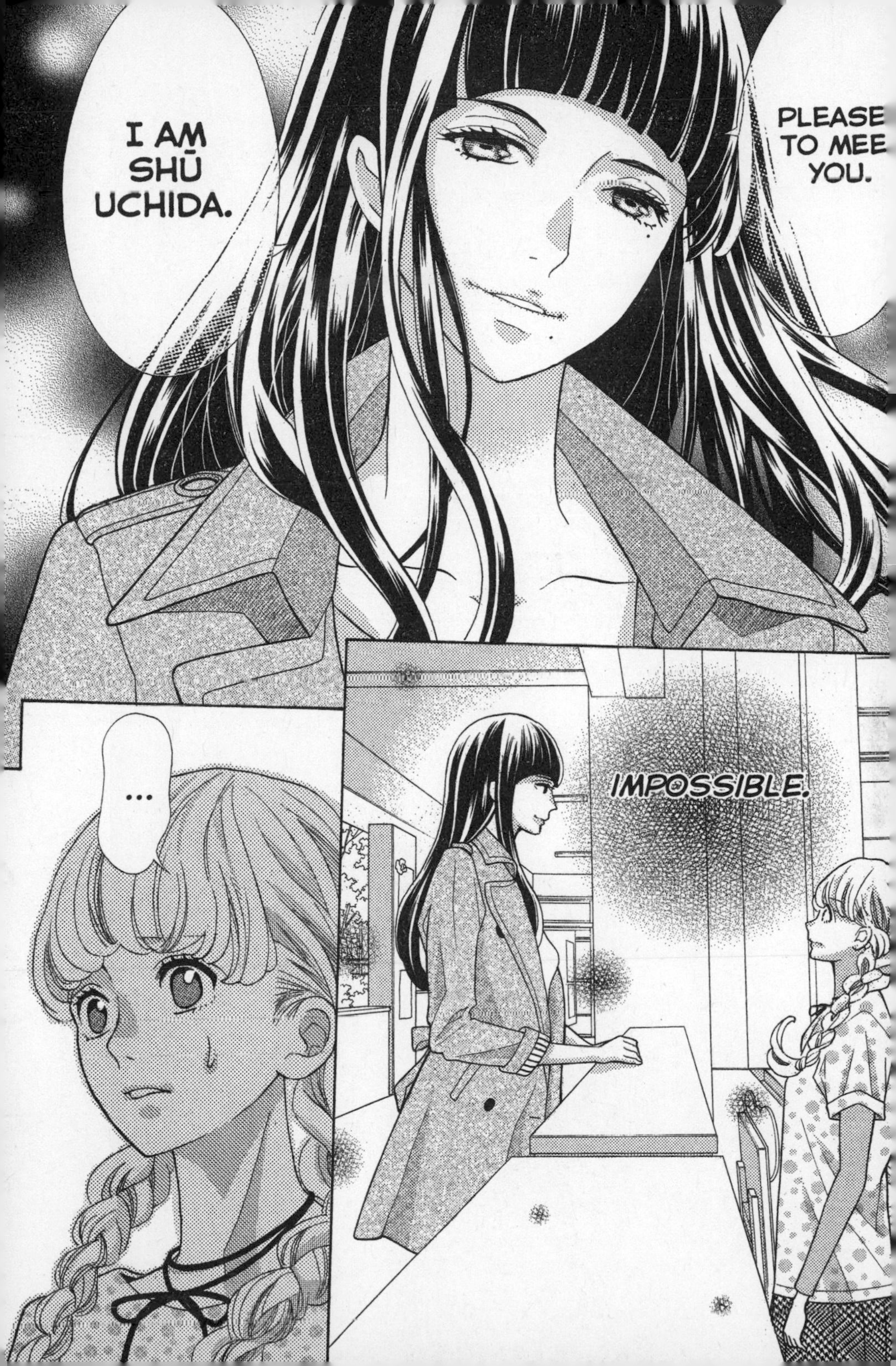
PLEASE TO MEE YOU.
I AM SHŪ UCHIDA.
IMPOSSIBLE.
...

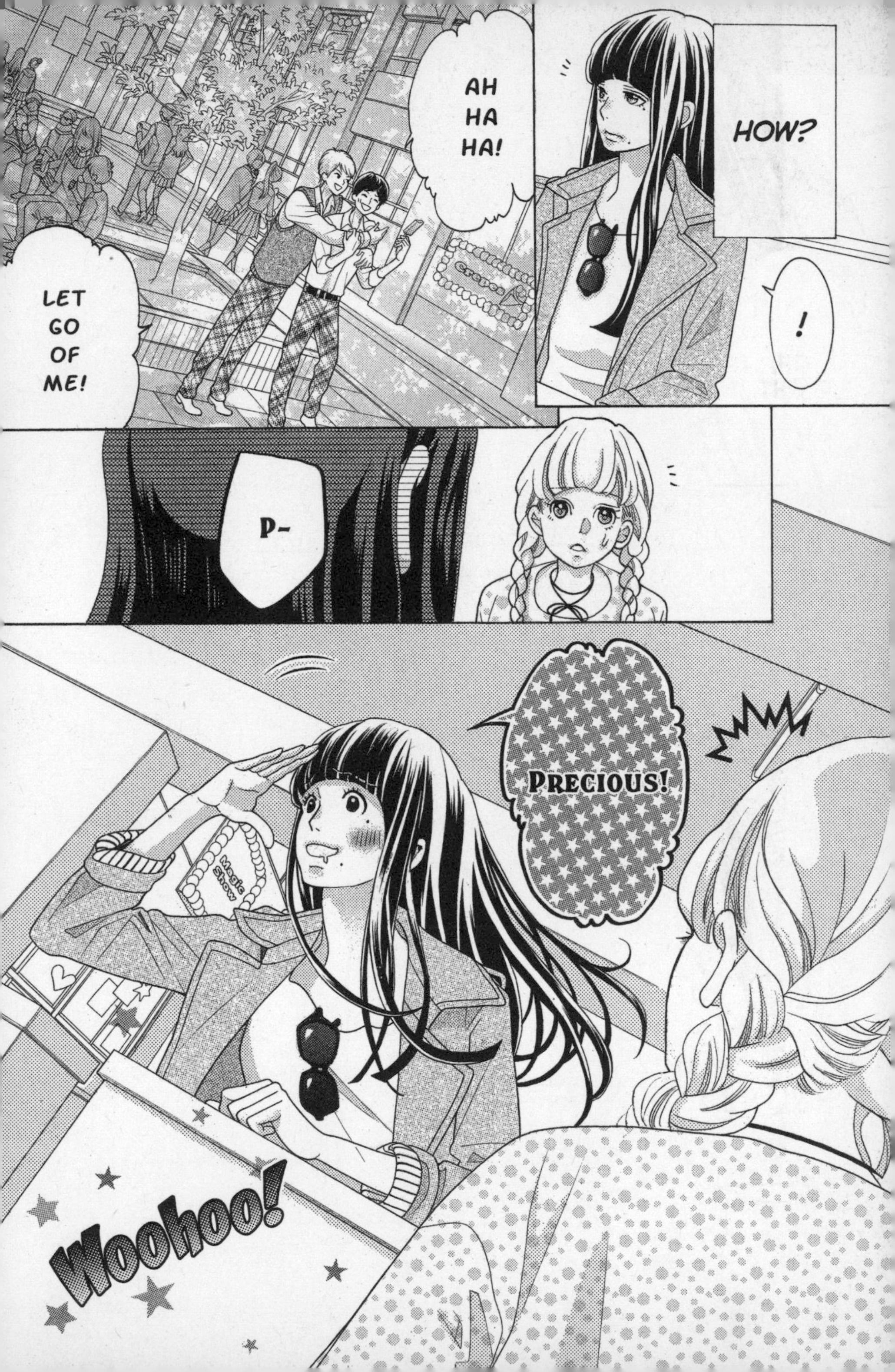
HOW?
!
AH HA HA!
Crepes
LET GO OF ME!
P-
PRECIOUS!
Magic Show
Woohoo!

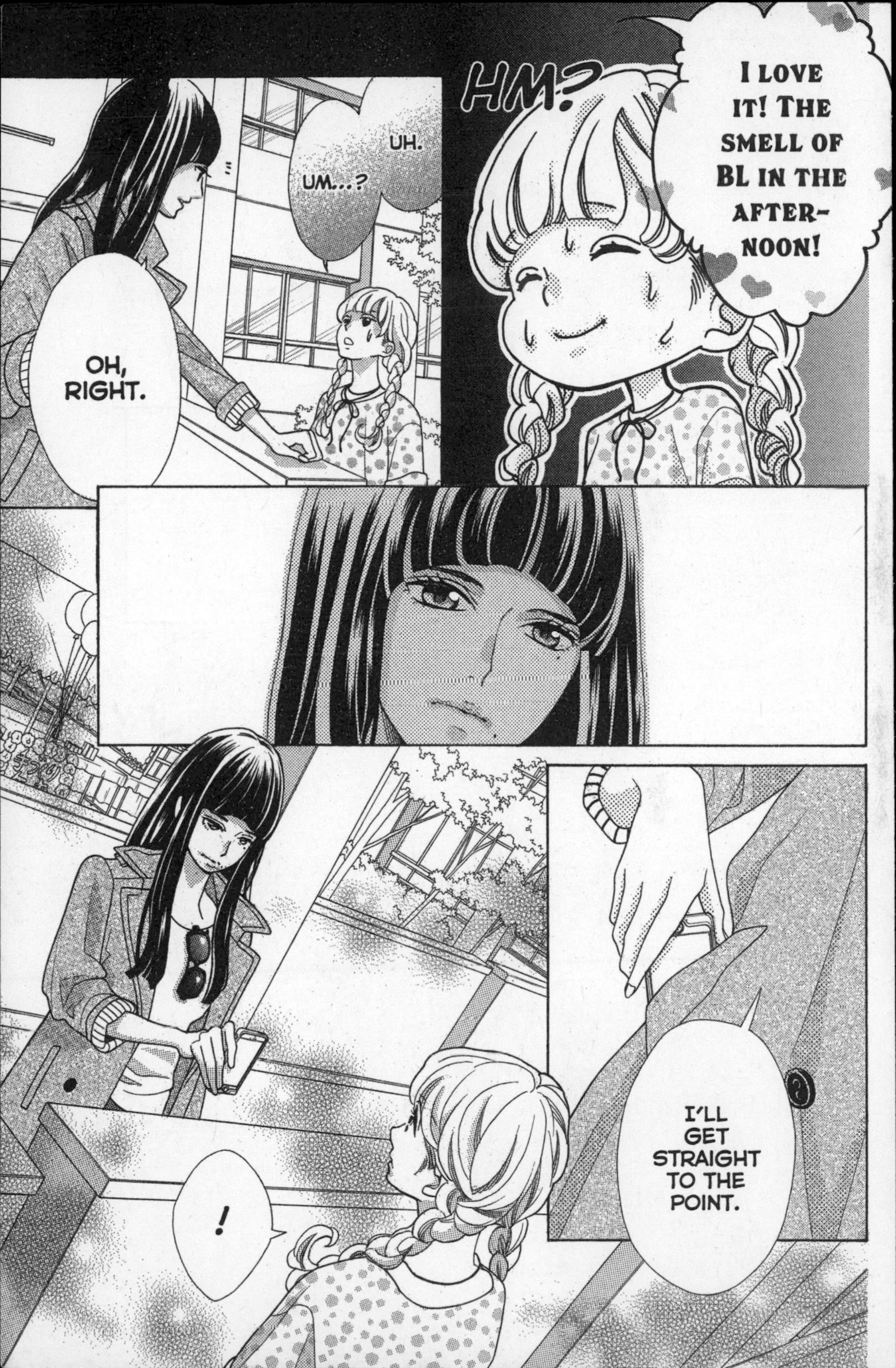
HM?
I LOVE IT! THE SMELL OF BL IN THE AFTER-NOON!
UH.
UM...?
OH, RIGHT.
I'LL GET STRAIGHT TO THE POINT.
!

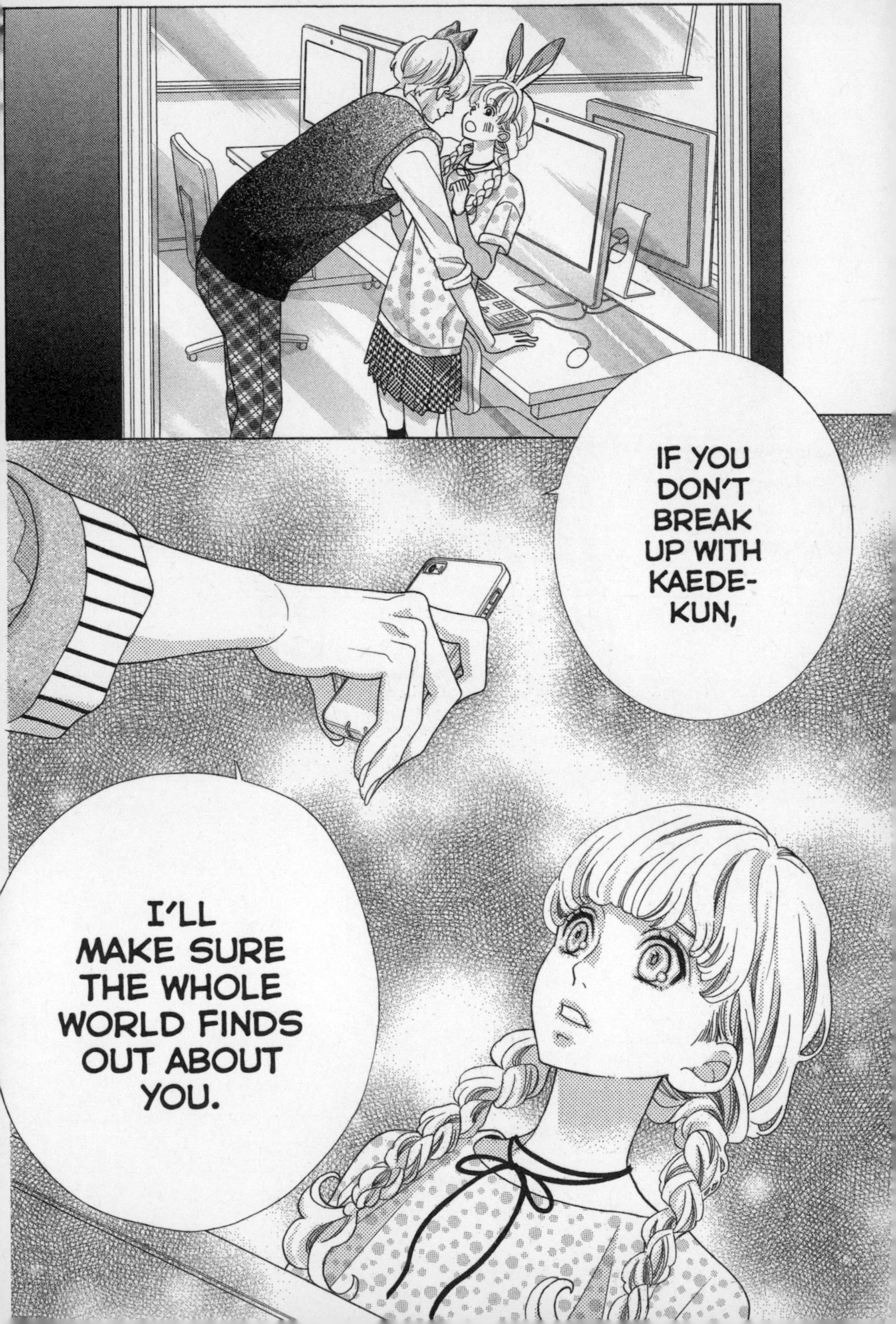
IF YOU DON'T BREAK UP WITH KAEDE-KUN,
I'LL MAKE SURE THE WHOLE WORLD FINDS OUT ABOUT YOU.

TO BE CONTINUED IN
KISS ME AT THE STROKE OF MIDNIGHT
VOLUME 6

AFTERWORD

HELLO, EVERYONE. HOW DID YOU LIKE VOLUME FIVE? I CHANGED THE COVERS SO THEY HAVE TWO PEOPLE!

THERE MIGHT NOT BE AS MUCH MAKING OUT AS THE LAST VOLUME, BUT I THINK THE STORY'S MOVED FORWARD A LITTLE.

INCIDENTALLY, THERE'S SOMETHING I'VE BEEN WANTING TO SAY FOR A WHILE, AND IT'S THAT I ACTUALLY MAKE A LOT OF MISTAKES! SOMETHING SOMEONE WAS HOLDING WILL DISAPPEAR, OR SOMETHING THAT WAS ON THE RIGHT WILL SUDDENLY BE ON THE LEFT. THEY'LL HAVE POCKETS AND THEN THEY WON'T. THANK YOU TO EVERY ONE OF YOU WHO NOTICED ALL OF THOSE THINGS AND PRETENDED THAT THEY DIDN'T NOTICE. I HOPE YOU WILL CONTINUE TO PRETEND YOU DIDN'T SEE ANYTHING! HA HA.

OR YOU CAN THINK THAT, IN THAT SPLIT-SECOND FROM ONE PANEL TO THE NEXT, THEY TORE OFF THEIR POCKETS, OR THEY MOVED THAT THING TO THEIR LEFT HAND, OR THEY THREW IT AWAY, OR THEY PICKED IT UP AGAIN. AH HA HA.

I WOULD APPRECIATE IT IF YOU WOULD LOOK KINDLY ON THESE EVENTS.

NOW THEN, IN THE NEXT VOLUME, THEY'LL BE ALL OVER EACH OTHER AGAIN, AND FINALLY WE'LL PLUNGE INTO THE FUNNY BONE ARC

I THINK.

I'M PRETTY SURE THERE WILL BE A LOT OF MEN.

IT'S GOING TO BE HARD TO DRAW...I MEAN, I HOPE IT'S LIVELY AND LOTS OF FUN!

PLEASE READ IT!

12.2016 -RIN MIKIMOTO

Special thanx

S.sato

H.saijyo

M.kawai

M.takayashiki

K.kaneko

Everyone on the staff

Everyone in the editorial department

Horiuchi-sama

Saiki-san

Editor-in-chief

Kanamori-san

arcoinc Kusume-sama

&U

I LOVE YOU

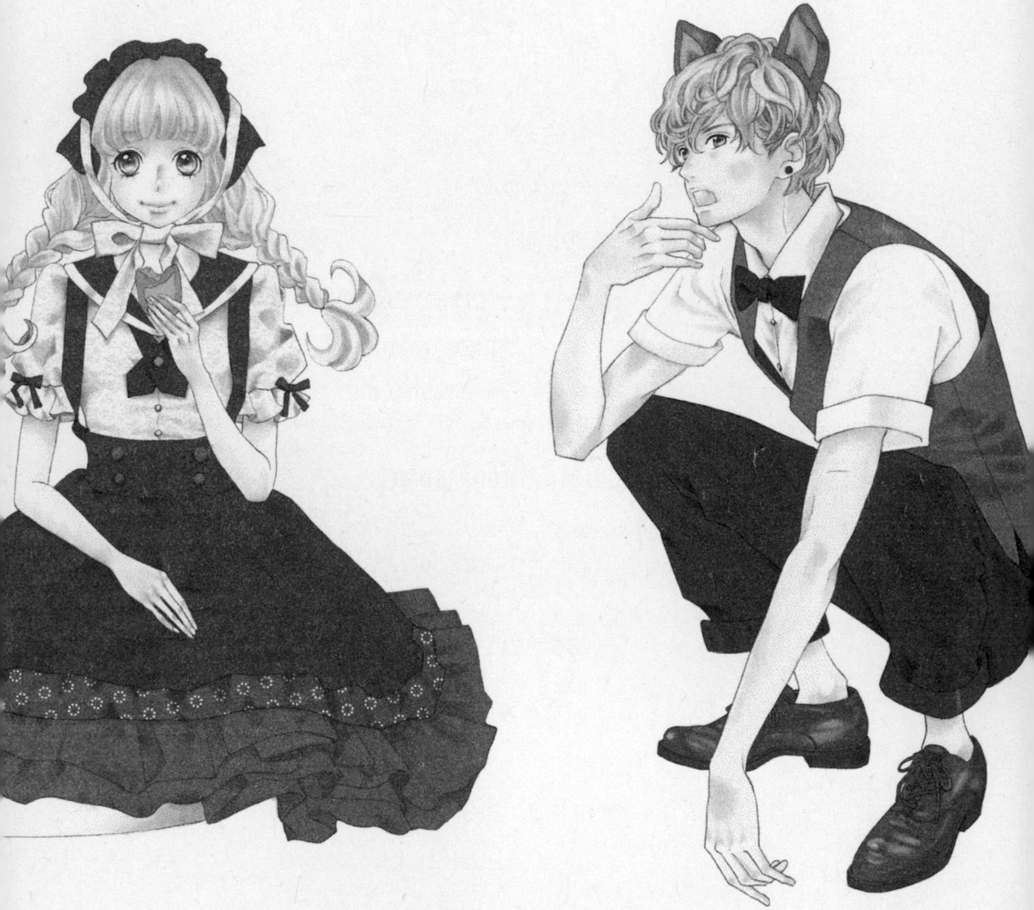

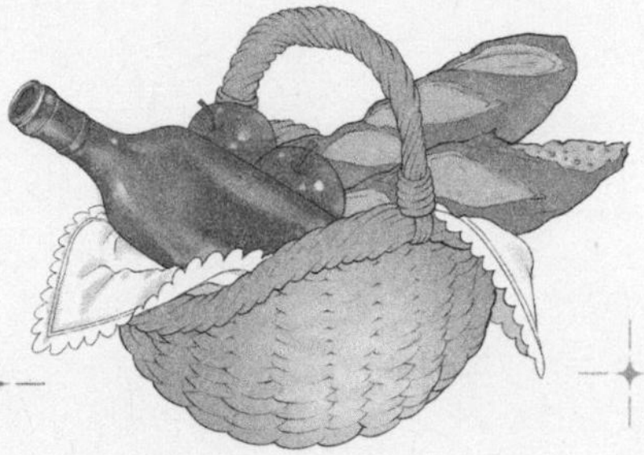

COMMENT

Starting with this volume,
I decided to put two people on the
cover. I might go back to closeups
after a while. We'll see how it goes.
The truth is, I did think about going
with a closeup of Ah-chan. I wonder if
he'll ever get to be on the cover.

RIN MIKIMOTO

TRANSLATION NOTES

TERU TERU BŌZU, PAGE 31
What Shū has made here is called a *teru teru bōzu*, or "shine shine monk" (or "shine shine bald head"), and is a lucky charm to keep rain away. They are usually made by children, out of a material like tissue paper, and hung in the window on the night before an outdoor excursion such as a school picnic.

PURIKURA, PAGE 105
Print Club (*Purinto Kurabu*), often abbreviated as *purikura*, is a kind of photo booth. You go in with your friends (or significant other), you take pictures, and then you have a few minutes to write or draw on the the images digitally, and add backgrounds, borders, and effects. Then the whole thing is printed out on a sticker sheet. It's a nice, quick way to make lasting memories together.

Kiss Me at the Stroke of Midnight

Having lost his wife, high school teacher Kōhei Inuzuka is doing his best to raise his young daughter Tsumugi as a single father. He's pretty bad at cooking and doesn't have a huge appetite to begin with, but chance brings his little family together with one of his students, the lonely Kotori. The three of them are anything but comfortable in the kitchen, but the healing power of home cooking might just work on their grieving hearts.

"This season's number-one feel-good anime!" —Anime News Network

"A beautifully-drawn story about comfort food and family and grief. Recommended." —Otaku USA Magazine

sweetness & lightning

By Gido Amagakure

KC
KODANSHA
COMICS

The award-winning manga about what happens inside you!

"Far more entertaining than it ought to be... what kid doesn't want to think that every time they sneeze a torpedo shoots out their nose?"
—Anime News Network

Strep throat! Hay fever! Influenza! The world is a dangerous place for a red blood cell just trying to get her deliveries finished. Fortunately, she's not alone…she's got a whole human body's worth of cells ready to help out! The mysterious white blood cells, the buff and brash killer T cells, even the cute little platelets—everyone's got to come together if they want to keep you healthy!

Cells at Work!

はたらく細胞

By Akane Shimizu

FAIRY TAIL S

For the members of Fairy Tail, a guild member's work is never done. While they may not always be away on missions, that doesn't mean our magic-wielding heroes can rest easy at home. What happens when a copycat thief begins to soil the good name of Fairy Tail, or when a seemingly unstoppable virus threatens the citizens of Magnolia? And when a bet after the Grand Magic Games goes sour, can Natsu, Lucy, Gray, and Erza turn the tables in their favor? Come see what a "day in the life" of the strongest guild in Fiore is like in nine brand new short stories!

**KC
KODANSHA
COMICS**

A collection of *Fairy Tail* short stories drawn by original creator Hiro Mashima!

LAND
OF THE
LUSTROUS

In a world inhabited by crystalline life-forms called The Lustrous, every gem must fight for their life against the threat of Lunarians who would turn them into decorations. Phosphophyllite, the most fragile and brittle of gems, longs to join the battle, so when Phos is instead assigned to complete a natural history of their world, it sounds like a dull and pointless task. But this new job brings Phos into contact with Cinnabar, a gem forced to live in isolation. Can Phos's seemingly mundane assignment lead both Phos and Cinnabar to the fulfillment they desire?

Kiss Me at the Stroke of Midnight volume 5 is a work of fiction.
Names, characters, places, and incidents are the products of the author's imagination or
are used fictitiously. Any resemblance to actual events, locales, or persons, living or dead,
is entirely coincidental.

A Kodansha Comics Trade Paperback Original.

Kiss Me at the Stroke of Midnight volume 5 copyright © 2017 Rin Mikimoto
English translation copyright © 2018 Rin Mikimoto

All rights reserved.

Published in the United States by Kodansha Comics,
an imprint of Kodansha USA Publishing, LLC, New York.

Publication rights for this English edition arranged through Kodansha Ltd., Tokyo.

First published in Japan in 2017 by Kodansha Ltd., Tokyo,
as *Gozen Reiji, Kiss Shi ni Kiteyo* volume 5.

Cover Design: Tomohiro Kusume (arcoinc)

ISBN 978-1-63236-559-0

Printed in the United States of America.

www.kodanshacomics.com

9 8 7 6 5 4 3 2 1

Translation: Alethea and Athena Nibley
Lettering: Jennifer Skarupa
Editing: Tomoko Nagano, Haruko Hashimoto
Kodansha Comics Edition Cover Design: Phil Balsman